THIS TIME
LET'S NOT
EAT
THE BONES

THIS TIME
LET'S NOT
EAT
THE BONES

Bill James
Without
the Numbers

Bill James

VILLARD BOOKS NEW YORK 1989

Library of Congress Cataloging-in-
Publication Data
James, Bill
    This time let's not eat the bones.
    1. Baseball—United States—
History. I. Title.
GV863.A1J37   1989   796.357'0973
88-33771
ISBN 0-394-57714-0

Manufactured in the United States of
America
9 8 7 6 5 4 3 2
First Edition

This book is for Susie.

Contents

Section III—People

ACKNOWLEDGMENTS

It has been several years since I have dedicated a book to my wife, in spite of which we are still married. When you write a book every year you can't dedicate it to your woman every year, but Susie is always the most important person in my life and always the person most responsible for helping to get this thing done, and thus always the most appreciated. This book ties a bow around twelve years of work and worry, and Susie has carried me through the crunches for twelve years. Dedication? That, ladies and gentlemen, is dedication.

The parts of this book are mostly lifted from the parts of previous books, and so I suppose I should acknowledge here all of the people who are acknowledged in any of those. This would be a bewildering undertaking, inasmuch as the 1983 book is dedicated to a list of about a hundred people (my old and early readers) and the 1987 book to another list of thirty-nine (the sales force of Ballantine Books). While all of you people are still appreciated, I hope you will understand if you are not all mentioned again individually.

Two other people have stayed with the books since 1982, those being my superstar editor Peter Gethers and my Hall of Fame agent Liz Dahransoff.

Other people who helped with one or more of the books in some way include Dallas Adams, Roger Angell, Pete Axthelm, Jim Baker, Chuck Berry, Marc Bowman, Dennis Dietz, Gary Brown, Walt Campbell, Jim Carothers, Craig Christmann, Clem Comly, Neal Conan, Steven Copley, Carmen Corica, Bob Costas, Bob Creamer, John Davenport, Bob Davids, Ted DeVrics, John and Sue Dewan, David Driscoll, Michael Duca, Russ Eagle, Eddie Epstein, Georgine and Wayne Ent, Jack Etkin, Tom and Jane Evans, Rob Fleder, Roger Friedman, Warner Fusselle, Colin Gage, Cappy Gagnon, Joe Garagiola, Gary Gillette, Laura Godfrey, Steven Goldleaf, William Goldman, David Guthmann, Alan Hendricks, Randy Hendricks, Art Hill, Ron Howard, Paul Izzo, Bill Jensen, Jim Johnson, Paul Johnson, Bob Jones, Chris Ketzel, Rob Klugman, Mike Kopf, Leonard Koppett, Dick Krinsley, Randy Lakeman, Bill Landman, Ward Larkin, Mike Lenehan, John Leo, John Lungstrum, Antoinette Machiabernia, Norman Mailer, Tim Marcou, Dan Marlowe, Mike Marrero, Jim McCarthy, Tom McCarthy, Mary McCarthy, Paul and Phyllis McCarthy, Brent McInnes, Patty and Steve Metzler, Stan Michna, Kenneth Miller, Tim Mulligan, Neil Munro, Mike Myers, David and Sherri Nichols, Dick O'Brien, Dan Okrent, Paul Olsewski, Pete Palmer, Mark Pankin, Charles Pavitt, Tom Peters, Mark Podrazik, Bud Podrazik, Sam Reich, Tom Reich, Raymond Riley, John Rinkenbaugh, Nell and Bill Ritchey, Steven Roney, Barry Rubinowitz, Perry Sailor, Paul Schwarzenbart, Scott Segrin, Audrey Simon, Gary Skoog, Randy Spence, Dennis Telgemeier, Jack Turcotte, Glen Waggoner, Susan Wallach, Chuck Waseleski, Phil Wedge, Robert Weisman, Jeff Welch, Carol and Melvin Wells, Jim West, Rosalie and Ned West, George Will, Robert O. Wood, Paul Worth, Craig Wright, Vic Ziegal, and Don Zminda. You are all listed here because you all contributed, in one way or another, to keeping the *Abstracts* going for twelve years, and that help has not been forgotten. And I shudder to think who I may have missed.

I have two of the sweetest children in the world, Rachel and Isaac. Rachel is two; Isaac is five months. Rachel decided last night, through a kind of quasi-logical process, that her birthday must be tomorrow; we haven't figured out how we're going to get it across that it isn't.

Thanks to the quiet people—D, T, B and M, I, LC, and DJ, the S and LF, TB, TB, C and MB. Thanks to Stokely and Isadora.

And most of all, I acknowledge once more a great debt to those who read.

Hi. My name is Bill James.

You have probably heard the story about what happened the first time pre-historic men decided to try to eat meat. See, there were these four cavemen sitting around one day getting hungry waiting for the tomatoes to get ripe; their names were Ugh, Umph, Arl and Mortimer, although some sources insist that Umph and Arl were women. Anyway, they got so hungry that they finally decided to kill an ox and put it in the fire and see how it tasted.

"Well," said Ugh, "that wasn't too bad."

"Beats starvin'," said Umph.

"It had some good parts," added Arl.

"Some tough parts, too," allowed Ugh, and they all did have to agree with that. Finally Mortimer spoke up.

"Next time," said Mortimer, "maybe we shouldn't eat the bones."

This is the *Baseball Abstract* without the bones. In the mid-seventies I wrote a number of articles about baseball which were published in places like the *Baseball Digest* and the *Baseball Bulletin*. As often happens to a young writer, what I wrote about and what I wanted to write about were on different planets of the same solar system. What I wanted to do was to pick up the things that baseball people were saying and examine them. I was interested in questions like "Is baseball seventy-five percent pitching?" and "Do base runners really steal on the pitcher or on the hitter?" and "Do left-handed batters really hit better against right-handed pitchers?"—as, indeed, were most baseball fans. What I wanted to do, though, was not to talk to baseball players or baseball insiders and collect their wisdom on the subject, but to examine the issue with the same kind of intellectual rigor and discipline that is routinely applied, by scientists great and poor, to trying to unravel the mysteries of the universe, of society, of the human mind, or of the price of burlap in Des Moines. I wanted, in short, to be a baseball scientist.

I decided to call the science of baseball sabermetrics, which wasn't a great decision but we'll leave that alone. Eventually I became frustrated with the limitations of the publications that I was writing for, with the things that one could not get published in them. When I developed scientific methods and procedures for the analysis of baseball, these methods had one of the same drawbacks that science has in any other field, namely, that you had to study them to understand them. Sabermetrics is not as easy to understand as journalism; it simply can't be. You have to work at it a little to get the message. I had no trouble getting published articles that I had written, which I didn't particularly like or respect, but if I wrote an article which I thought was good or important, I would be told that the public wouldn't understand this or didn't have the patience to sort through the data and reach a conclusion with me. The public, I was told, doesn't want to work this hard.

At the same time that I was being told that the public wasn't interested in this stuff, I would meet people almost every day who were interested in it—just people at weddings and on buses and in classes and at the factory. So I always knew that there was A public for the work that I was doing; maybe, I said, THE public isn't interested, but there is A public which is. Maybe it isn't *The Sporting News* public. Maybe it isn't the public that watches the *Game of the Week*, but then it doesn't have to be.

I asked myself a question: How many people do I need to be interested in this stuff to make a living from writing about it? I figured maybe two thousand, maybe four. I lived at that time in Lawrence, Kansas, a city of about fifty thousand people. If there was one person in each city the size of Lawrence who would buy it, I wondered, how many is that in a country of two hundred twenty million? The answer is a little over four thousand. In Lawrence, I knew at least twenty people who were extremely interested in the subject. So what did that mean?

What it had to mean is that the market was there; not *The* Market, but *A* Market.

At that point, I stopped worrying about the average reader, and began to concentrate on finding my market. I began to write an annual book, which I called *The Baseball Abstract*. What I wrote about, for the most part, was sabermetrics, the scientific study of baseball. It is important to understand this: I never wrote about statistics. I never wrote about "old statistics" or "new statistics" or any statistics at all. Although I have been described, referred to, labeled and introduced many thousands of times as a statistician, this is simply an error; I have never been a statistician. I have never compiled statistics, either for a living or as a hobby. I have never ever written about statistics, to any large extent. In the years of doing the *Abstract*, I wrote perhaps a dozen or so articles about statistics, certainly no more. I used statistics in exactly the same ways and for exactly the same reasons that an economist does or a sociologist or a physicist, except that rather than studying economics or sociology or physics, I was studying baseball. It really isn't any different to refer to me as a statistician than it is to call an economist a statistician, but "baseball statistician" was a recognized folder in which to put somebody that you didn't know what to do with, and therefore the label under which I was often filed.

The *Baseball Abstract* abounded in statistics, then, for precisely the same reason that a book about economics is almost always replete with economic statistics or a book about criminology is almost always filled with crime statistics. This was never hard for me, or for most of my readers; I would include statistical summaries and formulas and charts and technical references in paragraphs of ordinary prose. I was always aware that this made the book, for many people or even most people, indigestible—but I had decided not to worry about that; not *The* Market, but *A* Market. For many people the statistics were an absolute wall; they would get to the wall and not be able to see a thing beyond it. Reading the *Abstract*, for these people, was like trying to eat meat with the bones still in it, and thus many people were puzzled that the *Abstract* showed up on the best seller lists every year; puzzled, because they did not understand that who *doesn't* read a book and why they *don't* read it is irrelevant to its success. For a book to succeed it is not enough that it be accessible to everyone; it must exert a positive attraction to *someone*.

Well, there was a market out there, and eventually the market and I found each other; it was considerably larger than four thousand people. Ballantine Books began publishing the book in 1982 and paying me a living wage; I was able to stop working in factories and stuff and spend all my time doing my studies and writing them up. *The Baseball Abstract* ran for twelve years and engendered a variety of competitors.

However, while the *Abstract* was fundamentally about sabermetrics, it was not exclusively about sabermetrics; it was also about baseball history, about personalities, about the ethics and philosophy of the sport. Each book contained a year's research, but it also contained a few dozen essays having nothing to do with sabermetrics. In time I became more troubled by the fact that the *Abstract* erected barriers to so many people. I changed with the years; I'm near forty now, and not the same person I was at twenty-five. Sabermetrics was very good to me; the *Abstract* was very good to me. But I never made a decision that I wanted to do it for the rest of my life. Eventually I decided it was time for me to do something else, to reach out to a new audience.

This book is the first step in the effort to do that; it is a way of trying to introduce myself to the people who *didn't* read the *Abstract* because they just couldn't digest the bones. Most of the articles, essays, jokes, and libels in these pages have been published before, either in the *Abstract* or in some other forum. They have been edited for this edition. What I have done this time is take the bones out—or, to mix metaphors, to remove the wall that was a barrier to so many people.

It's been quite a trip, going through the books and articles that I've written and trying to put together a new book. In the beginning (1977–1981) I lacked the self-confidence to write as well as I was capable of writing. The first books with Ballantine (beginning in 1982) may be the most fun of the bunch, but I do find it hard to believe that I was so harsh, so cruel at times.

The 1984–85 books were a shock to review, and not a pleasant one. On reviewing them for pieces well enough written to republish, I found very little. When reviewing them for studies to summarize, I found few studies which retain interest. The books are somehow vaguely self-conscious and unduly concerned with the relationship of sabermetrics to the world at large.

It has dropped out of fashion to talk about the drawbacks and disadvantages of success, but for me, success was much harder to deal with than the struggle to get there. The years 1981–83, when success first hit us, were a lot of fun, and I think Susie and I both enjoyed life. But the years 1983–85, although I was making good money for the first time in my life, were miserable for me, surely the most unhappy years of my adult life.

When you're a young writer nobody expects that much of you. When you become successful, there is an explosion of demands on your time. All of a sudden, people were after me sixteen hours a day to do things for them, and I didn't know how to say "No." I'm still not very good at saying no, but at least I know how to stop worrying about it a little bit now. I have trouble dealing with things like letters. I feel like I should answer every letter that I receive, but try as I may I simply can't do it, so I walk around feeling guilty twenty-four hours a day (at some level) because I'm behind on my mail.

Although I myself was often a harsh judge, it was very hard for me to deal with the kind of criticism you receive when you're on the best seller list. I didn't have the sense to try to talk to anybody about it; I just bottled it up. I didn't take control of my career; I let things happen, and when they happened I got frustrated because they often didn't happen the way I wanted them to. I got involved in several projects, most notably a newsletter and Project Scoresheet, in which I immediately gave away the control that I needed, and as a consequence of that these projects consumed an enormous amount of time in nonproductive ways, which was an additional frustration to me. I was hard to live with or work with, was depressed most of the time and put on a lot of weight.

Until doing this book, I never realized how much that period affected my work. I guess I didn't read the books afterward, or if I did I didn't read them with clear eyes. In any case, by 1985 I began to pull out of it, and the 1986 book is a little better. The 1986–88 books are more even in terms of writing quality and contain more significant research, but by 1986 some of the fizz had gone out of my writing; it was more even but less volatile. I expected more of myself each year, which reduced the time I had to just sit and stew about stuff. The manuscript for the first Abstract was something like 600 pages, and many of the team comments were just 300–400 words; by 1988 the team comments ran 2400 words and the book manuscripts were well over a thousand pages—but as a consequence of this, and as a consequence also of having small children, I found it almost impossible to get the time or the solitude that writing well requires.

I quit doing the Abstract because I didn't feel that I was writing the best books that I was capable of writing. I wasn't writing them because the requirements of research (among other things) took time from the writing, and also because I was operating within a set of self-constructed walls.

The image of statistics as the bones of history has more

dimensions than often intended by the people who use it. What it is meant to imply is dryness, the absence of life. For many people statistics are as dry as . . . well, as dry as bones, dry and hard and devoid of life. What is less understood is that a baseball player's statistics, like bones, will be what is left when everything else decays. In the nineteenth century a player named Buck Ewing was regarded as a greater player than Cap Anson. Today Ewing is all but forgotten, not a hundredth as well known as Anson, simply because Anson did things which the statistics recorded, while Ewing did not. Statisticians are important because they are charged with the responsibility of creating the permanent image of a player's skills.

Are bones in fact devoid of life? Not at all—you have bones in you, don't you? Your bones are as alive as your heart. Our bones provide a structure for us—and, in the same way, baseball statistics structure the images of baseball players.

I've never really understood the tendency of people to put down what is outside their own group. I've never understood why New Yorkers put down California or why Californians put down the Midwest or why midwesterners put down New York. It's a manifestation of insecurity, obviously, but exactly why it makes people from San Francisco feel more secure to ridicule the lifestyle of Los Angeles . . . well, who knows? The same applies to our intellectual residences; scientists tend to scorn businessmen as greedy, businessmen look at artists as impractical, while artists portray scientists as narrow-minded and cold. I've never been able to understand that. In college I majored in Literature and also Economics; this was regarded by both camps as extremely strange, for reasons that I kept waiting to hear but never did. I never understood why Greeks looked down on independents or independents looked down on dormies. I've always tried to cross the barriers and embrace the truth wherever I found it.

And yet, I was still within my own walls. I tried very hard never to put journalists down—and yet, journalists often interpreted things that I wrote as being critical of them. I tried hard not to reject the wisdom of managers or scouts or players, the wisdom of experience—and yet I found that often the things I said were interpreted as putting down their point of view and discounting their experience. And perhaps, indeed, I really was. I guess you'll have to decide.

This book has five sections after the introductory stuff here. The first section, imitating the form of the annual *Abstracts*, contains comments about the teams, and will be headed "Teams." The second section contains comments about baseball players, active players at the time the comments were originally published, and will be labeled "Players." The third section contains articles about other people involved somehow with baseball, and will be labeled "People," which is not to imply that baseball players are not also people. The fourth section contains essays on anything and everything related to baseball, and will be headed "Essays." The final section contains brief synopses of studies done over the years, and will be headed "Research."

Nice to meet you. Let's go.

—Bill James
October, 1988

Section

1

TEAMS

Atlanta Braves

In retrospect, the trade of Butler and Jacoby for Barker was a three-player, five-pronged disaster for the Braves. Trading Butler opened up the left field spot in the field and the leadoff spot in the lineup; the two spots became glaring weaknesses, as 1) Komminsk failed to fill the left field job, and 2) everybody and his sister failed as the Braves' leadoff man. With Bob Horner out for almost the whole year, 3) third base was another major sore spot for the Braves—for which Brook Jacoby would have been the best solution they could have hoped for. But perhaps worst of all, the presence of Barker on the roster led almost directly to 4) the infinitely regrettable decision to release Phil Niekro. And then Barker 5) won seven games, lost eight, had an ERA worse-than-league-average and spent a good part of the season on the disabled list.

To these five factors, you can add in the money that the Braves gave Barker. Consider the fact that the trade was made to try to help win the race in '83, and the fact that Lenny was 1–3 down the stretch and the Braves fell apart right after the trade was made. Wow. That is what you call hanging yourself with a custom-fit noose.

—1985

Lord, what an awful team. Awash in mediocrity from the top of the organization to the lowest utility infielder, the Atlanta Braves trudged blindly through another disappointing summer in 1986. At no point did they seem destined to contend. No element of the team was strong. The team was not marked by outstanding talent, outstanding enthusiasm, outstanding management, or outstanding uniforms. It seems incredible that just a few years ago baseball fans were worried about baseball splitting into camps in which the rich grew richer and the poor grew livestock for the rich.

The Braves, you see, represent the rich. Having inflated the salaries of all baseball to draw players to Atlanta, Ted Turner is now saddled with an ugly, overpaid ball club that has no idea how to win. It must be easier for a camel to pass through the eye of a needle than it is for a rich team to win the division. If the powerhouse of the Dodgers is finished, at least it lasted almost a half century. The dynastic ambitions of Ted Turner flowered and died in two weeks in 1982, when the Braves opened the season by winning their first thirteen games. They have not been the same since. I'm not even sure what happened to all those free agents that the Braves were so excited about signing; the only people around who can actually play the game are those who have been here forever.

—1987

Baltimore Orioles

In 1984 the Baltimore Orioles had a disappointing season. After winning the World Championship in 1983, the Orioles dropped off to a record of 85 and 77. By the end of the 1985 season, one year later, the Orioles had changed regulars at five of the nine positions. Looking back on it now, it was a striking passage in the history of the team, one at which the collapse of the Oriole tradition was written large in the Western sky, had we not been too blind to see it.

The Orioles left in place what they saw as the anchors of their team, Ripken and Murray. In making changes at five other positions, they didn't want to risk trying out young, unproven players. In center field, they replaced John Shelby with Fred Lynn, a thirty-three-year-old free agent with an injury catalog in which you could find almost anything. At another outfield spot, they replaced Gary Roenicke with Lee Lacy, a thirty-six-year-old free agent. At second base they replaced Rich Dauer with Alan Wiggins, an established player who was available from San Diego because of drug and personality problems. At third base, they replaced Wayne Gross with Fat Floyd Rayford, a ten-year minor leaguer with a chronic weight problem.

These changes, rather than fighting off the natural aging process and the natural accumulation of incentive problems which occur within any lineup, made the team immediately older, less well-conditioned, less well-motivated and more injury-prone. There is no reason why this should not have been known at the time. At only one position, designated hitter, did the Orioles move to give a talented young player a chance to develop (Larry Sheets replacing Ken Singleton).

It is unusual for a team to introduce five new regulars in a season. It is extraordinary for a team to introduce five new regulars in an offhand way, without making a positive move to restructure the team. Facing what they saw as a disappointing year, the Orioles made five individual gambles, apparently without at the time seeing that the collective impact of this was to separate them forcefully from their past.

Then we look at the pitching staff. In 1984 their relief ace was Tippy Martinez, who was thirty-four years old and losing effectiveness. In 1985 they also replaced Tippy—with Don Aase, a thirty-year-old veteran who had been on the disabled list every year since the time of Cap Anson.

Then we look ahead to 1986, when the Orioles introduced onto their roster one new semi-regular—Juan Beniquez, then thirty-six years old. Or to 1987, when they introduced two new regulars, Ray Knight and Terry Kennedy. They hoped to make it three, but Rick Burleson didn't pan out.

It has been said that there is no event on record which a competent historian cannot make seem inevitable once it has transpired. I do not want to argue that the dissolution of the Oriole tradition was an inevitable consequence of these decisions. It was not inevitable. It was merely exceedingly probable.

This is so obvious that it embarrasses me to say it, but then I have said it a hundred times before and there is still no general acceptance of it. From the age of twenty-eight on, all groups of players are declining. Almost any group of players will lose 50 percent of their value, as a group, between the ages of twenty-eight and thirty-two. After thirty-two, the rate of decline accelerates rapidly. Some players of course do remain strong into their thirties, and the visibility of those who do causes the public to greatly underestimate the pace of decline in the normal case, but the fact remains that whenever you sign a player over the age of twenty-eight, you are buying into a market that is certain to decline.

If you see building a baseball team as being a matter of solving fifteen problems, then if you make a ten-year solution to each problem you've got to solve one or two problems every year. If you make a ten-year solution to a problem, then you have to solve seven or eight problems a year. Sure, it isn't easy to find that ten-year solution to a problem, but which do you have a better chance of doing?

—1988

Boston Red Sox

If history nags at the Yankees, it assaults the Boston Red Sox. Since 1938, the Red Sox have finished in the first division thirty times but have won only three pennants. This year Boston management, latching onto the Yankee secret, has analyzed the team and decided that having lost the pennant because of a lack of left-handed pitching, they should maybe get rid of their one left-handed starter and just go naked. Having disposed of Bill Lee, the prisoners of Fenway may now find themselves trying to win the division without a left-handed starter—something that no American League team has yet done.

Fenway Park, its charms notwithstanding, has become the Red Sox' inescapable fate. We start with two premises: one, that Fenway distorts the records of its players, and two, that you pay for believing everything which is not true. The first point is generally known, and universally underestimated. The Red Sox perpetually overrate their hitting and underrate their pitching and defense. The pitchers, shuttled into and out of 12–9 games like the white chips in a penny ante poker game, lose their rhythm and their confidence, while for everyday players, Fenway makes stars out of ordinary ball players —and, like stars, makes them hard to bench, hard to trade, hard to discipline.

But what to do? Three Red Sox regulars (Fred Lynn, Carlton Fisk, and Jim Rice) are in fact very good hitters, but the point has little to do with Jim Rice, for giving Fenway Park to Jim Rice is like arming Superman with a set of brass knuckles. The point has to do with Butch Hobson (.211 average away from Fenway, and an abomination on defense), George Scott (.178 in road games) and Dwight Evans (.219). Given Fenway Park to protect their records, such players are allowed to clutter up the offense for years.

—Esquire magazine
April 24, 1979

It will be up to Ralph Houk to make a ball club out of the reformulated Boston Red Sox. Houk has replaced Don Zimmer in what is surely the most subtle of the Red Sox' exchanges; the biggest differences between the two men are that 1) Houk carries his chaw in his left cheek and 2) Houk doesn't look as if he were stuffed into his doubleknits by a taxidermist's apprentice. Both Houk and Zimmer are able to handle the most treacherous responsibility of a manager, which is to gain and maintain the respect of the players. Both are decisive men who will carry through on a plan even in the face of criticism. But neither Houk nor Zimmer is an alert percentage manager, and neither has the ability to light a fire under a damp team. Neither can select and involve a twenty-five-man roster as adroitly as Weaver or Herzog. Like Walter Alston, both are corporate managers, the sort of men who can unblushingly conduct an interview while changing their pants. Neither will ever embarrass the corporation he represents, but neither will ever improve it.

—*Esquire* magazine
April, 1981

The Boston Red Sox led all of baseball in batting average and runs scored in 1981 but gave up too many runs to take full advantage. Yawn, Fenway. This image is indelibly stamped upon the Red Sox statistics, and it is difficult to know exactly how fine the offense is or how coarse the pitching. We do know that the combination has not often been fertile.

—*Esquire* magazine
May, 1982

California Angels

I used to work on a loading dock with a fellow named . . . well, to avoid offending any ethnic groups, we'll call him Vito. Vito Kowalski. Vito believed that one should never use an ounce of intelligence so long as one had the option of using a pound of force. We'd have to unload a railroad car, and since rail doors don't work very well, usually about a third of the job is getting the thing open. They can stick, jam, or lodge in about thirty places, but if you step back and look at them a second you can ordinarily figure out where the problem is and apply a crowbar to it. Vito would have none of that. His method was to grab hold of the handle and pull like hell, and if that doesn't work you pound on the handle with the crowbar, and then you hook up the handle to a fork lift, a chain hoist . . . on up to, presumably, a stick of dynamite. He would rush at breakneck speed from one of these remedies to the next, and nowhere along the line would he ever give a millisecond's pause to stop and consider what the problem was.

It's not that Vito was dumb. He wasn't dumb. He was bright. And, from the habit of using his muscles, strong as a rhinoceros. But the very idea of considering how to approach a problem, whether a rail door, an awkward traffic pattern, or a problem with a supervisor, seemed to profoundly embarrass him. It was unmanly, or something.

Vito eventually wound up in the state pen, charged with rape, which I kind of hate to bring up, because it ruins the atmosphere and all, and besides that it strains the analogy to the breaking point. But up to that point the California Angels were, it seems to me, a perfect baseball counterpart to Vito Kowalski. What so many baseball fans find unacceptable about free agency is that it simplifies the formula for building a winner; instead of spending X amount of dollars here to acquire a pool of potential talent and doing this and that and the other to bring the talent around so as to win maybe five years later, you simply pay the money and get the player. The simplification in my opinion is good for baseball and may even eventually lead to a revival of the minors, which are better off being out of the role of developing talent than being restricted to it.

But it is so . . . graceless, so inefficient . . . so brutal. It's not that the Angels' methods cannot eventually work; Vito would eventually get the car door open, at some cost to the equipment. The Angels believe in taking direct, forceful action to deal with the problem at hand, at whatever cost. Vito would unhesitantly use a fork lift to get the door open; the Angels will unhesitantly trade ten years of shortstop play for two months of relief help if what they need at the moment is a reliever. Any advantage to be gained by reflection, patience or acumen is regarded as practically dishonest.

The equation of success in baseball, while it may have been simplified (for the wealthy) by free agency, is not yet simple enough for the California Angels. That will be achieved, one suspects, when pennants are sold at auction at the winter meetings. With no sealed bids.

—1982

I keep a good distance from the California Angels, and consequently have little feel for the direction or momentum of the organization at any time. I see them play quite a bit—probably as much as any team except the Royals—and I have a real good feel for the *ball club*, but I just never have any idea of what the *organization* is going to do next. I always get the feeling that if I were ever to meet Buzzie Bavasi face to face we wouldn't be able to communicate; it would be like meeting someone who lived three or four planets down the cosmos, and only with a great deal of pointing and gesturing would we be able to get through simple messages like "I am here on a peaceful mission" or "I have come to eat your children and intend to take you back as a slave."

Anyway, with that qualification, the 1984 season seemed to me to be a watershed year in the history of the Angels, and to mark the end of the period begun in 1977 with the signing of mass quantities of expensive free agents. Reduced to an embarrassing 70–92 record in 1983, the Angels put several young players on the field and let them get a year of playing time. Tim Foli, a shortstop whose blood is still quite warm, was sent away so that Dick Schofield, Jr., could play shortstop. Mike Witt, a young pitcher of great promise, was given a good opportunity to get his career straightened out, and he did. A rookie centerfielder was allowed 140 games to show what he could do, and a young hitter named Mike Brown was allowed enough time to play his way into a role in the future of the organization. These actions are not consistent with the recent history of California baseball, and if you don't believe me I'll submit a brief list of players that you can ask: Willie Aikens, Richard Dotson, Rance Mulliniks, Carney Lansford, Ken Landreaux, Dennis Rasmussen, and Dickie Thon. A rookie pitcher, Ron Romanick, was given thirty-three starts; it was the first time since 1976 and only the third time since the late sixties that the Angels have given a decent shot to an unproven pitcher unless he was one of those guys like Ryan or Tanana who could throw a snowball through a blast furnace without its getting soggy.

The break with the past is still far from complete, but it moved further in that direction with the departure of Fred Lynn. Ron Jackson, the Angels' Ed Kranepool, was shown to the door in mid-season. In view of their age and recent performance, it seems likely that within a year it will be time to roll the credits on the Angel careers of Reggie Jackson and Rod Carew, and possibly Tommy John and Bobby Grich as well.

Where the new players will lead them in the standings it is real hard to say, but I will offer this. After the return of Gene Mauch as manager and before the loss of Fred Lynn, I would have picked the Angels to win the AL West in 1985. Mauch and Lynn have some things in common. It is true of each that early in his career too much was put upon him. What many people have forgotten about Mauch and what I suppose those of you under twenty-five probably don't know is that until September 15, 1964, Gene Mauch was the darling of the press corps; he spent most of the 1964 season trying to tell the reporters that he wasn't a genius. Eventually he demonstrated this to the satisfaction of all. Fred Lynn at first blush was supposed to be the second coming of Joe DiMaggio. When each proved to be human and fallible, some writers turned on them, exaggerating minor or imagined shortcomings and haranguing them for not being up to the impossible standards that had been laid out for them.

—1985

The California Angels are the smartest baseball team I've ever seen. In the late seventies, when the Angels were trying to stop the Royals by firing free agents at them, they would patch together a lineup out of two or three free agents a year and a couple of rookies and some guy they could pick up in a trade who had flashy batting stats in Boston or some place, and when this "team" didn't win they would fire the manager. The Angels changed managers in mid-season in 1974, 1976, 1977, and 1978. They also changed managers several times in the seventies between seasons. With each manager trying to "motivate" and guide a team assembled and instructed by somebody else, the Angels had no concept of executing fundamentals in a prearranged way. Since almost everyone on the team was either a free agent or a trade acquisition, there couldn't have been any "organizational" way of doing anything, so each player just did his own thing. Although they could hit and they had Nolan Ryan and Frank Tanana, each Angels game revealed a series of outfield collisions, dropped double play balls, basepath mixups, missed cutoff men, botched hit and run attempts, and pop-ups dropping in the middle of player triangles. When you bought a ticket to see the Angels play, you expected to see these things. It was so bad that even though I was a Royals fan and the Angels were the enemy and you wanted them to lose, it was irritating to watch a major-league team play this way. They were a team in name only, a team only in that they all wore the same uniform and got credited for driving each other in.

As a sinner becomes a saint and a radical becomes a Reaganite, with the passage of time the Angels have struggled away from that pole and reached the other. The talent on the Angels now is much less impressive (*Sports Illustrated* keeps picking them to finish fifth), but less impressive only in the sense of not being able to run as fast or throw as hard. I've never seen a team, anywhere, anytime, execute so well. Do Boone, DeCinces, and Downing *ever* make mistakes? Reggie is a smart player. Grich is a smart player. They make very few mistakes and turn the double play extremely well. Even the young guys are smart players. Wally Joyner plays like he taught first base at Stanford. When was the last time you saw Dick Schofield cost his team a run? The 1986 Angels were a great tribute to a great manager.

—1987

Chicago Cubs

Locked for two generations in the nether regions of the form chart, the Chicago Cubs exploded off the mat in 1984, pummeling the National League East left and right and center, and making off with their first divisional title. It was, however quickly passed, a moment of epic adrenaline, lending hope to the downtrodden of the earth and providing the first flesh evidence in years that the Lord still cares about the plight of the underdog. The moment arrived without any proper effort being made to prepare us for it; wallowing in sunlight and despair while starry-eyed adolescents turned into grandparents, the Cubs seemed as likely as not to let them return to dust seeing no more than a flirtation with promise. To the men who made the flag of '84 roar in the wind that flaps and flickers quietly so many others, to Ryne Sandberg and Rick Sutcliffe, to Dallas Green and Jim Frey, to Leon Durham and Gary Matthews and Bob Dernier, to Keith Moreland and Steve Trout and Dennis Eckersley and Larry Bowa, to Jody Davis and Ron Cey and Lee Smith and Scott Sanderson, let us render the honors that are due, and leave pass a decent interval before we ask of them anything more.

—1985

I don't think that enough has been made of the Sutcliffe/Borowy parallel. The last pitcher before Sutcliffe to win twenty games in the two leagues was Hank Borowy, who joined the Cubs in mid-season, 1945, to help them win their last pennant. Acquired by the Cubs on July 27, 1945 in a controversial $100,000 waiver deal ($100,000 then was a fair amount of money), Borowy won eleven games in two months to do basically what Sutcliffe did; he was 11–2 with a 2.14 ERA. He pitched only 122 innings—Sutcliffe, joining the team a little more than a month earlier, pitched 150—but at that time the ERA standard was ten complete games, so Borowy was, and is, the last Cub pitcher to win an ERA title. Borowy pitched a shutout in the first game of the 1945 World Series (the Cubs won 9–0), but then was hit hard and took the loss in the seventh and deciding game. Sutcliffe pitched seven shutout innings in the first game against the Padres, won by the Cubs 13–0, but then was hit for six runs and took a loss in the fifth and deciding game.

Fate, or chance? The Cubs in 1945 met the Tigers; the Cubs in 1984 would have met the Tigers if they had won one more game. Chance, or destiny? A new commissioner of baseball, Happy Chandler, was named in April of 1945, but had other commitments that kept him busy until that October; a new commissioner of baseball, Peter Ueberroth, was named in March of 1984, but prevented from beginning the job until October by other commitments. Coincidence, or fortune? Steve Trout won a five-hit victory for the Cubs in the 1984 playoffs; his father, Dizzy Trout, pitched a five-hit victory *against* the Cubs in the 1945 World Series. Luck, or predetermination? The 1945 season was the last hurrah for a popular Cub infielder named Stan Hack; the 1984 season was a last hurrah for a popular Cub infielder named Larry Bowa. "Hack" and "Bowa" each have four letters in their names, even if you spell them backwards. Coincidence, or sheer pap? The 1984 Cubs fired their television broadcaster, *Milo* Hamilton; the 1945 Cubs released a catcher named Len *Rice*; it goes against my grain to accept that as a mere coincidence. Goodnight.

—1985

The Chicago Cubs opened the 1986 season expecting to contend for the National League East title. Those expectations were unrealistic, founded in the fantasy that an injury-prone pitching staff would somehow spring to health and keep the opposition from abusing the friendly fences of Wrigley, and shingled over by the sheepish logic that what we did once, in 1984, we can do again in 1986. The season was a long, hard lesson that miracles cannot be repeated on demand, that the 1984 pennant resulted in part from a unique set of circumstances at a moment that came and went. The harsh summer split the Cub organization into bitter splinter groups which attacked one another in a season-long party game of Pin-the-Blame-on-the-Donkey. It was not a pretty time in baseball's prettiest park.

—1987

As this collection of non-talent wound its way toward a thoroughly unsurprising fifth-place finish, the games became a sideshow to the ongoing weirdness of an organization in turmoil. General Manager Dallas Green was unhappy with the effort given, which brings up a question: If Dallas Green thinks that lousy players are lousy players because they don't try hard enough, how does he explain his own career? On May 15,

Green was quoted as saying that Jim Frey must learn to criticize his players sometimes, holding them accountable for their performance. On June 5, Frey tried out Green's advice on Steve Trout, remarking that "In my opinion [his problem] is definitely not physical, so we know what's left." Apparently this carping came as too little too late, because on June 12, with the season a third gone and the Cubs only sixteen and a half behind the Mets, Frey was fired and replaced by Gene Michael.

The Cubs continued to lose. In July, ballgirl Marla Collins was fired for showing off some of her secret recipes in *Better Homes and Gardens*. Or was it *Redbook* . . . whatever; I didn't see them but I guess they were pretty exciting. I used to read those magazines, but after a while all the recipes started to look alike. In August, George Frazier and his 5.40 ERA were traded to the Twins; Frazier alleged that the problem with the Cubs was that Harry Caray and Steve Stone created a negative atmosphere among the fans. Harry Caray said that Frazier was inept. The Cubs were mathematically eliminated on September first.

—1987

Traditions die hard in Chicago, even bad ones. When operation Greylord revealed that Chicago courtrooms were still a sewer of bribery and favoritism not much better than when the signed confessions of the Black Sox disappeared from a State Attorney's file cabinet sixty-five years ago, Studs Terkel complained that these federal boys were messing around with a Chicago tradition, that this was just how things got done in Chicago. One gets the feeling that the *Times-Mirror* corporation feels the same way about the Cubs, that they've gotten along fine as losers for all these years so why bother to change anything, heh? It's hard to find anything good to say about an organization which dispatches a fine manager like Gene Michael and hires Mr. Potato Head to be their general manager. Despite their flash of glory, the Cubs have the twenty-third best record in baseball during the decade, and they're burrowing rapidly toward twenty-fourth.

—1988

Chicago White Sox

Let us start our account of the Ken Harrelson command where he started it, by moving the fences back at Comiskey Park. Moving further away from the fences, Harrelson felt, would be more accommodating to the kind of team that he wanted to have, a fast, aggressive team with outstanding pitching. It might have occurred to a more timid director of operations that he didn't actually *have* any of these things; he merely thought that it would be neat to acquire them. What he actually had was a slow team whose pitchers had control problems, and whose biggest assets were a few players like Harold Baines, Carlton Fisk, Greg Walker, and Ron Kittle, who didn't run well but did have power.

So anyway, the ChiSox now had an outfield of Baines, Kittle, and Law, none of whom could play center field in any park, and whose defensive abilities were stretched to the limit to cover the field in Comiskey as it was, although Rudy Law does run well. In order to get the maximum benefit out of this shrewd maneuver, Harrelson a) released the fastest player on the team, Rudy Law, over the vigorous objections of his manager, who thought Law was ready to have an outstanding season; and b) shifted his catcher to the outfield.

There is some controversy about who actually was responsible for the decision to move Carlton Fisk to the outfield, and the next person to step forward and take credit for it will be the first as well as quite certainly the last. You almost had the feeling that this was one of those acts, like leaving a bomb in a suitcase at an airport, that somebody should call up the newspaper and take credit for, but since no one did the maneuver is variously attributed to Tony LaRussa, Ken Harrelson, and Dave Duncan, the ex-pitching coach who apparently thought that Fisk's pitch selection was suspect. Maybe we should divvy up the credit among the bright boy who thought up the move, the genius who okayed it, and the powerful intellect who decided that the need to make this move was so pressing that it justified ramming it down Fisk's throat. In any case, before making this move the White Sox had:

1. One of the league's best offensive and defensive catchers in Carlton Fisk, who had hit 37 homers and driven in 107 runs in 1985; and
2. A slow, slugging right-handed-hitting left fielder/DH named Ron Kittle.

After making this move, the White Sox had:

1. No proven catcher;
2. Two slow, slugging right-handed-hitting left fielder/DHs; and as a special bonus:
3. One very unhappy veteran player, who just coincidentally had been the team MVP in two of the previous three years.

Any time you can make a trade like that, it's got to help you accomplish your mission.

As curious as these utilization-of-resources decisions were, what was most damaging about Harrelson's stewardship was his utter inability to evaluate talent. With the exception of the Britt Burns deal, which worked to the White Sox advantage because Burns wasn't able to pitch, every deal that Harrelson made, and he made a bunch of them, hurt the team. The fences can be moved back and Fisk can be returned to his position but the White Sox can't get Scott Fletcher or Joel Skinner or Ron Kittle or Rudy Law or Edwin Correa back. The legacy of Ken Harrelson in Chicago is an emaciated talent base that may take several years to rebuild.

There's an old saying that you should choose your enemies carefully, because that's who you will eventually resemble. We are a strange race, in that as we move through life we tend to switch roles with people we once despised. The abused child grows up to abuse his own children. The rowdy student grows up to be a strict teacher. Ken Harrelson ran the White Sox exactly the way that Charles O. Finley ran the Kansas City A's in the sixties, when Harrelson played for KC. To a fan of those teams, each Hawk blunder seemed familiar. Finley loved to move the fences in and out. Every couple of years he would have some new idea about the kind of team that he was going to put together to win big with, and the first thing he would always do was move the fences around to accommodate his notion. Then he would worry about the talent. Making trades on the seat of his pants without the advice and counsel of his organization, making personnel decisions on intuition and then forcing everyone beneath him to accept them, firing managers and general managers and assistant general managers to cover his own mistakes, getting down on players who were slumping or couldn't do what he asked them to do and trading them for half what they would have brought a year earlier, falling in love with unproven players and then giving up on them when they turned out to be ordinary—these were all very typical Charlie Finley moves. They didn't work twenty years ago, and they won't work twenty years from now.

Well, I could give a lot more particulars, but at this point to say more about Harrelson's direction of the Sox would be beating a dead horse's ass, so I'll move on to the characteristics of the team, such as it remained. . . .

—1987

One of the basic differences between a good organization and a poor organization is that a good organization will still get something out of a bad year. Rarely, if ever, have I seen a team get as much out of a bad year as the White Sox did in 1987.

The White Sox opened the 1987 season hoping to contend. "No one in the Western Division scares us," said Larry Himes, who also is not afraid of the Ty D Bol Man, the Tooth Fairy or the Keebler Elves. "When we left spring training the club had a good attitude. It thinks it can win." The problem with trying to win with an attitude is that the attitude changes from day to day, but that's another story. Early in the season it became apparent that this was not a year in which the Sox would win anything. By June 28 the White Sox were all but eliminated, with a record of 25–46.

The White Sox hit that floor and bounced off for two and a half months, hanging twenty to twenty-two games under .500 almost constantly from late June to mid-September. The major media story concerning the Sox was their attempt to enforce petty discipline from the front office. With the team in a slump in June, "at least three players were fined by General Manager Larry Himes for not wearing socks with their dress clothes in the home locker room" (*The Sporting News*, July 20, 1987). Various accounts, which may have been exaggerated, had the Sox posting a flunky in the clubhouse to check these details of appropriate attire. Several Sox players were unhappy about a ban on beer in the clubhouse; Carlton Fisk, for one, sounded off about that, and threatened (apparently in jest) to smuggle beer into his locker. Himes ordered security to check Fisk thoroughly when he came to the park.

Keep that good attitude, Larry, keep that attitude. I certainly wouldn't want to defend Himes for this kind of crap, but I do think it is unfortunate that the attention given to it has obscured some very real accomplishments. It's not that the White Sox are on the verge of emerging as a good team. They're not, or at least not that I can see. But just one year ago, I thought that Ken Harrelson had emaciated the Sox' talent base to such an extent that the White Sox would not be able to contend for the better part of a decade. I thought that in a couple of years they would be where Atlanta is now. Just to have avoided that fate is a very substantial accomplishment.

—1988

Cincinnati Reds

There is something strangely missing from the Cincinnati Reds, and it irritates me to admit that his initials are P. R. It has been two years since he packed up his scuffed-shoe and skinned-elbow charm and went off to save Philadelphia, and everything and everyone in Cincinnati seems smaller than it once did. His talents are replaceable, but no one in baseball can match Pete Rose's gift for baseball as theater. His stage gestures—the last out hurled violently into the turf when it could just as well slip quietly from his palm, the mad dash to first which has slowed to a furious waddle, the slight, tense quickening of his practice strokes at a key moment of the game, which passes *sotto voce* a sense of urgency to the dugout behind him, a sense of danger to the one across the way—all these may not fall directly into the stream of the action, but they rain heavily on the drainage area.

Which is prefatory to saying that the Reds may still, or again, be the best team in the National League, but how can one tell? Perez, Morgan and Anderson, men whose complex images were burned into the American consciousness, are gone; in their places are the faces of Who Driessen, What Oester, and Ida Know McNamara . . . .

—Esquire magazine
April, 1981

In the years 1980–82, the Cincinnati Reds organization was rocked by free-agent losses, personnel conflicts, an ongoing battle over uniform and dress requirements, and a series of misfortunes including the loss of a quality AAA franchise because of the Reds' insistence that their minor league teams not use the designated hitter rule, even when their opposition was using it. In July, 1983, the Cincinnati Reds fired General Manager Dick Wagner and replaced him on an interim basis with long-term GM Bob Howsam. Among Howsam's first acts was to hire Vern Rapp as his manager, an action which at the time was interpreted as meaning that nothing really had changed in the Cincinnati front office.

One of my rules for selecting articles for this book was that I did not want to reprint earlier articles of which it might be said that time had proven either that I was right or that I was wrong. My having been right or wrong in the past is not what this book is about. In this case, in time I was proven both right and wrong—wrong in arguing that Vern Rapp deserved another shot as a major league manager, but right in arguing that Bob Howsam was not just another version of Dick Wagner, and that something substantial had truly changed in Cincinnati. . . .

Among many baseball people, the name of Vernon Rapp had come to stand for "minor league manager," for the total experience of failure as a manager by one so dedicated to The Dream that he would pay for it in decades. I know a man who works in the front office of a National League team which recently interviewed a group of potential managers. A leading candidate came in and gave one of those ringing My-Way-orthe-Highway speeches, making a great impression on the owner and sending a chill down the spine of everyone else. "He really scared me," the guy said. "I thought we had another Vern Rapp situation on our hands." A couple of years ago I asked a player whether a coach who had been with the team the year before had potential as a major league manager. "He's got potential as a Vern Rapp," he sneered.

The return of Rapp to a major league dugout, then, was a bit of a shock, and was greeted with predictable derisive chatter from the nation's pressboxes. It was, so they said, a sign that nothing had really changed except the name plate on the GM's desk.

I beg to differ. It is certainly true that Bob Howsam has a taste for strict "disciplinarian" managers; he always has had. But that was not the defining characteristic of the Reds' organization under Dick Wagner. The defining characteristic of the Reds' organization under Dick Wagner was inflexibility. The fact that this rigidity was allied to old-line "disciplinarian" policies is certainly not incidental, but my point is that there have been any number of successful hard-line managers and organizations. If you keep the hard-line policies but get rid of the inflexibility, then you are dealing with a totally different situation.

When Dick Wagner made a decision, he wrote it down and closed the book. Wagner was concerned not with whether a decision was "working" or was "not working," but with whether it was "right" or "wrong." And if he made a decision, then it was therefore the right decision, and he was *not* going to review it. When the policy was adopted that the Reds would not use the designated hitter in the minor leagues, that was a reasonable decision. But what happened was, the costs of the decision escalated and escalated and escalated, while the policy was yielding returns that were not even visible; no one could see that the Reds' pitchers were hitting any better than anybody else's were. But Wagner refused to review the decision; it was the right decision, and therefore whether its benefits outweighed its costs was not a matter for discussion. To refuse to meet the salary expectations of established ballplayers was a right decision; whether or not it ruined the ball club was not important. The decision was made that Dan Driessen was going to play first base for the Reds, and Johnny Bench was going to catch—a reasonable decision at the time. But when Driessen didn't develop and Bench didn't want to catch, he wouldn't adjust; he would not review the decision.

Wagner could not understand that the contexts in which decisions were made were changing, and that therefore there was a need to review those decisions. He was concerned not with what came out of a decision, but with what went into it.

There is a word for people who think this way. It's a common word, something you always have on your person. Dick Wagner was like a man driving down a road who is stopped and informed that a section of the bridge over the river has collapsed, and who responds to this by saying, "Goddamnit, the county is supposed to maintain that bridge. I pay taxes. I've been driving over that bridge for thirty years, and I feel that I have a right to drive over that bridge." And so he does.

So the relevant question about Bob Howsam is not whether he too drives on that road, or whether he too pays taxes, or whether he too expects the county to maintain the bridges. The relevant question is whether or not he is flexible enough to choose an alternate route when a bridge goes out. Which, as he has demonstrated consistently throughout his long and distinguished career, he is.

—1984

The Cincinnati Reds now allow their minor league teams to employ the designated hitter. They have signed their first large free agent. They appear, in brief, to have abandoned all hope that Dick Wagner's adolescence will return, and have committed themselves to living in a world not of their own construction. Since the Reds are so conscious of symbols, so determined to maintain intact the integrity of their fifties image that they would rip the organization to shreds fighting internal battles over beards, shoes, stocking stirrups, and other details of proper 1956 fashion and attire, we here have been wondering how they could mark the transition forward in time with appropriate symbolic gestures. If you raise the fashions of 1984 to the level of a moral imperative, what do you get?

1. Any player reporting for a team flight without properly coiffed and styled hair will not be allowed to make the trip. A list of approved hair-fashion consultants will be maintained on a bulletin board in the clubhouse.
2. The wearing of earrings is an absolute must. Fifty-dollar fine for any player appearing before the public without his earrings.
3. If glasses are to be worn, they must be those ones that turn brown when you go out in the sun. This is a major league organization.
4. Proper on-field foot attire means either designer shoes, or

else some kind of shoe with the name printed on it large enough to be read from the third deck.

5. The uniform that is issued to you will include chains; you have your choice of a crucifix or a little gold spoon, or you may wear both if you prefer. Contact the equipment manager *immediately* if your chain is misplaced. (These chains do not need to be removed during showering or other intimate times).

6. If the temperature drops below sixty during the game, you will be allowed to button the top two buttons on your shirt.

7. Computer classes are available; the club will assist you in selecting one that fits your needs. Contact Jamie Lynn for details.

8. Wives are cordially invited to join us each morning for our special *Cincinnati Reds aerobic workout.* Selected wives might become eligible for valuable bonuses for cooperating in our community-wide aerobic program.

—Jim Baker and Bill James
1984

It's a pity that Bob Howsam and Dick Wagner weren't around a few years earlier to start protecting old-style baseball before it was already so corrupt. Just think about the things they could have saved for us. If the Reds management had been around in 1905, we would still be able to watch catchers playing without shin guards; a few years before that and they could have gotten catchers' masks, too. If Bob Howsam had been on the rules committee in 1950, we could still see fielders leaving their gloves in the grass at the end of an inning. If theses guys had been around in 1935, we would still have two stadiums without lights. If they had been around in 1920, maybe they could have arranged for the Reds' pitchers to be allowed to continue to throw spitballs. As recently as the 1930s, when there was a large crowd, fans would sometimes stand in the outfield behind ropes; the Reds could have preserved this practice for us. Perhaps, as a tribute to baseball history, the league could set aside all kinds of modern inventions, and allow the Reds to play with old, dirty gray baseballs and gloves without any padding to speak of, with bats made out of hickory and bulky flannel uniforms, a sort of living museum of baseball history. Their opponents would be free to elect these options as they chose.

—1985

Cleveland Indians

The Detroit Tigers have been in a building cycle since 1974. This does not impress the partisans of the Cleveland Indians, who have been rebuilding since 1957. Trying to get rid of a losing attitude in Cleveland must be like trying to stamp out venereal disease around an army base.

—*Esquire* magazine
April, 1981

Across the history of the Cleveland franchise a line is sharply drawn, and by that line the present condition of the Cleveland Indians, uniquely, can be dated to the hour. On April 12, 1960, the Indians ceased to be what they had then been for thirty-one years and became what they remain now.

What they had been since 1929 was a pretty damn good organization. In those thirty-one years they had finished with a losing record only six times, and even then they didn't lose badly. They were the perennial runner-up who would occasionally pull one out, having finished second six times in the nine years prior to 1960 and first twice in twelve years. They were coming off yet another second-place season. They were rebuilding a pitching staff that had long been recognized as the best in the game. The tradition of the Indians at that moment was very comparable to the tradition of the Boston Red Sox at this moment.

That tradition was blasted out of existence by what was called at the time the biggest trade ever made: Colavito for Kuenn. The Indians possessed a twenty-six-year-old power hitter who had hit 83 home runs in the last two years. In the major leagues. And they traded him. For what they traded him is not the point. The point is that the Indians possessed tradition, that Colavito was carrying a torch which had been passed to him from Earl Averill by way of Jeff Heath and Larry Doby, and when he was traded the fire went out. The point is that the Cleveland fans loved Colavito, and they did not love this fellow they were getting from Detroit. The point is that Colavito was both the physical and the psychological center of an offense which had just led the American League in runs scored and which did not need to be rebuilt at the moment, thank you. The point is that Colavito represented both the past and the future, and no one was quite sure of what it was that Kuenn represented. The point is that the Indians of 1959 knew they could win because they had always won, and they knew how to go about it. And when the leaders of their offense—Colavito and also Minnie Minoso—were suddenly gone, the Indians of 1960 did not know whether they could win or not, that a thirty-one-year accumulation of group confidence had been thrown carelessly out the window. The point is, in short, that the Colavito trade cut the center out of the Tribe tradition and that to this day they remain . . . a shell of talent wrapped around a void.

The Indians as of now have a core of good young talent. But then, they always do. On one minor league team in 1964, they had Sam McDowell, Luis Tiant, Tommy John and Tommie Agee. Among the people who played for the Indians in 1975 were Buddy Bell, George Hendrick, Alan Ashby, Rico Carty, Oscar Gamble, Rick Cerone, Duane Kuiper, Dennis Eckersley, Rick Waits, Gaylord Perry, Dave LaRoche, Jim Bibby, and Jim Kern. I will not bore you with more lists of names (like Chris Chambliss, Graig Nettles, Lou Piniella . . .) but the young talent has *always* been there, and it is there now.

Yet surrounding the young talent has always been, and is now, a list of players on the decline, players who were acquired and put onto the field at a moment when there was nothing much they could do except decline, players who could not by any stretch of the imagination be worked into the pattern of future excellence formed by the young stars, but who reserved their own section of the roster and by their very already-formedness defied any notion of melting into a core of shared experiences which might recast the missing center. The 1961 team which had Mudcat Grant, Jim Perry, and Johnny Romano also had Johnny Temple, Johnny Antonelli, Jimmy Piersall, and Bob Nieman, players who had made their reputation in the fifties and came to Cleveland to play out the string. The 1970 team mixed Graig Nettles with Vada Pinson and Dean Chance. Talent in odd lots and mismatched sizes; old mixed with young, seven singles-hitters with no speed and no one to drive them in, and then two steps later power all over the roster with no defense and no one on base.

In 1978 the Indians finished with a 69–90 record despite having a respectable batting average and ERA. Not good, but respectable. I remember that fall reading in *The Sporting News* that Gabe Paul felt that what the Indians needed was two things: power and speed. And so he traded for, you guessed it, Bobby Bonds. Also Toby Harrah, who had had 27 home runs and stolen bases just a year before that.

Now, in a narrow sense there is absolutely nothing wrong with that logic; asking the questions that he asks, he gets perfectly correct answers.

Q. What are our shortcomings?
A. Lack of power and lack of speed.
Q. Who can we trade for who will bring us power and speed?
A. Bobby Bonds and Toby Harrah.

The problem is, what does any of this "logic" have to do with the building of a championship baseball team? Nothing, nothing at all. To acquire a thirty-year-old middle-of-the-pack third baseman and a thirty-three-year-old outfielder (or a thirty-year-old Jorge Orta or a thirty-year-old Bert Blyleven) and to regard these as the building blocks of a championship team is pathetic.

In trading Colavito off just as he was entering his best years, the Indians were sketching a pattern that they would later trace time and again, reducing themselves often to a combination proving ground for players on the way up and halfway house for those on the way out. (The Indians five years later traded Tommy John and Tommie Agee to get Colavito back, just as he was leaving his prime period.) In that way, too, the Colavito trade is the beginning of the modern Indians. But in a broader sense, the Indians began then because that move marked the beginning of the notion that a baseball team is made up of interchangeable parts no more complex than lines of statistics.

In the first major work on sabermetrics, published a year after the trade was made, an opinionated metallurgist analyzed the Colavito-Kuenn trade at great length and with incomprehensible shallowness and reached the conclusion that the Indians had made a good trade. He couldn't have been more wrong. It was a classic example of what I call statistical idiocy. Statistical idiocy is the assertion that nothing is real except that which is measured in the statistics. That analysis of the trade ignored or dismissed as peripheral considerations every real or substantive issue that needed to be discussed, including the differences between Tiger Stadium and Cleveland Stadium, the differences between a twenty-six-year-old player and a twenty-nine-year-old player, the differences in defensive value, and, most importantly, the impact of the trade on the fans, the other members of the team, and on the players involved. That book set sabermetrics back by twenty years. This *tour de farce* of statistical idiocy reinforced the supposition that all statisticians were idiots, that the analysis of baseball by statistics must be one-dimensional and therefore unable to deal with the complexity of real-life decisions.

But it was not a statistician who made the trade! What I am trying to say is two things, which both amount to one: Not all statisticians are idiots, and not all idiots are statisticians. Frank Lane made the trade because he had been so successful as a trader in Chicago that he had come to believe more in his own genius than he believed in talent. He thought that he could move players around like they were APBA cards and turn a contender into a champion because he was smarter than anybody else. It didn't work because, even if he was smarter than anybody else, it was still the talent which had to go out on the field and win the games, and a bearskin rug stuffed with hamburger is not a bear. He was treating ballplayers like meat, and they played like meat. Genius or not, statistician or not, he was guilty of exactly the same idiocy. And that is the problem of the Indians until this tomorrow.

—1982

The Cleveland Indians are baseball's first bionic baseball team, if the image does not imply too much force or energy, a team assembled from the living scraps and donated parts of other baseball teams, without a heart or a soul or a reason for living, that you can tell. Mike Ferraro's assignment is to impart these things to them. I interpreted Ferraro's signing as a good omen for the organization, as I regard Ferraro as one of the best managerial prospects around. Then came the winter meetings, and the illusion that something might be different now was shattered. Ferraro will almost have to play Trillo at second for a year, which will hurt Perconte's chances of making it a year from now.

The Indians are the most difficult team in baseball to describe because their essential feature is that they are featureless, that they have no dominant character or type. They are not an old team nor a young team. They are not a power team nor a line-drive team, not an offensive team nor a pitching-and-defense team. You tell me: Do they have a particularly strong or a particularly weak infield or outfield? Do they have a past or a future? Is there anything to distinguish their starting rotation or their bullpen? They are not strong up the middle nor especially strong at the corner positions. They should change their name to the Cleveland Blahs. They'd probably get sued by a Blah Association and have to have a Blah Appreciation Day to settle the case, bring in a Blah singer (Jerry Vale) and a Blah actor and actress (Robert Wagner and Lois Nettleton), a Blah politician (Thomas Eagleton) and maybe some Blah ballplayers out of the past (Larry Brown, Duke Sims, Chuck Hinton).

What I want to know is, exactly what does Gabe Paul have to do before he gets fired? Trade Len Barker to the Yankees for Bye-Bye Balboni? Get arrested? Die? Trade Bo Diaz for Lary Sorensen? Deal off Von Hayes? At what point do you cry "Uncle"?

This is the man who, with the Indians heading into a crunching part of the schedule with seven pitchers on their roster, refused to call up a pitcher because he said the work would be good for them. This is the man who made his manager play the 1982 season with eleven minor leaguers on the roster.

There is still some good young talent on this team. I think Ferraro will do a good job with them. But "a good job" means 86 or 88 wins and third place if Andre Thornton and Toby Harrah don't go in the tank, eighty wins if they do. If I was an Indians' fan, I know exactly what I would do. I would set to work and build the largest, loudest and most abrasive fan organization in the world. It might not accomplish anything tangible, but it would serve a useful purpose anyway. It would prevent me from resorting to mayhem to put an end to the Chinese water torture of Gabe Paul's trades.

—1983

If the people who run the Cleveland Indians were in charge of foreign policy, I'd enroll in night school and start studying Slavic languages. The Indians have now accomplished something that many would have thought they never could: They've made their past brighter than their future.

That being said, it becomes increasingly difficult to make a positive comment about the team. Yet odd as it seems, the Cleveland baseball scene sometimes looks pretty good to a Kansas City baseball fan: no pressure, no tension, no hordes of blotto suburbanites trying to figure where their seat is and itching for a chance to let off some steam. Just a few hard-core baseball fans watching the summer ease by. You could get a ticket anytime and anywhere you wanted. Maybe we just could sit there and tell Gabe Paul jokes. (If Gabe was running a hospital, I'd invest in a mortuary. If I was on a ship and Gabe was the captain, I'd try to make friends with a shark. If Gabe was an investment counselor, I'd open up a pawn shop. If Gabe was selling furnaces, I'd sell smoke detectors.)

I suppose that's like the successful executive who goes to his twenty-year class reunion, sees a high school buddy who became a construction worker, and thinks that it looks like a good life—no pressure, when five o'clock comes the job's over and you go home to the wife and have dinner. Ah, the simple things in life.

Having been poor most of my life, I can assure you that, as long as you have your health, American poverty is not all that wretched; it's more irritating than anything else. But I'm in no hurry to get back to it. And I'm not going to move to Cleveland and root for the Indians, either.

—1984

I don't suppose that too many people are going to step forward and admit this, either, but I talked to a number of people last spring who thought that the Indians would contend in 1985, and to at least two people who thought they would win. They had won seventy-five games in 1984 and finished strong—they were over .500 the last two months—and they didn't look all that bad, what with four to six good young players in the lineup, an excellent rotation anchor in Blyleven, a relief ace (Camacho) coming off a fine season. The figuring was that if they could come up with a third starting pitcher behind Blyleven and Neal Heaton, their pitching would be about as good as anybody else's, and with the young hitters gaining a year of experience . . . well, you never know.

You sure don't. Once the season began, the Indians started out fairly well, for the Indians, if a little disappointing to those who expected a contender; they were 10–13 in early May. At this point, some bright boy in the Cleveland front office—we will discuss who in a moment—decided to solve the shortstop "problem" with Johnnie LeMaster, heh? Let's make a record of this for posterity. The Cleveland Indians already had an outstanding young shortstop, in Julio Franco. They already had a second baseman named Tony Bernazard, who was trying to get his game back together and was hitting .318 through May 7, when the Indians decided to move Franco to second, and acquire Johnnie LeMaster from San Francisco to play shortstop.

A few details of this story may help you to understand the reasoning behind the move. It was especially recommended by the facts that

1. Franco was twenty-three years old, an established star and leading the league in hitting at the time in question,
2. Julio Franco had never played second base in his life, and was thoroughly PO'd about being assigned to learn the position in mid-season.
3. Johnnie LeMaster, affectionately known to the masses as Johnnie Disaster, was a thirty-one-year-old lifetime .226 hitter who has avoided leading the National League in errors several times only by virtue of the fact that he couldn't hit well enough to stay in the lineup, and
4. LeMaster had made himself extra expendable to the worst team in the National League by becoming involved in conflicts with his manager.

I thought Tony Bernazard summed it up well. "I don't mean to be rude," he said, "but who the hell is Johnnie LeMaster?" Franco, despite being assigned to the second base position for eight games, managed to keep alive his record of never having played the position. Following this move, the Indians dropped out of contention in twelve minutes and seventeen seconds, and LeMaster was sent on his way in a few days, as soon as the Indians had a firm grip on last place.

It was the strangest, most incomprehensible organizational strategem in many years, and in view of this I was wondering who should be given the credit for it.

Of course, it goes without saying that if the Cleveland Indians had a manager who was worthy of the title he would have laughed and told the front office to go sleep it off. Since he didn't do this and no one else has come forward to take responsibility, the horrible suspicion persists that it may have been Corrales himself who initiated the move.

May have been, but not necessarily, for the Cleveland Indians front office is sort of like an All-Star roster composed of General Managers who have been fired by all of the worst teams in baseball for pulling crap like this. The Indians are the only team in baseball history which has more General Managers on their payroll than outfielders.

The Head GM is Peter Bavasi, who earned the position by having the worst record of all. At the time that he "resigned" from the Toronto czarship, Bavasi said that he was doing so to pursue other interests. I recommended that he sell shoes. Don't you always love that? . . . College football coaches are particularly good at it. Two weeks after they are fired they always pop up on the radio and report that they have received a number of attractive offers and are weighing their options. Seventy-three percent of the time they opt to sell life insurance.

Anyway, it should be pointed out in retrospect that during the years Bavasi was running the Toronto organization, the Blue Jays acquired nine of the players who played key roles on the 1985 American League East champions—Ernie Whitt and Garth Iorg (1976), Jesse Barfield and Willie Upshaw (1977), Dave Stieb and Lloyd Moseby (1978), Damaso Garcia and Tony Fernandez (1979), and George Bell (1980). If Bavasi can repeat that performance in accumulating talent, then with the young players the Indians already have this team is shortly going to be formidable. It should also be pointed out that Bavasi has now been a General Manager for six years with two organizations, and the best record by any Bavasi-led team was 67–95. While I haven't actually checked, this is a distinction which I am certain must be appalling.

Actually, before that Peter was listed for four years as the General Manager of the San Diego Padres, although at the time it was generally thought that it was his father Buzzie who made the tough decisions. But, not to be cheap about it, Peter can claim credit for them, too, if he wants it. They stunk, too.

The Cleveland Indians remind you of one of those movies that is supposed to be a metaphor for life, and the only thing you can think of while watching it is that if this is life I'm sure glad it isn't mine. In life, as in the Indians, we seem to waste so much of our talent, we seem to spend so much of our time bashing ourselves against entrenched and immovable forces. We make blind decisions about our lives and look back on them in awe of our own stupidity. They should call themselves the Cleveland Metaphor, or simply the Cleveland Life. I spent many years rooting for a terrible team, and I watch this team with a certain empathy. But I'm sure glad it isn't mine.

—1986

The Indians, as I am sure you know, were picked by *Sports Illustrated* as the best team in baseball a year ago. I dasn't twit the magazine too roughly about this, because I make predictions, too, and God knows I don't want to start comparing them; nonetheless, that's a pretty phenomenal accomplishment, the maximum possible error: Picking the very worst team in baseball to be the very best. Deluded by such predictions into believing themselves staring at the lips of glory, the Indians kicked off the campaign by making their annual hairbrained move involving the catching position. A year ago the Indians decided that Andy Allanson was ready to jump from the Eastern League into a starting job, and to put an exclamation mark behind this they released Jerry Willard, who had been their regular catcher the year before and had hit .270.

Allanson didn't exactly work out, so last year, as pennant insurance, the Indians signed Rick Dempsey as a free agent, even though this cost them their first round draft pick. Then they didn't even have the sense to platoon Dempsey; he started out playing every day and was struggling along with a .177 season until Bo Jackson crunched him at home plate in late July, putting his season out of its misery. I'm sure the Indians are about ready to try one of those infield-to-catcher conversions; the only question not yet answered is who will be the lucky schnook selected for the effort.

Pat Corrales' managerial career was one of the casualties of the season. The habit of changing managers in midseason is one of the ten warning signs of an inept organization. It is a warning sign, I suppose, if you change managers in the middle of the campaign to bring in a Sparky Anderson or a Jim Fregosi, somebody that you really want to be your next manager. If you change managers in mid-season to give the job to a coach who is there primarily because he was a buddy of the old manager and then leave him there because he seems to be doing all right, that's not a warning sign; that's sufficient for a diagnosis. When you see an organization do that, you know they're just playing it by ear. A team that can't get organized long enough to make a deliberate selection as to who should occupy perhaps their most critical position probably can't get organized long enough to plan out a trade or develop a training program or plan an amateur draft, either. Further evidence on this issue was provided over the winter, when the Indians went to Dallas with three third basemen on their roster (Jacoby, Snyder, and Williams) and with third basemen in demand, yet couldn't close a deal for a pitcher; when they came home they still had more third basemen than starting pitchers.

Another of the warning signs of an organization wandering in the desert is the inability to make a mature judgment about where they are. One can sympathize with the Indian front office for thinking that they were better than they were, because, after all, people were telling them that they were better than they were. Still, they made the mistake of believing it.

—1988

Detroit Tigers

The Tigers' future floats maddeningly on the horizon, a half-step always ahead of you while that which is at your feet is always sand. The World Champion Tigers of the future began to take shape in 1974, with the ashes of the last team still warm, when Roger LeFlore appeared. He was joined by Dave Lemanczyk; in 1975 the Tigers of the future were Danny Meyer and Leon Roberts, now the Mariners of the future, plus Tom Veryzer and Vern Ruhle. In 1976 there was the Bird, and also Jason Thompson. In 1977 there was Steve Kemp, aided by Dave Rozema, Bob Sykes, Tim Corcoran, and Fernando Arroyo. The class of 1978 might be one of the most remarkable rookie crops of all time: Lou Whitaker, Alan Trammell, Lance Parrish, and Jack Morris. Also Kip Young if you don't mind diluting the batch a little. In 1979 there was a fling of young pitchers (Robbins, Petry, Tobik, Underwood, Chris). In 1980 we will add Kirk Gibson, Dave Stegman, Rick Peters.

But . . . drip, drip, drip . . . when? It must be Chinese water torture for their fans, lusting for the better part of a decade after a championship that flirts toward you and dances away. To a disinterested party, it is a fascinating chance to study the cycle of decay and growth, development and disappointment that goes into putting together a ball club, for ordinarily the growth of one part is shielded by the foliage of another. The Tigers have exposed the innards of the process. An up-and-down cycle is not inevitable in baseball; it is perfectly possible to remain strong while moving from one team to another. But a down phase becomes inevitable *if you assume it is*, as the Tigers did in 1970.

And so they got down to nothing, right on down to where they didn't even have their skivvies left, and then they began the tantalizing piece-by-piece assembly with the whole world watching (and if I try to get one more figure of speech into this article, my typewriter keys are going to riot). See, now we have a first baseman, and we're this far along. Now what will happen if we add a double play combination? Excellent, excellent. Now, what's a starting pitcher worth? Is that all? Jack Morris goes from 3–5 to 17–7 and we don't gain anything? Ordinarily the process of development is concurrent not only with decline, but with a flurry of other marginally relevant activity that constitutes the day-to-day press fodder of the entertainment biz. Here there's none of that. It's like a watch with a glass back (Oops). Seriously, if you look at what has happened to this team, it really does show how much goes into the building of a complete team, because they've done it one thing at a time, without the shelter or confusion of mixed objectives.

And they will get there. The championship is not a mirage. The drip, drip, drip will not go on forever. The dancer's gonna kiss ya, the garden's going to grow, the cycle run complete, the full-dress uniform be assembled, the watch will run. Did I miss any? It is simply a long, long process to go from fifty-seven wins to ninety-seven, from zero players to thirteen to fifteen. But the production of the Tiger farm system has been prodigious, and their day will come. Maybe not this year, conceivably not even next year. But it will happen.

—1980

The Tigers react to modern salary demands like a schoolmarm on a date with a sailor.

—*Esquire* magazine
April, 1981

Houston Astros

The Astrodome, suggests Craig Wright, is a baseball time machine, jerking the game back to the days before Babe Ruth, before the home run came and forced all who did not choose to lose to adopt it. It seems an odd phrase for what we think of as an ultramodern structure, with the mythic private apartments of the old judge sealed up behind a concession stand somewhere. One hopes that we will always think of it as ultramodern. If more stadiums like it are built, the state of the art in domed construction will soon move past this: It can retain the ultramodern image only if it represents the furthest point along a road not taken, like the electric car.

But the Astrodome is the one park in baseball in which you simply cannot play long-ball successfully, and this takes the game back to the way it was played long, long ago. The bunt, the hit and run, the squeeze play . . . in the absence of more powerful weapons, these subtle plays attain a huge significance. In watching the 1980 NL championship games, I understood for the first time what the old-timers who felt that Babe Ruth had ruined the game were talking about. One cannot oppose a home-run hitting offense with a run-at-a-time offense; you'll get beat. Babe Ruth was a cyclone who swept up the precious strategies of the generations before him and scattered them in ruins.

As the mountains make Wyoming folk rugged and the cities make city folk guarded or defensive, this environment, too, shapes the character of its inhabitants. It has always been my feeling that the cliquishness of the Boston Red Sox, their surliness and impatience with the press (granted Ralph Houk has done wonders to control this, but he is the first Sox manager in decades to make any progress on the front), that this was the Curse of Fenway, that it owed its origins to a long-dead architect. An absurd theory? So it sounds, but hear me out. Fenway makes ballplayers look like better hitters than they are. That inflates egos. Inflated egos cause resentment, in particular among those not favored by the park; the team divides into clusters of the favored and the ill-favored.

The Astrodome is a negative image of Fenway, an exactly opposite park in almost every way one can imagine. Beautiful, ugly. Quaint, modern. Vibrant, sterile. Cozy, spacious. Hitter's heaven, hitter's nightmare. And for what were the Astro players of the fine teams of 1978 to 1981 known? Their openness with the press, their closeness and almost family-like atmosphere. Odd, isn't it? As the park knocks twenty points off every player's average, it humbles hitters, and it controls egos.

But even more than that, it is my feeling that the mere fact that in Fenway a hitter can create runs *by his own actions* tends to cause Fenway teams to pull apart over time. A key fact about the Astrodome is that it takes three players to make a run. In order to do your job in this park, you have got to see yourself as a part of a plan, a cog in a machine.

My feeling is that, over time, that changes the way that the Astro players think of themselves in relation to their team— but only over time. And thus, I believe, if the Astros are to win it is extremely important for them to keep a team together, to maintain a stable personnel. Tal Smith did that. He took the players who were with the team when he came here in 1975. And then slowly, ever so slowly, he wove new players into the pattern. Art Howe, the first baseman on that team . . . when did he come here? Enos Cabell, Terry Puhl, Cesar Cedeño, Jose Cruz, Joe Niekro, Ken Forsch, Sambito, J. R. Richard . . . they had all spent years together.

When the new management took over, they felt an immediate need to put their own stamp on the ball club. They weren't bad judges of talent. I don't see any specific trades here that I would regard as being especially bad. But there simply were far too many of them. Sutton . . . in and out; Whoosh. Knight for Cedeño, Thon in at short, Andujar gone, let's try Tony Scott, let's get Phil Garner from Pittsburgh to play second. These men aren't bad ballplayers. But they cannot yet have learned how to add three or four little acts together to make a two-run rally. They don't know what one another can do all that thoroughly. And that is how you have to play ball in the Astrodome.

In Fenway, again, the rule is just the opposite. In Fenway, the longer the players stay together, the more stale and lifeless they become. Fresh talent is constantly needed. After they have a good year or two, they forget all about playing together. Take a look at the teams that have been successful in Fenway Park. The 1975 Red Sox, the last champion, were led by two rookies (Lynn and Rice), and featured prominently a whole list of new and almost-new faces: Rick Burleson, Dwight Evans, Denny Doyle, Cecil Cooper, Rick Wise.

But the longer this collection of players stayed together, the worse they got. The same thing happened in 1967; the Sox won the pennant in 1967 with the youngest lineup ever to win the American League (six regulars were twenty-four or younger), but faded steadily in the following years. The Red Sox' last pennant before that was in 1946, with a team which had only one holdover regular from the previous year, a war year. With stability came decline; that Sox team never won again.

As ugly as it seems to many of you, as artificial as it is, the Astrodome should be treasured for the baseball it creates. It is just as unique and just as extreme as Fenway—and in a lot of ways, its baseball is more exciting. Was there ever a series more magnificent than the 1980 NL playoffs? I feel about the Astrodome much the way I feel about the turf that they invented for it. No, I don't like what it does to the ball parks. Yes, I know about the smell of the grass in Wrigley and Yankee Stadium. Yes, the dryness of Royals Stadium bothers me. But what it does to the *game*—that, I like. I like it a lot. The speed, the constant danger of the speed, the reflexes, the strategies, the stolen-base attempts—oh, man, I like those a lot. The stadiums that they tore down in the 1960s may be missed forever and I'm sorry I didn't get to see more of them—but I sure don't miss the baseball that they tore down with them. Babe Ruth's game reached its natural culmination in the 1960s, and it had to be the most god-awful boring brand of baseball ever conceived of, a whole decade full of .220-hitting shortstops who negotiated their contracts on whether they'd hit ten or thirteen home runs. If I never see another Dave Nicholson, I think I can live with it. I blame the whole decade on Spike Eckert. Baseball was so boring that people who should have been carrying banners saying, "Hit It Here, Willie," and arguing about who was going to be the NL's Rookie of the Year got all wrapped up in politics instead, and started carrying peace signs and worrying about evil and social injustice and stuff. Attendance suffered, and the nation with it.

—1983

The Houston Astros, I have decided, must be an acquired taste. You know what an acquired taste is, something like French cooking, modern sculpture, jazz, fat women, ballet, Scotch, Russian films . . . it's hard to define. An acquired taste is a fondness for something the advantages of which are not immediately apparent. An acquired taste in my part of the country is painted saw blades. Do they have those where you are? You go to somebody's house and you discover that above their fireplace they've got a bunch of old, rusty saw blades with farm scenes painted on them—look like a hybrid of Currier and Ives and Norman Rockwell. I don't really understand what the advantages are of having them around, but I figure that they must be an acquired taste. Or like Charlie Chaplin. I mean, W.C. Fields is *funny*. The Marx Brothers are *funny*. Charlie Chaplin is an acquired taste.

We all acquire a certain number of inexplicable attachments; mine include Bob Newhart, Jethro Tull albums, sabermetrics and Pringles potato chips. I am assured by other people in my life that all of these can be hard to get into if you have no history with them. If taken literally, everything in life is an acquired taste with the exception of a few basic staples like salt, sugar, sex, and slapstick comedy, which we all share an enjoyment of; however, the term is not usually applied to things which make an obvious display of their attractions—in the case of a baseball team, by doing things like winning lots of games, playing interesting baseball or developing exciting young players. One would never describe the New York Mets, for example, as an acquired taste. Acquired tastes have very subtle advantages. The expression "This must be an acquired taste," is quite useful, inasmuch as it can be adapted to hundreds of situations, meaning something a little different each time:

- If you hear the expression "Must be an acquired taste," on leaving a French restaurant, or any other restaurant in which the food costs more than twenty dollars a pound and tastes as if the oregano was left out, what it means is "I suppose you'd rather have stopped at Kentucky Fried Chicken, wouldn't you?"
- On a date, if you hear the expression "Must be an acquired taste," what it means is "This is the last time I'm going out with this bozo."
- In an art gallery, if you hear the expression "I guess it's an acquired taste," what it probably means is "What the hell are we doing here?"
- If you're discussing a fondness for some particular poet, painter, playwright, or breed of dogs with someone you are close to, and he or she says "I guess it's just an acquired taste," what that means is "I don't want to talk about it right now."

"It's an acquired taste" means either that I'm in the know and you're not, or that this is a particular type of sophistication to which the speaker does not aspire. I do not aspire to be an Astros fan. The Astros are to baseball what jazz is to music. Think about it:

1. Jazz is improvisational. Jazz musicians, uniquely among musicians I hope, sometimes string the elements of their music together as they go, with no particular plan or outline. Do you think the Astros know where they're going? Do you think there's a score for this?
2. Jazz ambles along without crescendos or refrains, going neither andante nor allegro and without reaching either fortissimo or pianissimo. A good piece of jazz only uses about

half an octave. The ultimate jazz tune is a saxophone player undulating slowly between D flat and middle C.

Similarly, the Houston Astros amble along at 80, 82 wins a year; in the last four years they've been 77–85, 85–77, 80–82 and 83–79. Since 1969 the Oakland A's have finished a total of 216 games over .500 in their good seasons, and 169 games under .500 in their bad seasons. The Houston Astros have finished 70 games over .500 in their good seasons, and 67 under in their bad seasons. The ultimate Houston Astros' season is one in which they lose on opening day, then win, lose, win, lose, win, etc., until they reach 81–81.

3. Jazz is usually played indoors.
4. Jazz uses comparatively few instruments. Jazz ensembles are rarely enlivened with sousaphones, steel guitars, oboes, bassoons, or any other instrument which might tend to break up the monotony. Similarly, the Houston Astros use comparatively few weapons, relying heavily on the stolen base and the starting pitcher, but with no power hitters, no batting champions, no Ozzie Smiths or Jack Clarks. Both jazz and the Houston Astros, in short, are boring.
5. All jazz music sounds pretty much alike to the uninitiated, that 99.97 percent of us who haven't acquired the taste; it's repetitious, depressing, ugly and inclined to bestow the recipient with a headache. Much the same can be said of the Houston Astros, well known for wearing baseball's ugliest home and road uniforms. Similarly, one Houston Astros season, one Astros game, and one Astros player looks pretty much like the next one.

No, I'm kidding, of course: the Astros have been a little boring in recent years, but they'll get over it, and I'm sure jazz is as beautiful, varied and enjoyable as real music if you happen to have a taste for it. It's just that . . . well, I'm a night person. During the *Abstract* crunch (a fifth season, unique to Winchester, Kansas) I start to work about 4:00 P.M. and I work until daybreak. About ten years ago we went through a period when the only thing on the radio between one and four A.M. was country music. I've never understood this. . . . I mean, if you don't like C & W in the middle of the afternoon, why do radio executives think you're suddenly going to be struck with a yen to hear some Merle Haggard at 12:59 A.M. ? Now it's jazz; I listen to a mixture of classical music, rock music, and talk shows as I work, and at seven o'clock every evening they all decide that I'd like to hear Count Basie. Public radio stations, usually a reliable port in a storm, have for some unfathomable reason decided that jazz is socially and morally uplifting, and that they have a responsibility to impose it on us. But if I want to listen to Mozart in the afternoon, why does anybody think I'd want to listen to Miles Davis all night?

Ah well, I've got my Jethro Tull and a stereo, and baseball season's coming. . . . What I should do is get a VCR and record a couple hundred baseball games, and play them back while I'm working. I might even acquire a taste for the Astros.

—1986

Kansas City Royals

The Royals' 1981 problems were more mystical than material, and for that reason are harder to diagnose and harder to react to than most. The Royals suffered from a seepage of confidence on all sides. They hit under .200 with men on base in the 1980 World Series, inducing self-doubt about their clutch ability and setting up a pattern of missed opportunities. The front office let a star player walk off without a replacement in sight, creating doubts about the front office. On top of that, the players were asked to have confidence in a generic manager (suitable for everyday use . . . may not react immediately when confronted with complex game situations). When confronted with a 17–1 start by their opposition, the Royals simply folded their tent.

—Esquire magazine
May, 1982

It is dangerous for a baseball team to have too many players with the same weakness, no matter what the weakness. To have two or three regulars who are bad defensive players may not cost much, but if you add one more you may be shoving a poor defensive player into a key defensive role. The ability of the good fielders to cover the mistakes of the bad ones will be overloaded, and the problem will blow up on you. To have three players who are slow may have a very minimal cost, but if you add one or two more who are slow, then you're going to be shoving people who are slow into offensive and defensive roles which require speed, and the incremental cost of the extra slow guy can be many times the cost of the first slow guy. The ability of the manager to adjust to situations in which speed is needed, such as a speed park or a running situation, diminishes greatly with each extra slow player; the ability to hide a slow player from the place where a slow player can't do the job is lost.

So in building a ball club, you have to be aware of the weaknesses of your stalwart players, and avoid duplicating those weaknesses among the replaceable parts. Willie Wilson used to be a good player and still does some things well, but his on base percentages have never been good and now are very poor. Frank White is a terrific player, but the ability to reach base is his weakest point. When you patch around those players with marginal talents like Larry Owen (on base percentage: .260), Angel Salazar (on base percentage: .219), and Steve Balboni (on base percentage: .273), then you've got five guys in the lineup who don't get on base, and then you can't hide from it. Vincent Jackson, regular left fielder for much of the season, had an on base percentage of .296.

This team's essential offensive problem remains what it has been for five years: They don't have enough people on base. During the 1986 season, the Kansas City baseball community talked incessantly about the need to get someone who could "bat behind Brett and drive in runs." If I heard that once, I heard it every day between June 15 and the Tartabull trade. You try to tell them: Look, this team is last in the American League in men on base. You can't drive in runners who aren't there. You don't score 780 runs when you only have 1800– 1900 runners on base. It can't be done.

So the Royals add Danny Tartabull. Tartabull is super, and what happens? The Royals are last in the league in runs scored. So what do people say? The Royals have to add more speed! No joke. The Royals have got to get back to "moving base runners, like they did when Whitey Herzog was here." What base runners? Look, the percentage of the Royal base runners who scored last year, given that this is a poor home run park, was *not* low. It was good. The number of Royals on base and the number who scored was virtually identical in 1987 to Whitey Herzog's first championship team (1976); actually Herzog's team had nine more men on base and scored two fewer runs. That level of runs scored was good in 1976, poor in 1987, but the relevant point is that with a given number of base runners, Herzog's team was no more successful than Gardner's.

In the June 18 broadcast from California, there occurred this exchange between broadcaster Denny Trease and Buddy Biancalana, sitting in the booth while on the Disabled List. Speaking of California rookie Mark McLemore:

TREASE—Very patient hitter. He takes a lot of pitches. Even in batting practice, he'll take pitches.

BIANCALANA—That doesn't go over too well with the veterans. Not on our ball club, at least.

TREASE—Get in there and swing, uh?

That's the problem in a nutshell, guys. Sure, it helps if you can add a Danny Tartabull, and it will help if Gary Thurman is as good as he looked in September. But as long as you consider it a moral imperative to swing at bad pitches, you ain't going to score runs.

—1988

Los Angeles Dodgers

The four Dodger infielders have been playing together longer than Johnson and Johnson. This is a considerably sounder approach than that of their Anaheim rivals, who change their infield more often than their underwear. . . .

—*Esquire* magazine
April, 1981

That which has ailed the Los Angeles Dodgers in recent years is, I think, essentially what plagued the Disney company in the years following the death of Walt Disney. Disney developed for his company a set of practices, guidelines, ethics, and operating procedures which pumped out success after success. He did not do things the way they were done in the rest of the entertainment business, but his formula worked for him because he knew what the elements of his product were, where to find them and how to combine them. He created a self-contained industry within the industry, and for thirty years during which the world and the industry changed enormously, he went on succeeding because he knew what his basic principles were and how to adapt his product without compromising those principles.

Following his death, however, the world kept changing, and his company no longer knew how to adapt. Lacking the self-confidence to ask "What needs to be done here, in this new and unique situation?", they tried instead to ask "What would Walt Disney have done here?" This was the wrong question not because Walt would not have known what to do, but because his successors couldn't really predict his thinking in his absence. They couldn't reach any consensus. Each understood his own place within the world that Walt had built, but no one felt confident enough to command the whole world or to guide it into the future. They got the conservative element of his thinking, but without the spark of genius that drove it.

So too the Dodgers, with the phenomenal stability of the Dodgers, with the Dodger way of doing everything, which unfortunately no longer works. In my twenty-seven years as a baseball fan, I don't know that I have ever seen a team put together such an awesome collection of castoffs, failed prospects, one-dimensional talents, and burnt-out minor players. All of the following men played for the 1987 Dodgers: Ron Davis, Phil Garner, Mickey Hatcher, Brad Havens, Danny Heep, Glenn Hoffman, Bill Krueger, Tito Landrum, Tim Leary, Lon Matuszek, Orlando Moroado, Tom Niedenfuer, Alex Trevino, Brad Wellman, and Matt Young. This doesn't even count the guys, like Jerry Reuss and Bill Madlock, who were a legitimate part of the team in the past and were still hanging around as the season started.

The impression that one gets is that the Dodgers can no longer recognize a prospect when they see one. They certainly can't find them in the draft anymore. The Dodgers have a young third baseman named Jeff Hamilton who is a fine hitter and regarded as a decent glove. The Dodgers keep piddling around with him, giving him a few at bats, a few games. He hasn't hit well yet, but who else do they have to play third base? While they won't make a commitment to a legitimate prospect in Hamilton, the Dodgers continue to insist that Chris Gwynn, who is a fourth-line prospect, is going to be a major league star, and that sooner or later Jose Gonzalez is going to learn to hit. In 1986 Mike Devereaux and Mike Ramsey were teammates in San Antonio. Devereaux hit .302 with 10 homers, 53 RBI, and 30 stolen bases; Ramsey hit .283 with 2 homers, 37 RBI, and 21 stolen bases while playing in four more games. Devereaux walked forty-five percent more often and struck out barely over half as much. Almost everyone in the league thought that Devereaux was a better player—but the Dodgers started the 1987 season with Mike Ramsey in center field, and Devereaux in double-A.

You can get by with that kind of crap, if you're right. *If* you know more than the stats and more than the common opinion, you can throw the stats out the window and base your decisions on your own reading of the players. But the other side is, if you're going to ignore what everybody else can see and base your decision on your instincts, you had damn well better be right.

—1988

Milwaukee Brewers

No one man possesses all of the abilities that are needed for an organization to win. Harry Dalton no doubt deserves a good share of the credit for what happened when he was in Baltimore, but then so do a few other people: Earl Weaver, Frank Cashen, Brooks Robinson, Hank Bauer, Jim Russo, Paul Richards, George Bamberger, Jim Palmer, Lou Gorman, Frank Robinson. It can get pretty thin. And Dalton deserves a share of the credit for what happened four years ago in Milwaukee, and we are about to find out how large a share of the credit.

Four years ago the Brewers materialized out of thin talent,

making the improbable leap from 67–95 to pennant contender in one year. Since then it has been Wednesday in Milwaukee. I get a sense of directionlessness about the organization, indecisiveness; the talent is not less impressive than it was two years ago, but the sense of orderly progression brought in by Dalton and Bamberger seems to have left with Bamberger. It is clear that the Brewers are standing on a doorstep. What is not entirely clear is whether they are going in or just leaving.

—1982 *Baseball Abstract*

As it turned out the Brewers were ready both to go in the door and out; they did finally take the division and league championship that year, but then immediately left the room where the pennant race was being run.

Minnesota Twins

In contrast to the comic ineptitude of Hawk Harrelson (see Chicago White Sox), there is something sad, something almost sinister about the ineptitude which guides the Minnesota Twins. For years, the Twins have had a collection of young power hitters which is the envy of the league. In 1986 the collection was enhanced when Kirby Puckett shocked the league with 31 homers among his 223 hits, while several other Twins had good seasons. The Twins hit more homers and had more total bases than any other team in the division—yet they were never in contention.

On the simplest level, the problems of the Twins are easy to pinpoint. They had the highest ERA in the major leagues. Living in terror of their bullpen, they led the major leagues in complete games while they were last in saves. They were hammered for 200 home runs, the highest total in the majors in several years.

It was said last summer that a point was reached at which Ray Miller was quoting Billy Gardner chapter and verse. Gardner, manager of the Twins from 1981 through 1983, didn't use his bench much and was never successful in developing a bullpen, so Miller entered the scene talking about the need to get all twenty-four guys involved in the game, improve the Twins' defense up the middle, etc. By the middle of last summer he was frustrated about the bullpen, complaining about the lack of a bench and how the poor team speed cut off his options—sounding, in general, a lot like Billy Gardner.

I had an on-air conversation in Minnesota with a radio personality who said that the experience of watching Miller and Gardner manage this team had led him to conclude that who was managing didn't really make much difference in the face of intractable team weaknesses. What I should have said, had I been alert enough, is that suppose you had a second baseman who couldn't hit for average and wasn't quick on the double play, and so you got rid of him and got another second baseman who couldn't hit for average and wasn't quick on the double play, either. Would you conclude from this that second basemen don't make any difference because they can't hit for average and don't turn the double play well?

Miller and Gardner happened to have some of the same weaknesses. Although neither Miller nor Gardner was one of them, there are managers who can study their options and create a bench. There are managers who almost never have serious bullpen problems, because they can look at the physical and mental makeup of the pitchers in camp, pick out a horse to ride and teach him what he needs to know.

The manager cannot carry all of the blame. The Twins' front office continues to display astonishingly little interest in solving their problems. It's a Minnesota tradition. They have allowed the team to go from season to season without any speed, without a proven shortstop or catcher. The Twins should play better this year, but then they should have played better last year and the year before, too.

—1987

Montreal Expos

The Montreal Expos of 1982 were a team that was never out of the pennant race and was never in it. They were never far enough away from the top of the division, from the first of May to the middle of September, that they couldn't have reached the top just by sweeping a couple of quick series. They could never do it. In retrospect, it might have been better for the team had they had a real bad spell, gotten ten games behind or so and panicked. They never did that, either. They hung around the fringes of the pennant race without momentum or direction from beginning to end, waiting for something to happen.

Perhaps I should just skip all of the numbers here, and abandon the floor to those who analyze pennant races in terms of "momentum" and "psychology," "guts" and "desire." It is my belief, as it must be everyone's, that there is a center to a ball club, that that center is formed by the feeling that each player has for the group as a whole. Jim Fanning's obvious failure to take command of the group, by such twerpish habits as changing his second baseman every week and asking his pitchers whether they wanted to pitch to Mike Schmidt or George Vukovich, induced severe doubts in each player about the group as a whole. No center, no momentum, no pennant.

Still, whatever the origin of the Expos' problems, those problems must still take the road of something tangible to make themselves known, as even a ghost must open and close doors and move furniture around or we would never know there was a ghost there. My friends who are Expo fans are convinced that too much has been said about the second-base matter already, that the press is using that as a catch-all for problems that really go much deeper. I can't agree with them. In essence, the Expos had the same posture that the Cardinals had before Herzog: tremendous strength at some positions negated by an unnecessary failure to plug a hole, like a girl with flashing eyes and a turned-up nose and three teeth missing. Nobody should lose a pennant for the lack of a marginal second baseman.

—1983

The Montreal Expos of Gary Carter's last years were a team with more holes than a porcupine's underwear.

—1987

The 1984 Montreal Expos, not meaning to slight Charlie Lea or anything, had essentially two strengths. In Gary Carter, they had one of the greatest catchers in the history of baseball. In Tim Raines, they had the outstanding leadoff man in the history of the National League. Raines hit .309, got on base almost 40 percent of the time, reached scoring position under his own power 130 times (with the help of 75 stolen bases and 38 doubles) and, playing center field, was second among National League outfielders in putouts. Raines scored 106 runs with a terrible offense coming up behind him, led the league in stolen bases and is now five years ahead of Lou Brock's pace as a base stealer. He doesn't throw real great, but if you've got to have a weakness that's a good one to choose, because it really doesn't cost the team a half-dozen runs a year. He is a great ballplayer, one of the ten best in baseball.

So what do they do? Of course: They trade off the catcher and worry about the center fielder's throwing arm. It's crazy, but if you're losing and you're frustrated, it seems logical. Losing ball teams focus their frustration on their best players in exactly the same way that a man who gets fired from his job and loses his house to the bank will then divorce his wife, who is the only thing in his life that's worth hanging onto. You know how the story goes from there.

—1985

For a while, the Montreal Expos made a good show of it. Picked by most to finish near the bottom of the National League East, the Expos arrived at May 11 with a record of 17–10 and eight consecutive wins. If you're going to have a streak like that you might as well enjoy it, and the Expos drank deeply of the excitement. Third baseman Tim Wallach opined that "We have more quality pitching than any other team in our division, and that includes the Mets." General Manager Murray Cook described the Expo offense as "intimidating." Bryn Smith said that he, Hesketh, Tibbs, and Youmans were capable of winning fifteen games apiece. It was observed by all that the attitude in the clubhouse was the best it had ever been, and Wallach thought the Expos would win a hundred games.

It would soon become apparent that the Expos would not win a hundred games, but they continued to play well; this was one bubble that was destined never to break, but to shrink slowly into nothingness.

—1987

New York Mets

The New York Mets have been sold; the new owners should be given five years to recover. The Orioles have proven that a shrewd team can survive on a budget, the Yankees, that an amateur can win if he spends enough money. But being cheap *and* ignorant is just too much.

—*Esquire* magazine
May, 1980

Does this say "Mets" all over it? John Stearns had 103 hits last year, and vaulted from tenth to seventh on the list of the Mets' all-time leaders. The men he passed were Rusty Staub, Tommy Agee, and Wayne Garrett. . . .

—1983

The New York Mets in 1986 had the talent and handled the pressure. Since leaping into contention in 1984—Dave Johnson's first season as manager—the Mets have consolidated their strengths and whittled away on their weaknesses. They opened the 1986 season as solid favorites to win the NL East, and broke away from the pack in the opening weeks of the campaign. By the end of May they had been virtually conceded the championship by fans, press, and opposition managers— at a point when they still had to go out and win another sixty or more games to convert that paper pennant into silk. Withering every challenge in its seminal stages, they managed gracefully the tricky task of *not losing* a race to which they had been granted premature title, so gracefully that the question of the tiger getting out of the cage never really came up. They were, in short, a great ball club, and a beautiful demonstration of what talent can do when assembled with planning and guided by intelligence.

—1987

There are important parallels between the 1986 Mets and the best of the bad-boy Raider teams. Those teams were portrayed, as were the Mets, as driven by arrogance and bad manners. They were in fact supremely talented, their arrogance and bad manners being not accidental (for this is clearly a part of the pattern by which they were assembled), not incidental (for the team would lack definition without these features), but simply irrelevant once the game begins.

—1987

I admire Davey Johnson. I enjoyed his book, *Bats*, with Peter Golenbock. But to my way of thinking, Davey Johnson in 1987 retreated a substantial distance from the positions which had made him a successful manager in the previous three seasons. When Johnson took over this team, he fought with Frank Cashen to commit the team to youth, to get Cashen to bring Dwight Gooden to the majors, to get a second chance for Wally Backman and to give up on Ron Hodges or whatever veteran catcher the Mets were using and give a shot to John Gibbons. The young players were essential to the development of his team.

He didn't do that last year. The Mets had two minor league shortstops, Kevin Elster and Gregg Jeffries, who were much better than the guy on the major league team. The difference between Rafael Santana hitting .220 and Rafael Santana hitting .255 is that when he hits .220 everybody knows he's not contributing. Johnson has to know anyway. Unless he has been struck suddenly stupid, Johnson had to know that Kevin Elster was a better shortstop and a better hitter than Santana. But Johnson either didn't fight for Elster, or he didn't fight hard enough for him.

Frank Cashen's theory is that everybody should spend at least one full year in AAA ball. My theory is that once a player has proven that he can play AAA ball, every extra game that he plays in the minors will make his career less than it would otherwise have been. The best players are those who get to the major leagues when they are young enough to learn major league skills to the depth of their bones. A player spends an extra year at AAA, he starts to wonder if he's really just a minor league player. Willie Mays didn't spend a full year at

AAA, and Mickey Mantle didn't, and Sandy Koufax didn't and Dwight Gooden didn't and Babe Ruth didn't and Robin Yount didn't and Kirby Puckett didn't and Tony Gwynn didn't and Reggie Jackson didn't and Pete Rose didn't and Andre Dawson didn't and Ozzie Smith didn't and on and on and on.

The position that every player has to play a full season of AAA ball is, I think, intellectually indefensible. The vast majority of the greatest players in baseball history played less than three hundred games of minor league ball. Every game you play in professional baseball before you reach the major leagues interferes with the clarity with which you see what happens when you do reach the majors. I think Frank Cashen may have cost the Mets the pennant last year by keeping Kevin Elster at Tidewater. (Actually, if I was running this organization I wouldn't open the season with Elster at shortstop, but with Jeffries, but I realize this is too much to expect from Frank Cashen.)

—1988

New York Yankees

There is a three-handed card game, known variously as sergeant major, pluck, or agony, in which the winner of one hand gets to pluck the best cards from his opponents to help him win the next. It's great fun while you're ahead, but when you get behind it's about as much fun as basic training.

The New York Yankees, for the moment, are baseball's sergeant major. Committed to a policy of signing whatever it is they least need, the Yankees have analyzed their strengths and weaknesses and decided, for the third straight year, to accentuate both. A pitching-and-power team troubled by advancing age and an offense that has declined, the Yankees this winter plucked two pitchers totaling seventy-four years or more, depending on who you believe about Luis Tiant's age. As Tony Perez remarked, "When I was a boy growing up in Cuba, Luis Tiant was a national hero. Now I'm thirty-six and he's thirty-seven." The Yankees point out that the ex-Dodger Tommy John is four years younger than Gaylord Perry, which is at least as relevant as pointing out that he's a year older than Denny McLain.

—*Esquire* magazine
April 24, 1979

The New York Yankees are trapped on a treadmill. Although they have not won anything since 1981, the Yankees have the best winning percentage of any team in baseball during the decade, or should I turn that around: Although they have the best winning percentage of any team during the eighties, the Yankees have not won anything since 1981. They are acutely aware of this, and so the winter of 1987–88 was spent in frantic preparations to make the 1988 season the one in which the nucleus of the team will be surrounded by a cast good enough to lift the Yankees off that 85- to 92-win tread-mill, and onto the championship rung. There is an irony in this, for it is exactly this philosophy which has created the treadmill from which the Yankees are now so anxious to escape.

I was appalled this winter to hear people saying that the Yankees had won the pennant on January 5 when they signed Jack Clark. Twelve years ago, at the beginning of the free-agent era, I tried to tell people that a single player just doesn't mean that much in the context of the thirty games or so that separate the best teams from the worst. I wrote articles arguing that a superstar might mean four to six games a year, but not more. People would say that Andy Messersmith was going to turn the Braves around, and I would try to explain why that was impossible.

I could understand why that was difficult for people to accept at the time. But after we have seen free agents change teams time after time after time without carrying pennants with them, after we have seen Andre Dawson go from Montreal to Chicago without Montreal getting any worse or Chicago getting any better, after we have seen Bruce Sutter leave St. Louis for Atlanta without the Cardinals getting any worse or Atlanta any better, after we have seen Lance Parrish jump from Detroit to Philadelphia without Detroit getting any worse or Philadelphia any better, after we have seen this time and again for twelve years, how can people still think that the *next* free agent is going to be the one who carries the mail? As I see it, Clark improves the Yankees' expectations by maybe a half a game, maybe two games at most. It's no big deal.

George reached a point at which he just had to scratch that free agent itch. Signing a free agent of Jack Clark's age (thirty-two) and injury history is the ultimate treadmill strategy. Like the Baltimore Orioles, the Yankees are investing in a market which is certain to decline. If you do that at a lower level, as the Orioles have, it is a disastrous strategy. If you buy the very best of the available players, as the Yankees have, it is a defensible strategy, but there is still that undertow, that treadmill, with the inevitable decline of players in their thirties pulling the Yankees away from their goal, while the development of young players in Boston, Cleveland, Milwaukee, and Toronto will be pushing those teams gently forward.

The problem with the Yankees is that they never want to pay the real price of success. The real price of success in baseball is not the dollars that you shell out for a Jack Clark or a Dave Winfield or an Ed Whitson or a Goose Gossage. The real price of success in baseball is the patience to work with young players and help them develop. So long as the Yankees are unwilling to pay that price, don't bet on them to win anything.

—1988

Oakland A's

We saw the A's play in Kansas City on June 23, and to be honest, I have not seen a team give such a pathetic effort since the Cardinals in early 1980. It was Rachel's first baseball game, and I remember I was focusing on Canseco all night, it being the first time I'd seen him, and thinking about how a rookie is like a baby, a mass of polymorphous potential that will be influenced by everything that happens, and thinking how sad it was that the A's were playing this way during the formative days of Jose Canseco's career, thinking that the A's had this wonderful gift in a rookie who could hit a baseball five hundred feet, and that in two or three years he's going to assume that this is all there is to it, that you just show up for the games and put your numbers on the scoreboard and forget all that crap about hustle and team play and trying to win.

What I did not know, of course, was that during the game

Dave Kingman had sent a rat in a pink box to a female reporter, Susan Fornoff, whose name spelled backwards would be Ffonrof Nasus. This puerile act highlighted a long line of disgraceful behavior from Kingman toward Ms. Fornoff, which harassment had already become a bone of contention between the Oakland organization and the Bay Area press corps. The Oakland management had cringed at Kingman's moronic actions, but the rat incident was too much; Sandy Alderson flew to Kansas City and informed Kingman that any similar actions in the future would terminate his contract, stopping off while there to fire the manager. For a few days the A's players, rallying to Kingman's defense, stopped talking to the press. This was a new role for Kingman, team leadership. Before, Kingman has always been dismissed as merely an immature jerk. It turns out that all he needed was the right team to bring out this new side of his personality, a team full of immature jerks. The A's were able to oblige.

Jeff Newman ran the A's, so to speak, for a couple of weeks during which they won a couple of games. To go by what was written in *The Sporting News*, Newman didn't make any pretense of knowing what he was doing, which was an improvement over the previous two Oakland managers, who did pretend to know what they were doing. On July 1, Cleveland manager Pat Corrales charged the mound and tried to practice his martial arts on A's pitcher Dave Stewart, who cold-cocked him. The A's were 31–52, fourteen games out, when Tony LaRussa was hired to bring some sanity out of the silliness.

—1987

The lesson of the Oakland A's is that you can, too, have too much pitching. I wrote a year ago that "the most serious question [here] is whether or not LaRussa can identify in spring training a group of pitchers who not only will pitch well for a time, but who have a shot at staying in the rotation and carrying the ball all the way. . . . If LaRussa can identify those five pitchers [from among Young, Haas, Stewart, Andujar, Codiroli, Mooneyham, Rijo, Plunk, Birtsas, Nelson, and Krueger], the A's will win this division."

Maybe the five men just weren't there, but in any case LaRussa didn't find them, and that was the story of the season. The A's opened April with a rotation of Young, Plunk, Codiroli, Stewart, and Rijo. Two of them were terrific. Three were terrible. Four hundred as a hitter is great; two for five in choosing pitchers won't get it done. Stewart and Young had a .623 winning percentage; the rest of the team was at .440.

The A's rolled to a two-and-nine start. They righted the rotation by inserting Moose Haas and Steve Ontiveros, and scrambled back into the race. By June 28 they were 40–33, seven games over. Then the rotation began to degenerate. Haas couldn't continue. Curt Young was out of action for three weeks, and struggled upon his return. When Andujar was ready to pitch (or was coerced into pitching, depending on who you believe), he wasn't effective. It was back to square one: Who do we try next?

If a team has only five candidates for starting jobs, that's trouble, because a couple won't come through. If a team has seven candidates, they have protection. If they have eleven candidates, they have confusion. All pitchers go up and down during the season. Having pitchers waiting in the wings undermines the commitment to work out the problems of the pitchers on the downswing. If a pitcher is struggling and Joaquin Andujar or Moose Haas is ready to come off the disabled list, the manager *has* to jerk the guy who is struggling out of the rotation and try Andujar or Haas. If he doesn't work out you try the next guy. It's real easy for the season to turn into a running experiment with the starting rotation. The ultimate example was Gene Nelson. Nelson didn't start until August 12, but when he pitched well his first three outings LaRussa was talking about his being a twenty-game winner in 1988. Then he had three more starts and it was back to the bullpen; his stint in the starting rotation lasted a little less than a month. If the guy happens to pitch well, like Dave Stewart, great, but if he doesn't you just try somebody else. It's unhealthy for the staff, I think, for there to be such a weak commitment to the rotation.

—1988

Philadelphia Phillies

Philadelphia owner Ruly Carpenter, realizing that Pete Rose at thirty-eight is no longer a player who can decide the pennant race, originally refused to pay what Pete was asking. But the TV station that carries the Phillies, concerned not with ability but with marketability, came up with the dough, and Rose became a Phillie.

It is an interesting alloy—television marketing techniques and baseball judgment—and it figures to snap like cold plastic in the pressure of a pennant race. The argument that Rose will have value in his role as Charlie Hustle would have real merit if it could be validated, but the Phillies are not schoolboys. The youngest regular is twenty-eight, and the pitching staff the oldest in baseball.

—*Esquire* magazine
April 24, 1979

History sometimes repeats itself, but usually not with the same cast of characters. The Philadelphia Phillies, 1976–78 division champions, will have the leaders looking over their shoulders until they prove irrefutably that last year's fourth-place finish was not a fluke, but it wasn't. The starting eight of the Phillies have nearly one hundred years of professional experience, which would be wonderful if they were in the real estate business. The Phillies are immensely proud of Larry Bowa, a thirty-four-year-old shortstop who never makes an error and has about as much range as the Birdman of Alcatraz. The Polish Anti-Defamation League should protest Greg Luzinski's being required to play the outfield.

—*Esquire* magazine
May, 1980

You know that ragged man that you meet on the street carrying a sign that says, REPENT! THE END IS NEAR! Chances are that he's a Phillies fan.

—*Esquire* magazine
May, 1982

Do you remember the story of the Devil and Daniel Webster? It's a story about a man who sells his soul to the devil for earthly success, but when the time comes to face up to his responsibilities, pack a trunkful of Coppertone and prepare for a long, dry summer, instead of just saying "Well, OK, you're the Devil and a deal is a deal," he says, "Nuts to you, I'm not going," and he calls in Daniel Webster to argue for him.

Well, the Phillies remind me of that story. The Phillies began to evolve into an old ball club four or five years ago, and a lot of people (including yours truly) have been waiting for them to collapse ever since. What you're supposed to do when you begin to accumulate thirty-five-year-olds on your roster is look to the future, begin breaking in some young talent so as to cushion the decline phase—like the Dodgers have done.

What the Phillies did instead was to start bringing in more old ballplayers, beginning with Pete Rose in 1979. Aha, we all said; you'll pay for this. Trying to stretch out your good times by a couple of years when you could be going to church on Sunday and bringing along some younger talent; you'll burn in the second division for this, Philadelphia.

But when their moment of reckoning arrived, and the aging of the talent became critical, the Phillies made a unique response: They sent for Joe Morgan. Instead of saying "OK, you're right; we've got to start paying for this now," they brought in even more, even older ballplayers to prop up the team until the next generation of talent was assembled. They challenged their liability head-on.

One of the marvelous things about baseball is that, after all the years I've been a fan, everything that happens is still new and surprising. I have never seen this before. I have never seen an organization, confronted with an aging roster, just decide that they would not yield to the problem, they would confront it.

And they got by with it. At the least, to this point they seem to have gotten by with it. The next generation of talent is here and ready to go. They've got Juan Samuel ready to go at second, and he looks great. Their backup outfield is probably one of the better outfields in the division. They've got Matuszek at first, Virgil to catch. They could lose a lot of talent, and not lose a thing on the field.

—1984 Baseball Abstract

Originally published under the title "The Devil and Joe Morgan."

What I am about to say should be obvious, but obviously it is not. Mike Schmidt's early September rip at Paul Owens' lineup juggling, while it may have helped to clear the air heading into the pennant race, could not possibly have been more wrong in content. Schmidt said that the Phillies had no sense of direction and no stability. Players like Pete Rose, Garry Maddox, and Joe Morgan, he said, were used to playing every day; they couldn't be expected to play their best playing four or five days a week. Because of that, he said, the Phillies were the least likely team to get hot in September.

Now wait a minute, Mr. Schmidt. The Phillies in 1982 used a set lineup. A very set lineup; at some spots it was set in concrete. Did they get hot in September? They had a strong sense of direction in September: straight down the toilet. Stability? Like a rock, they were.

Sure, Joe Morgan has played 150 games a year all his career. And he never hit a lick in September until he cut it out. Sure, Pete Rose has been playing 162 games a year for years, and he used to be a great September player. But he hit .234 in September of 1980 and .222 in September of 1982.

It is my belief that, in general, platoon teams play better in September than any other type of team. Weaver's teams did, and Stengel's did. But we're not talking about just any team here, but about an ancient team, a 1970s reliquary which has somehow, miraculously, survived into the mid-1980s. How on earth can you play them every day until they drop, and not expect them to drop?

The performance of the Phillies after Schmidt's outburst can be taken as proof that he was right or proof that he was wrong. I'll let you guess which way he took it. But remember what he said: He thought the Phillies were the *least* likely team to get hot in September.

—1984 *Baseball Abstract*

The Phillies, you will remember, went 22–7 in September of 1983, vaulting into the World Series.

Pittsburgh Pirates

Blessed with the best player in baseball in right fielder Dave Parker, the 1978 Pirates bobbled and baseran their way out of the divisional crown by committing sixty-three errors more than the Phillies, who still beat them by only a game and a half, and by adopting the stolen base as if it were more a test of masculinity than a strategic weapon.

—*Esquire* magazine
April 24, 1979

Since divisional play began in 1969 the Pirates have never been out of a pennant race. This dependability had given them an image of cold-blooded corporate efficiency, an image against which the Pirates of 1979 understandably overreacted, bathing their clubhouse in a flow of warmth and togetherness that would have been nauseating had it not been so welcomely out of step with the decade. There were times when the Pirates' success almost seemed to justify Disco music.

The success of the Pirates diffuses and escapes definition. The media have adopted Willie Stargell as the team's symbol, but in truth he seems as much the beneficiary of the team's success as its architect. The team has power, they have speed; they have starters, they have a bullpen; they have experience, they have youth. Nothing to excess, but everything in stock as needed.

—*Esquire* magazine
May, 1980

San Diego Padres

The Padres have averaged 96 losses a season throughout an eleven-year history afflicted by financial malfeasance, amateur management, and now, blatant nepotism. Club president Ballard Smith, who has experience as owner Ray Kroc's son-in-law, has traded for Dave Cash, thirty-one, and Willie Montanez, thirty-two, thereby committing the Padres to a successful past. But you've got to admit: It beats flipping hamburgers.

—*Esquire* magazine
May, 1980

Alan Wiggins was one of the key success stories for the San Diego Padres in 1984. Making the very difficult move from the outfield to second base, he had gotten along well defensively and contributed steadily on offense, enabling the Padres to get an extra bat in the lineup. In spring training of 1985 Wiggins confessed that he had developed a dependence on drugs, and needed to fight his way clear of it. The Padres were understanding about this, up to a point, but in the second week of the season Wiggins had a relapse, and had to seek further treatment.

It was late June when he was ready to return to the team, but by this time the Padres were playing real well, and they had reached the conclusion that they didn't really need Alan Wiggins—not only that they didn't need him, but that he did not deserve to walk among them anymore; yessir, they took a vote on it, and they decided that they just didn't want any of his kind around. The owner of the team took the same position, and took it with such determination that it was clear she would, if need be, fight in court for the right to throw Alan Wiggins away like a lump of rotten cheese.

Now that was, to tell the truth, a right arrogant, self-righteous attitude, and as I think I mentioned earlier in the book, it has been my experience that the Lord rarely wastes much time in punishing this particular failing in us. I mean, I've found that a lot of times it is just damned difficult to figure out what the Old Bugger is up to; I don't know too much about it, but I was raised to believe in God, and there are a number of areas which I was led to believe were his assignment to which it seems to me he don't pay as much attention as he might. He is, however, quite alert to punishing arrogance and re-instructing us in humility; in fact, I think this is the only one among his deific duties that he really enjoys, and I've found that he can be tremendously creative in accomplishing this task swiftly.

This was, by the way, about the eleventh consecutive season in which the story of the year for Dick Williams' team has revolved around the weird comings and goings of his second baseman. Some of Williams' actions there, such as the 1984 decision to release Juan Bonilla and shift Alan Wiggins in from left field, have been courageous and brilliant. Some, such as the time he tried rotating four men at the position and pinch-hitting for them whenever they were due at the plate, have been funny. Some, such as his 1973 decision to resign as manager of the A's over the shabby treatment of Mike Andrews, have been courageous and sad. Some, such as his dogged determination to play Rodney Scott in Montreal *and* San Diego, carried to the extent of claiming that Rodney was the best player on his Montreal team and pouting publicly when he couldn't have him for the Padres, have been courageous and stupid.

The 1985 decision was in the stupid category; courageous, but stupid. Now, it is important to note, lest I be accused of contradicting what I wrote about Chuck Tanner and Whitey Herzog, that Alan Wiggins had come to the Padres, had apologized for letting the team down and had asked for forgiveness. Darrell Porter got ahold of his problems, and Whitey Herzog was happy to have him on his team; Lonnie Smith faced up to his problem, and Whitey stuck by him until he was back on his feet. But the trouble with Wiggins was, as the Padres saw it at the time, that they had already forgiven him once. As I understand it, the team held a special meeting of their John Birch Society chapter, and they prayed for guidance and asked how many times they should forgive their brother, and the answer came to them that the appropriate number was seven times seventy, unless you had a platoon combination that could do his job just as well, in which case once ought to do it. I mean, this is God's own team, right? You can't have a doper on the same team with God and Steve Garvey.

Well, you see, the Lord was giving the Padres a little pop quiz, and that wasn't the right answer. It wasn't even close. Speaking of quizzes, you may have heard the story that when Alan Wiggins tried to demonstrate to the team the depth of his reformation they asked him to identify from photographs some of the nation's most respected religious leaders, but when Wiggins mixed up Oral Roberts and Pat Robertson they realized he was a hopeless miscreant; however, I count this an idle rumor, and doubt that there is more than a kernel of truth to it.

Anyway, the Padres had no sooner voted to drive Wiggins from their doorway than they realized that they had been struck slow. God-awful slow. Slow in the infield. Slow in the outfield. Catcher was a guy named Terry Kennedy, slower'n the fat girl chasing her chihuahua up the staircase. All of a sudden they couldn't buy a win. They looked around one day and said "Hey, you know, we ain't got no leadoff man." Tony Gwynn, who in 1984 had hit .406 with runners on base, suddenly lost about fifty points off his batting average. The team didn't have a bench; Wiggins, who would have been an invaluable bench man with his speed, switch hitting, ability to get on base and experience both in the infield and outfield, wasn't around. I'll get to more of the details in the next article, but in sum the Padres, who were 35–22 on or about the day they voted on Wiggins' right to return, went 48–57 the rest of the way. They were out of contention within forty-five days.

Well, I think you can safely infer from this that the Lord was not pleased with his Padres, and that's about all I had to say about it. At least Dick Williams had the guts to face up to it. He stated bluntly late in the season that the loss of Wiggins was the largest factor leading to the decline of the Padres. In other words, "We blew it, guys." I apologize if I offended anyone along the way, but for those of you who weren't offended, did you ever think that maybe we should form an entire league of teams with ecclesiastical monikers? I figure you could make up a good league with the Padres, the San Francisco Missionaries, the Atlanta TV Evangelists, the Houston Pastors, the St. Louis Cardinals, the California Angels and the Pittsburgh Men of the Cloth. I figure it would be a lot of fun drawing up the logos and all; for example, I reckon the symbol for the New England Deacons should be Fire and Brimstone, while the Cincinnati Clerics could be represented by a hand clutching a rosary. Any further ideas along these lines should be directed to the Commissioner's office.

—1986

WILL THE McMEETING PLEASE COME TO ORDER?

Mr. Billiard: Thank you for coming, gentlemen. The reason I called this meeting was to discuss what our conduct should be . . . um, what our policies should be . . . with respect to winter moves designed to restructure our team, which as you know has had a somewhat disappointing season. Before we begin, Mr. Toady has some remarks that he prepared after a conversation with Mrs. Crock, and I thought you should hear them. Frank?

Mr. Toady: Yes, Sir. To be as brief as possible, Mrs. Crock and I feel that there is a need for this organization to adopt some policies to protect ourselves against possible multimillion-dollar losses on long-term contracts. We have discussed this issue at length and have come up with two essential recommendations. Number one, the team should resolve not to enter into negotiations with any player who has a history of abuse of chemical substances. And number two, the team should no longer enter into negotiations for multi-year contracts.

Mr. Reasoner: Excuse me?

Mr. Toady: The team should no longer enter into negotiations for multi-year contracts. We feel, Mrs. Crock and I, that we should play it one year at a time.

Mr. Reasoner: Do you really think, Mrs. Crock and you, that that's feasible in today's market? And if so, how did you reach the conclusion that it was?

Mr. Toady: Evidence. We had some conversations with Larry Boner of the Player Relations and In-Laws Committee, who showed us figures which project that, at the current rates of growth, by the year 2000 major-league teams will be obligated to pay $148 billion a year to players who are no longer performing. We feel that to offer long-term contracts works to the benefit of the player, but exposes the club to additional financial risk, and thus is not in the interest of the club.

Mr. Reasoner: *Of course* it's not in the interest of the club. And while we're on the subject, it's not in the interest of the club that we pay the players, at all; it would be in the best interest of the club if they would just play for free. It would be in the best interest of the club if the players would pay for their own transportation and their own hotel rooms while on the road, not to mention if they would buy their own uniforms. There are times that it would be in the best interest of the club for certain players to be summarily executed. That doesn't mean that we get to do it. The point is that these things are arrived at through *negotiation*, and that in negotiations the club often agrees to do things that are in the interest of the player so that the player will do things that are in the interest of the club. Maybe if you worked hard enough at it you could even explain this to Mrs. Crock.

Mr. Toady: Oh, I don't think so. Mrs. Crock and I feel that it is in the best interest of the club not to commit ourselves to more than one year at a time.

Mr. Reasoner: Do Mrs. Crock and you understand that if we *don't* commit ourselves to more than one year at a time, all of our best players are just going to leave? Does Mrs. Crock also feel that it is in the best interest of our club if our best players all leave us?

Mr. Toady: Well, we haven't exactly discussed that point. I mean, we're willing to sign free agents and all. We're willing to put out good money on a one-year contract. As Mrs. Crock sees it, when you sell somebody a hamburger, they're not obligated to come back and buy another hamburger. And if we like what we get for our money, we'll sign the player for another year. What could be more fair than that?

Mr. Reasoner: What good does it do to say that you're willing to sign free agents if you're going to adopt a policy that will obviously preclude the possibility of signing any free agent worth putting cheese and pickles on? And by the way, I might point out that our GM, Trader Jack, has actually *saved* this organization hundreds of thousands of dollars by getting players committed to two-year and three-year contracts when they were coming off poor years and going into out-standing years. He's noted throughout baseball for his shrewd use of multi-year contracts. Does this mean anything to you?

Mr. Billiard: I think we've discussed this issue enough: Let's have a vote on it here. All in favor of adopting Frank's rec-ommendation, say "Aye." Seven to one? Okay, that's settled; I'll tell Jack about it first thing in the morning. Now, with respect to the possibility of acquiring additional talent through the winter . . . Ted, did you have some thoughts on that issue?

Mr. Reasoner: Well, there's this player in the National League named Tim Raines. Maybe you've heard of him? He's prob-ably the best player in the league at the moment, and he's expressed an interest in playing for our team. I think we should go after him.

Mr. Billiard: Sounds good to me. Anybody else here know anything about him?

Mr. Toady: I know all about him, and frankly I have to say that he isn't the kind of player who fits our present needs.

Mr. Reasoner: Doesn't fit our needs? But . . . but . . . but we need a leadoff man. And he's the best leadoff man in the history of the National League. And we need a left fielder, and he's the best left fielder in the league. And we desperately need team speed, and he steals seventy bases a year. How in the world can you suggest that he doesn't fit our needs? AND HE WOULD LIKE TO PLAY FOR US!!!

Mr. Toady: Well, we feel—Mrs. Crock and I—that there's more to it than just baseball skills. We feel that this team has a need for character and leadership. This Mr. Raines, he has a history of drug abuse, doesn't he? I sure don't think that shows the kind of character that we're looking for.

Mr. Reasoner: Four years ago, when Tim Raines was a twenty-two-year-old kid and *Newsweek* was putting cocaine on the cover and proclaiming it the nation's new recreational drug, Mr. Raines went through a brief period in which he abused drugs. But he got control of it—before it got control of him. He got clean, and he's been the most durable, dynamic, exciting player in the league over the last four years. You don't think that shows some character?

Mr. Toady: Well, I think what we're looking for is more in the nature of someone who has the character not to get involved with these things at all. I mean, how do we know he's not going to go back to it? We feel, Mrs. Crock and I, that for a baseball team to win, they've got to have character as well as talent.

Mr. Reasoner: Well, so do I. Sports are tests of character as well as talent, of course they are. But if you believe that sports are tests of character, then can you possibly explain how Tim Raines got to be a great player without having character? I mean, surely there's more to having character than being raised in the suburbs, isn't there? I might even suggest that I would think that Raines's experience, in that he overcame this temptation, might have a salutary effect on some of our younger players. It would make him a stronger role model. Anyway, how do we know that Terry Kennedy or Steve Garvey isn't going to start using drugs? For that matter, how do we know that you and Mrs. Crock aren't in there smoking banana peels? You've sure got to be on something. . . .

Mr. Billiard: Well, I think you've mouthed off about long enough there, Ted. Let's take a vote on the issue. Anybody else here who feels that we should make overtures toward this Raines individual? No? Well, that's closed. Any other new business, or can I go get my hair coiffed?

Mr. Reynolds: Mr. Billiard, I had a chance meeting this week with one of the Lord's Angels—

Mr. Toady: *(Intensely interested)*: Oh, really. Which one?

Mr. Reynolds: Grumpy, I think he said his name was. The Angel Grumpy.

Mr. Toady: A good man. I know him well.

Mr. Reynolds: I'm sure you do. Anyway, this angel said that, in view of the unique relationship that our organization has with the Almighty, he had been notified about a special dispensation on our behalf. It seems that the Lord is going to allow us, as a one-time thing, to choose a player out of the past and bring him back to earth at his prime. So long as we didn't put in artificial turf, saith the Lord. Apparently, Gabriel insisted on that.

Mr. Billiard: Gee, that sounds good. Just any player?

Mr. Reynolds: Any player out of the past.

Mr. Billiard: Well, um . . . Gee, that sounds great. What about Babe Ruth?

Mr. Toady: Babe Ruth? With all due respect, Mr. Billiard, I'm sure Mrs. Crock would want us to be consistent here.

Mr. Billiard: Is there a problem?

Mr. Toady: A large one, I'm afraid. Mr. Ruth was a known abuser of illegal chemical substances. Not just on occasion, but throughout his career. Besides that, his training habits were horrific, his education was limited, and his disrespect for team authority knew no bounds. I mean, even Goose Gossage never dangled anybody out the back of a moving 747. He was entertaining, but I'm afraid Mr. Ruth's impact on the team as a whole could be catastrophic and besides, our manager doesn't think he's fast enough.

Mr. Billiard: OK, scratch the Barnbuno. What about the . . . um, the Atlanta Peachtree, was he called?

Mr. Reasoner: Ty Cobb, you mean?

Mr. Billiard: That's him. What about Ty Cobb?

Mr. Toady: Mr. Billiard, with all due respect, Mr. Cobb is, if that's possible, an even more appalling suggestion than Mr. Ruth. Cobb was . . . well, little more than a common thug, really. He was involved in constant fights with opponents, teammates, butchers' clerks, even umpires. Sometimes he carried a gun. He was incredibly greedy. Many people believe that he helped to fix a game, for heaven's sake. I hardly think he exemplifies the kind of athlete we're looking for.

Mr. Billiard: Right. We could go for a pure hitter, instead. What about, um, this Mr. Williams, this "Freddie Ballgame"? What about him?

Mr. Toady: Mr. Williams was pretty hard to get along with, too. His attitude toward the press and public was very poor. He was quoted as saying that if you pour hot water over a sportswriter you'll have instant shit, and on one occasion he made an obscene gesture toward the fans. I think we'd better rule him out.

Mr. Reasoner: In my opinion, sir, I think we should go for a pitcher. What about Lefty Grove, supposed to be the greatest pitcher ever? I think we should go for him.

Mr. Toady: Another hothead, I'm afraid. A fine pitcher but an emotional adolescent, really, a guy who threw tantrums when things didn't go his way.

Mr. Reasoner: What about another pitcher? . . . How about that guy that Reagan played in the movie . . .?

Mr. Toady: Didn't you watch it? The man had a serious drinking problem. In the movie they made out like he got control of it, but he never really did.

Mr. Reasoner: Oh, right. How stupid of me. . . . Anybody have an interest in Mickey Mantle? He always seemed like a good guy to me.

Mr. Toady: Another overgrown adolescent. Training habits were very poor, honestly—in fact we have reports that he was hung over on the field at times. He drank more than the type of player we're looking for, which is to say that he drank more than Mrs. Crock does.

Mr. Reasoner: Willie Mays?

Mr. Toady: We have evidence that he missed church on a number of occasions. With no good reason, really.

Mr. Reasoner: How about Frank Robinson or Bob Gibson, somebody like that?

Mr. Toady: Oh, both of those guys were sheer heck to get along with, particularly after a loss. Also, wasn't Robinson involved in a DWI incident one time? Something like that.

Mr. Reasoner: Roberto Clemente, then?

Mr. Toady: Chronic complainer. Prone to injuries. Didn't get along well with some of his managers.

Mr. Reasoner: I guess outfielders are like that. What about one of those great middle infielders, like Honus Wagner or Rogers Hornsby?

Mr. Toady: Wagner was another man who enjoyed the night life, I'm afraid. Maybe it wasn't a problem, but I'm sure he could drink Mrs. Crock under the table. And Hornsby, he was a real attitude case, a guy who'd rip the front office or his own teammates if he took a notion. Couldn't nobody get along with him. We could have another Goose Gossage on our hands.

Mr. Reasoner: OK, I give up. Isn't there *anybody* who is acceptable to you?

Mr. Toady: Oh, my yes; I can name a number of acceptable candidates. . . . There's Amos Strunk, Tommy Thevenow, Joe Quinn. Our office has never received any negative information pertaining to any of these people. But we feel the ultimate, the perfect candidate to help our ball club is a player of recent vintage, an infielder of the 1970s who was taken untimely away. I refer, of course, to the great Danny Thompson.

Mr. Reasoner: Danny Thompson? Was that the Minnesota kid who married into the Griffith family? Is that who you mean?

Mr. Toady: A fine man and a fine player. I'm sure Mrs. Crock would be very pleased by his selection.

Mr. Reasoner: Let me get this straight. You've got a chance to pick up any player from the history of baseball, and, on the basis of the number of good-conduct medals earned, you're going to pick DANNY THOMPSON!!??

Mr. Billiard: That's enough, Ted. We don't want to get emotional about this. It sounds to me like Mr. Thompson will bring the team exactly the attributes we're looking for. Well, if there are no more suggestions, I'm late for my appointment with my hair stylist. Shall we go with Danny Thompson, then?

Mr. Reynolds: I'll tell Grumpy. Do you think we need to brief the media on this?

Mr. Billiard: No, I don't think that will be necessary. Just issue him a uniform and tell him when to report to Spring Training. If he's everything Mr. Toady tells us he is, nobody will ever know he's around.

—1987

San Francisco Giants

Over the years, the San Francisco Giants have been blessed with a string of general managers who couldn't break even on *Let's Make a Deal*. Last year, the Giants capped an incredible twenty-two year series by virtually giving away Bill Madlock, a lifetime .320 hitter, because he didn't like playing second base. This is understandable; bears don't like to roller skate, cows don't like to dance and the Pope rarely appears on game shows. Playing second base was not among Madlock's considerable talents. The Giants added an ironic touch by signing Rennie Stennett, the man Madlock had benched in Pittsburgh, for considerably more money than they were paying Madlock.

—*Esquire* magazine
May, 1980

The desire to build a domed stadium for the Giants has given birth to an odd, bass-ackwards advertising campaign for the Giants, a campaign that accentuates the negatives. It is an appropriate advertising campaign for a team that leads off a .240 hitter, plays an outfielder at second base and seems hell-bent on trading their best ballplayer when he is coming off his poorest season in several years. With respect to the team, all it seems necessary to say is that I now realize that my impression a year ago that the organization had gained a degree of purpose seems obviously over-optimistic. With respect to domed stadiums, a few thoughts.

1. We have moved into a distinctly different era of stadium construction, out of the time of Veterans and Riverfront and Royals Stadium—the stadiums called by some the sterile ashtray stadiums—and into an era in which stadiums are a) very difficult to get built, and b) most dreamed of and sought after in the domed condition. Seattle, New Orleans,

Minnesota and a couple of other places have succeeded in convincing the bankers; Cleveland, San Francisco, Buffalo, and many others are desirous but lackin' the backin'.

2. What is it, exactly, that attracts people so to the idea of putting a roof over a park? I know people who have lived in Minneapolis and gone to a good many baseball games there, and what they remember most is the weather, the wonderful warm evenings, sitting there at maybe 75, 80 degrees on a June evening, feeling in your face the same wind that carries the ball in from the track.

   And yet, incongruously, it was the weather that they wanted to keep out. Sometimes people become so problem-oriented, so focused on the worst side of a thing, that they fail even to see that in shutting out the bad weather, they are also shutting out the good weather, and that there is at least as much good weather as bad. An odd psychological mechanism is at work here, the perception of weather as inherently negative, something to be avoided.

   Somehow, I always thought people moved to San Francisco because they *liked* the climate. Why don't the Giants try to deal with it—play more day games, put up wind breaks to cut the chill, sell large mugs of hot chocolate along with the cold beer? Why do they want to spend $100 million to play baseball in a warehouse?

3. Getting back to the first point, I think that many people fear that the stadiums are losing their individuality, becoming more and more alike. I understand that fear, and I don't want to see the stadiums all wind up looking alike, either. But I think it's a fault of perception; I don't really think that stadium architecture is collapsing toward a center. It is certainly true that the stadiums opened in the eight years 1966–74 all look quite a bit alike; it is probably true that the stadiums built in any ten-year period have important similarities. If evolution in stadium design stopped at any moment, they would all bear the stamp of that moment.

But ask this question for yourself: Is the difference between all the stadiums less now than it was twenty years ago? I think there is far *more* variety in stadiums now than there was then. We still have a few of the gracious parks of the 1910–25 era, mixed in with quite a few postwar "relocation era" parks, a couple of converted minor league facilities, more than enough sterile ashtrays; now we are past that era and building domes. One thing can be said for domes: It's almost impossible to standardize their dimensions. But only if time stands still or if twenty-six stadiums are thrown up in a period of five years can we wind up with twenty-six identical parks. I don't think there's a tremendous danger of that.

Stadiums acquire an individuality more than they are built with it. When the stadiums of the 1966–74 era are redesigned a time or two to accommodate larger crowds, to provide better seating, to get rid of the turf and put in grass like the stadiums of the 1990s will have or just to repair the ravages of time, then they'll stop looking alike. Neighborhoods and trees will grow up around them. So let's not just focus on the negatives of the new stadiums. For a baseball purist to focus on the negatives of modern stadiums and fail to see the positives is really no different than for the Giants to focus on the negatives of the weather, and fail to catch the scent of salt water in the breeze.

—1984

I know of no parallel for what has happened here. I know of no other case in the history of baseball where any man has done what Al Rosen has done in San Francisco over the last two years. I would not have believed that it could be done. I would feel that I had failed in my responsibility as an analyst if I did not make you understand this.

To begin with, remember that just two years ago the San Francisco Giants lost a hundred games. In 1986 they improved from 62–100 to 83–79, a giant step for a single season though not a historic one. Teams which take a large step forward, however, usually follow up in the next season with a substantial step backward—just as Cleveland and Texas did in 1987. The Giants, early in the season, seemed likely to hold the ground they had gained in 1986, but no more. Rosen, however, did not accept that condition. He set to work, in the middle of the pennant race, to make the moves he would need to make to push this team over the top.

And he did it.

Now let me give you my prejudices. First, I don't think it is a good idea to restructure your team in the middle of the season. It is hard enough to evaluate the needs and abilities of the team at the end of the season, when everything is at rest, all the numbers are in the book and the sum of wins and losses which result from those abilities is known; it is hard enough, I say, to understand that mysterious relationship between individual abilities and team performance when nothing is moving. When every player is hot or cold or injured or pouting or trying to prove something to Detroit, it's just too confusing. It's a kaleidoscope, changes every three seconds. It's dangerous to make decisions about that picture; it's a Cleveland Indians strategy. It's too easy to wind up paying through the nose for a pennant that you don't really have a chance to win.

Second, I think it is dangerous to try to build a ball club too quickly. It is a rule of nature that things which are built too quickly will not endure. A young tree grows a foot a year; if something grows seven feet in one summer, that's a weed. They can slap up a house now in two days, but I would not want to live in any house that was built in less than a couple of months. Any relationship that goes from "What do you do for a living?" to "Do you want to get married?" in less than six months is a good bet to wind up at "What's your lawyer's number?" in another six months. People Express, the airline that went from startup to a power in the industry in five years, went bellyup in another five. Baseball teams illustrate this rule as well.

Yet if there is a fundamental weakness underlying the San Francisco success of 1987, if this team was built too quickly or if something was left out of the mix because it was built in motion, I certainly can't see it. Rosen got all the pieces put together. This, ladies and gentlemen, is an excellent ball club.

—1988

Seattle Mariners

The Seattle Mariners, it is useful to recall, were born as a result of a lawsuit, which is an infernal conception if ever there was one. One can trace a fairly direct line between that fact and the present pointless drifting of the organization. Because the American League was forced to give a franchise to Seattle, it was not in a position to insist, as it normally would have, on solid ownership for that organization. Because the Mariners did not have good financial backing, they have been forced to live a sort of hand-to-mouth existence, without the strength to chart a course and force their way along it.

—1982

There is absolutely no truth to the rumor that the new skipper of the Seattle Mariners will be the Ty D Bol man.

—Esquire magazine
May, 1982

Whew! Am I glad O'Brien's gone. Danny O'Brien had been conducting for three years a dastardly campaign to confuse the sportswriters and sports fans of this country, to render them utterly and hopelessly unable to keep straight who his players were. The Mariners had playing for them at the start of 1983 a double-play combination of Cruz and Cruz, Julio Cruz and Todd Cruz. He dispatched both of them in midseason, sending them (suspiciously) to the two teams which were on their way into the playoffs, causing further identification problems for anybody who might have trouble keeping them straight. The two best hitters on the team were two outfielders named Henderson, Dave Henderson and Steve Henderson. In addition to a "Todd" Cruz and a "Julio" Cruz, a "Steve" Henderson and a "Dave" Henderson, he had on his roster in 1983 a "Rod" Allen and a "Jamie" Allen, a "Jamie Nelson," a "Rickey" Nelson, and a "Gene" Nelson. His roster included an inordinate number of people with names like "Moore," "Clark," "Thomas," "Putnam," and "Reynolds" and enough people named Bill, Bob, Jim, Dave, and Rickey to staff the reunion shows of *Ozzie and Harriet, Leave It to Beaver, Father Knows Best, My Three Sons,* and *Lost in Space.*

Further, the *Baseball Abstract* staff of investigative reporters has now uncovered evidence that many of these people were, in fact, not major league baseball players at all, but hired "ringers" or "rhymers," as they are called, imported specifically to confuse the public. An unnamed source has told us that, as recently as August of 1981, eleven members of the 1983

Seattle Mariners were working in the tobacco industry. Investigator Paula Fastwon in Strawberry Hill, North Carolina, found this advertisement in the help-wanted section of the August 17, 1981 edition of the *Strawberry Sunday News:*

> Growth-oriented company looking for a few young men to come help us fight forest fires in the Pacific Northwest. We have a lot of spare time to kill, *so only those with some familiarity with American sports jargon need apply.* Prefer applicants to have at least average manual dexterity and foot speed; those forest fires can come at you pretty fast, you know. Contact Dan at P.O. Box 1392, Strawberry Hill.
>
> (Emphasis mine)

Don't think that's suspicious? Well, consider this: 47 percent of the people who live in Strawberry Hill, North Carolina, are named "Henderson"! Apparently, O'Brien hoped, once he had the rest of the league properly confused, to get seven people on his roster named "Dave Henderson," and then go to the winter meetings and start trading them; promising each opposing general manager that he was getting *that* Dave Henderson. O'Brien planned to keep the real Dave Henderson, release everybody in his system named "Nelson" or "Allen," and make his bid for *The Sporting News* Executive of the Year award. The plan was uncovered by an alert security guard at the Kingdome, Dick Henderson, who contacted Danny Kaye, who passed the word to George Argyros. O'Brien pleaded for a chance to see his plan through, but was fired after uttering the unforgivable words, "What else did you expect me to do, you moron, you can't make a ball club out of moussaka."

—1984

The Seattle Mariners treat talent as if it were a free resource. About five A.M. one winter morn some sixteen years ago I rolled out of bed with a hundred or more equally disaffected strangers. We gathered in front of the barracks, made a formation and marched over a mile. Spreading out, we meandered down a half-mile grass strip between the two lanes of a highway, "policing the area," which is military talk for picking up all the little bits of paper and trash. This took maybe twenty minutes, but with the formation and the march to and the march back it took well over an hour, every day. I estimated that the Army was spending about eighteen hundred dollars a week (nearly eight thousand dollars a month) to keep the paper picked up on this little stretch of grass between the two lanes of a highway.

The problem was that the generals were in the habit of thinking of manpower as a free resource. Economists used to refer to things like air and water, which could be used by anyone without charge, as free resources. They were assumed to be available in unlimited supply. At one time grazing lands were a free resource. Probably at some point in the early history of man, the land was a free resource. Now it is realized that even air and water are limited, and I don't think economists even use the term anymore.

Military officers didn't use the term, either, but when I entered the Army I was paid something like seventy dollars a month. If one man got killed or served his time or ran away, they just drafted another one; they didn't worry about what it cost. My monthly salary rose rapidly, however, not because I was a good soldier but because Congress was regularly raising the salaries of lower enlisted men. This was toward the end of the Vietnam era, and it no longer seemed viable to draft men and pay them nothing. The society would no longer accept it. With the draft discontinued, soldiers were being paid substantial sums of money to reenlist—and the generals, once those men had reenlisted, were ordering these expensive soldiers to march in circles about two weeks of each month, at a cost of billions of dollars.

Being treated for two years as if my time had no value impressed upon me a lesson: The more talent available to you, the less respect you have for it. The Seattle Mariners farm system over the last five years has been as good as any. Last year Danny Tartabull, a 1986 graduate of the Seattle farms, hit .309 with 34 homers and 101 RBIs—for Kansas City. Ivan Calderon, a 1985 graduate, hit .293 with 28 homers and 83 RBIs—for the White Sox. Both men are young, and one might think that the Mariners perhaps would project what their team would look like with those men in left and right fields over the next ten years, slap themselves in the forehead and say, "We can't let that happen again."

The Mariners, however, still have all kinds of young talent, so they think it's a free resource, never going to run out. Not properly chastised for having disposed of Tartabull and Calderon, they went for the hat trick with Phil Bradley. The failure of this team to improve dramatically despite producing talent is in part due to the organization's failure to perceive a simple reality: that young men who can play baseball are precious to baseball teams. You shouldn't give one away unless you also acquire one.

—1988

St. Louis Cardinals

In retrospect, what is curious about the John Claiborne era in St. Louis is the appearance of design that Claiborne gave to the accumulation of talented losers, as if this were all he had in mind. Claiborne grew up in baseball in the Oakland A's organization, in the days when they would have fistfights in the locker room an hour before a World Series game. He came to believe, one might infer, that such things as character and team spirit were mere oriental dragons envisioned by an occidental press corps. You take the boys who have character, he seemed to say, and I'll take the ones who can hit and run and throw. A man eventually becomes a parody of the things he once believed in, and thus a series of exchanges that are individually defensible are collectively incomprehensible. Garry Templeton, the most talented young player one can imagine (if attitude is not considered a talent), was surrounded by every influence he didn't need, the Christmas apple stored in a barrel of rotten fruit. The Cardinals emerged as baseball's con artists, able to affect to the last cuff link the appearance of successful ballplayers, but having no taste for the actual work of going out and winning baseball games. Whitey Herzog acted shrewdly in cashing in half of his players for what people thought they were worth.

—Esquire magazine
April, 1981

In the attempted first game of the NL playoffs—the game that, as Howard said, "proved not to be capable, meteorologically speaking, of resumption"—there was a beautiful illustration of why people overrate the stolen base so badly. The first inning went like this:

Tom Herr. . . . . single
caught stealing
Ken Oberkfell . . . popped to left
Lonnie Smith. . . . . triple
ball got to the wall; Smith could have scored
Keith Hernandez. . . . . . . Out 5–3
lined off Horner's chest; ran it down and threw him out

The Cardinals committed three base-running mistakes in the inning and didn't score, the third being that Hernandez wasn't running down the line. Hernandez' failure to hustle down the line cost the Cardinals a run, and both Lasorda and Al Michaels pointed that out. Smith's failure to watch his third base coach cost the Cardinals the same run, and Lasorda pointed this out *four times*, once when it happened, again after the Cards were retired, again in the fourth when the Braves mounted a threat, and again when the rains came with the Cards trailing one–zero.

But Herr's attempt to steal a base cost the Cardinals *two runs and a win*—and not one word was said about it. Not only would Herr have scored on the triple, but with only one out Smith would easily have scored on the ground-out, giving the Cardinals a two–one win.

How many two-run innings do you have to lose before the stolen base becomes a bad gamble? Damn few. People overestimate the value of the stolen-base gamble because they fail to make a reasonable accounting of the cost of a caught-stealing. It's an invisible loss; you don't really see the runs you don't get, whereas you do see it when it pays off. But I've noticed something about those big innings that win ball games. You hardly ever see anybody caught stealing in the middle of a three-run rally.

—1983

I think Peter O'Malley is on to something here, I really do. The Dodgers are refusing to sell Busch beer in Dodger Stadium this year because it was that mean old August Busch, Jr., who wouldn't let Bowie Kuhn stay on as commissioner of baseball. Susie and I have talked this over and decided that we, too, want to do our part to support Bowie, and we have been discussing what our options are to hit Gussie Busch right where it hurts, right in the old pocketbook. We have decided on the following, unprecedented actions:

1. We're going to drink more wine and less beer, and we're going to sample some of Busch's competitors' products if he hasn't driven them all out of business.
2. If or when we go to spring training this year, we are not going to make a side trip to Busch Gardens' Dark Continent, or if we do go we are not going to put any money into any of those machines that make those neat little plastic monkeys.
3. We're going to go take the tour of the Budweiser plant four or five times next summer, and every time we do we're going to gulp down as much free Michelob as we can at the end, even though it might make us sick, because we know that it costs them money to provide this service. Also, we plan to stuff our pockets full of those funny little pretzels before we leave.
4. When we go to see the Cardinals play, we're not going to park in their parking garage.
5. We are not going to buy any souvenir batting helmets or anything that has "St. Louis Cardinals" on it.
6. Whenever we see a parade and the Clydesdales are in it, we're not going to watch. We're going to turn off the television set until they're past. Also, we don't plan to laugh at any of Ed McMahon's jokes or buy any of Leon Redbone's records.
7. Finally, we plan to get a can of spray paint and make up a little stencil that says "Welcome to Miller Time" and spray it on our sidewalks, just so that our neighbors know where we stand on this issue.

It might take a while, but in time these actions, if followed by hundreds of people, will constitute an effective boycott, drive Busch to his knees and make him plead for Bowie Kuhn to quit playing darts and come back to lead baseball to greater and greater heights of prosperity. Support Bowie Kuhn. The next time you see a Budweiser truck parked at a liquor store, go let the air out of the tires.

—1984

Some will argue that if the Cardinals can go from 101 wins to 79 in one season, it must be possible for them to get back to 101 in one more season. Perhaps, but if a man is thrown from a horse in a half-second, does it follow that he must be able to get back on the horse as quickly? If you wrap your car around a tree, can you put it back together as quickly as it was torn apart? It is a rule of nature that the processes of destruction, such as fire and violence, act more quickly than the processes of growth and development, and it can be shown that this rule also applies to baseball players and baseball teams.

—1987

Texas Rangers

As the California Angels in 1986 seemed an incarnation of the concept of experience, the Texas Rangers seemed to embody youth. With three young pitchers and young players at eight positions, the Rangers overpowered their own reckless mistakes with the cockiness of young men quite unaware that the world was not ready to step aside and watch them win.

A year ago this winter, the Rangers were blistered in the papers when they traded for Pete Incaviglia, who had refused to sign with Montreal because Montreal was going to send him to the minors. The going line about this trade was that 1) the Rangers had made it more difficult for everybody else to sign their number one draft picks, who were now liable to demand trades; and 2) Incaviglia had a big swing and wouldn't hit major-league pitching anyway. The second point proved to be false and the imminent disaster in the first has failed to materialize, so this petty controversy could well be forgotten now, were there not so much to be learned from it.

It simply is not true that every player has to go through a minor-league apprenticeship in order to play in the majors. It never has been true. There have always been some players (probably many players) for whom the minor leagues were just a nuisance from which they learned nothing and in which they lost twenty to forty percent of their productive life as ballplayers. But the problem is that the most dangerous thing you can do in any learning process is to expose the student to a situation that he or she can't handle. If the young player gets in over his head his confidence can be destroyed, and fears can be set loose in his mind that can never be put away.

And so, understandably, major-league executives become hypercautious about bringing along their young players. It eventually reaches the rather silly point of many organizations insisting that every player stop at every level in his path to the majors, regardless of his individual needs. When they make an exception to their rule by jumping a player across one level—bringing up a rookie all the way from AA ball—they feel like they're doing something bold and innovative. And when an organization does try unsuccessfully to bring a player along quickly, as the Rangers did with Jeff Kunkel, then that organization will be the subject of harsh criticism from the press for having defied the sacred belief that every player should be nurtured slowly.

Throughout baseball history there have been repeated cycles of suddenly rediscovering this truth, rediscovering that some players are ready to play in the major leagues at a young age and without much minor-league experience, and then very gradually burying that secret again under the fear of destroying a player and the fear of criticism. When the cautious attitude is dominant, as in the eighties, then it takes a player of the brashness of Incaviglia to confront it, to say, "No, damn it, I *don't* need to go to the minor leagues. It's a waste of my time and talent." It takes an organization of the self-confidence and imagination of the Texas Rangers to provide an opportunity for him. And so, in a sense, the marriage of Incaviglia and the Rangers was inevitable, because the Rangers were the only organization that was equipped to meet Incaviglia's very legitimate needs. And there we get to the nub of the matter—the arrogance of the young, the insufferable cockiness of young men for whom there is no place in the world but who will not accept that there is no place for them and who go about shoving rules and habits aside to make their place.

—1987

That was some ugly baby. Before the 1987 season Ranger veteran Larry Parrish said that "people expect the labor pains to be over. They expect to see the baby." It was an ugly baby from the first squall. The Rangers lost ten of their first eleven games, and never got above .500.

There is no team in baseball whose failures in 1987 are easier to diagnose, or could be. Texas pitchers walked 760 men, which was 25 percent more than the next-worst team in the American League.

—1988

Toronto Blue Jays

And yet, they did not die. The Toronto Blue Jays in 1986 were harder to kill than Rasputin. The Blue Jays left the gate with a rookie manager, an unreliable bullpen, a starting rotation that was a shambles, and a controversy about who should be their leadoff man. Early in the season the Blue Jays buried themselves in what seemed like an impossible position, yet they were able to scramble back and give the Red Sox all they wanted in their battle to retain first place. Though it was a disappointing season for Blue Jay fans, it was a season that demanded courage, resilience, tenacity, and the sacrifice of personal goals from the Jays' players, and one in which those players answered the challenge in a style that must be admired. For the fans, there will be better years.

—1987

The problem is that you acquire a past. In the beginning what needs to be done is so clear, so obvious. When you have no players you must acquire the best young players that you can find and when they are ready you put them in the lineup because the people who were there before them are just a holding action, just waiting until the future is warm. When you have no past you have no loyalties, no debts. You know exactly where you are in the cycle. You have no memory of yesterday's dreams which still might flower tomorrow, and thus there is no confusion of tomorrow with yesterday, hopes with plans or plans with dreams or what is right with what is best for the team. On September 20, 1987, the Toronto Blue Jays had a clean slate. They never will again.

What happened? It happened, that's all. It happened like a car wreck or a rape or an aneurism in the brain, an arbitrary punishment selected by an unseen God for an unknown reason, a punishment which could have happened to John or Joe or George Bush or the St. Louis Cardinals, but which sought out the Toronto Blue Jays and sat upon their shoulder with wings of iron. In many respects the period just ended in Toronto is like the Dick Williams era in Montreal, the years from 1977 to 1981 when the Expos had the best young team in the National League and, for two or three years, the best combined record in the league, but weren't able to win the close races. When the Expos moved out of the era, they moved into an era of mediocrity, when their pitching staff dissolved, they were unable to hold on to Gary Carter and their farm system stopped producing. While there is no executive in baseball for whom I have more respect than Pat Gillick, one would be foolish not to acknowledge that the same thing could happen here.

But I will be rooting for the Toronto Blue Jays in 1988. I feel like this city and this team and this front office and these fans deserve a World Championship. We have had ten World Champions in the last ten years, but no team has worked harder, no fans have supported their team any better, no front office has been smarter or more decent. Good luck to 'em.

—1988

Section

II

PLAYERS

Willie Aikens

A year ago I wrote that if there was a worse defensive first baseman in the majors than Willie Aikens, somebody must be playing first with a machete. I must report now that Aikens was one hundred percent improved defensively in 1981; he was all the way up to dreadful. He had greatly improved mobility, and he made a handful of legitimately fine defensive plays (most of his good defensive plays are merely plays that any other first baseman would make routinely) in 1981. Lord, is he awful. He has three particular plays that he makes game-in and game-out. On any throw from right field to home plate, if Aikens can get to the ball he figures he is obliged to cut it off, or at least knock it down. I don't care if the throw is right on line, the play is close, the catcher is set, and there is nobody else on base to worry about. If Willie can get to the ball, he's going to cut it off. Somebody should explain to him that this is an option; nobody's going to laugh at you if you let it go through.

The second one is the high pop-up. Willie fixes his stare on any ball popped up in the infield and stalks toward it like a man possessed. He never gives a thought to the notion that there might be somebody else around; I've seen him knock Frank White into center field on balls hit twenty feet from second base. If the ball's hit high enough, the other infielders hold a meeting and decide who gets to tackle Willie.

The third specialty of the horse is coming a half step off the base to catch a throw and then looking around not for the base but for the runner. Willie loses about eight runners a year by standing four inches off the base and trying to tag the runner before the runner can touch the base. If the runner slows up this is pretty easy, but if he is coming full tilt it is damned deadly difficult and in any case the runner moves faster than the base does and I've never yet seen a base take evasive action, so you might as well go for the one that doesn't move.

He has a wide variety of habitual misplays; I don't mean to overemphasize these three merely because they're his favorites. I also don't mean to make light of the fact that the man can hit. You put him in Tiger Stadium and he'd have a real good shot at hitting around .320 with 35 home runs.

—1982

Just for posterity's sake . . . I noted a year ago that Willie had never hit a triple in the major leagues, and wondered in print if this was a record. It was. I made a journey through the encyclopedia to check, and with the help of an old box score concluded that the previous record of the sort was held by Ed (faster than a speeding bureaucracy) Herrmann, who tripled in his third at-bat on May 4, 1973—1,282 at bats into his career. Herrmann, who may have been the slowest player I ever saw, was eventually to amass four triples lifetime.

Anyway, Willie had topped this nonperformance by the beginning of 1982, and I pointed this out in a note for *Sports Illustrated*. This apparently didn't set too well with Aikens, and there was a stretch early in the season (June 6–12, to be specific) in which Willie was thrown out three times in a week trying to stretch a triple into a triple. Toward the end of a 14–1 rout in Yankee Stadium he hit a massive high drive to right center, a thing of beauty it was, which bounced off the wall and away from Dave Collins. Collins ran it down and three-hopped it to the vicinity of the shortstop, who chased it down and relayed it to third. It was a close play, but I thought he should have been called safe.

It was August the twentieth, and the wife and I were for some odd reason up in the cheap seats when the historic moment finally arrived. It was Willie's 1,717th career at-bat. Gus Triandos was not in attendance. Willie speared a fastball and launched it straight toward the tacky water fountains in center field. Susie and I both realized before Willie was out of the batter's box that if it didn't clear the wall this might be *it*, and so we jumped to our feet and began screaming wildly for Willie to get it in gear. This drew considerable consternation from the surrounding fans, most of whom I think were there on a bus tour or something, because it was 11–3 in the bottom of the seventh and nobody had seen anything worth cheering about since the departure of Chico Escarrega in the fifth. Rudy Law was in center field, which will not come as a surprise to those of you who have seen Rudy Law throw. There was a play, but it wasn't close.

Willie in 1982 was taking a lot of crap for his fielding, for which I feel personally responsible, but the strange thing was that he was fielding a lot better than he ever has before. If he was an F three years ago and a D− in '81, he was . . . what, a D+ last year? It wasn't that bad. But he wasn't hitting a lick for four months, and when you don't hit that magnifies the other weaknesses in your game. I really like the guy; he seems hard-working. It's fun to watch him struggle so hard to overcome his inherent limitations; almost inspiring, in a comical way. I'd a lot rather have him out there than Mike Squires.

—1983

Webster's Thesaurus suggested the following words as possible synonyms or related words for error: mistake, inaccuracy, miscalculation, miscomputation, oversight, slip, blooper, blunder, boner, bull, bungle, fluff, lapse, miscue, misstep, rock, slipup, trip, faux pas, bevue, fault, misdoing, misjudgment, stumble, boo-boo, botch, fumble, muff, howler, screamer, impropriety, and indecorum. Their list of suggested synonyms for *inept* is even more generous. It includes awkward, bumbling, maladroit, unhandy, wooden, infelicitous, graceless, ill-chosen, unfortunate, unhappy, improper, ill-timed, inappropriate, inapt, unapt, malapropos, undue, unseasonable, unseemly, unsuitable, unadept, undexterous, unfacile, unhandy, unproficient, inefficient, incapable, incompetent, inexpert, unexpert, unskilled, unskillful, and unworkmanlike. Just a note to the Toronto press corps: You never know when one of these words might come in handy. You never know when a few minutes spent studying this list now might save you valuable deadline-pressure seconds during the course of the long, long, long season. I particularly like "botch," "howler," and "unfacile." I also like "fluff" and "bevue," although I don't really know how to use them. I'm sure you'll have the opportunity to work them in somewhere, though.

—1984

Joaquin Andujar

I worked on Joaquin's salary arbitration case three years ago. When you do an arbitration case you go through the player's whole career game by game, looking for anything—any patterns, any counts, any oddities—that might be of use to you in trying to convince Mr. Arbitrator (that is really what you call him, by the way). One of the things we found about Joaquin was that he had pitched very well when he was in rotation, on three or four or five days' rest, but very poorly when he was being shuttled back and forth between bullpen and rotation. In particular, his control was excellent when he was in rotation, but bad when he was not.

So why didn't they leave him alone? Basically, because they didn't like him. The Astros couldn't resist the continual temptation to try to teach him a lesson, make him a little more normal. I asked David Hendricks, one of his agents, about him a year later. He said, "You know, Joaquin has really been a pleasure to deal with. You go to dinner with him, he'll pick up the check; likes to do things for you. He just goes nuts when he's not pitching." Herzog was smart enough to look at what he could do on the field without being blinded by the man's reputation as a head case.

—1983

Marty Barrett

In the military, drill sergeants and other power mongers will set up little tests for you, make you do some stupid, irrational, and painful thing just to find out how you react to it. If you pass their little test, then they'll always think you're OK, regardless of whether you're worth a hoot or not, because they have reached a prior conclusion that this is the moment at which they're going to find out about you.

I was at a game in KC last May in which Barrett had a couple of hits early, just took pitches on the outside corner and guided them softly over the first baseman's head, the two hits being identical. When he came up the third time I was saying to myself that now they'll make him hit the inside pitch, and they did. The pitcher threw him two pitches on the inside corner, and he turned on the second one and hit the thing a mile (well, maybe 430 feet) for his first major league homer. I was really impressed by that, although logically I knew that it didn't mean any more than anybody else's first home run, because in my mind I had made a prior decision that this was Barrett's test as a major league hitter.

This is a good example of the kind of gut-level decision making that sabermetrics intends to render obsolete . . . .

—1985

Tony Bernazard

You know your career probably isn't going to be made into a movie when they bench you so that Mike Fischlin can play second base . . . .

—1985

Vida Blue

You want to know something funny? My *wife* analyzed this trade better than I did at the time it was made. I was like an eight-year-old, calling up people saying, "Hey, did you hear? We got Vida Blue!" My wife kept saying, "I don't know, Bill; I've heard you point out so many times how people get burnt on trades by trading off prospects to get some old guy." "But honey, it's *Vida Blue*," I protested. . . . The Royals may not have gotten burnt, but I'd sure trade him back to get Atlee Hammaker, and looking a few years down the road . . .

1083

Bruce Bochte

I wrote an article for *Inside Sports* last summer of which the central thesis was that managers tend to select their lineups on the basis of images that they inherited with their first can of Desenex, and not on the basis of any logic or analysis or even reflection as to which combination of hitters will produce the most runs. Your leadoff man, now, he's a speedy singles hitter, little guy most of the time; the guy batting second has to have good bat control, middle infielder if you've got one. Then in the middle of the order you've got the big slow guys.

There are good reasons why these images have evolved, and thus a lineup selected on the basis of these images will probably be at least reasonably well-ordered probably 70 percent of the time. Bruce Bochte is a classic counter-example. Bochte's on base percentage in 1982 was .382, which is outstanding. Despite the fact that he is a big fella, he does not have the kind of power a third- or fourth-place hitter needs. His career high in home runs is sixteen, and that in the Kingdome. The Mariners had several players who could do at least as good a job of bringing people around, including Al Cowens, Dave Henderson, and Richie Zisk.

Yet the Mariners led off their offense with two players who got on base very little (Julio Cruz, on base percentage of .317, and Manny Castillo, on base percentage of .291), and had Bochte batting third. Why? Why start off the offense with two people who don't get on base, and then bring up somebody who isn't particularly good at driving runners around?

Images. Speed, bat control, big slow guy. Bochte batted in the middle of the order because he was a big slow guy.

—1983

Oil Can Boyd

On July 10, 1986, the American League announced the pitchers selected for the All-Star game. Despite shaky credentials (he was 11–6 with a 3.71 ERA), Oil Can Boyd was certain he would hear his name. When he didn't, The Can threw a temper tantrum and left the park, for which he was suspended. As this storm was ready to pass, Boyd mixed it up with two narcs, one of whom filed a complaint alleging that the flyweight pitcher had assaulted him. That complication got infected with charges of drug use, racism, financial distress, press bias and organizational arrogance, out of which the only thing to emerge clearly was that Oil Can Boyd doesn't use drugs, his having passed more drug tests than a race horse. (Didn't you always wonder how they teach those horses to pee in a bottle?)

Anyway, by the time the Red Sox were ready to let Boyd pitch again, it was early August and the Scarlet Hose were clinging to a two-and-half game lead. The division had closed up to where the Sox, once leading by nine games, were only nine games away from last place. There was a strong feeling that the Red Sox must inevitably fold. A Baltimore sportswriter wrote that the Red Sox were choking, just as "they" had choked so many times before. (Casually linking together four decades of diverse frustrations, one is urged to conclude that the Red Sox uniforms must be too tight.) The pennant race became a deathwatch; the nation waited for the Red Sox to self-destruct. It is a tribute to them that they didn't panic and stampede for the exits under the month-long scrutiny that commenced with Boyd's suspension.

—1987

Phil Bradley

If anybody really understands what the trouble between Bradley and Dick Williams was about, he never wrote it up so I could understand it. Williams talked about Bradley being a cancer on the team, a clichéd image which does absolutely nothing to explain what the problem was. All it says is "I don't like him." You wish that these people would go so far as to say that he's a cancer on the colon of the team, or a cancer in the breast of the team, or something. Give us a hint. A cancer on the wallet, perhaps.

—1988

George Brett

What has happened to George over the last two seasons is unusually simple to explain, and can be traced unmistakably in the records. It all began on October 10th, 1980, and no, that is not the date of Dickie Noles' knockdown pitch. That is the date on which, after the nation had just spent three days listening to Billy Martin (working the series for ABC) explain how his pitchers had stopped George in 1980 by a steady diet of breaking balls, Goose Gossage delivered a 98-MPH fastball, and George Brett deposited it in the third deck. And it is overstating the case, but not by much, to say that that was the last fastball that George has seen.

Pitchers, basically, like to throw fastballs. Most of them are in the major leagues because they have strong arms and can throw hard. They are proud of the fact that they can throw hard. They like to. When a pitcher throws breaking stuff and changes speeds a lot, the hitters will sit in the dugout and scream at him, essentially, to fight like a man. Challenge the hitters, that's the spirit. Besides that, the fastball is easier to control than a breaking pitch, and it doesn't put as much strain on the arm.

I have known since 1976 that George Brett was basically a fastball hitter, and so, I suspect, has every pitcher in the American League. But there's knowing something, and then there's *knowing* it. Before 1980, the fact that Brett was a fastball hitter represented a challenge to the pitchers. It didn't dissuade most of them from throwing their fastballs, it simply caused them to try to throw harder. But when the Goose loaded up and threw him the best fastball that he had and George said Whoopee, that did it. Billy's bragging about getting George out with slop took on a whole new meaning. Throwing him a fastball was no longer regarded as a challenge, it was regarded as suicidal.

Before 1980, he didn't walk much; since then, because breaking pitches are harder to control, he walks quite a bit (seventy-one times in '82). Because he is taking more pitches, he is also striking out a lot more (fifty-one times in '82, about twice his pre-1981 average). Through 1980 he was an amazing clutch performer; now, with men on base he gets impatient and lunges at off-speed pitches. Whereas he used to hit one hundred points better in Kansas City, he now does better on the road where the fences are easier to reach if a curve ball hangs.

But watch out, he is adjusting. I think there is a definite limit to how many curve balls you can show the man before he starts rocketing them all over the park, and I think we're pretty close to reaching that limit.

We'll see. There is more to the story than just that, of course; there's a Roger Maris Syndrome involved. I think that the irate locals who portrayed George's contract disaffection as an act of infantile temper were making a more profound point than they realized. George is a man whose masculine family— his father and his brothers—are everything to him. He is a bachelor. In the Herzog years, the Royals were a close team, with a warm, we're-all-in-this-together sort of atmosphere— exactly as the Cardinals arc now. They're not that way any more; Howser is a fine manager, but he's just different. I think George misses that terribly. How does he feel when he sees Jamie Quirk, whom he's been with since the low minors, pushed out of the nest? Like it's time for him to go, too, I suspect. He wants the Royals to tell him that they love him, and instead they tell him it's a business. Sure, he's a spoiled kid, but we're not all too adult to sympathize with those feelings, are we?

—1983

Bill Buckner

A year ago I wrote that Buckner was a batting champion in the noble tradition of Pete Runnels, Ferris Fain, and Bubbles Hargrave. My mail has been about evenly divided between those who think I was maligning Buckner and those who think I was maligning Ferris Fain.

—1982

Al Bumbry

Bumbry and Singleton are an essay on what is wrong with the notion of the "complete player." The complete player is a fluke, a once- or twice-a-generation thing that has nothing to do with the ordinary ballplayer. You don't judge a player by the things he can't do, but by the things he does—how many of them there are and how well he does them. Bumbry's arm was never good, he never had any power. Singleton's arm is just fair and he may be the slowest outfielder in the major leagues. But in their prime they were great ballplayers, because they did the things that they were capable of doing every day.

—1982

Enos Cabell

How can you play full time if you don't do anything? The guy hit .255 (the league average was .255), hit only two home runs, drew only ten walks, had more caught stealing than stolen bases, and played the least demanding position on the field. Badly. Why would a team keep somebody like that in the lineup?

—1982

When Enos Cabell was hot early in the year, you'd ask Sparky Anderson about him and Sparky would say "Enos Cabell is a *we* ballplayer. You don't hear Enos Cabell saying 'I did this' and 'I did that.' " I think that's what drives me nuts about Sparky Anderson, that he's so full of brown stuff that it just doesn't seem like he has any words left over for a basic, fundamental understanding of the game. I want to look at a player on the basis of what, specifically, he can and cannot do to help you win a baseball game, but Sparky's so full of "winners" and "discipline" and "we ballplayers" and self-consciously asinine theories about baseball that he seems to have no concept of how it is, mechanically, that baseball games are won and lost. I mean, I would never say that it was not important to have a team with a good attitude, but Christ, Sparky, there are millions of people in this country who have good attitudes, but there are only about two hundred who can play a major-league brand of baseball, so which are you going to take? Sparky is so focused on all that attitude stuff that he looks at an Enos Cabell and he doesn't even see that *the man can't play baseball*. This wee ballplayer, Sparky, can't play first, can't play third, can't hit, can't run, and can't throw. So who cares what his attitude is?

—1983

You may not believe this, but Enos Cabell and I have friends in common. I happened to be visiting last fall with some people that Enos had been staying with just a few days before. He apparently has taken my remarks about his abilities in stride, and left an unfriendly but good-natured gesture with an intermediary. Public life is rougher than you think it is; you learn to accept those things.

Everybody tells me that Enos is a hell of a good guy, and you know, you can tell he is. His abilities being what they are, would he be in the major leagues if he wasn't? Tom Reich insists that if the Tigers don't re-sign Enos, it will cost them ten games next year because they'll lose Enos' steadying influence on some of the other players. I don't deny it; I just don't have any way of knowing about it. I'm an outsider. And I find that the closer I get to becoming an insider, the harder it is for me to tell the truth about players, the harder it is to resist their distortions and misjudgments. So I spray a little acid around, make a few enemies. It helps keep me honest.

—1984

To recap his career briefly, Enos was an outstanding player in the years 1977–78, when he hit for a good average, hit a few homers, hit about thirty-five doubles and stole about forty bases a year. That's a good offensive player in any park, and in the Astrodome it's a heck of a player. After that he lost the power. Then he lost the speed, and he kept trying to steal bases when he wasn't making it half the time. Then he lost the average. He didn't walk, at all. By 1982 he was probably the worst player in the major leagues, hitting for a .260 average that was as empty as Al Oliver's .300.

It was at this point that I wrote a synopsis of Cabell's contribution to this team—an extremely accurate synopsis, by the way—which is one of the more controversial things that I've written. Cabell is a generally well-respected individual, and a lot of people felt that it was damned impolite of me to point out that he was a terrible player; nonetheless, that was not the essential point that I was trying to make with the comment, and I would not have come down so hard on him if it had been. The essential point that I was making is that ball games —all ball games—are won and lost on the field of play. "Attitude" and "leadership" are very real things; they are on the same plane of existence as "talent," "desire," "training," and "experience," which is to say that they are very valuable *if you can turn them into on-field results.* If you don't turn them into results, and Enos was not at that time, they're meaningless words. Mike Ivie had enormous talent, but that's a poor excuse for keeping him in the lineup if he doesn't produce—and the same goes for Enos Cabell and his "leadership." If you score three runs and the other team scores four, you lose, period; how much "leadership" and "ability" you have does not have one blessed thing to do with it. If you lose a ball game on the field you cannot win it back in the clubhouse, and anybody who thinks you can is a loser.

I thought that to an intelligent reader, it would be clear that that is what I was trying to say, and that it was not my purpose to hammer on Enos. But to people who know Enos and work with him and respect him, the point that I was trying to make was less important than the fact that I hammered on Enos in order to make it. The same applies to the Doug Flynn in Montreal comment a year ago, and I can understand the feeling; it's not reasonable to tell an athlete that he's a terrible player but shouldn't take it so personally. The comment was not inaccurate, but it was unkind, and I regret that.

Threatened with professional extinction, Cabell has arrested his decay, and gotten back some of what he lost. He has hit .300 for the last two seasons, which is just one part of his game but it still beats hitting .260, and he hit with some power in 1984. His defense at first base has improved. He's in the middle of the pack.

—1985

Rod Carew

The year after Carew hit .388, I commented that all dramatic successes in baseball are imitated and come to shape the way the game is played in future generations. I never anticipated that the influence of Carew would be as quick or pervasive as it has been. It's not just the occasional Cecil Cooper who adopts the whole program that I'm talking about, but that elements of his style—in particular the pointed lead foot, the heel turned and poised like a dancer's—are catching on among an alarming number of hitters. I think that Carew has shown people that a stance which is natural and relaxed and normal-looking is *not* necessarily the position from which one can bring bat into contact with ball in the quickest possible motion.

I, for one, *like* unusual batting stances. I think that if you look at a hitter who has tremendous ability but isn't getting out of his ability as much production as seems to be possible, eight times in ten you will see a hitter who is using a very conventional batting stance: flat footed, balanced, bat perpendicular to the shoulder. I think that hitters like John Wockenfuss or Brian Downing who have the guts to do things in an odd or different way very often wind up being better hitters than they have any right to be. I think that someday some struggling young player is going to adopt a Wockenfuss or Downing type of stance and, with better luck, become a superstar. Anyway, Carew at the moment is my best example. Great players are those who construct the conventions of the future, not those who accept the conventions of the past.

—1982

Gary Carter

A year ago (re: Gaylord Perry) I had a comment about why players' careers were getting longer, suggesting that it was primarily an economic phenomenon. This explanation struck a chord, was picked up by the media and ran the gamut from theory to accepted wisdom to cliché in about three months. Usually when something strikes like that, it's a sign that there is some truth in it; at the same time, you should see that there is another side to it, the Gary Carter side. Before the free-agent era, I don't think there is any way that a player as valuable as Carter would have been worked as hard as he was worked from 1977 to 1982. The Expos a) are paying Gary Carter a great amount of money, and b) do not own his future. In those circumstances, they are inclined to take more chances with Carter's future than they otherwise might. They are risking a future that doesn't belong to them anyway to get their two million dollars a year's worth. For this reason and for others, the long-term career implications of baseball's economic restructuring are very, very different than the short-term implications, which are all that we have seen yet.

—1984 *Baseball Abstract*

Marty Castillo

Marty filed for arbitration last year after hitting .119. I don't know if that qualifies as chutzpa or chutzpidity.

—1986

Cesar Cedeño

In the summer of 1982, Cincinnati executive Sheldon Bender gave a celebrated interview in which he blamed the Reds' dismal season on three players. The storm at the time centered on the propriety of his comments. I chose to focus instead on their perceptivity.

The amazing thing about Chief Bender's controversial radio interview last summer was that he only got one out of the three right. He was looking for people to pin the blame on without getting holes in his shirt, so he chose Cesar Cedeño, Jim Kern, and Johnny Bench. Kern was a silly idea, because you've got your number three reliever there with the best ERA on the staff, so who is going to believe he's the reason you're in last place? Bench was terrible at third, so we'll give Bender some credit there without arguing about whose stupid idea it was to put him at third. But Cedeño? That's ridiculous. Cedeño was the team's leading hitter at .289, with 35 doubles and 10 game-winning hits, both figures also leading the team, and he was sharing the outfield with a .221 hitter. The rest of the lineup was burgeoning with truly terrible ballplayers like Alejandro

Trevino and Eddie Milner, Tom Seaver was getting the devil beat out of him regular as clockwork, and you're going to blame the season on the .289 hitter? Regardless of what kind of expectations they had for Cedeño, most intelligent people could figure out that Householder's failure to hit .230 had more to do with the Reds' season than Cedeño's failure to hit .320.

—1983

Rick Cerone

At catcher, the Yankees have replaced the late Thurman Munson with Rick Cerone. Cerone is to catching more or less what Thurman was to aviation . . . .

—Submitted in an *Esquire* article
Deleted as being in bad taste

Ron Cey

I think Cey suffers some from the Yogi Berra syndrome. Berra was a funny guy, odd build and odder face and such a good character story that regardless of what he did on a ballfield he was always a character first. Whereas many ballplayers evolve into legends after they are retired, Berra's image as a ballplayer seemed to fade gradually behind his image as a comic-book reader. "How good a ballplayer was Berra?" asked a friend. "Take Thurman Munson and change ten outs a year into home runs," I replied. I would say that the two greatest catchers in history were Yogi Berra and Johnny Bench.

Ron Cey, like Berra, suffers in reputation from having such an automatic identity that whatever he does, his identity remains. But the Dodgers have been in four World Series in the last eight years, and I can't think of anyone who deserves more credit for that than Ron Cey.

—1982

Ron Cey won the Lou Gehrig Award in 1982. The qualifications for winning this award are (pick one):

1. Getting hit in the head by a Rich Gossage fastball.
2. Playing major-league baseball for twelve years despite the fact that your knees are the height of a seven-year-old's.
3. Having your name drawn out of a hat by the appropriate committee; or
4. Putting up with the second-hand opinions of Frank Sinatra for six years without cracking under the strain.

Maybe this comment is fatuous and absurd, but it seems to me that to imply an equality between battling against Amyotrophic Lateral Sclerosis and any of the above is equally so.

—1983

Will Clark

Will Clark be a great player, or won't he? If Gary Ward was a basketball player, would that make him a Ward of the Court? Can Vance Law ever be repealed? Why didn't Danny Darwin ever evolve into the pitcher people thought he would be? Can Rick Honeycutt the mustard anymore? Is Dale's horse any better today? How about Moose's Haas? What does Ron Cey about being retired? Do you think this will be the year Billy Beane sprouts?

—1988

Henry Cotto

See, on the one hand you've got your Henry Cottos, and on the other hand, you've got your Ken Phelpses. If Henry Cotto is a major league ballplayer, I'm an airplane. Cotto is one of those guys who runs well and throws pretty decent, and one year he hit .270-something, and even though it was an empty .270 in Wrigley Field in not very many at bats, you'll get guys like Don Zimmer who will rave about this great young prospect and keep trading for him, so he'll get about eight chances to play in the major leagues before they figure out he can't hit. At first when he doesn't hit they'll say he just needs more playing time, and then they'll say that he needs to stop wiggling his elbows while the pitcher is in motion or some little thing like that, and then they'll say he needs to point his lead foot and learn to keep his weight back, and then they'll say he needs to be more aggressive at the plate, and then they'll say he needs to go back to wiggling his elbows like he did when he had the good year with the Cubs. They always figure that if you can run and throw they'll teach you to hit. Of course they can't teach anybody to hit, but they always *think* they can, so they keep trying.

Then on the other hand you've got your Ken Phelpses. Ken Phelps has been a major-league ballplayer since at least 1980; through 1985 he had 567 at bats in the major leagues with 40 home runs and 92 RBIs. The Mariners didn't want to let him play. See, the problem was that Chuck Cottier, in his day, was a Henry Cotto, a guy who could run and throw, but couldn't play baseball. Most major league managers were those kind of guys. Ken Phelps, on the other hand, can't run particularly well and doesn't throw well, and if you're that kind of player and want to play major league baseball you'd better go seven for twenty in your first week in the major leagues, or they'll decide it's time to take another look at Henry Cotto. Ken Phelps in his first two shots at major league pitching went three for twenty-six. This cost him several years of his career.

—1987

Eric Davis

When Eric Davis leaves this game
What shall be written beneath his name?
Shall we old men, o'er a glass of ale,
Legends tell and stats detail
Of wonders worked in the Cincy sun
Or merely the record of another one
Who had a chance and didn't take it,
Made us dream, but didn't make it

Up that mountain, built of hope
(Lord, it is a treacherous slope).
When Eric's time has come and gone
Some other youth will claim the dawn
But none of us will be the same,
What shall we see, beneath his name?

—1987

Andre Dawson

There are occasions in your professional life which make you think you're not making any progress. The election of Andre Dawson as the National League's MVP is one of mine. One of the ironies of editing the *Baseball Abstract* is that I am occasionally attacked for placing too much faith in baseball statistics and missing the other elements of the game, the things that "statistics can't measure." The reality is that the essential work of this book is to try to teach people *not* to trust statistics. It was never my idea that we needed to look more carefully at baseball statistics because statistics are the best way to look at baseball. It was my point, rather, that people *do* make judgments about baseball players primarily by statistics, not should but do, and because they do they need to have a better understanding of what those statistics really mean.

The selection as Most Valuable Player of Andre Dawson, who couldn't have been one of the thirty best players in the National League, is an excellent illustration of this. How did Dawson get to be the MVP? Obviously the decision was primarily based on statistics. Dawson led the National League in home runs and RBIs, and the RBI count is the one largest factor in determining who wins the MVP vote—much more important, for example, than playing for a championship team.

Now I'm certainly not suggesting that driving in runs is not an important function of a baseball player, or that RBIs are not a meaningful statistic. I am suggesting that you would have a better chance to evaluate a player fairly if you looked at the entire statistical package, rather than one or two statistics:

1. Dawson's batting average, .287, was neither a positive nor a negative. Among the thirty-six regular National League outfielders, Dawson ranked nineteenth in batting average.
2. Dawson's on base percentage, .328, was a major negative. Dawson drew only 32 walks, while striking out 103 times. His strikeout-to-walk ratio was one of the worst in baseball.
3. Dawson hit only 24 doubles and only 2 triples, both figures well below average. He stole 11 bases.
4. Despite the 49 homers, Dawson scored only 90 runs, meaning that he scored only 41 runs when not hitting a home run. This is a direct result of his failure to get on base consistently.

The way in which all of these things—the walks, the doubles, the batting average, and the home runs—can be evaluated along a common scale is to look at the impact of each on the number of runs scored by the team. Dawson created an estimated 111 runs, tenth in the National League. He made 463 outs. Of the nine men who created more runs for their team than Dawson, all nine did so while using fewer outs. All of the following people were more productive players, in terms of runs created per out, than Andre Dawson: Mike Aldrete, Jack Clark, Will Clark, Kal Daniels, Eric Davis, Pedro Guerrero, Tony Gwynn, Von Hayes, Chris James, Dion James, Howard Johnson, John Kruk, Dale Murphy, Tim Raines, Randy Ready, Mike Schmidt, Darryl Strawberry, Tim Teufel, Andy Van Slyke, and Tim Wallach.

This, however, is without adjusting for illusions of context. After you look at the entire statistical package, you need to look at the illusions which go into making a player's statistics what they are. Some ball parks are much easier to hit in than others. Dawson's statistics were tremendously inflated by playing in Wrigley Field. In Wrigley Field, Dawson hit .332 with 27 home runs. On the road, he hit .246 with 22 homers.

So why did he win the MVP Award? I know what some people will say. It wasn't Dawson's statistics, it was his leadership and his throwing arm. People will say that, but you know it isn't. You don't give an MVP for "leadership" on a last-place team. Half the time, the MVP Award goes to the league leader in RBIs. That's not leadership; that's statistics.

And if they really understood his statistics, they wouldn't have done it.

—1988

Bo Diaz

Pat Corrales last spring described Bo Diaz as the best young catcher in baseball. Also, one might add, the *oldest* young catcher in baseball. Diaz is now thirty, a year younger than Darrell Porter, a year older that Gary Carter. But Corrales deserves a lot of credit for this remarkable season. Corrales got in Diaz' corner years ago, has been telling anybody who would listen that Diaz was going to be an outstanding catcher. You can't reasonably dissociate Corrales' enthusiastic support for Diaz from the season that he had, but many people never make the connection at all, and instead blame Corrales for burning out Diaz, by not giving him more days off in August. OK, Diaz did collapse late in the year, so that's fair, but on balance he had a season that was far above any reasonable expectation.

—1983

Brian Downing

There are few players in baseball for whom I have more respect than Downing. I was thinking of Downing when I was writing the comment (see "On Drugs in Baseball") on the immense difficulty of a player's making a big change in the level of his skills after he reaches the majors; he is perhaps the one player in the major leagues who is a clear exception to what I was saying there. Ten years ago, he looked like he was nothing, a no-hit catcher with a mediocre arm. By lifting weights, he's built himself up physically. By experimenting with different odd batting stances, he's made himself a much better hitter, and probably a smarter hitter, than he was ever supposed to be. By playing hard every inning of every game, he's constantly stretched his abilities, like Pete Rose. He's proof that, by sustained effort in a variety of directions, a player can grow and change after he is physically mature. To me, he embodies the virtues of Rose without the incessant theatrics and grinding self-promotion.

You ever notice how much he looks like Christopher Reeve?

—1985

Mark Eichhorn

Eichhorn is a unique player, a man whose career was going nowhere until he adopted his oddball motion a few years ago —a sidearm, almost underhand motion which he completes by hopping toward first base. I wonder if you would mind if I used Eichhorn to make a series of points which are only vaguely related.

In the very early history of baseball, pitchers threw underhanded. It has been my belief for many years that at some point in the future of baseball, throwing underhanded or low sidearm will return, and will again become the dominant mode. There are several reasons for thinking this, the most basic of which has been cited by many others, that being that it is a more natural motion and a motion which puts less strain on the arm. While that is merely an arguable advantage, not extensively tested by experience, there are other reasons for suggesting this:

1. There have been more successful underarm pitchers in baseball history than many people realize. Carl Mays, a brilliant pitcher of Babe Ruth's time, stood upright on the mound and threw straight underarm. Eldon Auker, who won a hundred and thirty games in the American League in the thirties and early forties, was a submariner. Ted Abernathy, who saved twenty-eight games with a 1.27 ERA for the Reds in the sixties, sometimes scraped his knuckles on the pitching mound. In our own time, of course, Kent Tekulve and Dan Quisenberry have turned in good careers.
2. These pitchers have surprisingly little in common other than throwing underhanded. Mays threw like a softball pitcher but had a blazing, frightening fastball which ex-

ploded past hitters. Auker's delivery was a little bit like a tetherball spinning around at a twenty-degree angle to the pole; his stock-in-trade as I understand it was a very heavy forward rotation on the ball, which tended to cause anything that was hit off of him to burrow into the ground. Abernathy twisted his torso so that his arm was almost perpendicular to the ground, but he was actually throwing sidearm, upper body bent severely to the right. Tekulve throws low sidearm, sort of flying his arm like a flag. Quisenberry is similar to Tekulve but faces the hitter more and throws with less body motion; he also threw a sidearm knuckleball for a couple of years.

This diversity suggests, to me, that an underarm motion is not simply a trick or a novelty, but an alternative that will support a variety of motions and pitches—just like throwing overhand.

3. Those pitchers who have thrown underhand have been disproportionately successful for their numbers. Abernathy, Quisenberry, and Tekulve have all had seasons in which they pitched a lot of games with ERAs in the ones. They have shown, as a group, exceptional career longevity.

4. With the exception of Abernathy with his contorted motion, all of the successful underhanded pitchers have had very good control. Quisenberry's control record is probably the best of any pitcher of the lively ball era.

5. These pitchers were, as a group, the most marginal of talents. They were, like Eichhorn, pitchers whose careers were going nowhere until they got down and dirty. *That much* success from *that little* talent has got to be trying to tell us something.

Suppose that you had a group of light-hitting infielders who discovered that they could do something (let's say, start using a bottle bat) which would turn them into .300 hitters. Wouldn't you think that would be of considerable interest among marginal talents?

6. Let us assume that it is true that one can throw harder overhanded than underhanded. But let us assume, at the same time, that one can manage better control underhanded than overhanded. Which is more important to quality pitching: power or control?

Baseball men love to tell you that the important thing is

control—but there is a great reluctance to follow up on that. No serious person doubts, I think, that a control pitcher without a good fastball must overcome a tremendous prejudice to earn a chance in the major leagues.

7. Quite apart from control, I believe that the natural trajectory of an underhanded throw has advantages. An overhanded throw is naturally thrown on a line, descending from shoulder height (plus the mound) into the strike zone. An underhanded toss can both rise and fall, meaning that an underhanded pitch can be thrown with an amount of top-spin which would make an overhanded pitch uncontrollable. In my opinion, that is potentially a tremendous advantage to an underhanded pitcher.

Now, having said those things, I have to add that I have been somewhat surprised that the underhanded motion has not shown more signs of catching on. I would have thought that the success of Quisenberry and Tekulve would light a brush fire among pitchers whose careers were endangered. The spark hasn't shown signs of catching—yet neither has it gone out. Counting Eichhorn, we now have three pitchers who sometimes throw underhanded. It is easy to see how three could grow to ten and ten to fifty and fifty to two hundred. But it hasn't happened.

—1988

Ken Forsch

When I was kid I used to think that the true test of a baseball fan was being able to spell "Schoendienst." Now I think the real test is if you can keep the Forsch brothers straight. Which one is 6'4", 200, and which one is 6'4", 205? Which one pitched his no-hitter in April of 1978, and which one in April of 1979? Which one finished 11–7 in 1981, and which one 10–5? In the three years before that, which one won thirty-three games by winning ten, eleven, and twelve, and which one won thirty-three games by winning eleven each year? Which one has a career total of eighty-nine wins, and which one has ninety-three? The answers are Bob, Ken, Bob, Ken, Ken, Bob,

Ken, Bob, Ken, and Bob, respectively. Bob's the one who won twenty once, pitches for the Cardinals. This is the other guy.

—1982

Gary Gaetti

In 1984 Gary Gaetti, who had hit 46 homers the previous two years, hit only 5 home runs while playing 162 games, while Hubie Brooks, whose previous career high in home runs was 5, hit 16.

NEWSFLASH . . . Compton, California, December 23, 1984. Gary Gaetti's home run swing, reported missing by the young third baseman during spring training, was recovered by police today from a trash can three blocks from the Compton home of National League player Hubie Brooks. Police, acting on a tip from an anonymous caller who was described as "practicing his French accent," discovered the missing upper-cut moments before it would have been emptied from the dumpster and ground into tiny pieces. Gaetti expressed relief over the recovery of the swing, which was valued at approximately six million dollars but could not be insured, while manager Billy Gardner said he was elated by the recovery, and described it as "the best Christmas present a manager could ask for." No suspects are in custody, but the investigation is proceeding.

—1985

Ron Gardenhire

When Ron Gardenhire was called up to the Mets last fall, he sent his pet cat to stay with his in-laws here in Lawrence, Kansas. This is not strange. What is strange is that *The Sporting News* reported that Ron Gardenhire had sent his pet cat to stay with his in-laws here in Lawrence, Kansas. I am not making this up. It is right there in black and white—October 3, 1981 edition, page 8, column 2:

*The day after he arrived in New York, Gardenhire decided
to send his cat, Tigger, a plain old alley cat, to Ron's in-laws
in Lawrence, Kansas.*

I have no idea why they reported this, but I am, as anyone
would be under the circumstances, absolutely convinced that
it must have been done for my benefit. I mean, if you lived in
Muskegon, Wisconsin, and you read in a national publication
that Ron Gardenhire had sent his pet cat to stay in Muskegon,
Wisconsin, wouldn't you rather fancy that this information
must have been provided expressly for you? I don't know who
Ron's in-laws are or what the cat looks like (there was a drawing in The Sporting News, but it wasn't in color, and all cats
look pretty much alike in black and white), but I want to tell
you, I have been driving *carefully*. Can you imagine what it
would look like if there was an accident: GARDENHIRE'S CAT
SMASHED BY WRITER!! And just beneath the banner, "details on
page 4: Sabermetrician denies malice; claims Tigger jumped at
his tire." I may give up driving entirely. Or maybe I'll give up
reading The Sporting News. Whichever it is, Ron, if you're ever
in town, stop by and say hello. And, by all means, bring your
cat.

—1982

Steve Garvey

What is it about Senator Garvey that rings so false when you
know in your heart that it is probably as genuine as the con-
tented look on the face of a cow and as deeply held as Hallow-
een candy in the hand of a child? I have a cousin who strikes
me exactly the same way, and I'll bet you do too; we'll call
mine Wally. Wally graduated from high school with highest
Hosannahs and went straight to Harvard, where he met and
married a reasonably pretty girl with an awfully sensible head
on her, and then he got his master's degree and went to work
in corporate America, shinnying rapidly up the ladder of success and making oodles of money and saving it so that his
children will never have to worry about who will pay for their
next orthodontist's appointment. Wally is an awfully nice man

and he has never said an unkind word to me in his life, and he is brilliant, and I avoid him at all costs. There is something about the very sensibleness of his life that seems to any normal person to be almost accusatory, for sometimes I am chubby while he retains an accusing trimness, and sometimes I am underemployed while he rests in accusingly attainable affluence, and sometimes I might neglect to have my teeth looked at for a decade or two because of an irrational fear of dentists while I know without a thought that if Wally had such a fear he would deal with it directly, and if he didn't his wife would spin him around and kick him in the butt and send him on the way to his appointment anyway, so that you would never know the difference.

It does not ring false, perhaps, but hollow, that since the very essence of life is a mystery, life seems unreal without self-doubt, and we must see that self-doubt in others before we can accept that they share our humanity. Garvey never allows the question marks to rise into his eyes or to afflict his performance, and thus he seems . . . what is it that people say about him? Plastic? A robot? A programmed performer? How can he be a human without doubting himself, without yielding to periods of frustration and futile anger? It is not only Garvey's chin which seems chiseled in granite, but his values, which were given to him while he was in grade school along with the rest of us. But while the rest of us have eroded ours by turning them over and over and examining them in different ways, Garvey seems, impossibly, to have let his stay untested and unworn.

One might think that when this period is in the past Garvey will be humanized somewhat by what the networks refer to as his "mental torment," by his accompanying sub-Garvey seasons. Self-doubt comes directly from pain, as ashes are left by a fire. What is so unnerving about Wally and Steve is to think that they have never lost a year or two out of their lives because they were wondering about something, got their values confused, never sifted through the ashes before. 1981 and 1982 were the years Garvey lost in the fire, and one might hope that he will have the sense not to hide that from us. Welcome, Steve; welcome to the human race.

—1983

Dwight Gooden

There were reports last year that Mel Stottlemyre had persuaded Dwight Gooden to stop trying to strike out every hitter and to try to concentrate on getting more ground ball outs. His thinking was that going for strikeouts was placing a strain on Gooden's arm, and that in the long run he'd be more durable as a ground ball, control-type pitcher.

That's a common belief among baseball men, but it is dead wrong. Among all of the hundreds of issues that I have studied in the ten years I have been doing this, the *most* definitive evidence that I have ever found on any issue is the evidence that the career expectation for a strikeout pitcher is dramatically longer than it is for a control pitcher, a ground ball pitcher or any other class of pitchers. *Virtually all pitchers who are durable over a long period of time begin and become successful as strikeout pitchers.* In some cases, like Warren Spahn, they will become ground-ball pitchers as time passes, but in most cases they will remain strikeout pitchers as long as they are effective.

If you take two pitchers of the same age, same ERA and same won-lost record, the one who strikes out more hitters will go on to have a better career almost 80 percent of the time. The greater the difference in strikeouts, the greater will be the difference in their future careers. The exact number of strikeouts that the pitcher gets is an excellent indicator of exactly how long he will last. Nolan Ryan and Steve Carlton, two of the greatest strikeout pitchers of all time, have also been two of the most remarkably durable pitchers of all time. Look at Walter Johnson, Tom Seaver, and Bob Gibson. Look at Marichal and Sutton and Ferguson Jenkins. Look at Blyleven. The guys who move the ball around in the strike zone, like Catfish Hunter, Randy Jones, and Mike Flanagan, will have some good years but almost never last as long as the power pitchers. Even Tommy John as a young pitcher was over the league average in strikeouts—as, of course, was Hunter.

Even Stottlemyre himself. People think that Stottlemyre was a durable pitcher, and he was, but he won only 164 major-league games and had his last good year at age thirty-one.

Stottlemyre came up in mid-season, 1964, and went 9–3 in thirteen starts. Luis Tiant, one year older than Stottlemyre, also came up in mid-season, 1964, and went 9–3 in sixteen starts (as well as 1–1 in relief). It's as good a matched set as you can hope for, the difference between the two being that Stottlemyre was a groundball pitcher and Tiant was a strikeout pitcher. Stottlemyre won 164 games but was finished by 1973. Tiant lasted until 1979 (effectively); he made about 30 percent more starts, pitched 30 percent more innings and won almost 40 percent more games.

Why? Maybe for this reason: As a pitcher ages, his strikeout totals almost always decline. They go up for two or three years after entering the league, but, with the exception of an odd case like Mike Scott, then they decline. Once the pitcher is below average in strikeouts, he must be outstanding in some other respect in order to keep pitching, so that you might generalize that once a pitcher is below the league average in strikeouts, he usually has only two or three years left as an effective pitcher. If you visualize this as a line on a graph, the height at which the line starts to decline and length of time that it takes to reach the bottom are going to be very closely correlated. Stottlemyre came into the league at 4.6 strikeouts a game, and went up to 5.3 (1967), after which he began to decline. By 1973, striking out only three men a game, he was putting tremendous pressure on the other elements of his game. Tiant came into the league at 7 strikeouts a game, and went up to 9.2 (1967–68). In 1972 he was still striking out 6.2 men a game. In 1976 he was still striking out 4.2 men a game, and so he was still effective. But there just really aren't very many effective pitchers who strike out three men a game.

I've reported on the studies before and won't repeat them, but I'll say this: The separation of data on this issue is so dramatic that you can't miss it. If you study the issue, no matter how badly, no matter how carelessly, you can't possibly miss seeing that the strikeout pitchers last a lot longer than the control-type pitchers. There are a lot of factors which will determine how long Dwight Gooden will pitch, and you have to be concerned about a pitcher who has been worked so hard at such a young age. But if Mel Stottlemyre wants Dwight Gooden to last as long as possible, he'd better stop this crap about throwing ground balls and tell him to concentrate on striking out as many batters as he can.

—1987

The useful lesson of the Dwight Gooden story is that the age of the hero is not over. When Dwight Gooden was on top of the world two years ago, we read and heard constantly about what a level-headed, mature young man he was, what a great set of values he had and how he represented so much that was good about America. Looking backward, it is painfully obvious that Dwight never was what we tried to make him out to be. He was exceptional in that he could throw so hard and in that he could throw the ball where he wanted it to go and in that he learned so quickly, and because he had those qualities people who didn't really know him or understand him imputed to him qualities of character equal to his preternatural skills. The lesson we have learned is not that he is a bum but that he is a human being, and thus that despite all we have read over the last twenty years about the lack of heroes in American society, about this being the age of the anti-hero, the fact remains that as a nation we desperately wanted Dwight Gooden to be a hero. We wanted him to represent our values.

Some Met fans will tell you that Gooden should shoulder the blame for the Mets' failure to repeat, which is a part of the same syndrome. You can't be thinking that way, guys; it's a loser's logic. The Cardinals lost John Tudor for a lot longer than the Mets lost Gooden, but they still won. Gooden last year was off by a game and a half. Ron Darling was off by two games and a half, Fernandez off by three games. Orosco and McDowell were way off, as were several non-pitchers. The critical blow was not any of these but the loss of Bobby Ojeda. Why then was it Gooden's fault?

Because he was supposed to be a hero, and turned out to be a human being.

—The Great American Baseball Stat Book (1988)

Did you ever think of Strawberry and Gooden as the Whitey and Mickey of the eighties? Well, think about it . . . the great young outfielder, held up always to impossible comparisons, the great pitcher, the best of friends, in New York City, on the best team in baseball. Of course, Strawberry and Gooden are always getting into some kind of trouble, while Whitey and Mickey were choir boys. I'd like to think that in thirty years we will look back on this time and remember them fondly, warts and all but with the warts not put under a magnifying glass and blown up as big as a house. I would hope that Dwight and Darryl would grow old and respectable and write books full of wild stories about the things that happened to them when they were young rogues and had the world by the tail. Keith Hernandez will play Phil Rizzuto (the classy veteran, looking on with a bemused expression). Yogi appears to be as yet uncast, but we're looking carefully at Mookie.

—1988

Ron Guidry

One of the tricks of journalists used to cast agents in a bad light is to describe anything that an agent says as a "demand." Thus it was when Guidry's agent made public the considerations which would decide where Guidry played in 1982. He wanted to play for a contender, he wanted to play for a team with a good bullpen, a team that could score some runs, and as to the money . . . well, it would depend on what the situation was.

This was as intelligent a free agent posture as I've ever seen. Guidry showed a recognition of his own limitations. He showed a willingness to decide the issue on the basis of something other than raw dollars. I always think how different the careers of Oscar Gamble and Richie Zisk might have been had they used their freedom to get into situations where they could succeed, rather than joining desperate organizations in parks that were terrible for them because that's where the most money was.

The press characterized all of the things that Guidry was looking for as "demands." A free agent doesn't "demand" anything; he is in no position to offer any ultimatums. All a free agent can do is look the offers over and decide which one he likes. It was a shame to see such a classy statement so grossly distorted.

—1982

Toby Harrah

The Toby-Harrah-for-the-All-Star-team controversy . . . how can the entire country get so confused about these things? Let's review the facts: Toby Harrah plays in the major leagues for roughly forty years, during which he clearly and unmistakably establishes that he is *not* an All-Star. George Brett, over a period of several years, establishes beyond any shadow of a doubt that he *is* an All-Star. Toby Harrah has a hot streak early in the year, on the strength of which he carries a .336 batting average into the All-Star break with 17 home runs and 45 RBIs, while George Brett was stumbling along barely over .300 with only 10 homers. Nevertheless, the nation's baseball fans elect George Brett to the All-Star team, which strikes me as an act of abundant good sense, because everybody in the country knows that George Brett is a better ballplayer than Toby Harrah.

But what comes of this? Why do we have to put up, every All-Star season, with these asinine editorials about why is this guy on the All-Star team when his numbers are only this when this guy isn't on the team when his numbers are this and this and that guy has done this. Was there one of you out there who really thought that Toby Harrah had become a .336 hitter? And if you didn't think that he was a .336 hitter, why did you think that he should have been on the All-Star team? Would you be happy if we schedule an All-Mediocrities-Who-Had-Good-First-Halves Game? We could play it in Cleveland every year.

There is a debate that goes along with this every June and July about the "relevance" of this season's statistics and the "relevance" of career statistics to the question of who belongs in the All-Star Game. I can see how this would be a difficult issue to resolve, particularly if you haven't stopped to think about the subject for thirty-five seconds before joining the debate. If you have, the resolution of the debate is absurdly obvious.

Q. What are baseball statistics? What do they mean?
A. Baseball statistics are valuable as evidence about the ability of baseball players.
Q. Why do we keep them?

A. We keep them to tell us how good a baseball player somebody is.

Q. Which statistics are relevant to the selection of an All-Star team?

A. *All statistics are relevant to the extent that they provide credible evidence about the abilities of the player involved.*

That's it. That's all you need to know to put an end to this whole stupid argument. If you're comparing an unknown quantity—a Kent Hrbek in 1982–to an old, once-great ballplayer—Carl Yastrzemski in 1982—then by all means, the seasonal statistics are relevant evidence. When you talk about career records, Carl Yastrzemski's 1967 season is clearly and obviously irrelevant, because no sensible person would use what happened in 1967 as evidence about what kind of a ballplayer somebody was in 1982. A sensible man, looking at the 1982 statistics of Kent Hrbek, could very possibly conclude that he was a better ballplayer than Yastrzemski. If Toby Harrah had been hitting .383 and George Brett .250, then that would have been credible evidence that Harrah had become the legitimate All-Star. But just because somebody goes on a hot streak early in the year . . . who cares? There is no reason to let it confuse you.

—1983

Rickey Henderson

We are living in the age of the great leadoff men, and I think it's important to appreciate that. I grew up in the sixties, and we had all of those awesome power pitchers—Gibson, Koufax, Drysdale, Maloney, Veale, Sam McDowell. I had no sense of historical perspective, as a child doesn't, and I didn't understand that it hadn't always been this way and wouldn't always be this way. Now they're mostly gone, of course, and I feel like somebody should have told me to appreciate them.

—1984

George Hendrick

I did a once-a-week radio show last summer on KMOX in St. Louis, the flagship station of the Cardinals. A caller asked me to evaluate George Hendrick as a fielder, and I do not recall exactly what I first said about him. It wasn't very derogatory, but it was to the effect that I didn't regard him as a great outfielder. Two or three calls later, some nerdwit called up and demanded to know how I could criticize George Hendrick's fielding when I didn't even live in not only not St. Louis, but not a National League city.

To back up a minute, I had done the show a few times earlier with Bob Costas and Bob Burns, radio veterans, when another listener had called in with some twisted version of what one of us had said. What both of them did in that circumstance was to turn on the guy instantly. Costas would chew the caller out for about two minutes for dragging the level of the conversation down; Burns would just snap at him, but set the record straight. But I thought I'd be nice about it, which was my first mistake, and use the opportunity to get a little spirited debate going on the show, which was my second mistake. So, to be nice about it and give the show a little contrast in viewpoints, I said, "Well, if you live in St. Louis and see him play a lot, then I'll accept your word for it, but . . . " That was my third mistake.

For about three weeks after that, I felt like the new guy in the cellblock. That comment, of course, was intended to set a polite tone for the discussion that followed, and also to put an end-point to the discussion by making it clear that I didn't have a closed mind on the subject, and would be happy to learn what the Cardinal fans had to say. The third mistake, though, was to assume that I was dealing with an intelligent audience. There is an intelligent audience out there, but sometimes they call and sometimes they don't. There was another audience out there, which interpreted this deferential opening as a sign of weakness, and therefore as a signal to attack.

There are still several thousand baseball fans in St. Louis County who are convinced that Kenny Reitz was an outstanding third baseman and a productive hitter who was driven out of baseball by an establishment conspiracy. In Kansas City, their cousins still espouse the cause of Pete LaCock, and I am not making that up. These people, take my word for it, do not wish to be educated. The sole criterion of baseball expertise which these types recognize is, "How many Cardinal games did you see last year?" I was introduced to a good many of these people last May; another thing which I learned about them is that they don't really listen to the show, but it doesn't matter much. I received perhaps a dozen calls which could be recorded quite literally as "I wasn't listening to that show so I don't know what you said, but you sure shouldn't say something like that unless you see a lot of Cardinal games." It is also very important to these people to register their sentiment personally, even if those sentiments are not distinguishable from those of the last eight callers.

By the middle of the summer, of course, Hendrick had begun to play right field in the manner to which he has long been accustomed, and we were receiving calls every week about what a lackadaisical right fielder George is, and why doesn't somebody do something about it? I didn't say a word; just chuckled during the commercials. I'm not complaining; over the course of the summer, we received a lot of good calls, with thoughtful comments from intelligent people. I enjoyed talking to them. But if you ever hear me doing a radio call-in show, by all means, reader, call in. Because if you don't, the ignorant shall inherit the air waves.

—1983

Keith Hernandez

It was noted last year that, with the Mets having a young pitching staff and a rookie catcher, Keith assumed what has traditionally been the catcher's role of "handling" the pitcher, watching his mechanics and supervising his pitch selection. It is surprising that we haven't seen any other team in a long time take this fairly simple and logical step. Why do you *have* to have Bill Schroeder worrying about handling the pitcher when you have Cecil Cooper at first base? Taking that responsibility away from the young catcher reduces the number of things he has to worry about while he is trying to establish himself as a major league player, and at the same time places the responsibility in the hands of someone who has the experience to do the job.

Everything old becomes news again. While writing the historical *Abstract*, I noticed that prior to 1920 it was not uncommon for the first baseman to do this. The basis of Frank Chance's reputation as an on-field leader and player/manager was exactly that—he was regarded as an exceptional handler of the pitching staff. Because of his position on the field, his view of the pitcher and the strike zone, the first baseman was in many cases considered a kind of an automatic captain; other first basemen in this period who became player/managers included Fred Tenney, John Ganzel, George Stovall, Jake Stahl, and Hal Chase. Sometimes a first baseman would be criticized by the press because he was considered deficient in filling his role as a field leader.

—1985

Joe Hesketh

On June 17, Joe Hesketh's ERA was 7.14, and the scouts all know it is bad luck to have the ERA of a jetliner.

—1987

Teddy Higuera

Higuera, I suspect, is one of the half-dozen pitchers in our generation who can work eight or ten innings a start without being destroyed by it. The way that managers have tested the limits of starting pitchers for the last century is quite a bit like the way they used to test for witches, by pond dunking. You ever read about that? If a woman (or a person, usually a woman) was suspected of being a witch, they'd tie her to a pole and dunk her in the pond. If she survived for several minutes underwater, then she was a witch and should be stoned or burned at the stake or whatever. If she drowned, then you knew she was innocent. Of course, the woman was dead, but at least you knew where you stood with her.

That's how managers used to test starting pitchers, and to some extent still do—just throw them out there and let them pitch. In each generation there are a handful of pitchers who can start thirty-five or forty times a year and pitch seven innings a start—a handful, but no more than a handful. If you try that and it ruins the pitcher's arm, then you know he's not one of those pitchers. Managers establish as a normal workload the workload that Jack Morris and Teddy Higuera are capable of handling, but which destroys most pitchers in a year or two. They're a little better about it now, but there are still an awful lot of young pitchers whose arms are ruined by managers who are under pressure to win now, and who don't see any point in making sure that the pitcher isn't overloaded.

—1988

Butch Hobson

Of all the differences between baseball and other games, the most rudimentary is that baseball is played every day. It is this original source, though we never pause to consider it, which creates most of the differences between baseball and other sports. One of the most striking things about baseball is the lack of violence in it, the shortage of collisions and crunching bones. Because there is always a game tomorrow, baseball men have found it unprofitable and shortsighted to create situations which risk injury. Many people think that there is something inherently violent in the nature of football, something about the design of the game which necessitates the use of force. But that's not it; it's just the playing schedule. In the early days of the sport, the elements of violence in baseball were much larger than they are today. A batter was originally put out by being hit with a thrown ball. My favorite story from nineteenth century baseball, which is attributed to Honus Wagner, concerns a time when Wagner hit a triple against the Baltimore Orioles. He said it would have been a home run except that the first baseman bumped him, the second baseman tripped him, the shortstop gave him a couple of shots as he went by and when he got to third, John McGraw pulled out a shotgun.

It was a rough game. The elements of violence and force have been gradually weeded out of the game because of the paramount importance of keeping people healthy. This process is still going on. Hit batsmen per game dropped a third between 1967 and 1980. The rules on taking out the pivot man on a double play have been tightened up in the last few years. And it is my impression, at least, that there are far, far fewer on-field melees now than there were fifteen years ago.

At the same time, the elements of violence in football have taken hold and been allowed to grow gradually larger. An innovation of just ten years ago on defense is the bump and run. The players have gotten bigger and bigger and stronger and stronger, for a simple reason: the better to inflict pain upon one another. Starting from points relatively close together, the two games have evolved in opposite directions. The nation's third major sport, basketball, is right between the two in the frequency with which it is played—and right between the two in the degree of in-game use of force. It is played less often than baseball; it is more physical than baseball. It is played more often than football; it is less physical than football.

Another unique quality of baseball is that it is the most unpredictable of games, the game in which, as they say, "form does not hold." There are no upsets in baseball (in a single game); there are no expectations firm enough to create upsets. Again, this is a function of the number of games on the schedule; time is a leveling force. If baseball teams played sixteen games a year, then it would be of paramount importance to win those sixteen games, and the better teams would dominate. Each team would have only one or two pitchers, so that all of the Phillies' games would be started by Steve Carlton. Baseball allows quality to seep out of its cracks because the schedule permits it; if the schedule didn't allow it, strategy would adapt to that. Again, basketball falls right between the other two in this regard.

These two factors join in several ways. The great number of games diminishes the importance of each game, and that makes each game less worthy of risks. I commend to your attention one play in baseball: the collision at home plate. Why doesn't the same collision take place at the other bases? Why doesn't the second baseman block second base, and the third baseman third? The rules applying to the play are exactly the same for other fielders as they are for catchers; catchers have no exemption from the rules regarding base runners. The collision at home is simply a reflection of the value of the run, as opposed to the value of possession of the other bases. They fight over home plate because the evolving ethics of the sport have decided that in a close game, home plate is worth fighting over. The other bases are not. In the same way, the great abundance of games and plays makes each play less worth fighting over.

In football, the scarcity of plays—the few number of plays which go into making a successful season—changes the relationship between the value of the player and the value of the play. In football, every game must be won at all costs. If you make the play and lose the player, well, that's the way it is; you still have to make the play. In baseball, the relative abundance of plays makes the player more important than any play.

The abundance of plays—what a phrase! The cornucopia of plays, spilling forth over the months and creating a leisurely pace in which there resides a poetic warmth. The wild cheering and constant noise of football games are a manifestation of the magnified importance of each series in a short season. The Japanese notwithstanding, the same would be inappropriate at a baseball game; over time it would become insufferable. It is commonly observed that baseball players train much less than other athletes, that whereas football players lift weights and run drills and practice patterns *ad infinitum* and basketball players do the same with less fanaticism, baseball players don't really work all that hard at conditioning. Again, a product of the schedule: Football players practice more because they play less. If you see somebody running in the outfield before a baseball game, who is it? It's likely to be either a pitcher or a utility man, somebody who doesn't play every day.

The overriding consideration in baseball is always this: There is a game tomorrow. That is what leads, eventually, back to the subject, which is Butch Hobson, and leads to the different psychological types which succeed in baseball and in other sports. Baseball demands a different makeup than football; it demands a Steve Garvey rather than a John Matuszak. It demands a *percentage* player.

And yet, and this is the central point of this essay, many fans do not realize this or will not accept it. The fans don't go to the game every day. They don't feel the pain if something gets torn. To them the only thing for an athlete to do is to go out and give it everything he has on every play; if he doesn't play that way, he's not doing what he should be doing. He's not earning his pay. If the ball is in the seats, he's supposed to dive in after it. If it requires him to go to the wall, he is supposed to hit that wall. A player who plays all out will always be a fan favorite; a percentage player will never be accepted by the audience unless he is able to overcome that impression some other way.

Remember now what they used to say about Butch Hobson up in Boston? The *fullback* attitude. Get it? He's a football player; he is the poorest percentage player of our time. He's all-out, into the wall, take out the baseman, dive for everything. Butch always plays as if there were no game tomorrow, and the fans love that.

The problem is that there *is* a game tomorrow, and one the day after. I will never understand why baseball fans admire a player who runs into walls. Running into walls is a stupid waste of talent. Playing hard in baseball is so much admired that people make up lists of players who play hard, with the implication that this is a good to be sought after in its own right.

The problem is that eighty percent of the people on those lists are dyed-in-the-doubleknit losers, and the ones who aren't losers are players like Brett and Molitor who spend a third of the season on the disabled list. Nobody will ever convince me that Butch Hobson has gotten out of his talent anything like what he had the potential to be. Everything about him—his batting style, his defense, his baserunning—is gung ho. And ill considered. The only thing he knows about defense is run hard toward the ball and throw it as hard as you can throw it. That kind of play just does not provide a fertile ground for the development of refined skills.

Two years ago I saw a game in Kansas City in which the fans lustily booed Amos Otis, who had only given them about ten good years, because in one inning he pulled away from two balls that he might have caught. First he shied away from the wall on a drive that hit the wall about seven feet high. Then he pulled up and played a ball on a hop when he might have caught it had he dived. *Might* have caught it, I say. The Kansas City fans will never forgive Amos for being a percentage player, but the Yankees would score only one run in that inning, and Otis would drive in two runs before the night was over and the Royals had won. And some people will always admire Butch Hobson because, come hell or high water, he always tried for everything. But I'm not among them. My favorite player is Amos Otis.

—1982

Charlie Hough

"Casey Chases a Knuckler"

Rough, tough, Charlie Hough
All eight innings had his stuff
Floating light from Charlie's cuff
Breaking late and just enough
To keep the scoreboard bare.

And yet, the Mudville fans did dare
To hope that foul would soon turn fair.
A single here, an error there,
Casey stood on deck and glared
At rough, tough Charlie Hough.

Casey snorted, loud and gruff,
"I'll knock that busher on his duff.
Bring him on, I'll call his bluff;
How dare he aim that piece of fluff
At Casey's mighty stick?"

A home run now would tie it quick.
Charlie gave his wrist a flick;
Casey took a mighty lick.

The hearts of Mudville landed sick;
Just three pitches did the trick
From rough, tough, Charlie Hough.

—1987

Art Howe

The Astros' second baseman, using the term loosely, is Art Howe. Last year Howe hit extremely well, and pivoted on the double play almost as well as Bobby Doerr. Doerr was one of the greatest pivot men ever, but he is now sixty-one years old, and he gave up the game some years ago, when he began to pivot like Art Howe . . . .

—*Esquire* magazine
April 24, 1979

Glenn Hubbard

I am absolutely baffled by why the Braves' managers have so much trouble seeing what a good ballplayer this guy is. I mean, I know he's slow and doesn't hit for average, but look at the positives:

1. Excellent strike zone judgment.
2. Tremendous ability to turn the double play—as good as anybody in the game today.
3. A little power, enough to hit 30 doubles and 10 homers in a good year.
4. Avoids grounding into the double play very well.
5. Tremendous hustle on defense.
6. Intelligent, heads-up baserunning.

You would think that Atlanta managers, struggling with this awful, inept, inert team, would just love to put Glenn Hubbard in the lineup and let him him play, hoping that his attitude would infect some of the rest of the team. Instead, they seem determined to replace him. Last year's manager played

Ken Oberkfell at second base in part or all of forty-one games, playing Rafael Ramirez at third and Andres Thomas at short. In what respect does this improve the team? What can an infield of Horner, Oberkfell, Thomas, and Ramirez do better than an infield of Horner, Hubbard, Thomas, and Oberkfell? Hit singles? Commit errors? Fall down? Fall down and commit errors?

If you watch the Braves for about two weeks, you will understand perfectly why Ted Turner would think that *Casablanca* would be a better movie in pastels. The man loves mediocrity. He worships mediocrity. He sends his announcers to mediocrity school, where they spend sixteen hours a day listening to tapes of Jay Randolph and Curt Gowdy. He collects mediocre players and mediocre pitchers and hires mediocre managers to direct them. *Colorless* mediocre players. I mean, it's no wonder their attendance is terrible, and no reflection on the fine people of Atlanta, who are merely exercising a modicum of good taste in not taking this team to their hearts.

—1987

Mike Ivie

A short sermon on the worth of raw talent in baseball: There probably are not ten players in baseball today who have as much natural talent at hitting a baseball as Mike Ivie.

Our topic for next Sunday: John Mayberry is one of those ten.

Our topic for the Sunday following: Pete Rose isn't.

—1983

Bo Jackson

We didn't handle it very well, guys. None of us—fans, players, manager, front office, ownership, media. Bo Jackson represents, to an organization, a unique collection of possibilities and problems. As of July 2, 1987, the athlete of the decade was hitting at a rate that projects for a season .269 with 34 homers and 90 RBIs. He was playing fairly well in left field, with his tremendous throwing arm and speed compensating for his predictable mistakes. A whale of a rookie year, let's say.

How we got from there to Jackson winding up as the scapegoat for the season is a long story with no heroes. We all made mistakes. The ownership, to begin with. Jackson in the fall of 1986 didn't look anything like a major league player, and it was assumed that he would most likely open 1987 at Omaha. Jackson worked hard during the off-season, however, and showed well in spring training. The front office still thought he would benefit from AAA experience, and announced the intention of sending him down.

Royals co-owner Avron Fogelman, however, decided not to let that happen. He was, he said, afraid that it would break Bo's spirit to send him down after he had worked so hard all winter and played so well in the spring. He talked to John Schuerholz, and the decision was made that Jackson would stay in the major leagues.

That, looking backward, was the first mistake, or at least the first one we'll count. The subsequent story became a case history to teach owners why they should not intervene publicly in personnel decisions: because if you do, it undermines the authority of everyone between the owner and the player on the club's organizational chart.

Jackson is a difficult personality, a man whose ego is as well developed as his thighs. When former manager Mike Ferraro introduced himself to Jackson, Bo reportedly turned his back and walked away without speaking or shaking hands. I have asked myself many times why a man would do a thing like that, and I can't come up with a credible answer. Whatever the reason, the gesture was interpreted on the level of appearances, and it certainly didn't look very good.

So Jackson was playing well, early in the year, but in the back of his mind he had to have figured out that he had the upper hand on his manager. He knew that his manager couldn't send him down. He knew that even the owners couldn't really hurt him, because he could always go play football. In early July he went through a minor slump, losing about fifteen points in batting average in a week. It was reported as a major slump, but that was just more Bo stuff; everything gets blown out of proportion. Anyway, he was frustrated.

On July 10 in Toronto, Thad Bosley pinch hit for Jackson. Jackson cleaned out his locker, perhaps intending to quit baseball, perhaps intending only to threaten to quit so as to obtain the right to play football in the off-season, which was prohibited under his contract. Perhaps he wanted a guarantee that he wouldn't be pinch hit for anymore; who knows. Avron Fogelman flew to Toronto. A deal was negotiated: Jackson would stay for the season, but would be allowed to play for the Raiders after the season ended.

At the time, I thought the club had done the right thing. If I had known how it was going to turn out, obviously I wouldn't have thought that. What I had not anticipated, and what made this the second mistake, was that the reaction of so many people would be so immature. George Brett had two quotes about the subject, both of which were so restrained that no one bothered to re-quote them, but which I thought summed up perfectly what the mature reaction would have been. The two quotes were "Life's too short to choose up sides," and "I can't decide what he ought to do. It's his life."

Brett's reaction was, like Brett himself, restrained, intelligent, and mature. Willie Wilson's reaction was, like Wilson, loud, opinionated, and childish. "I guess he got the last laugh, didn't he?" said Wilson. "He got us to believe him, and now we're fools." Other Royals were reportedly upset, but Wilson, who himself was a spectacular football player in high school, but was told by the Royals that he would have to give up football to take the money, was the loudest.

Unfortunately for everybody, the community chose to follow Willie Wilson, rather than following George Brett. That was the third mistake. Jackson was booed every time he moved. The fans hooted when he took the field, howled when he came to bat, screamed when he struck out. Fans threw toy footballs on the field. New York fans held up a sign: LT'S NEW HOBBY: TYING BO INTO KNOTS. The local fans were no kinder.

Somewhere in there, trying to explain the decision, Jackson had described his football playing as "just another hobby, like hunting or fishing." I'm not sure if this word was used only once or was used a few times. Jackson is not an articulate speaker. He stutters badly, and just doing an interview is an obvious effort for him. He refers to himself as "Bo," in the third person, as people with speech impediments are sometimes taught to do to avoid saying "I." He often doesn't say things exactly as he wants.

In any case, this word "hobby" was picked up by the media and repeated and repeated and re-phrased and re-quoted and re-framed again and again and again; from a quiet utterance, it found its way into a thousand headlines. Network commentators who deal with sports only in passing would pick up this word, hobby, and cast a snide remark toward anyone who would be so impertinent as to describe playing professional football as a hobby. Talk show hosts and minor league broadcasters and editorial writers all gave us their opinions of professional football as a hobby; their opinion, perhaps I should say, since there was only one opinion, signed by ten thousand claimants. Jackson was treated as if wanting to play both professional baseball and professional football was criminal as well as stupid beyond any description. The cartoonist for the local newspaper, a mean-spirited bush leaguer who has never drawn a funny cartoon in his life, drew a "cartoon" which consisted of three pictures with the headlines: baseball, football, screwball.

Maybe I don't understand something here, folks, but I don't know how you all can live with yourselves. I mean, I know I've got a mean streak. I've written some awful things about ballplayers over the years, for sins no more heinous than falling down chasing a fly ball or running the bases with one's head down. But Lord help me, I never abused a man this way for searching his vocabulary and choosing the wrong word. Alright, it was a poor choice of words, by a young man under tremendous pressure who isn't famous for his ability to choose words. But to pick up that word and hammer him with it and hammer him with it until the pain is tattooed on his forehead . . . well, I just don't understand it. I know that Bo is awfully well paid for being a public figure, and in that case there is an argument that anything which is true is fair. But is it true, or is it a distortion, to rip a word out of a man's sentence and blast it out of the headlines as if it were his philosophy?

What was lost in the rush to judge Bo is that the man never stopped hustling. I have always thought, as a baseball fan, that if a player works hard on the field, he's entitled to a break on anything else. If a player doesn't hustle and pulls a rock, boo him, but if a player gives you everything he has and makes the same mistake, maybe you ought to give him a break. I don't mean that Bo does what is expected of him, but that I see a lot of Royals games, and if you asked me which Royal gives the best effort, start to finish, every ground ball, I'd have to tell you it was Bo Jackson. When the booing started, when the toy footballs started coming out of the stands, I couldn't understand, and I can't understand, why that didn't count.

Can Jackson excel, over a period of years, in two sports? Probably not. If he were to play two sports year-round for several years, there would certainly be a price to pay in terms of performance in either sport. But what puzzles the hell out of me about all of these people is the presumption that they know more than Bo Jackson does about what that price would be. Let's take that sign: LT's new hobby: tying Bo in knots. Now, who knows more about what it is like to be hit by Lawrence Taylor: Bo Jackson, or the guy who held up the sign? The same idea showed up in about thirty letters to the editor in the *Star and Times* sports pages: I wonder how Mike Singletary is going to react to a guy who talks about playing pro football as a hobby. Well, who knows more about tangling with Mike Singletary: Bo Jackson, or the guy who wrote the letter? Who understands better the price of trying to play both sports: Bo Jackson, or the morning disc jockey? It's obvious, isn't it? How can these people be so arrogant as to assume that they know more than Bo does about the costs of his decision?

This is not to say that the Royals organization doesn't have the right to tell Bo to make a choice. If they want to say "We'd love to have all of Bo Jackson, but we don't want half of him," that's their option. In retrospect, it couldn't have worked out much worse—understanding that Bo's option is not only to go play football, but to talk to the other twenty-five baseball teams as well.

Sports fans, as a group, have an inordinate amount of trouble coming to grips with a fundamental principle of satisfactory relationships: that I don't own anyone's talents except my own. A hundred times a year, someone will ask me, about one aging ballplayer or another, "Don't you think he should retire now? Isn't he hurting his reputation and his image by trying to hang on this way?" My answer is always the same: "Hell, I don't know what he should do. It's his life. It's his talent. It's his reputation. It's none of my business what he does with it."

I'm damned if I'm going to let anybody else make those decisions for me, and because of that I recognize that I don't get to make those decisions for anybody else.

About the time that Bo signed with the Raiders, I was reading the biography of Moe Berg, a major league catcher in the twenties and thirties. In addition to being a baseball player, Berg was a scholar. He graduated from Princeton and the Sorbonne with degrees in languages, of which he spoke somewhere between fifteen and twenty. He was a leading authority in his day on Sanskrit literature, which was one of his main passions, another being medieval French. Berg read about twenty newspapers a day, in a wide variety of languages, and seemingly remembered everything in them. On a radio quiz show in the late thirties, experts attempted to stump Berg by asking questions like "Who was Poppea Sabina?", "Who was Calamity Jane?", "Who was the Black Napoleon?", and "Who or what are the Seven Sleepers, the Seven Wise Masters, the Seven Wise Men, the Seven Wonders of the World, and the Seven Stars?" Berg answered these questions in great detail, giving the astrological reference points of the Seven Stars, the real name of Calamity Jane and throwing in where she died and where she was buried. Berg wrote articles for publications like *The Atlantic Monthly,* and also took advantage of his facility with languages to do serious high-level espionage prior to and during World War II.

Now, if you were to ask, "Is it possible to be, at the same time, a linguist, a scholar of repute, a spy, a compendium of limitless miscellaneous information, and a major league baseball player?"—if you were to ask this, I say, in the same way that we now ask "Is it possible for a man to compete successfully in both major league baseball and major league football?" one would ordinarily have to answer, "No, it isn't possible." It wouldn't be possible for any ordinary athlete. It was possible for him. Certainly, Berg's decision to play baseball hurt his career as a scholar enormously, and the time he spent in the off-season learning Japanese and sneaking around Tokyo in a kimono taking pictures of military installations no doubt cut into his success as a ballplayer. But what the hell, it was his life, wasn't it? It didn't cost us anything, did it? If Bo wants to have half of a baseball career and half of a football career, what do we as fans have to lose by letting him take his shot?

Jackson stayed with the Royals, but it would have been far better had he not. The furor over Jackson became the center of the season. Facing intense hostility from fans, his manager and some teammates, Jackson stopped hitting. He started dropping fly balls in the outfield. On July 28 in New York, Jackson beat out a bunt single with two out, nobody on and the Royals trailing 2–1, top of the sixth inning. Gardner, under pressure from the front office to be tougher in his handling of players and unhappy with Bo anyway, was furious. He felt that Jackson was playing for his own stats, not interested in the team. He told reporters after the game that "we" had talked to Jackson about this before, presumably meaning that he had asked Hal McRae to talk to Jackson about it. He threw in a gratuitous insult for the two hitters coming up after Jackson (Salazar and Macfarlane) describing them as "Lou Gehrig and Babe Ruth." But two days later, Gardner acknowledged that he still had not talked to Jackson about the incident. Somehow, I don't think this is the rcommended way to handle this, is it, Billy?

After that Jackson's play deteriorated to such a point that there was simply no issue as to whether or not to play him. He disappeared. Billy Gardner got fired.

None of us understands Bo very well or probably ever will, but I think a key toward understanding is to remember that every unusual strength that we develop in life, in my experience, we develop as a way of covering a weakness, much as a blind man learns to use his ears. Bo didn't develop the ego he has because he wanted to have an outsized ego. He developed that ego, I suspect, to cover a center of self-doubt. Another key, I think, is the stuttering. Stuttering, as I understand it, is in many cases a manifestation of a deep-rooted psychic scar; that's why stutterers may have trouble saying "I." What seems to be arrogance in Bo may be, I suspect, in fact a manifestation of insecurity. Or perhaps that is redundant, for perhaps arrogance is always a manifestation of insecurity.

My sister Rosalie, who is not a baseball fan, asked me a simple question: Why is it that everybody is mad at this man who wants to play both baseball and football? It seemed to her, as it does to me, that there was something rather magnificent about a man's trying to do something that nobody else can do. Why were people so mad?

I told her that I thought there were two reasons: 1) That

people thought they had been lied to when Jackson seemed to speak definitively about playing baseball, and 2) that Jackson signed with the Los Angeles Raiders, the most hated rivals of the Kansas City football team. If he had signed with the Chiefs, the reaction would have been positive; if with a neutral team like the Cleveland Browns, a less intense reaction. A third answer would be that that is the way people react to arrogance: They feel the need to poke a hole through it, and to expose the raging self-doubt underneath.

That's what happened, but it's a pretty sorry excuse, isn't it? Look what we did: We destroyed the player, at least temporarily, and we destroyed the season. The fans, the owner, the front office, the manager, the teammates, the media—we all behaved badly. Bo made mistakes, but we didn't deal with his mistakes in a way that was mature or intelligent or that did anything positive for anybody. I say, let's face up to that. We had a unique and wonderful talent out there busting his butt for us, and we booed him and ridiculed him until he broke. What good did that do? If Bo is back with the team this year, let's try to do right by him.

—1988

Danny Jackson

I wanted to say a couple of things about pitching motions, or "Why I Love To Watch Danny Jackson Pitch." Let's start by talking about the trailing leg. When a left-handed pitcher starts toward home plate, he steps out with the right leg, committing the momentum of his body forward. Almost all pitchers will plant the lead foot, push off the other foot onto the lead ankle and pivot the entire body over that ankle, with the load leg being stiff. When the pitcher's torso (his main body weight) passes from behind the front leg to ahead of it, the trailing leg has to fly forward to maintain balance.

The way in which the trailing leg does this is interesting for many different reasons. It is a sort of an "index" to what the pitcher is doing. As a general rule, the faster the pitcher's body moves forward, the more violently the trailing leg has to jerk forward to counterbalance it.

Most pitchers—not just some, but most—will kick the leg less energetically when throwing an off-speed pitch than when throwing a fastball. Pitchers have to carefully disguise everything that happens *before* the pitch is thrown, so as to avoid tipping the hitter about the pitch. But after the pitch is thrown it doesn't make any difference, so they don't bother to disguise it. Thus the movement of the trailing leg, the last part of the delivery, is often the only thing a fan can see which will tell him, even up in the cheap seats, what the pitching patterns are.

The movement of the trailing leg is an indicator of how hard a pitcher throws—not a perfect indicator, but a valuable indicator. A real old guy, like Phil Niekro or Woodie Fryman, may not throw the leg forward at all, but just bend from the waist and step up at the conclusion of the pitch. If you see that, you know the guy isn't throwing eighty miles an hour. When a pitcher is warming up, you can tell how hard he is working by watching the trailing leg. Many relief pitchers will come in and just flip the ball to the plate a few times, not working hard enough to make themselves throw the trailing leg, whereas Lee Smith will come in and throw just as hard as he will throw when the game starts.

Most importantly, *the movement of the trailing leg is often the first indicator of when a pitcher is tired.* When a pitcher gets tired, he'll start to conserve energy by diminishing the force with which he propels himself forward; the end result of this will be a dramatic reduction in the movement of the trailing leg. *Many managers pay no attention to this, and will allow a pitcher to stay in the game, even with men on base and the game on the line, when it is very obvious, from the movement of the trailing leg, that the pitcher is tired.* The pitcher disguises everything he does before the delivery, and after the delivery the manager, like everybody else, moves his eyes to follow the pitch. I don't know how many times I have seen pitchers lose games (and quickly) after they started dragging the trailing leg, but before they started doing the things that the manager was waiting for them to do to show fatigue, like dropping the arm or getting pitches up in the strike zone.

Then, on the other hand, there is Danny Jackson. Danny's delivery is unique; there is no other major league pitcher with a delivery that is even vaguely similar. Danny starts out with a very long stride, and plants his right leg way out in front of him. But as he vaults forward, rather than pivoting the body weight over the planted foot (the right foot), he bends the right leg at the knee and throws his body downward into the foot, with the leg acting as a "spring" to absorb the shock of the delivery. His center of balance never does pass in front of the right leg, thus there is no need to throw the trailing leg to compensate. He completes his delivery facing directly toward the plate, sometimes almost collapsing onto the right knee, but usually springing up off the knee.

Sometimes when I talk about this people say, "Oh, like Tom Seaver," because Tom Seaver lectures on absorbing the shock of the pitching motion with the legs. But Seaver flies off the mound; Seaver uses the large muscles of his leg to vault forward, thus reducing the strain on the arm. It's not similar at all. Koufax and Warren Spahn had deliveries that were somewhat similar.

Anyway, because there is no radical alteration in the pitcher's center of balance, there are no sudden movements to adjust and rebalance the body. This makes the delivery, rather than being a series of related jerks and spasms (to overstate the case), into a continuous, fluid, graceful movement. How it will affect him over a period of years, how it will affect his arm and his knees, this I wouldn't pretend to know. But it's gorgeous. I mean, sometimes he winds up a little off-balance and looks like he's going to wrench his knee, but most of the time it's a smooth, beautiful, reliable delivery. Make it a point to watch.

—1986

Reggie Jackson

Reggie said an interesting thing about Eddie Murray in the World Series when Eddie was struggling, trying to get untracked. He said that he thought Eddie had the "character" and the "determination" and the "fortitude" to fight his way out of this thing and make his presence felt. You get it? What he's saying is, "I didn't hit all those homers in the World Series play because I happen to be a great athlete. I didn't win two

World Series MVP awards because I am strong and have a quick bat and saw a few pitches I could hit and hit them. Oh, no. I did that because I have *character* and *fortitude* and *determination*. I succeeded because I was a better human being than those other people out there on the field."

You hear that stuff every day, although most athletes are smart enough to disguise it a little better. Many athletes truly believe that they are successful at what they do not because God made them strong and fast and agile, but because *they're better people than the rest of us*. And in order to believe that, they must believe that the games themselves are not merely contests of skill and luck, but are tests of *character* and *determination* and *will*. That's where all of the bullshit about clutch ability comes from. Clutch ability is that thing that wells up from inside of you when the game is on the line, that thing that separates the "winners" from the "losers," that thing *which only an athlete can possess*, and therefore only an athlete can understand.

The problem with that is that when the public is sold enough cow manure in little plastic bottles marked "character" and "attitude," the public is going to stop buying any little plastic bottles marked "character" and "attitude." I had a long conversation with a friend of mine, a highly intelligent and successful attorney, who tried to convince me that such things as "character" and "attitude" and "wanting to play baseball" had nothing to do with winning a pennant, that they didn't even exist. He reminded me about the way that Clemente when he came up and Joe Morgan when he came up and Frank Robinson in his early years got labeled "attitude problems." Then, of course, as soon as Clemente learned to hit a curve ball, he was a great human being, and the "attitude" label went away. Did his "attitude" ever really have anything to do with it?

But *of course* "attitude" is real, and so is "character" and "determination" and "will." Wanting to win a pennant has *everything* to do with winning a pennant. Just as there are people in your school or people in your law firm or people in your Gay Rights activists group who have the ability to be outstanding students or lawyers or Gay Activists but who don't really want to do it, there are people in baseball who have the ability to be outstanding baseball players, but have bad attitudes.

But if athletes keep debasing those qualities by focusing them on ridiculously small moments in a person's life, if they keep using them to explain every dramatic success and every dismal failure, then they're eventually going to convince the public that they don't exist, at all. Every time a favorite player delivers a key single to bring a win closer, and the announcer delivers a speech about the "courage" and the "determination" and the "guts" that the player has shown, then those words become a little cheaper, and the act that they describe becomes smaller and less significant. Reggie Jackson is an ordinary human being, glib but of average intelligence at best, of character unshining and fortitude unknown, who has hit ten home runs in World Series play and who is not, on that basis, entitled to the stature of a demigod.

—1984

Cliff Johnson

What the career of Cliff Johnson shows us is how much timing and circumstances determine who will emerge as a star. If Cliff Johnson had been given the opportunity of a George Scott, installed at Fenway Park and at first base at age twenty-two, it is not at all difficult to imagine him turning in a Hall of Fame career. And people twenty years from now will say "Cliff Johnson a Hall of Famer? That's crazy." But it isn't.

Johnson had two misfortunes: He played for the Astros, and he played in the Astrodome. A lot of organizations would have taken note of Cliff Johnson when he hit .332 and led the Carolina league in HRs and RBIs in 1971, then hit .382 in twenty-two games of triple-A ball. The Astros sent him back to the Southern League. They tried for six years to make him a catcher, a position for which he had just enough talent to get out of spring training. The Astrodome has frustrated some of the best offensive talent in the game—Morgan, Mayberry, Wynn. The combination of liabilities didn't leave him much to work with. Still, throughout his career Cliff averaged 31 homers and 110 RBI per 620 at-bats.

One can always say that Johnson didn't help himself, that he could have made it as a catcher if he had really wanted to and Joe DiMaggio became the biggest of stars with no help from Yankee Stadium. I don't think there are a lot of successful 227-pound catchers in the game, and while Johnson is no DiMaggio, his talents are roughly comparable to those of Harmon Killebrew. Harmon should be thankful he never played for the Astros.

—1982 (data updated for current edition)

Somebody Named Johnson

What I want to know is just where the hell are all these Johnsons coming from? Is there a Johnson factory down there in the Sun Belt somewhere? In 1980 there were only four Johnsons playing in the majors—Cliff, John Henry, Lamar, and Randy (John Henry is one Johnson), and Randy only batted twenty times. Last year we had at least five R. Johnsons alone —R. Johnson of Atlanta, R.R. Johnson and R.W. Johnson of Montreal, plus Randy Johnson of Minnesota (I think this is Randy I'm supposed to be writing about here), and Ron Johnson of Kansas City, with at least eleven total Johnsons around the majors. How are we supposed to keep track of all these people? Maybe we should start assigning them distinctive nicknames, Clicker and Turkey Shoot and stuff like that. Howard Johnson of Detroit, needless to say, is exempted from this requirement. And Drungo Larue Hazewood languishes in the minors. What a waste.

—1983

Matt Keough

Matt Keough pitched a three-hit complete game victory against the Kansas City Royals last September 11, in the midst of which a strange and marvelous thing happened. Keough struggled some early, but his outfielders took good care of him, and after Oakland scored three runs in the sixth and three more in the seventh, he took the mound in the eighth with a 6–1 lead. His first two pitches missed the strike zone, and Billy Martin popped out of the dugout and headed for the hill. By the time Martin crossed the line Keough's cap was pumping up and down like the bobbin-head doll in Freddie Prinze's routine, saying, "I know, I know. Throw strikes; big lead, throw strikes." But Martin didn't stop; he strode to the mound like an angry father, wagging his bony fingers up and down and gesticulating vigorously at Mike Heath's mitt. *Because of two lousy pitches!* At that moment any other manager in baseball would have been reclining in the dugout, might have bestirred himself to shout a few words of encouragement or glanced nervously at his bullpen. Martin reacted immediately and with uncomfortable force, and thus this comic opera scene, complete with stage gestures, with Keough saying, "I can do it. I know. I know what I'm supposed to do," and Martin responding, "Well, goddammit then, *do it.* Do what you are capable of doing."

But when you look at the Oakland A's, what do you see? You see a whole team of people who are doing what they are capable of doing. You see Rickey Henderson, who is a little guy and years away from being a polished hitter, but what he can do is he can run like hell, and he will go into a crouch which gives him a strike zone about the size of a cigarette pack, and if you don't throw it in there he will walk and drive you nutty on the base paths, and if you do, he will slap it past the third baseman, who has to play in about twenty-five feet to keep him from bunting .450. You see Tony Armas, who will strike out once a game and hit a three-run homer to win the game for you anytime you make a mistake. You see Cliff Johnson hitting his home runs and Rob Picciolo scooping up every ground ball that he can get to.

More successfully than any other manager, Martin has been able to make an entire collection of athletic young bodies into an expression of his own will. Like everything else Martin does, this is the short-term strategy, for each of the players in truth has his own will, his own desires and goals and ambitions, and while he may allow those to go into remission for awhile, they will return to the fore within a few years. Matt Keough doesn't know it yet, but he's going to get awfully tired of having his butt chewed every time he doesn't do exactly what Billy thinks he ought to. Successful teams over a period of years are built on a successful merging of individual wills into group strength, not on the obliteration of anything that opposes the manager's master plan. But tomorrow may be a dream or a nightmare or it may never be. If you want to win *today*, Billy Martin is the best manager there is.

—1982

Ron Kittle

Tony Kubek said during the playoffs that a lot of people have been surprised at what a good outfielder Ron Kittle is. How in the world could anyone possibly be surprised by what a good outfielder Ron Kittle is? What would your expectations for such an outfielder have to be? Saying you're surprised by what a good outfielder Ron Kittle is is like saying you're surprised at how nimble Willie Aikens is while running the bases. Being surprised by what a good outfielder Ron Kittle is is like being surprised by how good Elizabeth Taylor looks in a bikini. Being surprised by what a good outfielder Ron Kittle is is like being surprised by what a with-it, snappy kind of guy James Watt turned out to be. This ranks right up there with being adrift in a rowboat for two weeks and saying, "Gee, somehow I always thought the Pacific would be bigger than this."

Defensively speaking, Ron Kittle is the worst young outfielder I have seen since Greg Luzinski came up. I don't mean to be unkind or anything, but when they take a guy out in the late innings so that leftfield can be patrolled by Tom Paciorek or Jerry Hairston, you don't exactly figure he's going to be the one who keeps bringing up defense during salary negotiations. He fielded .964 and had the range factor of a three-toed sloth. I'm sure that he made some nice plays from time to time, and I'm sure that Elizabeth Taylor occasionally skips lunch. But she makes up for it over the weekend.

—1984

Ken Landreaux

Baseball statistics are fascinating, among other reasons, because they form crude but detailed images of realities which are in origin psychological or mental or physical or emotional or . . . who knows. If the people who believe in biorhythms were scientists rather than suckers and charlatans, they would find in baseball their perfect laboratory, where the ebbs and flows and highs and lows and double-highs and triple-whammies of thousands of players, date of birth known, have been recorded in unconscionable detail for over a century. The psyche that is imitated in the month-by-month log for Ken Landreaux is among the most unique. Ken is a .280 hitter, but not your basic .240-to-.320 range .280 hitter; he mixes up a fascinating string of .415 months with .160 months. His good months are so good that if he could just stay within a hundred points of top form from beginning to end, he would be dropping bread crumbs on the road to Cooperstown.

Mixed up with his streaks, unfortunately, are months that Mark Belanger wouldn't sign for. What is he? Moody? Lazy? Manic-depressive? Given to fits of depression and weeks of exhilaration? But I see every set of numbers as a puzzle, and some puzzles can be solved in too many ways.

—1983

Tim Laudner

Name rhymes with "Podner."

—1983

Ron LeFlore

An odd contrast between Ron LeFlore and my favorite center fielder, Amos Otis, occurred to me last summer. Their throwing arms, I think, are very similar. The odd thing is that Amos has a reputation for having a good throwing arm, and it was good when he was younger, but really it isn't all that good any more, pretty good on short throws but if he has to throw long the ball is not going to be where it is needed most of the time. LeFlore, on the other hand, has a reputation for having a very bad throwing arm, but he throws out a lot of people on the base paths, and if you watch him you will see him cut loose some decent throws. It's not a great arm, but . . . well, it's about like Amos's, mediocre to poor.

Why the difference? One play, but a play that a center fielder makes about a hundred times a year, I'd guess: runner on second, ball hit into shallow left-center or right-center. The center fielder can try to make the throw home, which is going to be too late or off-line or dropped by the catcher the huge majority of the time, or he can throw to second, concede the run and hold the runner at first. The difference is this: Amos will throw to second 90 percent of the time, throwing home only if the run is crucial. LeFlore will throw the ball home 90 percent of the time. Le Flore's throw home will get the runner —and thus get an assist for LeFlore—maybe ten times a season. Another five or seven times a season LeFlore's throw will be so bad that he draws an error on it, hence his career .968 fielding percentage. Another forty or fifty times a year, I would guess, the runner goes to second. Otis doesn't get the assists, doesn't get the errors, and keeps the runners on first. But also, he does not expose the weakness of his arm. LeFlore's continual attempts to make the very difficult throw home put the weakness of his arm on constant display and lead to his bad-arm reputation; Amos is making the much easier throw to second, which protects his reputation.

Who is doing what is better for the team? I don't know. I don't think you could figure it out without actual data on how many errors result on this play and how many runners advance to second. I would guess that it's fairly even, but not knowing any more than I do, I'd rather have the play made to second and keep the inning under control.

—1983

Aurelio Lopez

This guy must have one of the greatest arms that God ever made. He's thirty-five, threw about nine million pitches in the Mexican League before he came to Los Estados Unidos, where he has been working sixty games a year since 1979, and he trains on beans and beer with three side orders of meat, and he can still blow his fastball by good major league hitters.

—1984 *Baseball Abstract*

Lopez in 1984, the year after this was written, worked seventy-one games and had the best season of his major league career. And he continued to blow that fastball by major league hitters for another three years and another twenty pounds after that.

Joe Morgan

For years and years, Joe Morgan was the best ballplayer in the National League. In 1972 he hit .292, had an on-base percentage of .414, hit 16 homers, stole 58 bases, fielded a league-leading .990 at a key defensive position and led the league in runs scored with 122. For this incredible performance—Bobby Grich with speed and another 30 points on his batting average —he finished fourth in the league's MVP voting. I will grant you that there were a lot of people having good years. So in 1973 Joe repeated his season and tagged on another 10 home runs and another 12 doubles and another 9 stolen bases and 14 more double plays at second so he could lead the league in that, too. Again, he finished fourth in the MVP voting. So in 1974 he did it all again. He finished eighth in the MVP voting.

I have written that Amos Otis is the only player in baseball who can be evaluated in the nine basic areas of performance and come up with nine positives. But has there ever been a player who had so many double positives and triple positives as Morgan? For exceptional performance over a wide range of skills, I can't think of anybody who compares to him. Sure, Henry Aaron had twice as much power, but did he steal 60 bases a year and turn the double play? Or walk 120 times a year?

Yes, Morgan did win two MVP awards—after he towered over the league like Babe Ruth in a Babe Ruth league. In one season he hit 27 home runs, averaged .320, drove in 111 runs, drew 114 walks, stole 60 bases, won a gold glove award at a key defensive position, led the league in the two most important offensive categories (on base percentage and slugging percentage), and for good measure threw in league-leading totals in sacrifice flies, stolen-base percentage and fewest grounded-into-double-plays. Who the hell else are you going to give the award to?

And so, for a brief time, the public became dimly aware that Joe Morgan was a great ballplayer, which they quickly and happily forgot as soon as he was no longer the greatest player in the game. You hear every ten minutes about winning teams following Reggie around, with incessant and interminable and unending explanations about his taking the pressure off everybody else and hitting in the clutch and breeding a winning atmosphere. Reggie's teams in Oakland, Baltimore, New York, and California have a combined record of 914 wins, 650 losses in the last ten years. Morgan's teams in Cincinnati, Houston and San Francisco have a record of 913 wins, 655 losses. Do you hear a word about winning teams following Joe Morgan around? Reggie and Grich won the division in California with a supporting cast of seven all-stars: Morgan and Jack Clark won 87 games and missed by 2 with a cast of seven Bozos. Which is the more impressive accomplishment? I'm not saying this to rip Rose or Schmidt or Bench or anybody else, but no player since Mantle in the mid-1950s has reached a peak of performance as high as Morgan's in the mid-seventies. It's a shame that the only effect of that has been to cast a shadow over the rest of his brilliant career. The three greatest second basemen ever are Hornsby, Gehringer and Joe Morgan.

—1983

Phil Niekro

Did you know that Phil Niekro is five years older than Denny McLain? Phil Niekro is older than Ron Santo. Phil Niekro is older than Joe Torre. Phil Niekro is older than Lou Brock or Carl Yastrzemski. Phil Niekro is older than Joe Pepitone. Phil Niekro is older than Richie Allen.

Jeff Torborg was dismissed in his third season as manager of Cleveland; that was seven years ago. Phil Niekro is older than Jeff Torborg, two and a half years older. Phil Niekro is older than Bobby Cox or Pat Corrales.

Do you remember Zoilo Versalles, who was the American League's MVP twenty-one years ago? Phil Niekro is older than

Zoilo Versalles. Do you remember Jose Azcue, the great Azcue? Phil Niekro is older than Joe Azcue. Phil Niekro is older than Bernie Allen, Gene Alley, Mike Shannon, Dave Nicholson, or Roger Repoz. Phil Niekro is older than Tony LaRussa, Doug Rader, or Ken Harrelson of the White Sox.

We can do this by teams. . . . Let's do the Cardinals. You probably know all of the current Cardinals; Steve Braun is the oldest of them. Mike Torrez, who started with the Cardinals and then pitched for everybody else before dropping out of the game, was older than Steve Braun. Rick Wise, another peripatetic pitcher of similar talent, was older and earlier than Torrez. Jerry DaVanon, a utility infielder of the same era, was older than Wise. Jose Cardenal, a teammate of DaVanon's in 1970, was older than Jerry. Tim McCarver, who caught for the Cardinal champions in '64, '67, and '68, was older than Cardenal. Ray Sadecki, a teammate of McCarver's early in that period, a twenty-game winner on the 1964 World Champions, was older than McCarver. You may remember Dick Nen, who hit the gigantic home run which buried the Cardinals the year before that, 1963. Nen was older than Sadecki. If you think hard enough, you may remember Julio Gotay, the Cardinal shortstop before they traded for Dick Groat. Gotay, who was most famous as the man who dropped his mail in a green-painted trash bin for several weeks before Curt Flood noticed him doing it, was older than Dick Nen. Von McDaniel, the Cardinals' pitching sensation of 1957, was older than Julio Gotay. But Phil Niekro is older than Von McDaniel.

Phil Niekro is older than Claude Osteen, the veteran pitching coach, or Milt Pappas. Phil Niekro is older than Sammy Ellis, one of the Yankee pitching coaches, or Dick Ellsworth. Phil Niekro is older than Tommie Aaron, except that Aaron is dead and you can't get any older than dead. I remember a few years ago at spring training, when Tommie was a coach with the Braves, he was hitting fungoes one day, his claim to alphabetical supremacy stretched across his back. Susie and I were sitting and watching him. A little woman about fifty yelled out from behind us, sounding for all the world like a character in the background of an old movie, "Haank. Oh, Haannk." She had a camera. At length, Tommie turned around and gave a dutiful, patient half-smile. She took a picture and yelled, "Oh, thank you, Hank." Then he died, a year or so later.

You remember Don Kessinger? Phil Niekro is older than Kessinger or Beckert. Glenn Beckert got the job as Cubs' second baseman after Ken Hubbs was killed in a plane crash in the spring of 1964. Phil Niekro is three years older than Ken Hubbs would be. Phil Niekro is older than Felix Millan or Sonny Jackson or Rico Carty. Phil Niekro is older than Martin Luther King or either of the Kennedys were at the time of their assassinations. Phil Niekro is older than Boog Powell. Phil Niekro is more than ten years older than I am.

Funny thing, though. He don't look a day over sixty. . . .

—1986

Ron Oester

The government has a category of "discouraged workers" for people who have been unemployed so long that they have given up trying to find work. Maybe we should have a category of "discouraged ballplayers." Oester's got talent and I think he could help a good ball club.

—1983

Al Oliver

On March 31, 1982, the Texas Rangers traded Al Oliver to Montreal for Larry Parrish and Dave Hostetler. The Rangers, 57–48 in 1981, lost 98 games in 1982. The following comment clearly qualifies as 20/20 hindsight.

Another trade that hurt both teams . . . I don't think I would ever make a trade like this, where you give up somebody who is the heart of your offense (Oliver) right at the end of spring training, because it seems to me that such a trade would just be psychologically devastating. I think that to win a pennant you have to do basically three things: get talent, deploy the talent correctly and build up group confidence to where the talent feels that it can win. The first two are the ones that I write about 99 percent of the time—who has talent, what talent, how it should be used—but I still recognize that the third element is really the tricky one. You can have all kinds of talent—indeed, the Rangers did have all kinds of talent—and still lose if the players don't feel that they can win. It seems to me that to take a team all through the process of getting ready for the season with a hitter like Al Oliver in the center of the lineup and then suddenly to tell the team that you're opening the season without that player, that you've traded him for two complete strangers with unimpressive records . . . well, that's suicide, isn't it? Isn't that a commercial for self-doubt?

—1983

Joe Orsulak

Did you ever notice that if you say Orsulak over and over (Orsulak Orsulak Orsulak Orsulak) it sounds like the noise you hear inside of a train? Another one of those is Quisenberry. If you say Quisenberry over and over and tap the table with a pencil on the "Q" and the "b" it sounds like windshield wipers. . . .

—1987

Amos Otis

In the years that Amos Otis was in Kansas City you would occasionally, maybe once a year, see a note in the letters section of the paper that went something like this:

> As I was leaving Royals Stadium after the Royals/White Sox game of June 13, I experienced car trouble and was stranded for twenty-five terrible minutes in the heat beside I-70 as the postgame traffic rolled by. I was wondering how we would ever get out of there when a car stopped behind me and the driver asked if we needed help. To my amazement, the driver of that car was Amos Otis.

Amos has been cast by the media as a moody and unapproachable man, and that he is; he is moody, and he is unapproachable. In his last three or four years as a Royal, I can never remember hearing him interviewed on the pregame show. This wasn't because Denny and Fred didn't want to interview him. I tried to interview him myself a time or two and got nowhere much. He might consent to interviews in spring training, but once the season began the evasions began, the "No Interviews" sign went up and came down and went up again. He always said that he didn't like to talk to the press when he was going good and they never wanted to talk to him when he was going bad.

Yet anytime I was in the clubhouse, I always enjoyed watching him talk to the other players. I remember seeing him explaining to John Wathan how he hit Len Barker. "Fastball," he said, swiveling his head to watch the imaginary pitch go by. "Fastball . . . slider . . . fastball." Then he yelled "Change-Up" and his eyes blazed and his hands leaped into action and an enormous smile seized hold of his face.

His Kansas City career came to a sad end when he cleaned out his locker in mid-September with the team on a road trip, denying the fans a last at-bat or a last cheer or a turn and wave good-bye. We all felt a little cheated, and we all felt that Amos had been a little selfish walking out that way, and I think he was. But it would have been out of character for him to do it any other way.

Amos was an intensely private man living an intensely public life. He disdained showmanship—probably he hated showmanship—of any type and to any extent. He could never quite deal with the fact that his business was putting on a show. This is what is called "moodiness" by the media. Yet there is a rare, deep honesty about him that was his defining characteristic both as a man and as a ballplayer. He could not stand to do anything for show. He could not charge into walls (and risk his continued existence as a ballplayer) after balls that he could not catch. He could not rouse the fans (and risk his continued existence as a base runner) with a stirring drive for a base too far. He never in his career stood at home plate and watched a ball clear the fence. McRae and Brett, they did that sort of thing; Otis would sometimes turn away interview requests with a sardonic comment, "Talk to Brett and McRae. They're the team leaders."

It went further than that. Amos could not quite walk down the line when he hit a pop-up (that, too, would be dishonest), but he could not quite bring himself to run, either. Because it was false, you see? He wouldn't have been running for himself or for the team or for the base; he would have been running for the fans, or for the principle that one always ran.

But what you must also see is that the same honesty which denied Otis the indulgence of flair, the same feeling which required that he keep his kindnesses out of the view of the public, this is what built the wall around Amos. He could not give interviews because he could not recite clichés, and he could not recite clichés because they are false. We're eight and a half behind on September eighth, and somebody asks you if you think we still have a chance to win, and you're supposed to say, "Absolutely. We've got to go out and play hard every day and not be watching the scoreboard."It would have turned Amos' stomach to recite that stuff; it wasn't fair of us to expect him to do it. There is truth in it, but there is falsehood in it, too. Amos could not digest the falsehood to be nourished by the truth. It is a way of putting out your hand and feeling the wall there, and when you reach out and you can't feel the wall there anymore, custom or maybe it really is common sense requires that you pretend that there is still a wall there. If there is no wall, then you have no support, and you will fall.

But Amos could not pretend to feel the wall. He could not mime the wall; he could not put on the show.

And what is running out a pop fly ball to Manny Trillo, but a cliché in action? George and Hal, that was their schtick. Amos was the one that the young black players on the team, U.L. and Willie and Al Cowens, always grew to admire. Amos was the one who picked you up at the airport when you had to come to town in the winter. Amos was the one who led quiet workouts in the offseason, far out of view of the press. (It is to laugh that there were charges late in his career that Otis was not in shape. He was as trim and strong the day he left the Royals as the day that he arrived. Only he was thirty-seven years old.)

And yet, Amos ached for the recognition he denied himself. It bothered Amos that others were regarded as the leaders of the team. And how did they reach that position? By showmanship, disreputable showmanship. It ragged at his heart that players no better than he got far more recognition because they put on the dog. He had a tendency, in his rare moments of communication with the press, to whine about those things.

Yet even Amos' playing talents were shaped by the need to

avoid attracting attention. Amos could have hit 30 home runs (with a lower average) or he could have hit .320 (with less power) or he could have stolen 70 bases (with 25 times caught stealing). He would take a day off in the last week of the season with 93 RBIs. If his average was at .301 with a week left, he'd decide to become a power hitter. To give in to those numbers, those attention-getting goals, that was not honest enough for him. His goals were private; you never knew whether he had reached them or not.

Amos could not often bring himself to protest a particular scorer's decision, because that would be admitting that he cared about the show. So instead, he would grumble in a general way about the scorer's treatment of him.

He was a purposefully unburnished silver player. If the public wanted to love him, he would make them do it privately; he would brook no flashy displays of affection. A small man with effeminate cheerleading gestures sat behind home plate wearing the number 26 for three years; Amos, interviewed on the subject, spoke cuttingly about the strange things people would get it in their heads to do. If you reject them first, of course, they have no chance to reject you.

His tender ego and his suffocating, defining honesty made him a lesser ballplayer than he might have been, and a greater ballplayer than he probably should have been. But it was, on the whole, an enjoyable ride; there were quite a few change-ups in there among the fastballs. Baseball needs Hal McRaes and George Bretts, but it needs Amos Otises and George Hendrickses, too. It needs people who cannot stand to recite clichés. His ambivalence toward public life was harder for him to live with than it should be for us.

—1984

Dave Parker

I wanted to say something about weight clauses. Incentive bonuses in baseball are a negotiating tool, used by both sides to resolve an impasse and put an agreement on the table. To people who are involved in the negotiations, the criticism that so often is directed at them seems puzzling and at times more than a little bit bizarre.

What happens initially is that the player and his agent will make a decision, based on the information that is available at that time, to ask for a certain amount of money—let us say $450,000. The player has just had a good year; he has finished nineteenth in the voting of the MVP award, third at his position in the voting for the AP post-season All-Star team, and he is beginning to think of himself as one of the better players in the league at his position.

Meanwhile, the owner and his agent, who is called a General Manager, will meet and make a decision about what to offer the player. As they see it, the young man has shown some progress, and he is in the general class now with Chico in Chicago and Abdul in Atlanta and Herman, our own young infielder. Chico is in the second year of a three-year package averaging $265,000 a year, Abdul is unsigned but played last year for $160,000, and Herman is knocking on the other door asking for $345,000. Owner and GM mull this over, and they come up with what they think is a very fair offer: $275,000 for one year, or $650,000 for two.

A phone call is arranged. Offers are exchanged, and then grimaces. This one ain't going to be easy.

They begin to talk. Reasons are given. Strengths of the ballplayer are pointed out by the agent; weaknesses of the player are pointed out by the GM; weaknesses of the comparable players are pointed out by the agent; strengths of the comparable players are pointed out by the GM; alternative sets of comparable players are introduced by the agent (look at Bob in Boston and Louie in LA); strengths and weaknesses of these comparable players are elucidated *ad infinitum*. Weeks pass; calls are being made every day.

And as each man talks, he becomes more and more convinced that he is right—convinced that if the case must be sent to an arbitrator, he is going to win it. Irritation grows; positions harden. Eventually an offer is declared Our Final Offer. $310,000; that's it. You're not getting a penny more.

Well, says the agent, this is Our Final Offer: $425,000. Take it or fight.

Silence reigns. A week goes by with no contact. War preparations are begun. Arbitration cases are being written, and that means sixteen-to-eighteen-hour days for both sides. Another week of this begins to wear on the combatants. Ten days until the arbitration schedule begins. Both agent and GM have other things to do, other contracts to worry about.

But while the positions are not changing, the information bank is. Abdul in Atlanta signs a contract which undercuts the team's position; Bob in Boston signs a contract which nullifies his value for the player's position. The club reaches an agreement with Herman at $325,000. The agent asks the statistician who is working on the case whether or not he can sustain the comparison to Louie in LA; the statistician says I doubt it. The GM looks carefully at Herman's stats, and realizes that he would have a tough time explaining to an arbitrator why he is paying Herman more than he is paying this guy.

Both sides now realize that they cannot defend the positions they have taken.

Both sides now realize that they cannot present a solid arbitration case at the figures given—but, unfortunately, they can't get out of them. Because when they convinced themselves that they were going to win, they also convinced the people whose money it was. The GM has convinced the owner (or the assistant GM has convinced the GM) that $310,000 is a generous offer, a winnable figure in arbitration. The agent has convinced the player that he deserves every bit as much as Bob in Boston, and he's not about to take what Herman got. The owner has got another arbitration case on a pitcher with the same amount of experience, and if he settles this one at $400,000, it's going to hurt him on that one. Neither side can move, and neither side really wants to fight this thing out.

So what can they do? I was not in any way connected with those negotiations, but it certainly is not a coincidence that the precedent-setting weight clause in the Bob Horner contract grew out of a situation in which the two sides of the negotiation had hardened to an unusual extent. Incentives. Bonuses. They serve as a bridge between the solidified positions. The GM finally goes to the owner, and he says, "You know, I wouldn't mind paying this bozo something like what he's asking for if we just didn't have to worry about conditioning. He had a pretty good year last year, but you know he tends to put on weight in the offseason, and I just don't feel like we can count on his having as good a year again."

And the owner says, "I thought we were in a good position on this one?"

And the GM says, "We should have been, but then that moron in Atlanta gave all that money to Abdul, and I'm afraid it's going to kill us. You just never know what an arbitrator is going to listen to."

And the owner says, "Well, maybe we can come up a little if we can get some guarantees—a weight clause, some performance clauses. I don't mind paying him if he has a good year, just as long as we don't wind up paying through the nose for a bad one."

Presto. A contract is agreed to within twenty-four hours—$310,000, plus $50,000 in incentives based on playing time, plus $40,000 in weight clauses. The war is avoided; the GM doesn't have to go into arbitration and tell the player why he doesn't deserve more. His staff can concentrate on the other case. He doesn't have to explain to Herman why he gave a bigger contract to somebody else. He doesn't really have to back down on his "final" offer, a practice which could kill him in future negotiations if he makes a habit of it. He has gained a measure of control over the player's conditioning program; at least when he thinks about the player's conditioning, he has a reason for optimism. The player is happy; as far as he's concerned it's a $400,000 contract as long as he keeps his weight down. The team has acknowledged that he's a better player than Herman is. He can now go to spring training and concentrate on playing baseball. The agent is happy; he feels that he's done the job for the player—not like that guy who represents Chico in Chicago, who has the guy playing for $265,000. Good feelings emanate all around; an agreement is made to meet in June and talk about a long-term contract.

And then some old plaster brain working for the local paper, who knows as much about negotiating a contract as he does about playing the French horn, will write a column in which he rips you all to shreds—the greedy player and his greedy, greedy agent who expect to receive $40,000 a year for just not getting fat, the stupid owner and his stupid, stupid GM who yield to this kind of blackmail, and I remember Stan Musial used to do jumping jacks all winter just to keep his ankles in shape and nobody had to pay him anything to do it, and isn't the world just going to shit these days when you have to pay an athlete an extra $40,000 just so he won't O.D. on Twinkies and chocolate bars.

Well, friends, Stan Musial was not a typical ballplayer from the 1950s. And if I had a ball club, just about everybody on it would have a weight clause. Why? If you were managing the Pirates over the last three years, wouldn't you have wished to God that Dave Parker had a weight clause in his contract? Allow me to point out that Dave Parker is not the first fat ballplayer who's ever played the game. He's not going to be the last. Mickey Lolich and Smoky Burgess and Dick Radatz and Ernie Lombardi and Bob Fothergill and Piano Legs Hickman and Wilbert Robinson—as far back in the history of the game as you can see, they've always been there.

Weight clauses are an intelligent attempt to deal with a problem that major league teams have been attempting to deal with from day one. The need for their existence says a mouthful about human nature, but it says not a word about the decade that we are living in.

—1984

There were charges of "negative leadership" leveled at Dave Parker by Rose and Murray Cook in 1987. This seems to be a coming code word, but what exactly it means could be anything from not showing up at the park on time to not taking an interest in younger players to something more serious. Certainly Rose was not pleased when he wanted Parker to move to first base and Parker wouldn't, and he shouldn't have been pleased, in that that may well have cost the Reds the pennant. Parker is an awful right fielder, slow and unreliable. The Reds needed a first baseman who could put runs on the scoreboard; they were playing Dave Concepcion and Terry Francona at first base. Parker wouldn't move.

I think that to have a key player on any team who won't do what the team needs for him to do for the good of the whole is tremendously damaging. Earl Weaver tells in *It's What You Learn After You Know It All That Counts* that when he was a coach with the Orioles Frank Robinson didn't like to sign baseballs. You know, people are always requesting signed baseballs, and the Orioles (like most organizations) bring boxes of baseballs into the clubhouse for the players to sign. When

Weaver took over the Orioles Frank Robinson came to him and asked what he could do to help Weaver out. Weaver told him to sign baseballs. It was symbolic, but it was important, because there was this daily sign that we're all going to pitch in here and do what has to be done. Parker's refusal to move to first base sent the opposite message: My ego is more important than the good of the team.

—1988

For further evidence on the damage that a key player can do if he openly refuses to subordinate his ego to the team goals, consider the Toronto Blue Jays of 1988.

Gary Pettis

As much as I admire Gene Mauch, I think he completely missed the boat with this guy. You know that expression about "playing within yourself," which I guess a lot of people think is a cliché, but cliché or not there aren't very many good ballplayers who don't know what they can do and what they can't do. The managerial equivalent of that is playing within the limits of your ball club, not asking people to do what they're not capable of doing. "You've got your mules, and you've got your race horses," Billy Martin says, "and you can kick a mule in the ass all you want to and he's not going to be a race horse." Gene Mauch is often credited by the media with not asking players to do what they're not capable of doing—but in this case, that's just what he did. Gene Mauch could never accept that Gary Pettis is what he is.

Pettis strikes out a lot. He's not a bad player. He's the best defensive outfielder in baseball, and a decent offensive player as well, because his on base percentages are pretty fair. He gets on base a lot more often than Willie Wilson, let's say; if Wilson outhits Pettis by sixty points Pettis will still be on base as often. That enables Pettis to make some use of his speed on the base paths.

Mauch could never accept that. He wanted Pettis to be a different type of player—a contact hitter, a guy who would choke up on the bat and slap the ball to the opposite field. I agree that it would be wonderful if Pettis was that type of player, but he simply isn't. As a twenty-six-year-old rookie in 1984, he struck out in almost 30 percent of his at bats. You simply cannot tell a man at that age to stop doing one thing and start doing another, and teach him to be a successful major league hitter. I submit that there has never in the history of baseball been a player who learned how to hit at the age of twenty-seven. There are a few cases where people think that is what happened, like Matty Alou, Pete Runnels and Harry Heilmann, but if you really understand the situation, you know that that's not what happened. I've seen players who pushed themselves to higher and higher levels over a period of years, like Brian Downing, Alan Ashby, and Frank White, but I've never seen a player just learn to hit, or learn a hitting style, after the age of twenty-five. I submit that it can't be done, that the game is too hard for that.

Gene Mauch, however, was determined that Gary Pettis was going to be the first. Pettis is an excellent number nine hitter, perfectly designed for the spot. The thing to do with him was to put him in the number nine spot, see if he could increase from 65 walks a year to 85, see if he could push his batting average up about 20 points. Forget about the damn strikeouts; they don't matter, anyway. Not good enough for Mauch; Mauch wanted him to stop striking out, hit .300 and become a lead-off hitter. And he worried about that, and he worried about it, until he pushed Pettis back to AAA.

—1988

Darrell Porter

There is still a great deal of crying and moaning in Kansas City about the Royals' failure to re-sign Darrell Porter, a decision which no doubt contributed in some part to the team's poor 1981 season. Joe Burke is convinced that the salary that Porter got was inflationary, out of line with established salaries. I am convinced it was not. I was talking with an agent about Porter in October, 1979, a month and a half before he signed, and we both made guesses at what he would get. We didn't miss by much. Burke and John Schuerholz simply didn't or don't want to admit that the salary structure of the free agent pool is what it is; they were looking at contracts signed by Fisk and Bench and Bob Boone and the like two or three years earlier and thinking of that plus twenty or thirty percent as the prevailing level.

At the same time, try to see Darrell Porter's career as it will look in retrospect. If you look at Porter's career as it will appear twenty years from now, you'll see that it was the Milwaukee Brewers who did the cooking and the Cardinals who picked up the bill for the ingredients, but it was the Royals who ate the cake. The Brewers signed Porter for a big bonus, trained him, suffered through his early struggles. The Cardinals rewarded him for the big seasons and suffered with his decline. But it was the Royals who got the three good years, and for those three years he was some player.

—1982

Well Jeez, Darrell, if you were going to win the World Series for somebody, why couldn't it have been us? We're the ones who took you in when you were down and out, watched you grow into a star, stayed behind you and poured out our warmth and friendship when you had your troubles. You go put yourself in an institution and not one joke did I ever hear about it in Kansas City. You had a miserable year for us, we didn't boo you.

The national media chose Willie Wilson to be the goat in the 1980 World Series, but anybody who has studied the scoresheets knows who really lost that series for the Royals. Twice you come tiptoeing into home plate like an old lady trying to sneak into bed with the gardener; you bat eight times with men on base and don't drive in one damn run, and you don't throw worth a hoot. We didn't need you to be the series MVP—Amos was taking care of that—we just needed you to do your part. And then the St. Louis fans give you absolute hell for two years, and you give them a World's Championship—their (ouch) ninth. There's no justice.

—1983 Baseball Abstract

Darrell Porter was the MVP of the 1982 World Series, while playing for the Cardinals. He finally paid the Kansas City fans back in 1985.

Kirby Puckett

Probably no other player in any city is as popular as Kirby is in Minnesota. They just love the guy up there—children, teammates, bankers and bureaucrats. He's hard not to love. What other major league superstar would let his teammates rub his head for luck? Who else would say, when asked what he would wish for by *USA Today*, that he would like to have a body like Glenn Braggs? Is his phone number still in the book?

Young players are often bathed in a transcendant innocence which makes them attractive. Then they start doing commercials, trading on that attraction, and we know it's just a matter of time until they are caught trying to capture some chemicals or are hit with a paternity suit and start fighting with the club over money. Willie Mays played stickball in the streets of Harlem for only one year. When he came out of the army in '54 he didn't have time for that anymore—and yet we remember those stickball games as a central part of his identity; even more, as an image of the era. Willie played stickball in the heart of the McCarthy era with America at war. We use that image to scrub up our memory of the time, to make it simpler and more innocent than it was. Innocence is the sugar coating which makes history palatable, as evil is its medicine. Part of the charm of Kirby is that his skin of innocence seems thicker than usual, and seems to be wearing off more slowly.

—1988

Randy Ready

One of the most inscrutable managerial moves of the year was Lachemann's unwillingness to take a long look at Randy Ready. When you a) are blown out of the race by the first week of May, b) lose your regular third baseman for the season with an injury, and c) have a rookie who everybody has been raving about who just happens to be a third baseman, how smart do you have to be to piece this together? Instead, I saw the Brewers play in the first two weeks of the season, and they had Ted

Simmons at third base. Lachemann announced in early June that he had decided to make Roy Howell his regular third baseman. I'm not making a judgment here, but does this make sense to you?

—1985

Jeff Reardon

There is something to be learned from the incident of Reardon's wife, which was that Mrs. Reardon, having completed a given amount of charity work, stood up in front of a Montreal crowd and was, her husband not having pitched well of late, greeted with a chorus of boos. This scorched any bonds of kinship Reardon might have felt for the Montreal fandom, and inasmuch as he learned a lesson by it, so might we all.

The lesson is this: Public life is rougher than you think it is. It all looks smooth from the outside. Public men make a lot of money, often for not working very hard and for working at things less distasteful than, say, collecting garbage, working in a steel mill or selling life insurance. People recognize them on the street and deluge them with get-well cards when they are in the hospital.

Publicity magnifies the good things that come into your life —but it also magnifies the bad things. It is people like me who make it rough, with our caustic comments and our cold analysis. And as I do to Doug Flynn and Enos Cabell and Bucky Dent, other people do to me at times, and others to them, and it doesn't feel so good. The IRS takes a special interest in you if your name is in the papers; they live by promoting the fear that you might always get caught, and they would love to use a Jeff Reardon or a Norman Mailer to advance that fear. Willie Wilson goes directly to jail for an offense that would draw a stern look from a judge if it were you or I, because somebody is using him to prove a point. Strangers will stop you on the street or call on the phone and want something that you can't give them, and if you get famous enough they will actually start shooting at you.

About my small acre of fame I am certainly not complaining, just trying to make you see a little clearer what comes with the title. Willie Wilson's comment, while being led away in handcuffs, was "expletive publicity"; it is not reported whether he made the same remark at the time of signing his $4 million contract. And as to Mrs. Reardon, well, my sister has devoted her entire adult life to working with homeless and destitute people, and she doesn't stand up in front of no crowd and expect them to applaud on Sunday. When you decide to be a public figure, you take what comes. You cannot control it, and you cannot choose it.

—1984

Craig Reynolds

The next time you read one of those cranky articles about the spoiled, no-good modern ballplayers, taking a million dollars a year and behaving like children, just remember Craig Reynolds. He was an All-Star, one of the best in the business in the late seventies. When he lost his job to a prospective superstar, he went quietly to the bench; I read no stories about his throwing tantrums in the clubhouse and demanding to be traded. I don't know what he was doing for those two years, but I could make a pretty good guess in view of the fact that when the time came that he was needed again, he stepped quietly back into the lineup and quietly reestablished himself as one of the best. What more could anyone ask for from an athlete?

—1985

Angel Salazar

A talented player, he projected as a rookie who would hit a year ago, but didn't seem to react well to the challenge of earning the job. . . .

Well, let's not be coy about it. I don't know how much truth there is in this, but what I was told in Montreal is that Salazar, with a job virtually handed to him, displayed what we might call a Miguel Dilone Syndrome. He wouldn't put out any extra effort as a show of good faith, wouldn't take extra hitting practice or work on his defense; he just acted like the job was his. The worse he played, and he played quite badly indeed, the less receptive he became to help.

When a young player does that, people say that it doesn't seem like he wants the job. Well, of course he *wants* the job; every young baseball player wants to play. What this behavior suggests to me is a player with a deep-rooted lack of confidence. Men who are consumed with a fear of failing often protect themselves from the failure that they subconsciously anticipate by adopting a pose of indifference and hostility; any attempt to reach out to such a player would be interpreted as an attempt to force him to make an emotional commitment to the job, and thus would feed the fear and force the player to fortify his defense mechanisms. Such a player would exhibit external signs of self-confidence, and would refuse to make any special efforts to cooperate, as to do so would be a tacit acknowledgement of his unsteady position. Not until the player sheds the label of a hot prospect, and nothing more is expected of him, will the fear subside and the ability once more begin to assert itself.

What can be done about it? I don't think anything can. If a twenty-two-year-old athlete doesn't believe in himself, deep down, I doubt seriously that there is anything anybody else can do about it that will change that fact. Salazar has terrific talent, and he can play shortstop in the major leagues. He might have a big year sometime. If he can have two straight big years, he might even grow into the confidence that he needs. But I doubt that anybody will ever be able to control his talent.

—1985

Tom Seaver

I'm always kind of fascinated by strategies that go out of fashion. Remember Ted Lyons, the Sunday pitcher? Pitched every Sunday for the White Sox for several years, pitched great. In the period 1935–50 there were a number of old but skilled pitchers who would start twenty to twenty-five times a year, not because they were injured, but just because it was felt that that was the way they could be most effective. They were, by and large, damned effective—Ted Lyons was from 1934–42, Grove from 1939–41, Red Ruffing pitched that way for a couple of years, Spud Chandler for a year, Freddie Fitzsimmons and Carl Hubbell for several years each. They were all at the tag ends of brilliant careers, and they weren't really strong enough to hitch up to the plow every fifth day, but they were effective at the level of twenty starts a year.

For some reason, the strategy fell out of favor about 1950, and I don't really understand why. I keep waiting for somebody to try to revive the idea. Tom Seaver last year was 3–2, 4.13 ERA when he was starting on long (five days) rest. He was 2–11 otherwise with an ERA over six. You've got a team going nowhere; you've got Soto and Berenyi to build the pitching around. Why not pitch Seaver once a week, see what he can do? Indeed, why not set Sunday aside for him? Maybe there's a good reason the strategy went out of use, but I don't know what it is.

—1983 *Baseball Abstract*

I eventually figured out why the strategy fell out of favor. In the time of Ted Lyons, teams played doubleheaders almost every Sunday, and thus to use a "Sunday pitcher" for one game of the doubleheader had a stabilizing effect on the starting rotation, which otherwise would have had to cough up an extra starter for the doubleheader. But after doubleheaders became less common, and eventually uncommon, the use of a Sunday pitcher would have destabilized the starting rotation, rather than stabilizing it, by forcing an irregular turn for one pitcher. This is not to say that it couldn't work, but at least you can see why they stopped doing it.

Ted Simmons

You may recall that one of Whitey Herzog's first official acts in assuming control of the St. Louis Cardinals was to trade away Ted Simmons, the Cardinals' biggest star. At the time, the move was extremely unpopular in St. Louis.

One of the many wonderful moments in the movie *Ragtime*

occurs just after the terrorist group has seized the library, and Jimmy Cagney, the police chief, has arrived on the scene. A stranger breaks through the crowd and informs Cagney with great urgency that he is the curator of the library, and that it is a priceless collection that must be handled with the utmost of care. Well, says Cagney, why don't you go tell those fellows that? To which the poor man replies, are you trying to be funny? And Cagney replies, my good man, so long as those guys are in there, you are not the cur-a-tor of anything.

I was just amazed last summer by the intensity of the anti-Herzog, pro-Simmons sentiment in St. Louis. The Cardinals had the best record in the division in '81 and were in contention all the way last year, but every time they lost two games in a row the Simba-ites would come out of the woodwork.

But look at the situation as it must have looked to Herzog. You've got a highly talented team that isn't winning. The team doesn't hustle; it doesn't execute fundamentals, it doesn't play very good defense. You've got a player who is universally recognized as the leader of that team. He is a public idol. He is on the board of directors of the art museum. He is, reportedly, good buddies with the owner. He is a .300 hitter with power. But, unfortunately, he is a catcher, and he is not a good one. So you sign another catcher, and you tell him that, for the good of the team, he is going to have to move. And he says, "No, I won't do it. The hell with what's good for the team." What are you going to do?

I don't know what you'd do, but I know what I would do. If I had to trade that man for five cents on the dollar, I'd trade him. You don't have to be in baseball to relate to that circumstance. Suppose that you are the new manager of an office, or a loading dock, or the new plant manager in a factory, and things aren't running worth a hoot, and people are bitching and moaning a lot instead of working together, and you approach your highest-paid employee, who is also the most popular, visible man in the organization, and who is also a friend of your boss, and you tell him that you're going to assign him some different duties. And he tells you to stick it. What are you going to do?

De facto authority, that is the message. You either get rid of that son of a bitch, or you accept the fact that he is running the show and you are not. If Whitey Herzog didn't have the guts to run Ted Simmons out of St. Louis, he might as well have quit on the spot. Because if he didn't, from that moment on he was not the man-a-ger of anything.

—1983

Don Slaught

The five most reasonable explanations that I can think of why anyone would trade Don Slaught for Jim Sundberg:

1. Don Slaught is a secret hemophiliac and his hobby is playing with chain saws.
2. Don Slaught likes to jump out of airplanes and frequently forgets to put on his face mask before the start of an inning.
3. Don Slaught made a pass at Ewing Kaufmann's wife.
4. Don Slaught made a pass at Ewing Kaufmann.
5. Don Slaught's agent carries a razor.

If none of these conditions applies, then I really don't understand the trade.

—1985

Lonnie Smith

I would try to tell you what a bad outfielder Lonnie is, except that I confess that I would never have believed it myself if somebody had tried to tell me. I will say, though, that the real cost of Lonnie's defense is not nearly as great as the psychic impact of it. He makes you wail and gnash your teeth a lot, but he doesn't really cost you all that many runs.

One reason for that is that he recovers so quickly after he makes a mistake. You have to understand that Lonnie makes defensive mistakes every game, so he knows how to handle it. Your average outfielder is inclined to panic when he falls down chasing a ball in the corner; he may just give up and set there a while, trying to figure it out. Lonnie has a pop-up slide perfected for the occasion.

Another outfielder might have no idea where the ball was when it bounded off his glove. Lonnie can calculate with the instinctive astrophysics of a veteran tennis player where a ball will land when it skips off the heel of his glove, what the angle of glide will be when he tips it off the webbing, what the spin will be when the ball skids off the thumb of the mitt.

Many players can kick a ball behind them without ever knowing it. Lonnie can judge by the pitch of the thud and the subtle pressure through his shoe in which direction and how far he has projected the sphere.

He knows exactly what to do when a ball spins out of his hand and flies crazily into a void on the field. He knows when it is appropriate for him to scamper after the ball and when he needs to back up the man who will have to recover it.

He has experience in these matters; when he retires he will be hired to come to spring training and coach defensive recovery and cost containment. This is his specialty, and he is good at it.

—1986

Ozzie Smith

I was surprised and disappointed in the National League MVP vote for 1985. Meaning no disrespect to Willie McGee, to my way of thinking it was obvious that the Most Valuable Player in the N.L. in 1985 was Ozzie Smith.

Before the 1985 season, it was widely written that the Cardinal pitching was weak. With the loss of Bruce Sutter and poor late-season pitching from Joaquin Andujar, many felt that the Cardinals didn't have the pitching to win. I approached the issue in this way: There are three things which beat pitchers. Those are walks, home runs, and balls in play which are not handled. The Cardinal pitchers would be receiving huge breaks on two of the three. Busch Stadium would help control the number of home runs allowed. With Ozzie Smith behind them, Ozzie Smith and Willie McGee and Tommie Herr, they would be receiving a huge break on balls in play. Therefore, as long as they didn't walk people, the Cardinal pitchers would be all right. And Whitey won't use a pitcher who walks a lot of people; he'll instruct his pitchers to go after the hitters, and get rid of those who won't.

Given those advantages, and given the presence on the staff of Andujar, John Tudor, Ricky Horton, and Danny Cox, it seemed to me that the Cardinal pitching would be perceived as outstanding. Ozzie Smith would save the Cardinal pitchers enough runs that they could win—not Ozzie alone, but Ozzie as the lynchpin of a strong defense. The Cardinals would win, and Ozzie would be the MVP.

But nobody saw it.

If Ozzie Smith wasn't the MVP, then can any player of his type ever be the MVP? It is hard to see how. Ozzie is unquestionably the greatest player of his type, isn't he? He is generally regarded as the greatest defensive shortstop ever to play the game. He has the best defensive statistics of any shortstop to play the game.

Of his species—the light-hitting defensive wizard—he is one of the best offensive players. He isn't a high average hitter or a power hitter, but he hits for a decent average (second best in the league at the position), his strikeout and walk data are exceptional (the second-best in baseball, exceeded only by Mike Scioscia), and he is an excellent base stealer. Looking at the entire picture of his offense, he was clearly the best-hitting shortstop in the National League.

So what you have is

1. The greatest defensive player ever
2. At one of the two most important defensive positions
3. Who is also the best hitter in the league at his position
4. Having his best season offensively as well as perhaps defensively
5. Holding together a team expected to collapse
6. And leading them to the league championship.

That is about as good a definition of an MVP as one can write—yet Ozzie finished eighteenth in the MVP voting! He was mentioned on only two ballots, placing eighth and ninth on those two.

I didn't expect that. I don't understand it. I can't justify it. And I don't think it reflects very well on the award or the men who did the voting.

—1986

Marc Sullivan

I am sorry if this is harsh, but there is nepotism here, and petty as it is, it offends me. The Red Sox in 1979 blew a second-round draft pick on Marc Sullivan, the son of Red Sox then-vice president Haywood Sullivan. After young Marckie hit .203 with one home run in 117 games in the Eastern League (1982), the Red Sox had the effrontery to dress him up in a major league uniform and foist him off as a major league player, in two games late the same season. After he went back to the minors and hit .229 and .204, they decided he was ready to play for the major league team. In 1985 and 1986, as a part-timer, Sullivan hit .174 and .193. In 1987 he opened the season as the Red Sox' regular catcher. We should all find our opportunities so abundant.

What I would like to know is, where the hell does Haywood Sullivan get off trying to make his precious little boy an exception to the rules that the rest of the baseball world obeys? The most basic rule of sports is that in the effort to win, you put the team goals ahead of your personal agenda. The public posture of every major league team is that they expect their players not to play for their own statistics or their own greater glory, but to do what the good of the team demands. They would be appalled if a player stated publicly that he was playing for himself first and didn't much care whether the Sox won or lost. But Haywood Sullivan wants to add, "Of course, that doesn't apply to me."

And where is the watchdog? What does the press say? They tell us that Marc Sullivan is such a nice kid. Well, who the hell cares if he is a nice kid? Do you have any idea how many nice kids there are in AAA ball? It is not fair to those kids to tell them that Marc Sullivan is playing by a different set of rules than they are. It is not fair to Red Sox fans, and it's not fair to their other players.

Al Campanis' son was a catcher, too; he was about as good as this kid, a lifetime .147 hitter. When Campanis took over the Dodgers his first official act was to trade his own son. He didn't love his son any less than Haywood Sullivan does. He just had the character to say, "Son, the rules are just the same for you as they are for anybody else." And if Haywood Sullivan was half a man, he would have done the same thing.

—1988

Jim Sundberg

As a Royals fan, I had a sick feeling when it was announced in the winter that the Royals had traded Don Slaught and Frank Wills to acquire Jim Sundberg. It isn't that Jim Sundberg isn't a good player. In 1984, at least, he was a very good player; he hit well and was, as he has always been, one of the top defensive catchers in baseball.

It wasn't, either, that I think Don Slaught is going to be a big star; I used to think that, but I don't anymore. Slaught in 1984 drew only 20 walks and hit only 4 homers, and as an analyst I know that with those peripheral numbers, he'll have to hit at least .285 to be much of an offensive plus. He might do that; he might not. He might hit .320; the odds are he won't.

It was, rather, this: the unavoidable acceptance that I am, as a fan, rooting for an organization whose philosophies are diametrically opposed to my own, not only as to the question of *whether* you succeed, but as to the question of *how* you succeed. I like to watch young players grow and develop into stars, as I watched Amos Otis and George Brett and Frank White and Dennis Leonard. I take pleasure in seeing what they can do one year that they couldn't the year before; this is what, as a fan, I enjoy.

As an analyst, I have always espoused the human concept of the player, the eccentric notion that athletes are not static batting lines that can be moved around to accommodate needs, but rather are changing, complex combinations of skills and psyches that "function" best when knitted together young and allowed to grow as one. I have always believed that the future of any organization lies in the hands of the young men on the make, that once a player passes thirty absolutely the only surprise he can give you is to grow suddenly old. It was the Royals' organization which taught me this in the seventies, when they brought together young men without names or reputations and grew them into a championship unit. Perhaps, in the eighties, the Royals' organization will teach me differently, will teach me that success comes from cashing in the raw material of potential for the hard wealth of established talent. I'm afraid I shall find this lesson hard to enjoy.

—1985

Frank Tanana

Tanana was one of those pitchers they used to compare to Sandy Koufax at the same age. Remember those? It's so stupid. The whole point about Koufax is that he *became* a great pitcher. It's like comparing Robert Redford to Ronald Reagan at the same age.

—1983

Danny Tartabull

There was an interesting contrast in the reaction to the Tartabull trade as reported in *The Sporting News* and *Sports Illustrated*. Moss Klein in the December 15 *TSN* wrote that "Tartabull has obvious talent . . . but the Royals had better correct his attitude. He refused to make adjustments in his swing even though he had the worst strikeout ratio in the league . . . and he'll probably be a defensive liability at any position." Klein was trying to make sense of a trade that doesn't make sense on the surface by whittling away at Tartabull, but his comments are wide of the mark. I don't know what he means by saying that Tartabull "had the worst strikeout ratio in the league." Tartabull struck out in a little less than 31 percent of his at bats, which was about the same as Canseco, Cory Snyder and teammate Jim Presley and less than Incaviglia, Rob Deer and Gorman Thomas. For a power-hitting rookie, there is nothing in the least remarkable about Tartabull's strikeout rate. Reggie Jackson and Mike Schmidt both struck out more often as rookies than did Tartabull, and Schmidt still struck out more in his third season in the league. If Klein meant strikeout-to-walk ratio, Tartabull wasn't one of the ten worst in the league.

As to the comment that Tartabull "refused to make adjustments in his swing" to curb the strikeouts: Tartabull struck out in 41 percent of his at bats in April and 36 percent in May, but cut it to 26 percent in July and 28 percent in September. Hell, it took Reggie five years to make that much progress in cutting his strikeouts. Most power hitters strike out much more in their first couple of years than they do later on, but Tartabull was cutting the rate down remarkably well as the season progressed. More to the point, if you were a rookie and you were hitting the way Tartabull was hitting, how anxious would you be to start fooling around with your swing? If you were a manager and you had a rookie who was hitting like Tartabull, how anxious would you be to have somebody else fooling around with his swing? I know I wouldn't tolerate it.

Each man is the conservator of his own talent. No one else has developed Danny Tartabull's abilities to where they are. No one else will suffer the consequences if the adjustments that he makes throw him into a tailspin. So long as the man is succeeding and contributing, I don't feel it's appropriate for anyone else to snipe at the way that he chooses to develop his skills.

Peter Gammons in the December 22–29 *Sports Illustrated* took just the opposite approach to the trade, highlighting the riddle of the trade by stretching Tartabull's credentials while diminishing those of the new Mariners. Tartabull was now a "rare young right-handed slugger who knocked in 96 runs as a rookie despite a month's illness" who was handed over for "diminutive breaking ball pitcher Scott Bankhead, utility outfielder Mike Kingery and ten-year minor-league veteran pitcher Steve Shields." The "diminutive breaking ball pitcher" weighs fifteen or twenty pounds more than Ron Guidry and has a good fastball, and the "utility outfielder" has never been used in a utility role, having been a regular since being called up in midsummer and having played well enough that the Royals, or at least their media, had projected him as a regular in 1987. Gammons lengthened the gap between the players traded to emphasize the point that the Mariners "were looking for cheap help . . . they got just what owner George Argyros wanted—seven players each making under $100,000 a year."

I don't know what truth there is to the allegation that the Mariner trades were economically motivated. In baseball it's not the kind of thing you say about your friends. It's an "allegation." You don't announce that you've made a trade to save money, but over the history of baseball there have been a hell of a lot of fine trades that were made with one eye on the balance sheet. The trade was made, at least in part, because Dick Williams evaluates talent differently than other people do. In my part of the country there used to be a basketball coach named Jack Hartman. He was a fine coach and his teams would win, but a lot of times his players didn't look like they were good athletes. Sportswriters talked a lot about how much Hartman did with so little talent, which was intended as a compliment but became a tiresome one after a while, and Hartman finally said, "Look, what is talent? Talent is just being where you are supposed to be and doing what you are supposed to do." What he was saying, in essence, was that you may think that talent is being able to run fast and jump high and stop and start quickly, but I think that talent is blocking out on the boards and cutting off the passing lanes and hitting your free throws. You recruit the guys that you think have talent and I'll recruit the guys that I think have talent, and we'll see who wins.

Williams is like that. He takes a somewhat different view of what constitutes talent than do most other managers. If you think that talent is being able to throw ninety-two miles an hour, fine; you take the guys who throw ninety-two miles an hour and work behind the hitters, and Dick will take the guys who throw eighty-seven miles an hour and work ahead of the hitters. Scott Bankhead struck out ninety-four men and walked thirty-seven in 1986. To Dick Williams, that's talent.

The economic explanation for this trade doesn't make a lot of sense to me. If you just want cheap help, you can pick that up anywhere; you can always bring players out of the minors to play for $52,000. The trick is to find players who don't make a lot of money and can produce. Tartabull will not be eligible for salary arbitration for two more years, and it is generally assumed, among baseball men, that the most productive phase of a ballplayer's career, dollar for dollar, is the years two through five. Rookies are paid hardly any money, but then a lot of them can't do the job, and after five years a player's salary has reached its peak, while his skills often are beginning to decline. If you were very interested in getting good value for the dollar, it seems likely to me that Tartabull would be the first player you would want to keep, rather than the one to trade.

—1987

Garry Templeton

The Cedeño of the eighties. Templeton is reportedly going to be traded, but Herzog's handling of him has been courageous and appropriate. Templeton is never going to be the ballplayer he should be unless somebody confronts him with the fact of his misbehavior and makes it clear to him that talent is not an excuse for immaturity. If he'd had a manager who would have chewed his butt about two years ago it would never have come to this. Can you imagine one of Billy Martin's players saying he wasn't going to hustle this year because he wasn't being paid enough? You'd want to reserve a hospital bed in advance.

—1982

Mike Torrez

He's a mystery. He doesn't strike people out, he walks too many, he gives up too many home runs, doesn't get particularly good double play support, doesn't hold base runners well, gives up over a hit an inning, and has long stretches during the season when he can't get anybody out. Yet his winning percentage has been better than .550 in seven of the last eight years, and he has 165 career wins. He just seems to be able to smell a win; you get him a lead, he gets you a W. He can be in the middle of yet another career-endangering slump and zip off six victories before you can say "Steve Crawford."

—1982

Ellis Valentine

Ellis is starting to remind me of Downtown Ollie Brown. You remember Ollie? He used to warm up by sort of casually lobbing the ball from the warning track to the third baseman, took two infielders and a bat boy to get it back to him. He was a big guy, like Ellis, had some power and ran well, but his career just drifted away among inconsistent offense and too many strikeouts. About 1976 somebody asked him if he still had that great arm. He said, "Yeah, and I'd sure like to trade it for a great bat."

—1983

Frank White

Did you ever notice that players name "White" are almost always black, and players named "Black" are usually white? Why is that? The last White major leaguer who was actually white was Mike White, who played for Houston in the early sixties. Since then we've had Bill White, Roy White, Frank White, and Jerry White, all of whom were black; Mike White probably would have been black except that his father played in the majors in the thirties and they didn't allow you to be black then. The Royals also had a Black on their roster, Bud, who of course is white; in fact, the Royals had to set some sort of record by having four colored people on their team, White, Black, Blue and Brown. Scott Brown is not any browner than anybody else, Vida is definitely not blue, nor for that matter is Darryl Motley. I suppose that it is the nature of names, as with Peacekeeping Missiles and Security Police, to disguise the truth more often than they reveal it. Horace Speed stole only four bases in his career. Vic Power was a singles hitter, Bill Goodenough was not good enough, and Joe Blong did not belong for long.

—1983

Alan Wiggins

Turned in an impressive year at second base. He made some errors early in the year, wasn't real quick on the double play, but he showed good range there all the way and by the end of the season he was fine. . . . My ignorant fan's opinion is that he's not doing his batting any favors with all the bunting, and would be a little better hitter if he'd cut the bunt attempts back to about two per game. But he's a good player.

The release of Bonilla is a classic Dick Williams move. Almost any other manager (let's make that categorical) . . . *any* other manager in baseball, given the situation the Padres had, (an excess of outfielders but an unproductive second baseman) would *at best* have hedged his bets, kept Bonilla on the roster just in case the Wiggins experiment didn't work out. When was the last time any major league team released outright a twenty-eight-year-old player who had batted over 550 times the year before? I'll bet it hasn't happened in ten years. What many managers would have done, and what a lot of fans and sportswriters were doing a year ago, is to make excuses for Bonilla's performance, and to talk about his injuries and his problems and his potential rather than facing the fact that the man was not getting the job done. They would have kept him in the lineup and given him another sixty or seventy games to redeem himself; at the very least, they would have said, you've got to have a defensive replacement around for the late innings of a close game.

The universal theme that cries out from Dick Williams' managerial record is that decisions work best when you commit yourself to making them work. To any other manager, moving an outfielder into second base is an experiment, and as such you want to protect yourself if it doesn't work; this is known in the business world as a fallback position, and in the military as CYA (Cover Your Ass). Williams' attitude is the heck with that; if my decisions don't work they're going to fire my ass anyway. I don't want Alan Wiggins looking over his shoulder. Williams is the one manager in baseball who never hedges his bet, and never vacillates on a decision once it is made.

—1985

Mookie Wilson

Talk about your eerie coincidences. Mookie's real name is William Wilson, but they can't call him that, for obvious reasons. There is another major league player who does and doesn't do exactly the same things that this guy does, and who is the same age and color, and that man's name is Willie Wilson. To use the same name would invite unnecessary and unattractive comparisons.

Edgar Allan Poe wrote a story about a man who was haunted by another man of the same name, same build and talents and face. The idea was that you were supposed to catch on that his personality had split, and he was merely projecting himself into another character of the same description. The two men's names? William Wilson. Swear to God.

—1982

Forty-eight players named "Wilson" have played in the major leagues. Among their familiar names are Hack, Tack, Hickie, Artie, Grady, Icehouse, Chink, Fin, Highball, Maxie, Zeke, Mookie, Mutt, Gomer, and Squanto. Gomer was called Tex, Fin's real name was Finis. The player who was called Icehouse Wilson was really named George Peacock Wilson. There was also a Frank Wilson, who was nicknamed Squash, and a Charlie Wilson, who was called Swamp Baby, probably not to his face. One Wilson, Hack, holds the record for runs batted in in a season. Another, Chief, holds the record for triples. A third, Willie, holds the record for at-bats.

—1984

I suppose I shouldn't comment on this, but don't you reckon Mookie Wilson and George Foster has got to be the ugliest platoon combination in the history of baseball?

—1987

Butch Wynegar

You may not believe this, but the November 1977 issue of the *Baseball Digest* contains an article solemnly entitled: "How the Tigers Missed Out on Drafting Butch Wynegar." The Tigers in 1974 drafted Lance Parrish in the first round and were planning to pick Wynegar in the second until the Twins, drafting two ahead of them, picked him. The Tigers, according to the article, "still cringe when they recall how close they came to claiming the switch-hitting Wynegar." I haven't asked, but I reckon they've given up cringing since then.

—1984

Robin Yount

I am reliably assured that Robin Yount is not, in addition to his other virtues, a brilliant man, but he made the one most perceptive comment that I heard on television in the summer of 1982. When asked who he thought should vote for the All-Star game, the players or the fans, he said, "I can't really answer that question because I don't know who the game is supposed to be for. I don't know if the game is supposed to be for the fans or if it is supposed to be for the players." You see the point? You know those people who run around saying that the players should elect the All-Star teams because look at this vote and look at that one and there are all kinds of people who don't deserve the honor who wind up in the starting lineup? Those people are making an assumption, without even realizing that they are, that the purpose of the All-Star game is to honor the players, and therefore that the desire to honor the right people takes precedence over the desire to put in front of the fans the people that the fans want to see. Is the game basically an honor for the players, or is it basically an entertainment for the fans? The answer that you select to that question will tell you who ought to elect the teams. People simply leap over that question and construct their reasoning from beyond it; Yount sliced up the argument with a deftness that William Buckley should envy.

—1983

Section III People

Jack Aker

In the "Does this make any sense to you?" department, an October 18 note from *The Sporting News*:

> Former major leaguer Jack Aker, a manager in the Mets' organization since 1975, was dismissed after leading Tidewater to the International League championship. "Jack Aker has done a fine job," said Mets' Vice President Lou Gorman, "but we felt it was in Jack's best interest to seek challenges in another organization."

Huh? Is one of us cracking up? What about the best interests of the Mets' organization? Let me get this straight . . . You fired the guy for his own good?

—1983

George Bamberger

Comment written in 1982, as Bamberger assumed the job with the Mets.

It is the second coming of The Man Who Saved Milwaukee ("A city ravaged in a baseball sense," to quote Cosell), and there is nothing else in prospect for the 1982 season that excites me as much. What will he attempt to do? How will it work? Can he find another Gorman Thomas? Can he do for Pat Zachry what he did for Mike Caldwell?

George Bamberger shares credit with Harry Dalton and others for what happened in Milwaukee, and what happened in Milwaukee in 1978 was fairly astonishing. The exciting thing for a Mets fan is the chance that Bamberger can do it again. The exciting thing for the rest of us is *finding out* whether he can do it again.

—1982

Peter Bavasi

Peter Bavasi resigned last winter as General Manager of the Blue Jays with the incredible parting comment that the thrill was gone and that therefore it was time to move on to new challenges. I would suggest farm work, maybe buy a gas station, sell shoes or something. Well, yes, Peter, I can understand how the thrill would go out of losing 105 games a year after about five years. I mean, I know that first 57–105 season has got to be a rush, but after a while I suppose it gets to be routine, like anything else. The truly amazing thing, Pete, is how you managed to enjoy it as long as you did. It seems to me that any normal person would get sick and tired of losing two games out of three after a year or two, but you positively wallowed in it for five years. . . .

Peter Bavasi believed in stability, commitment to young players and orderly progress for the organization. That's putting it mildly. *I* believe in stability, commitment to young players and orderly progress. The difference is that Bavasi did not recognize the existence of any competing virtues. His method was simple: Find young players, put them in the lineup and wait for them to develop. And wait. And wait.

—*1982 Baseball Abstract*

Originally published under the title "A Solid Financial Footing for Toronto," or "A Man's Outhouse Is His Castle If He Holds His Nose and Pretends the Flies Are Pigeons."

Harry Caray

Cable television has arrived at this distant Balkan outland I call home, and I have been watching Harry Caray whenever I get the time. It's the first significant exposure to Harry that I've had in fifteen years, and I realize with a sense of shock how much of my own attitude about the game and about my profession, which I thought I had found by myself, I may in fact have picked up from hundreds of hours of listening to Harry Caray as a child.

Or perhaps it is a false pride, but I love Harry Caray. You have to understand what Harry Caray was to the Midwest in my childhood. In the years when baseball stopped at the Mississippi, KMOX radio built a network of stations across the Midwest and into the Far West that brought major league baseball into every little urb across the landscape. Harry's remarkable talents and enthusiasm were the spearhead of their efforts, and forged a link between the Cardinals and the Midwest which remains to this day; even now, some of my neighbors are Cardinal fans.

This effect covers a huge area and encompasses millions of people, many times as many people as live in New York. A Harry Caray-for-the-Hall-of-Fame debate is in progress. To us, to hear New Yorkers or Californians suggest that Harry Caray might not be worthy of the honors given to Mel Allen or Vin Scully is a) almost comically ignorant, sort of like hearing a midwesterner suggest that the Statue of Liberty was never of any national significance and should be turned into scrap metal, and b) personally offensive. That Harry should have to wait in line behind these wonderful men but comparatively insignificant figures is, beyond any question, an egregious example of the regional bias of the nation's media.

But besides that, the man is *really* good. His unflagging enthusiasm, his love of the game and his intense focus and involvement in every detail of the contest make every inning enjoyable, no matter what the score or the pace of the game. His humor, his affection for language and his vibrant images are the tools of a craftsman; only Garagiola, his one-time protégé, can match him in this way. He is criticized for not being objective, which is preposterous; he is the most objective baseball announcer I've ever witnessed. He is criticized for being "critical" of the players, when in fact Harry will bend over backwards to avoid saying something negative about a player or a manager. But Harry also knows that he does the fans no service when he closes his eyes and pretends not to see things. A player misses the cut-off man, Harry says that he missed the cut-off man, the player complains to the press, and some sweat-licking journalist, trying to ingratiate himself to a potential source, rips Harry for being critical of the player.

Harry is involved in another controversy now over the firing of Milo Hamilton, onetime heir apparent to Jack Brickhouse. Hamilton as a broadcaster is a model of professionalism, fluency, and deportment; he is, in short, as interesting as the weather channel, to which I would frequently dial while he was on. Milo's skills would serve him well as a lawyer, an executive or a broker. He broadcasts baseball games in a tone that would be more appropriate for a man reviewing a loan application. He projects no sense that he is enjoying the game or that we ought to be, and I frankly find it difficult to believe that the writers who ripped the Cubs for firing Hamilton actually watch the broadcasts. Is Harry to be faulted because the fans love him and find Hamilton a dry substitute?

People confuse "objectivity" with "neutralism." If you look up "neutral" in the dictionary it says "of no particular kind, color, characteristics, etc.; indefinite. Gray; without hue; of zero chrome; achromatic. Neuter." That pretty well describes Milo Hamilton. To Harry Caray, the greatest sports broadcaster who ever lived. This Bud's for you.

—1985

Pat Corrales

When I began the *Baseball Abstract* in 1977, my position was that I would not criticize baseball managers. Managers, I reasoned, were professional men. They had seen a lot more baseball games than I had. There was no reason why a team would hire an imbecile to run the show, and therefore it must be assumed that they were not imbeciles. If I were to criticize a baseball manager, why would an interested third party believe that I knew what I was talking about, rather than the manager? Better to remove the discussion to the more impersonal realm of strategies and tactics and definite, quantifiable truths than to join the journalists in discussing individuals. The thing to do with a manager was to try to listen to him and learn from him; better to be a student at his feet than a pygmy at his heels.

And then there was Don Zimmer. . . .

This position has gradually eroded over the years, not entirely of my own choosing. Evaluating managers—evaluating anybody, for that matter—is something that the people who run magazines and talk shows and morning editions are always after you to do. My view of it is that by piling up mountains of facts, making pile after pile of absolutely true, verifiable statements, one builds a little respect in the public's eye, that when you say something people will believe that you know what you're talking about. That respect is the currency by which I live. When I indulge in criticism of managers, I am spending that currency. And editors and talk show hosts . . . well, the more of it you spend with them the happier they are.

Perhaps, sometimes, I have spent that currency a little foolishly, and will have no one but myself to blame if the public stops believing anything I say. I regret, in particular, an evaluation of Pat Corrales as a manager that appeared in an article in *Sport* magazine last summer. The evaluation said, I think, "D+; has the personality of a doberman pinscher; would be more effective if he were more knowledgeable." That isn't actually what I wrote; what I wrote was funnier than that, but *Sport* was afraid that Corrales would sue them if they printed it. I will respect the advice of their lawyer.

Anyway, Corrales is now under fire for his handling of the Phillies in a pennant race, and I find myself, to my surprise, leaning in the direction of his corner. I simply cannot look at the Philadelphia Phillies of 1982 and see a better team than Corrales got out of them. His managerial performance in Texas looks a lot better when contrasted with the job that Don Zimmer did than it looked when we had only the performance of that team under Billy Hunter to compare it with. I am far from convinced that Corrales is a good manager, but I am not convinced that he isn't, either.

My position with respect to managers now is that I recognize fully that there are many things that they must be able to do that I don't know a thing about. I couldn't begin to help a hitter with his batting stroke. I couldn't teach fundamentals. I couldn't . . . well, a million things. But between what a manager does for a living and what I do for a living there are certain overlapping areas. It would be silly and false to assume the pretense that the managers, being professional men, know more about all of those things than I do. I work too hard for that. I hope, with those areas of overlapping knowledge, to be able to explain to the public what some of the differences are, what this manager does differently from that one. And I can't resist firing off an opinion now and then; I'm an argumentative SOB by nature.

—1983

Jim Davenport

It was generally felt, in the Bay Area, that Jim Davenport was a good baseball man but not a particularly good baseball manager. Specifically, many people felt that Davenport had more than the usual amount of trouble with such things as selecting the right lineup, knowing when to bunt, when to pinch hit, when to send runners and where to put the infield. Davenport had limited managerial experience—three years in the minors, a long time ago—and it is not especially surprising that he should have some trouble here.

I thought, in connection with this, how odd it is that a baseball manager should be at a disadvantage to his fans on issues such as these, how completely unnecessary it is for a manager to arrive at the major league level unprepared in this respect, when there is available a perfect tool to educate a manager in these things. I refer, of course, to table games like APBA and Strat-O-Matic. In many other professions, simulations are much prized as educational tools; a major airline would never think of sending a pilot up with the lives of passengers in his hands unless he had pulled a few dozen planes out of simulated crashes. And what is an APBA game, anyway? Why, it is a simulation of a manager's job, nothing more or less.

And from playing one of these games, any competent table manager would know that if you bat a guy with a .287 on base percentage in the second slot, you're going to lose runs, there being no way that you can add enough runs by moving base runners to compensate for the ones the number two hitter himself doesn't score. Any table game manager could make a good instinctive guess about when to issue an intentional walk, how likely it is to blow up on you.

Why is it, then, that an inexperienced manager is not simply instructed to manage his team through a thousand or so games of table baseball before he really takes the field, just to get the feel of what works and what doesn't?

Because those games are for *fans*, that's why. We're *professionals*, you know; we don't have anything to learn from these *fans*.

In *Good Enough to Dream*, Roger Kahn reports on his minor-league manager who says, whenever confronted with the notion that there may be a better way to do things, "You always think you know baseball. *I* know baseball. *I'm* the manager." Baseball is something that everybody has an opinion about, and so it develops that to baseball men the distinction between professional and fan is blinding, obliterating all other distinctions. Professionalism is the sun around which all baseball knowledge must revolve.

I know that if I proposed this table-game theory to any general manager, I would probably get a lecture on the differences between managing the table game and managing the real team. In the table games, players' levels are fixed; they don't fall into slumps. They don't have pitchers who have the whammy on them, or pitchers that they can tear apart. Pitchers in table games lose their stuff at known and predictable stages of the game; in the real game they may lose it gradually or suddenly. In the table game pitchers can be brought into the game without being warmed up. In the table game, players are not going to quit on you if they don't like the way they're being used.

Of course, all of that is true and much more. The table game teaches only the course, and not the winds. But is it an argument against using the table game to teach those things which it can teach? Isn't it a better argument that a major league manager should be so thoroughly grilled in the normal percentages, the normal "course," that he can navigate through the normal case blindly, and thus free his mind in a real game to concentrate on the complicating factors? Couldn't a general manager say, "Look, I don't want my manager sitting there trying to figure out what the percentages are. I want him to *know* what the percentages are like he was born with them. Then he'll be able to clean his mind out and work on those subtler things that complicate the game on the field."

Of course, you wouldn't ask Earl Weaver, who managed in the minor leagues for twelve years, to go play a few hundred games of APBA—or then again, maybe you might, just to learn his team. An airline doesn't assume that because you've got a thousand hours in a twin-engine Cessna you don't need to do the simulator before getting into a DC-9. But I know that I've seen major league managers who would finish sixth in a good table league. That seems to me an unnecessary price to pay for defending one's professional status. A command of the percentages is not the whole job—but one would think it was one of the prerequisites.

—1986

Jim Frey

Jim Frey's handling of his three catchers (Wathan, Grote, and Quirk) ranks somewhere between "maladroit" and "lunatic." Rarely does a manager have such an abundance of options. The three men all do different things. Frey could have platooned Wathan, a right-handed, and Quirk, a lefty. That would have given most of the at bats to Quirk, and Wathan is probably a notch ahead of him, so he could have used Wathan full-time in Kansas City, where his speed and line-drive hitting are most valuable, and platooned them on the road, where Quirk could make some use of his power. Or he could have used Wathan full-time against good base-stealing teams, as Wathan can get the ball to second better than the other two, and then platooned against teams which didn't run as much. After Hurdle's injury, he could have sent Wathan to right field to clear up that mess and platooned Quirk and Grote. One option that I particularly like would have been to assign the veteran Grote, who worked with the young Tom Seaver and Nolan Ryan, to work full-time with Rich Gale, who has a great arm but desperately needs direction. Grote could catch Gale and work with him between starts; Wathan could catch Gura, who likes to work with Wathan, and otherwise platoon Wathan and Quirk. This would reduce Quirk's defensive responsibilities to receiving Splittorff and Leonard, who are the two easiest pitchers on the team to catch. Or he could have platooned Wathan and Quirk, but switched to Wathan on defense after the fifth any time he had a lead. Or he could have made Wathan the regular except when facing a right-handed pitcher in a left-hander's park (New York or Detroit) or a park which emphasizes the home run. Or he could have simply chosen a regular. Or he could have combined these strategies in a limitless variety of ways.

You know what he did? Nothing. He never did make a

decision. Whoever had had the last hit was his regular catcher. Any of these options would have maximized strengths and concealed weaknesses. Frey would have Jamie Quirk catching against a left-handed pitcher in a poor HR park against a running team, thus forcing Quirk to do everything he could not do and denying him the chance to do what he could. He would have Larry Gura trying to lead Grote through his complex guessing game when the only man in the world who can think with Gura, John Wathan, was in right field. None of them knew what his job was, what he was expected to do, when he would play again or who he would be catching. None of them knew what his pitcher was trying to do. All of them were degenerating defensively as the season wore on.

Frey was in a classic situation in which *any* decision is better than *no* decision. He made the wrong choice. He couldn't decide.

—1982

If God had intended for this to be a logical universe he would never have entrusted Jim Frey with a baseball team.

—1988

Calvin Griffith

A friend of mine last fall offered to bet me $100 that I wouldn't be able to write one hundred words about the Minnesota Twins. I didn't take him up on it. The Minnesota Twins at this moment consist of a group of players who are either new to the major league scene, and hence devoid of history and functional description, or so bad that to say anything at all about them other than that they are bad would be to risk being ludicrous. I do not believe in saying things which are obvious or generally known, and the shortcomings of the Twins' organization which are obvious and which are generally understood are of a nature and size that crushes all other truths. How can I write about the subtle nuances of failure in a situation like this? It would be like reporting on a hotel fire and writing about the damage to the wallpaper. What is the point in talking about the characteristics of Minnesota's organization over the years when everyone associated with what the Twins did in better days has run for cover? How about writing about Billy Gardner as a manager? Sure.

The only thing about the Twins which seems to be really remarkable is the extent to which Calvin Griffith is able to shut out reality and continue to put out self-congratulatory BS in the face of the most stark realities. Calvin loves to tell reporters how good he is at dealing with player agents. "They come around here with their average-salary business, they try to tell me that so-and-so is the average salary for third basemen, I won't listen to it. I tell them, 'Yeah, but in there you've got Mike Schmidt and he's getting so much, and you've got George Brett and he's getting this much.' They're not putting that stuff over on me." Oh no, nobody's putting anything over on Calvin. Of course, he *has* lost a ballplayer or two. "I take pride in the fact that we run an efficient organization," he loves to say. What the hell is so efficient about getting your brains beat out? It's like running out of gas in the middle of a desert and congratulating yourself because you were getting forty miles to the gallon. "I'm the only businessman left in the game," he will tell you. "I don't have a lot of money to throw around like some of these guys. I've got to try to make a living off the game." Well, Calvin, if you're such a damn good businessman and Steinbrenner isn't, then how come you're losing money and he's making it? Somehow I thought it was supposed to be the other way around. Not all businessmen look exactly alike, you know. What you really are, Calvin—somebody should have explained this to you before—is not a businessman; you're the north end of a southbound Brontosaurus. And the best thing you could possibly do for the rest of us, if you wouldn't mind, is to quit your living sermon on the virtues of being miserable, and go quietly about the business of becoming extinct.

—From the 1982 *Baseball Abstract.*

The memory of Calvin Griffith has undergone a remarkable transformation in the years since he has relinquished control of the team. Griffith, generally seen while active as an unholy combination of buffoon, tyrant and racist, has emerged in retirement as a kindly father figure to Minnesota baseball, revered as one of the last links to an era of professional sports on a human scale and yet also respected for his keen baseball acumen. I don't know quite what to make of this singular passage, other than to observe that there is probably almost as much truth in one view as in the other. The romanticization of Griffith results from the habits of mind that lead to the glorification aspects of the past in other ways. Whenever people tell me that they wish they had lived in the eighteenth century, I always want to ask if they would particularly have enjoyed having their teeth pulled with pliers and no anesthetic. Griffith, like the past itself, is easy to admire so long as you don't actually have to deal with him.

Whitey Herzog

It was not a good year to be a Whitey Herzog fan. As the 1982 season, like a soft light on the face of an aging woman, brought out all of Whitey Herzog's strong points as a manager, the 1983 light glared down from over his head, and pointed accusingly to all of his shortcomings. The temptation is to say that he was not as good a manager as he appeared to be in 1982 and is not as bad as he appeared in 1983; the truth is more likely that he is every bit as good as he appeared in 1982, and better, and he is every bit as bad as he appeared in 1983, and worse.

The watershed of the season seems to be the Keith Hernandez trade, so let's talk about that a moment. If you look at the Keith Hernandez trade on the basis of the talents exchanged—Hernandez for Allen—then the trade doesn't seem to make a lot of sense. Allen is certainly a better pitcher than he seemed to be at the moment of the trade, but he doesn't look like MVP material, either. But if you look at the move as being representative of the things that Whitey Herzog believes in, as all moves present an image of the philosophy that guides them, then the trade makes perfect sense. Hernandez lacks the speed that Herzog values so highly, at least in Busch Stadium. Hernandez is a thirty-year-old ballplayer whose reputation was made four or five years ago; Whitey Herzog has always preferred to rest his fate with hungry ballplayers, with aggressive young men who play as if they had something to prove. But at any stage in his career, Hernandez simply never was one of the hustling, aggressive types of players that Herzog has always preferred to have. He doesn't challenge the defense on balls hit down the line; he won't run out ground balls if his manager doesn't insist on it. Most fans, many sportswriters, and a few managers can successfully turn a blind eye on that. Losing managers often insist that their teams are hustling when they very clearly are not. Herzog just isn't made that way.

If you were to sum up Whitey Herzog as a manager and as a man in one word, the word would have to be "aggressiveness." When he was rebuilding this ball club at the winter meetings in 1980 and 1981, his aggressiveness in making deals stunned a baseball community which had become so cautious that many had concluded that it was no longer possible to make big-name player deals. Most of the agents that I deal with can't stand Herzog because he is so aggressive in contract negotiations. When things stall, he won't hesitate to call up the player himself and lay it out for him, put pressure on him to make a decision. He can't stand for people to waste his time warming up; he wants them to get to the bottom line. He doesn't get involved in the negotiations to negotiate; he gets involved to settle things. He has no use for anyone or anything who is tentative, indecisive.

And on the field, he's exactly the same. The 1982 Cardinals played their average nine-inning game in two hours, twenty-two minutes, the fastest in the majors. Whitey does not want his pitchers out there nibbling at corners; he wants them to be aggressive, go after the hitters. His base runners are noted for their aggressiveness in asking for an additional base from time to time. In his first year as a manager, in 1973, he had Jeff Burroughs on the roster, whom Ted Williams had been trying to teach to be selective at the plate. Whitey didn't want that; he wanted Burroughs to be more aggressive at the plate. He made a wager with Burroughs, in which if Burroughs swung at a strike and missed he would pay him a dollar—but if Burroughs took a pitch in the strike zone, he owed Whitey a dollar. Burroughs had his first good year that year, hitting 30 home runs.

I have mixed feelings about all of that aggression; 1982 shows the good side of it, 1983 the bad side. Aggressiveness puts the pressure on the opposing defense—but it takes the pressure off the opposing pitching staff. The sequence begins with the ball in the pitcher's hand, and the pressure on him to throw a strike; an aggressive hitter sometimes too willingly takes that pressure on himself in an attempt to pass it on to the defense. Whitey will stay for a long time with a hitter whose aggressiveness at the plate is costing him runs; Willie McGee is one example, Frank White another. At the same time, Jeff Burroughs' walks might be valuable, but his career would almost certainly have been better than it has been if he had stayed a little more aggressive at the plate, instead of sitting back on his heels waiting for a pitch he liked. Whitey's base runners often make very poor percentage gambles, but over a period of time they learn what they can do and what they cannot do, who they can take advantage of and who they can't. They wind up being able to do more than they otherwise would have. A poor percentage move can still have positive psychological consequences, and Whitey's teams can get awfully hot in September.

—1984 *Baseball Abstract*

Obviously, Keith Hernandez in New York was a changed ballplayer. Stung by the events of 1980–83, Hernandez emerged as an alert, aggressive player which, combined with his native intelligence, made him a tremendous asset to the Mets for five years. The description of his play in St. Louis remains accurate.

Whitey Herzog may be baseball's most controversial manager, which is probably one of the reasons I feel drawn to the man; I've little use for your button-down company men in any area, and no use for them at all in sports. Whitey has strong opinions about almost everything, and fortunately lacks the good sense to keep them to himself. He got in trouble last summer because somebody asked him why he traded Keith Hernandez, and he told them.

In principle, the media admire candor. They celebrate this admiration by boiling the candid in the juices of their own indiscretions, until they learn to give appropriate responses like "Keith's always been a great player, but we were in a position where we had a young man on the bench that I thought was going to be outstanding, and at the same time we were desperate for pitching help. I guess I made a mistake, but

I've always had the greatest of admiration for Keith, and I'm glad he's been so terrific for the Mets.'' After all, Whitey *did* make a mistake there, and he might as well admit it.

—1985

Dick Howser

When condemned prisoners are being moved through the inmate population at San Quentin, the accompanying guards shout "Dead man coming through" to clear the walkways. The Kansas City Royals opened spring training with a dead man managing the team. One of the ways that sports contribute to society is by the creation of a community of interest, which can be a wonderful teaching vehicle. Through Len Bias and others, we have all learned something about the dangers of cocaine that we might never have learned through public education projects throwing out statistics and studies.

Through the experience of Dick Howser, we in the Kansas City area learned a great deal about brain tumors. There was no good news along the way. At first we were told that the big difference was between benign and malignant tumors. Dick's was malignant. Then we were told that there was a big difference between those tumors which were and those which were not deeply rooted. Dick's was deeply rooted. Then we were told that even among malignant tumors, there were four different grades of malignancy, from those which grew rapidly to those which hardly grew at all. There was no announcement about the grade of Howser's malignancy. They said there would be an announcement the next day, and then they said they'd decided not to divulge it. Anyone could interpret that. Although the Royals carried out a charade of hope for Howser's benefit, an experienced manager was on hand to step into the role when the inevitable could no longer be denied.

—1988

Ken Keltner

A committee has been established which begs us to examine the Hall of Fame credentials of a Cleveland Indians' star of forty years ago. I received three cards in my December mail, which from the outside could easily have been mistaken for Christmas cards from some near-forgotten ex-neighbor had not the name "Ken Keltner" appeared on the envelope. The first card was shaped like a bat, and said "We need you to go to bat [open card] for nominating KEN KELTNER to the National Baseball Hall of Fame." The card outlined Keltner's career batting accomplishments and informed us that he had more RBI than Jackie Robinson, a higher lifetime average than Eddie Mathews and more lifetime hits than Ralph Kiner, plus he hit "the home run that helped to win the 1948 American League Pennant." It bore the printed signatures of The Party to Put Ken Keltner in Cooperstown—Lou Boudreau, Bob Lemon, Paul Schramka, Bud Selig, and Warren Spahn. It accomplished this in just 142 words, which is several less than are used in this paragraph.

The second card was shaped like a ball, and it said "We're making a pitch to you [open card] to nominate KEN KELTNER to the National Baseball Hall of Fame." This card briefly recounted Ken Keltner's fielding accomplishments, and reminded us that he was the player who "examined the stitches on the ball before firing to first." It was signed by Lou Boudreau, Bob Lemon, Paul Schramka, Bud Selig, and Warren Spahn, and used even fewer words than the first.

The third card was shaped like a glove and said "We hope you've caught our message [open card] because KEN KELTNER belongs in the National Baseball Hall of Fame." This card recounted the highlights of the previous two cards, and bore the signatures of Lou Boudreau, Bob Lemon, Paul Schramka, Bud Selig, and Warren Spahn.

I don't know how I got on these people's mailing list, but I like it. Flattered as I am by the implication that someone with a Hall of Fame vote might actually pay attention to something that I wrote, the issue of whether or not a player belongs in the Hall of Fame is one of the questions that I have always had some trouble discussing. There's a long article on the subject in the historical book, but the gist of the problem is that I can follow the logic of the discussion only this far:

Q. What is a Hall of Famer?
A. A Hall of Famer is a player of the quality usually elected to the Hall of Fame.
Q. What is the quality of player who is usually elected to the Hall of Fame?
A. It all depends.

It all depends on a lot of things—the committee that is doing the selecting, the era in which the player played, and whether or not the player has died recently. Among the eligible electors and boards, there is no generally accepted functional definition of what a Hall of Famer is; outside of those discussions, there are no written guidelines. The longer article proposes some alternative definitions of what a Hall of Famer should be, and uses those in the course of discussing the credentials of several hundred former players.

Ken Keltner, I missed. Keltner was the third baseman for the Cleveland Indians in the late thirties and forties. He was a good player; of this there can be no doubt. He played in seven All-Star games and was one of the stars of the 1948 Indian infield that some regard as the greatest infield ever. His two defensive gems on July 17, 1941 interrupted Joe DiMaggio's hitting streak after fifty-six games.

The logic of the argument proposed by the PTPKKIC is, as the logic of advertising tends to be, almost comic in its transparency. The comparison to Jackie Robinson's RBI count is an obvious red herring, since Jackie Robinson is not in the Hall of Fame because of his credentials as an RBI man; likewise, Eddie Mathews is not a Hall of Famer because of his career batting average, and Ralph Kiner is not in because of his career hit total. By the same logic, one could argue that Walt (No Neck) Williams should be in the Hall of Fame because he hit more home runs than Rabbit Maranville, stole more bases than Harmon Killebrew and hit for a higher average than Luis Aparicio. That Eddie Mathews' career batting average was only .271 has absolutely nothing to do with the question of whether or not Ken Keltner should be in the Hall of Fame.

But what does? In the absence of any better direction, what

I recommend is a kind of common-sense approach, based on finding the answers to a list of fairly simple questions, no one of which is the fine line separating in from out, but the answering of which is useful for clarifying where the player stands. Among the questions that I would suggest are these:

1. Was he ever regarded as the best player in baseball? Did anybody, while he was active, ever suggest that he was the best player in baseball?
2. Was he the best player on his team?
3. Was he the best player in baseball at his position?
4. Did he have an impact on a number of pennant races?
5. Was he a good enough player that he could continue to play regularly after passing his prime?
6. Was he the best player in the league at his position?
7. Is he the very best player in baseball history who is not in the Hall of Fame?
8. Are most of the players who have comparable career stats in the Hall of Fame?
9. Is there any evidence to suggest that the player was significantly better or worse than is suggested by his statistics?
10. Is he the best player *at his position* who is eligible for the Hall of Fame but not in?
11. How many MVP-type seasons did he have? Did he ever win an MVP Award? If not, how many times was he close?
12. How many All-Star-type seasons did he have? How many All-Star games did he play in? Did most of the other players who played in this many go into the Hall of Fame?
13. If this man were the best player on his team, would it be likely that the team could win the pennant?

A similar concern, which I won't list because it is too hard to answer objectively, is "Was the guy really famous?" That seems to me to be a minimal consideration for the Hall of Fame —that the guy have a degree of fame. That's one thing you have to say for Don Drysdale: The man was famous. When I became aware of baseball in my youth, Drysdale had neither won nor seriously threatened the standard of twenty wins a season—yet he was one of the best-known players in the game.

None of these questions is unanimously accepted as a criterion of Hall of Fame selection, and I'm not suggesting that it should be. I am suggesting that the questions here are a hell of a lot more germane to the issue than "Did the guy have more hits than Ralph Kiner?" If you review this set of questions for a player of the calibre of Mantle, Mays, Schmidt, or Dale Murphy, you'll find that almost every answer is positive. It seems to me that if a man doesn't meet any of the standards outlined here, you've got to ask yourself why you are considering putting him in the Hall of Fame. Let's look at Keltner's qualifications:

1. *Was he ever regarded as the best player in baseball? Did anybody, while he was active, ever suggest that he was the best player in baseball?*

    A tough standard, but the answer, obviously, is no; nobody ever suggested that Keltner was a better player than Musial, DiMaggio, Williams, *et al.*

2. *Was he the best player on his team?*

    Obviously not, no; the best players on the Cleveland team at the time of Keltner's peak were Bob Feller and Lou Boudreau. Keltner was one of the players who would have vied for the spot as the number three star on the team, along with (at various times) Jeff Heath, Joe Gordon, Bob Lemon and Mel Harder.

3. *Was he the best player in baseball at his position?*

    There's an easy way to answer that. *The Sporting News* polls the nation's sportswriters and selects the best players at each position every year, and has done so since the 1920s. While these votes, of course, are not perfect, they provide an objective record of what is seen and thought about the player's ability while he is active; if the player's defensive skills or clutch performance or leadership qualities are outstanding enough to cause him to rate higher than his statistics show, these are the people who are in a position to know that.

    The writers selecting that team never considered Keltner to be the best third baseman in the major leagues, not even once, not even in his best year. The third basemen who were selected in the years 1938–50 were Red Rolfe (1938–39), Stan Hack (1940–42), Billy Johnson (1943), Bob Elliot (1944, 1948), Whitey Kurowski (1945; Keltner was in the service) and George Kell (1946–47, '49, and '50).

4. *Did he have an impact on a number of pennant races?*

Keltner had an enormous impact on the pennant race in 1948, when he had his best season (.297, 31 homers, 119 RBIs), and hit a home run and a double, driving in three runs to help the Indians win the playoff game (8–3) after the race ended in a tie. One must conclude that without Keltner, the Indians would not have won the pennant in 1948.

With the exception of that one season, it would be difficult to say that he ever had a positive impact on the pennant race. The only other seasons in which the team that Keltner was on finished closer than 13½ out were 1940, 1949 and 1950. In 1940, when the Indians lost the race by one game, Keltner had one of his poorest seasons, hitting just .254 with 15 home runs, and the Indians lost the race by one game. By 1949 he was finished.

5. *Was he a good enough player that he could continue to play regularly after passing his prime?*

He didn't, anyway. He was finished at thirty-two.

6. *Was he the best player in the league at his position?*

In 1948 he was, and during the war years he was; otherwise he was not. Keltner played in the All-Star games in 1940 and 1941 as a late-inning replacement for Cecil Travis, a career .314 hitter. When Travis went into the service in 1942, Keltner was probably the best third baseman left in the league.

7. *Is he the very best player in baseball history who is not in the Hall of Fame?*

Again, that's a tough standard, but obviously, he wasn't. He can't be rated with guys like Slaughter, Ed McKean, Herman Long, Pete Browning, Billy Williams, Jim Bunning, and Thurman Munson. I would also suggest that several of his contemporaries, including Joe Gordon, Bobby Doerr, and Hal Newhouser, would have to be rated ahead of him.

8. *Are most of the players who have comparable career stats in the Hall of Fame?*

Using the method called similarity scores, the ten players most comparable to Ken Keltner in terms of offensive production and defensive position are 1) Harlond Clift, 2) Doug DeCinces, 3) Richie Hebner, 4) Pinkie Whitney, 5) Don Money, 6) Willie Jones, 7) Frank Malzone, 8) Tony Cuccinello, 9) Travis Jackson, and 10) Red Kress. One of the ten comparable players (Travis Jackson) is in the Hall of Fame; the other nine are not.

9. *If not, is there any evidence to suggest that the player was significantly better or worse than is suggested by his statistics?*

There are two good reasons to say that Keltner was a better player than his offensive statistics show. First, he was by reputation a fine defensive player, which is substantiated by his defensive statistics. His defensive statistics are probably the best of any third baseman of the 1940s. It is unfortunate that there were no Gold Glove awards given at the time, but on the basis of what I know I am willing to consider Keltner to have been the American League's Gold Glove third baseman from 1939 to 1943. (After George Kell came up, I'm not so sure.)

Second, the ratio of Keltner's RBIs to his other batting stats is quite good—one could even say unusually good.

On the other hand, one must remember that, in playing defense or having other outside-the-books advantages, Keltner is hardly unique. The same is true of many of the other players whose names have come up in this discussion or will do so. The best objective test of the impact that these things had on those who saw him play is the player's performance in contemporary award voting, such as the annual votes for *The Sporting News* All-Star team and the MVP Award.

10. *Is he the best player at his position who is eligible for the Hall of Fame but not in?*

Ken Keltner's 1948 season was your basic Ron Santo year—.297 with 31 home runs and 119 RBIs. You can take the full statistical line for that year (89 walks, .969 fielding percentage, 312 assists) and stick it in the middle of Ron Santo's career, and nobody would guess that it didn't belong. To a lesser extent, the same is also true of Keltner's other best seasons, 1938 and 1941.

But in the context of Keltner's career, the 1948 season does stick out; Keltner never had another year of anything like the same quality. The 1938 and 1941 seasons, excellent years for Keltner, would have been somewhat subpar for Santo in his prime.

Defense? Ron Santo won five Gold Glove awards.

One of the reasons that is proposed for Santo's failure to draw support as a Hall of Fame candidate was that his batting stats were inflated by playing in Wrigley Field—and that is absolutely true. They were. Santo hit 216 home runs in his home parks, "only" 126 on the road. Yet even Santo's "road" total *by itself*, is almost as high as Keltner's career home run total.

I see no logical alternative but to conclude that Santo was a better player than Keltner, and the same argument applies to Ken Boyer; Ken Keltner's 1948 season fits in with Boyer's career a whole lot better than it fits into Keltner's, and Boyer also won five Gold Glove awards. And what about all the people who were regarded, while Keltner was active, as the outstanding third basemen in the major leagues (that is, the people who kept him off *The Sporting News* post-season All-Star team)? What about Stan Hack, whose career batting stats are far better than Keltner's, and who hit .348 in four World Series, and who had a much greater impact on pennant races? What about Bob Elliott, who did win an MVP award? I think that if you go down the list of these questions for Bob Elliott, you're going to turn up a surprising number of "yes" answers.

I would have to rate at least a half-dozen other third basemen ahead of Keltner in Cooperstown's line—including Santo, Boyer, Elliott, Hack, Clift, Bando, and possibly Cecil Travis.

11. *How many MVP-type seasons did he have? Did he ever win an MVP Award? If not, how many times was he close?*

Keltner never won an MVP award; in fact, he never finished in the top ten in the voting. His best performance in MVP voting was in 1939, when he finished twelfth.

12. *How many All-Star-type seasons did he have? How many All-Star games did he play in? Did most of the other players who played in this many go into the Hall of Fame?*

Keltner played in seven All-Star games, which is one of his strongest credentials. He started the All-Star games in 1942, 1943, 1944, and 1948; he was a late-inning sub on three other occasions.

Excluding pitchers, players who were in mid-career when the All-Star games began, and players who played in multiple All-Star games in one year, there are twenty-five players who played in six to eight All-Star games. Five of those twenty-five are in the Hall of Fame—George Kell, Roy Campanella, Pee Wee Reese, Jackie Robinson, and Duke Snider. The other twenty are not.

13. *If this man were the best player on his team, would it be likely that the team could win the pennant?*

Again, this one requires a degree of subjective judgment, but I would say that if Ken Keltner were the best player on a team it would be almost impossible for that team to win a pennant. I would also submit that it would be very difficult to name a pennant-winning team whose best player was not demonstrably better than Ken Keltner.

The gentlemen who are running the campaign to put Keltner in the Hall of Fame (Lou Boudreau, Bob Lemon, Paul Schramka, Bud Selig, and Warren Spahn) are unquestionably well-meaning and probably well informed in their own way. The roots of their effort, one suspects, are in the best of human traits: in kindness, in generosity and friendship. If these virtues were married to better arguments, it would give me great pleasure to join in the effort.

But do we wish, in kindness, in generosity, in friendship, to put the third-best player on an also-ran team in the Hall of Fame? A judge in deciding a landmark case must deal not only with the good and bad that will come of his decision, but with the ultimate consequences of the legal theory that is established. In the fight for access to the Hall of Fame, every decision becomes a landmark. If the judges of baseball immortality accept the legal theories which would qualify Ken Keltner, they must face the fact that those same theories would qualify a thousand or more players. If a thousand players are in the Hall of Fame, there will not be a schoolboy alive who can tick off the names of the Hall of Fame third basemen. And will the Hall of Fame then be what it is?

—1985

Bob Lemon

Like a great work of literature, it can only be fully appreciated with the benefit of hindsight. As Bob Lemon is let out to pasture, let it be noted that in 1977, Bob Lemon won ninety games with this lineup:

1B   Jim Spencer
2B   Jorge Orta
3B   Eric Soderholm
SS   Alan Bannister
LF   Ralph Garr
CF   Chet Lemon
RF   Richie Zisk
C   Jim Essian
DH Oscar Gamble

His starting rotation was Francisco Barrios, Steve Stone, Ken Kravec, and Chris Knapp. His relief ace was Lerrin LaGrow.

How? He had a bad infield, a bad outfield, an awful starting rotation and Jim Essian at catcher. Kravec had the best ERA of any starter, 4.10. The team finished last in the league in double plays, first in errors, and last in stolen bases. The pitching staff threw three shutouts. It had to be one of the best managerial accomplishments of the decade.

Lemon also brought the Royals in in 1971 at 85–76 with a team prominently featuring Gail Hopkins, Paul Schaal, Joe Keough, Jerry May, Bob Oliver and Ed Kirkpatrick. His top home-run hitter that year hit fifteen, and only one other player was in double figures. The only starters to win more than eight games were Dick Drago and Mike Hedlund. The more you look at these accomplishments, the more remarkable they seem.

—1983

Denny Matthews

Among the pleasures of being a Royals fan, few rank any higher than turning on the radio each evening to receive the seven o'clock greeting of Mr. Denny Matthews. My goal about each team is to try to bring to light something about the team which is not generally known. After years of post-season play with basically the same team, not much about the Royals has slipped through the network of the country's information services. But behind their microphone, all but unknown to the nation, sits one of the most skilled and gifted men that the craft has ever produced.

His gifts, I suppose, are moderate, if well adapted to the task. His voice has a pleasant timbre which suggests a cheerful occasion. Its natural inflection rises and falls constantly, so that over the course of countless hours it acquires neither the grating quality of forced enthusiasm nor the drone of forced interest. He has a dry, understated humor that drifts through much of his audience undetected. One cannot learn these things at a microphone; they are given. But heck, I talk to people with pleasant voices every day, and Denny isn't Bob Uecker, by any means. These are not the things that lift him out of the class of the competent announcers, and into the class of the great ones.

Fred White, the Royals' other announcer, is good too. But what are the acquired skills, I got to wondering, that make an announcer? If Denny and Fred are not quite paragons of the things a baseball announcer should be, they are an acceptable substitute. So what do they have, exactly?

1. (And by far the most important) An intense focus on the game that is being played in front of them. I score games some-times, even over the radio, and when I do I try to record a variety of information other than the stuff you can get out of the records. Sometimes I try to do this with other announcers, and I am amazed at the information they leave out. "Base hit!" says the announcer. Base hit? Where? Scooting by the short-stop into center? Drilled to left? I'll be listening to another game, and there will be runners on first and third in the fifth, and I will wonder if the manager is going to bring the infield in—and be astounded that the announcer doesn't tell me. There will be a single to center and I will be sitting there trying to visualize the play, and when I look for the throw . . . no throw. The voice has not told me where the throw went. I find out two pitches into the next batter that the other runner is now on third, and I wonder if the announcer didn't see him go over there, or what? The color man breaks in and tells you that the runner was able to get to third base because he was off with the pitch. Well, if he was off with the pitch, why didn't you tell me? This leaves me wondering if he was off with the pitch the previous two times, when the ball was fouled off.

And you know why so many announcers don't tell you

these things? *Because they don't see them.* Because they haven't ever learned, really, to become the eyes of the listener. I was just amazed, in the World Series, when an announcer told us that Darrell Porter's batting stance "looks a lot like Rod Carew's." Darrell Porter's tense, pigeon-toed, cocked-arm, locked-wrist stance like Rod Carew's pointed lead foot, loose wrist, relaxed batting style? They have open stances and they crouch a little and they point the bat in the air. That's the end of the similarities. I saw an American League rookie do an absolutely perfect impression of Rickey Henderson at the plate last summer and the announcer's comment was "Hmm. Funny-looking batting stance."

Denny Matthews tells you, batter after batter

1. What the pitch was.
2. Where the pitch was.
3. What kind of a swing the batter had at it (fought it off, flicked at it, tried to hold up, had a good rip but swung over it).
4. Where the defense is.
5. What the runner does.
6. Where the hit goes.
7. Where the throw goes.

If the wind is blowing in, he tells you; if it shifts, you hear about it. He describes the batting stance of each player, in very specific terms as well as the impression it gives, once each year. He describes the delivery of the pitcher in specific terms. If the throw to first was a low throw or a high throw or a wide throw or a good throw, he tells you. If the fielder fields the ball on the second hop or the third hop, on a high hop or a short hop, to his left or to his right, he tells you. If the batter breaks his bat, if he squirts the ball off the end of the bat, he tells you. In the batter's first at-bat, he tells you what the batter has done in the last few games; after that, he tells you what the hitter has done earlier in the game. After a while, you get used to knowing stuff like that.

There is one thing that happens about once a week that tips you off on how intense Mr. Matthews' concentration on the game is. What does your announcer say when the scoreboard count gets mixed up? Does he never notice it, and just read the count off the board? Does he say, "Now wait a minute . . . I thought the third pitch was called a strike." Does he debate the color man about what the count was? Denny dismisses it with a six-word phrase: The scoreboard has the count wrong.

2. The other main thing that I like about Denny is the things he *doesn't* say because he is too busy describing what he sees. Let's go back to the first-and-third situation where the announcer doesn't tell us what happened. What is he saying, while he is not telling us where the hit went and where the runner went and where the throw went? The worst announcers, and you know they do it, will launch into a sermonette about a) the character of the man who got the hit, or b) the bad run of luck we've been having lately, how we're in one of these stretches when balls like that that aren't really hit that well just fall in between the fielders. The competent announcers tell you what they see, and then break into generalities about the people involved in the play, and talk about "concentration" and "fundamentals" and stuff.

Some people actually criticize Matthews because he's not judgmental about what he sees. They want the announcer to tell them that Ron LeFlore has a bad arm, and Denny will tell them that the throw was off-line and then move on. But what is an announcer doing, when he makes those sort of judgments? My view is, if the announcer sees the man make a poor throw, he should say so at the time; if he doesn't see it, he shouldn't be talking about it. I don't want an announcer passing on to me the stuff he heard in a bar last week. I don't want to know what some scout said about the guy's arm. I can make those judgments for myself; indeed, I prefer to. That's all right if the announcer knows what he's talking about, but two times in three he doesn't.

3. Denny works consciously against the pace of the game. If the game is dull, he starts giving you more and more information about the game, the players. When the game is on the line, he lets the situation speak for itself. If it's a blowout, he starts telling stories.

Nobody's perfect. He moans a lot about the length of the games and how slow the pitcher is working, and I wish he'd shut up about it. A lot of the fans complain about his giving meaningless stats, and I think sometimes that the stats he gives are not always meaningful (but then again, he doesn't state them in a way that makes that judgment for you). But he works hard at his craft; he truly loves the game. He gets his ego and his theories and his preconceptions out of the way, and becomes a tube through which the game splashes out into your room, pure and clean and complete. That's too easy for most announcers, and too hard.

—1983

—1983 *Baseball Abstract.*

As good as I thought Denny Matthews was at that time, I must say that he has improved markedly in the last six years. After I commented that Denny moaned about the length of the games too much, he stopped doing that. As he has become more comfortable in his job, Matthews has become more willing to use his humor. Fred White is a pretty funny guy, too, and when the Royals are out of the pennant race (which seems to happen earlier each year) they really cut loose. The last month of the season will involve several games which are considerably funnier than an average edition of The Tonight Show.

Gene Mauch

The difference between Gene Mauch and Earl Weaver is that Earl Weaver believes in platooning as a strategy and Gene Mauch believes in platooning as a religion . . . .

—Esquire magazine
April, 1981

Gene Mauch had a beautiful line last fall when somebody asked him if he wouldn't almost have been happier losing than having to face all those questions about what does it feel like after all these years. Gene didn't like that question either, so he snapped, "Nobody in this room is smart enough to analyze me." Nobody in the world is smart enough to figure out why Gene Mauch does some of the things he does, including Gene Mauch.

Mauch has been managing in the major leagues long enough to have become a legend in his own time. He hasn't become one, of course, but he's been managing that long. You want to know how long Gene Mauch has been managing in the major leagues, consider this: Alvin Dark played for him. Mauch might have become a legend—he certainly had the personality for it—if only he had won a little more often.

But, as I am so fond of saying, records are only meaningful in the context in which they are compiled, and that is no less true for Gene Mauch's wins and losses than it is for Bob Horner's home run rates or Pete Vuckovich's wins and losses. And in the context in which it has come, Gene Mauch's record ain't half bad.

Mauch took over a terrible team in Philadelphia, and had them in contention in three years; he left and the team was as bad as ever. That is a fact. His record in Montreal is far better than the normal performance of an expansion team. That is a fact. That he is under .500 lifetime as a manager, that he went twenty years without winning anything . . . these are also facts. But that he should have done this in 1964 or that he should have won so many games in 1977; these are only opinions.

And I have my opinion, too. Gene Mauch's problem, in short, is that he has taken over too many challenges and not enough ball clubs. Mauch's reputation as a manager, and even as a managerial prospect before he was a manager, was good enough to have given him some choice in which jobs he took. Mauch was either too impatient to wait for a good job to be offered, or too arrogant to realize that even *he* could not lift a bad team single-handedly all the way over the pack. But there never was anybody in the room who was smart enough to tell him that.

A bad manager? Not at all; a good judge of talent, an excellent psychologist and motivator, a fine handler of pitchers who built generally superb bullpens, an intense and capable in-game strategist who worked too hard on that phase of the job, and did not always respect its limitations. A master of details, a master of small things. He may have analyzed ball games somewhat better than he analyzed pennant races. I am a little sad to see him depart the scene without one of those rings on his finger. For his arrogance, he paid with his reputation.

—1983

Gene Mauch in 1985 turned in the archetypical Gene Mauch season. Mauch, the only remaining major league skipper who

managed Elmer Valo, took over a team which in the previous
two seasons had finished twenty-two games under .500, and,
through his extraordinary short-sightedness, poor judgment,
and compulsive over-managing, prevented them from winning
the World's Championship. That, at least, is the story of the
season as it seemed destined to be written before *Sports Illustrated,* in its October 7, 1985 issue, rose to the level of journal-
istic nobility. In a fine article by Ron Fimrite, *SI* wrote that
"once again, as he has so relentlessly in the past, Mauch is
flogging an under-manned and over-matched team to exceed
itself in a pennant race."

The magazine speaks for no one but Time Inc., but they do
occupy a unique position in sports journalism. In so writing,
Sports Illustrated issued public forgiveness to Gene Mauch for
his years of irritation and bitterness, and recognized what
seems to me to be the unavoidable fact of his failure to win a
pennant: The man has never had the horses. In response to
this there were the inevitable letters from Minnesota Twins
fans, and others, clinging to the more popular interpretation of
the 1977 season: Gene Mauch failed to win the pennant in
1977 even though he had the league's Most Valuable Player,
the league's two leading hitters, in Rod Carew (.388) and
Lyman Bostock (.336) and the league's leading RBI man in
Larry Hisle. It hardly seems worth pointing out that before
Gene Mauch came to Minnesota, the Minnesota fans had been
treated to several years of Rod Carew attempting not very successfully to play second base, in which effort he was frequently injured. Gene Mauch shifted the batting champion to
first base, where, able to stay in the lineup and concentrate on
his offense, Carew *became* the Most Valuable Player.

It hardly seems worth pointing this out, because anybody
who is interested in looking at such facts in their true context
probably already knows it. By the by, *Sports Illustrated* erred
in saying that the Twins, in strong contention in early September "lost 18 of 27 games to finish fourth, 7½ games behind
Kansas City." It was seventeen and a half, not seven and a half;
while the Twins were losing eighteen of twenty-seven, Kansas
City was turning in one of the greatest stretch runs in baseball
history, winning twenty-three of twenty-four at one point. The
Twins would not have won in 1977 even had they won 70
percent of their games in September and beaten the Royals in
their head-on matchups, a performance which would have

been pretty remarkable in view of the fact that they were working with a four-man pitching rotation of Dave Goltz, Paul Thor-
modsgaard, Pete Redfern, and Geoff Zahn.

—1986

John McNamara

McNamara is the father of the minimalist school of managing;
his forthcoming book on managerial strategy is sure to be entitled *Let Them Play and See What Happens.* It is appropriate
that the most controversial moment of his managerial career
came not when he made a move, but when he failed to make
one, failing to pinch run Dave Stapleton for Bill Buckner.

—1988

Frank Robinson

If you had never heard that the San Francisco manager had
once played and coached for Earl Weaver, you wouldn't have
to be too smart to figure it out. The signature of Earl Weaver is
written large and small all over this team.

First of all, I am, among sabermetricians, not an enthusiastic proponent of walks as an offensive weapon. I think that
players who walk a lot tend to be slump-prone. The runs-
created method, if used to rate hitters, will rate a player who
walks frequently lower than any other reasonably sophisticated offensive rating tool that I know of—lower than Barry
Codell's Base-Out Percentage, lower than Boswell's Total Average, lower than Thomas Cover's Offensive Earned Run Average, lower than Pete Palmer's OBA + SP (On Base Average
Plus Slugging Percentage). But the public at large doesn't even
seem to realize that records are kept of who walks how often,
or else thinks that it is just a sort of random result of being at
bat when a pitcher is stricken with control trouble. Given that,
it must often seem to the public that I am referring to the walk
column constantly, overrating all of the people who walk a lot
and underrating those who don't.

My view of walks as an offensive weapon is that I don't wish to be an advocate of any position on the subject at all, but. The immense defensive importance of walks is universally assumed. You listen to any game where one team issues four or more walks and loses, and I guarantee you that the announcer will cite the control troubles of the losing pitcher as one of the keys to his defeat (oh, those bases on balls). The fact that bases on balls have both an offensive and a defensive origin—that the batter can do every bit as much to put himself on base by that route as the pitcher can—is equally obvious, and is a fact that any analytical review of the game will constantly thrust upon you. To reach the conclusion that walks have an immense offensive importance is only a tiny logical step. Until the public learns to take that step by itself, it simply is not possible to make an intelligent review of the game without beginning the discussion with that step.

No manager has ever understood this better than Earl Weaver. Craig Wright has described isolated power and walks as the sabermetric virtues, a phrase with which I feel rather uncomfortable; I don't really want to be in the position of advocating one type of offense as opposed to another.

I prefer to think of them as the Earl Weaver virtues. Earl Weaver's teams rarely hit for a high batting average. Only one EW team ever led the league in batting average; usually they were below the league average. Several times, Weaver's teams had fewer hits in the season than did their opponents, and over the course of his career they exceeded their opponents in hits by only 5 percent. But every team that Earl Weaver managed in the major leagues drew more walks than did their opponents, an average of 24 percent more (not including Earl's ill-fated comeback in 1985.) This has both offensive and defensive components, of course. His hitters drew walks; his pitchers didn't issue them. All of Weaver's teams but one hit more home runs than their opponents, an average of 22 percent more.

The San Francisco Giants of 1982 were, down the line, an Earl Weaver team. The team was led by four ballplayers, three of them old, whose batting averages represented an unusually small part of their offensive value—Joe Morgan, Reggie Smith, Darrell Evans, and Jack Clark. They all walk a lot, they all have power; they are generally good percentage base stealers. And because of that the 1982 Giants were able to post a winning record despite being outhit by their opponents by a very substantial margin.

—1983

George Steinbrenner

My friend Randy Spence, who is an excellent chess player, once told me that each game of chess is like an intense, ferocious argument without words—an argument about how chess should be played. In the ledger of bad ideas of historical magnitude, enter now the name of George Steinbrenner, cited for his 1981 argument that the era of the home run was over, and that the Yankees were to become a slashing, speed-based team in tune with the 1980s. The chance that this would work was roughly equal to the chance that Ronald Reagan might elope with Joan Baez. All successful ball teams adjust to the design of their home park, and this park is not designed for speed. It is designed for left-handed power. And no Yankee team has ever won a pennant—not even once—without having that left-handed power, and a bunch of it. Throughout their history, the periods when they have not had left-handed power and the periods when they have not won coincide perfectly.

—1983

Susie

Each edition of the *Baseball Abstract* must be written, typed, figured, proofread, and sent on its way within a period of a few months, climaxing in two or three crushing and boggling weeks. No one person could or should do this alone, and my wife during this period kindly consents to become as crushed and boggled as I am, at which I am awed and grateful. I love my work at two o'clock in the afternoon, but it does get a bit tiresome at four A.M. morning after morning, and I've no idea how anyone else can endure it. But Susan McCarthy does, and at the heaviest moments finds new burdens to pick up.

—From the Acknowledgments, 1982 *Abstract*

I am still married to Susan McCarthy, who remains (you will be happy to hear the yearly update on this), who remains the best wife in the world. Yes, it's true; the computerized rankings were just released on Tuesday by the WWRS (World Wife-Rating Service), and Susie is ranked first again, edging out a Polynesian woman named Baktal á Sepatoli, whose husband was attacked by a shark while he was swimming, and who dived into the water and gave that shark wherefore and whathaveyou until the terrified fish gave back her husband's hand and agreed to pay all of his medical bills. This service is nothing compared to what Susie does for me—figures the catchers' stats, for example, and reads all the articles and makes corrections, and takes care of the details of life for the months known (we will not miss this expression) as the Abstract Crunch. Among husbands, by the way, I rated 912,474,384th, between a Yugoslavian alcoholic and a Jamaican guy who's been dead for several years. I think it was a misprint.

—From the Acknowledgments, 1988 *Abstract*

Chuck Tanner

TANNER'S SPRING

In his first managerial role, Chuck Tanner's team blasted its way out of mediocrity, moving into contention in two seasons after losing 106 games in 1970. The key to this accomplishment was the acquisition of Dick Allen, a man of considerable intelligence and charm and a truly great ballplayer who was available cheap at that time because he was a manager's Excedrin headache #1—insubordinate, irresponsible and injury-prone. The three I's; everything a manager wants in a superstar. To give Tanner due credit, this was not the *only* key to the 1972 season; Tanner moved Wilbur Wood out of the bullpen into the starting rotation, saving the team a woodpile of runs—maybe as many as forty or fifty—and helping cut the staff ERA from 4.54 to 3.12.

Tanner was the baseball manager for the seventies; his approach to "handling" Richie Allen was just not to worry about Richie's little eccentricities. He had seen Gene Mauch and several other managers, challenging Allen on some minor point, find themselves locked in tooth-and-nail ego battles that divided their teams. If Richie wanted to spend spring training at Hialeah and batting practice at Arlington Park, he just wasn't going to worry about it. If it feels good, Richie, have at it. Allen responded to this revolution in managerial morality with his best season, and the White Sox won eighty-seven games to challenge the formidable A's in 1972.

Chuck Tanner received, and deserved, great praise for the progress of the Chicago team. It developed in time that the White Sox castle was built on sand; Allen signed a record-breaking contract early in 1973, was hurt for most of 1973 and "retired" in September of 1974.

Worse, several of the White Sox young players, notably Carlos May, began to emulate Dick Allen's casual attitude toward the game of baseball. Tanner's other key pitcher in 1972 had been Stan Bahnsen, who over a two-season period (1972–73) made eighty-three starts with a 39–37 won lost record (21–16, 18–21); his arm proved incapable of sustaining this workload. Wilbur Wood worked even harder, but, being a knuckleballer, wasn't destroyed by it; however, Wood became champion of the White Sox fat brigade—excess flab was another thing that Chuck had decided it didn't pay to nag about —and his effectiveness also declined rapidly.

In three more seasons under Tanner the White Sox never beat .500 again—yet the press never reneged on its praise of Tanner. Chuck Tanner, it turned out, was a heck of a nice guy, many say the nicest in baseball. His reputation survived the poor years in Chicago. Everybody who interviewed him came away from it finding something *nice* to say about such a *nice* manager. Tanner managed one year in Oakland, and the A's failed to win the division for the first time in six years and had their poorest record in eight years, yet in truth it was an extremely difficult summer in Oakland, and Tanner's reputation survived this.

Tanner was traded to Pittsburgh in 1977. The Pirates had been a very successful team, and they remained one for three years, winning the World's Championship (again) in 1979. Since then, lacking any sense of discipline or direction, the Pirates have unraveled, and Chuck Tanner has become Exhibit A in Leo Durocher's brief, a walking lecture on why nice guys finish last, how nice guys finish last, and how long it takes them to reach last if they start out with a good team. Nice guys finish last because nice guys don't go up to their players and tell them that they're going to lose fifteen pounds or fifteen hundred dollars. Nice guys finish last because nice guys don't tell the clowns on the bench to shut up and pay attention to the game. Nice guys finish last because nice guys don't go up to their players and tell them to keep their shabby friends out of the clubhouse.

Every good manager effectively threatens his players with professional extermination if they don't give him the best effort that they are capable of giving; Casey Stengel, Billy Martin, Whitey Herzog, and Earl Weaver are masters at it, as was Durocher. They are *not* nice people. They are manipulative, cunning SOBs, hard and crass and they drink too much. Nice guys finish last because a nice guy is not going to coldly exploit the insecurities of his players. Nice guys finish last because a nice guy is not going to kick an old friend out of his comfortable sinecure the minute that old friend becomes a milli-second too slow on the fastball.

Of course the generalization contains as much falsehood as truth; the point here is only that it contains much truth. For if you believe in sports, then you must believe in stretching abilities to the limit. What is the sporting arena, but a world in which the best is demanded from each and every one; what else? If you believe in sports, you must believe in using the best players that you can find and demanding from each of them all that he can give, because without that sports would have no interest and no meaning. The sporting world is a refuge from a universe of laziness and sloth, indecision and lack of commitment, hedged values and shortcuts, a corner in which individuals are commanded to reach down inside and find the best that's in there, and apply it to . . . this nothing, these games, these silly rules that tell them where to run and when to run there. Athletes are heroes; that is their job.

TANNER'S FALL

We come then to the summer of 1985, and to the bizarre confluence of news stories which joined at the Allegheny and the

Monongahela. On the one hand, there was the story of the on-going drug investigation centering on Pirates and former Pirates; on the other, a steady stream of stories about what a hell of a job Chuck Tanner was doing of managing the Pittsburgh Pirates through their nightmare. The theme of these stories was "He's just the same. I interviewed him in '79, when the Pirates were in their glory days, and I interviewed him in '85, and he's the same now as he was then."

The logic of this argument misses me. Would you defend the pilot of a crashed jet-liner by saying that he flew the plane just the same through a thunderstorm as he had on a sunny day? Would you defend the general of a slaughtered infantry by saying that he marched his men into a hail of bullets just as if they were marching in a Fourth of July parade? Would you defend a doctor by saying that he treated you the same when you were healthy as when you were sick? What kind of moron is going to manage a team like this just the same as he managed a World Champion?

I know I write too much about Whitey Herzog, but what I am struck by is the extreme similarity (to Tanner) of the challenges that Herzog faced after having successful teams in Kansas City and St. Louis, and the 180-degree difference of his reaction to it. After winning three divisional titles in Kansas City, Herzog began to have drug problems with the team, as well as having players who put on weight. The record of the Pirates in 1980 (83–79) is almost the same as the record of the Royals in 1979 (85–77) and the Cardinals in 1983 (79–83).

In response to potential weight problems, Whitey adopted, and enforced, weight limits for all players, a practice which I think he continues in St. Louis. As the Pirates began to degenerate into a collection of fat and lazy players, the Pirate front office got involved in a couple of nasty hassles when, burned by big contracts given to Dave Parker, Jason Thompson and Bill Madlock, they tried to include weight clauses in new contracts. But every time I heard about the Pirates trying to put a weight clause in somebody's contract, I kept wondering where Chuck Tanner was.

A few years ago, writing about Dave Parker, I came to the defense of weight clauses in contracts, describing them as "an intelligent attempt to deal with a problem that major league teams have been attempting to deal with from day one." (See

Dave Parker.) In retrospect, I'm not so sure. One of the problems with a weight clause is that it sets the price of being overweight. If a player has, let us say, an $800,000 contract with a $15,000 weight clause, it is difficult for the team to take any further action against the player on this account. Suppose, if push came to shove, that the team released the player and refused to pay the balance due him, arguing that the player had violated the contract by being out of shape. The team would be quite within their rights to do this, but *if the contract contained a weight clause*, they would almost certainly lose the case in front of an arbitrator. The arbitrator would almost certainly rule that by agreeing to pay the player $800,000 plus $15,000 for meeting his weight, the team had in effect agreed to pay the player $800,000 even if he failed to meet the weight. The weight clause effectively sets the price of being overweight at $15,000, which would amount to about $2.56 to the player once the lawyers, the bankers, the agents and the government get done with it.

In retrospect, I would still defend the Pirate front office for attempting to deal with the problem—but confronting the player about conditioning is something which has traditionally been the province of the manager. In this case, Tanner was conspicuously absent from the debate.

As I see it, there's just a whole lot of people around this year who owe Whitey Herzog an apology. With the revelations in Pittsburgh, we are in a position to see some things that we couldn't have seen clearly before. We can start with the Kansas City front office. When the KC players began to experiment with chemicals, Herzog confronted the problem—just as he later would in St. Louis. First there was John Mayberry; then there was Keith Hernandez. In actions speaking much louder than words, Herzog sent a clear message to everyone in his organization: Stay away from drugs, or *Get Out Of My Life!* He didn't say "I wish you would clean up your act." He didn't say "John, I'm concerned about your health." He said "Look, you mess with drugs and I'm going to ruin your career. I don't care how good a player you are. I don't give a damn how much money the front office is paying you. I don't care what the public, which doesn't know what you're putting up your nose, says about it. I don't care what your friends tell you about it not affecting your game. I don't care what the press says. I don't care if I have to give you away in a trade. I don't care if I have to play some kid out of AAA ball in your place. I don't care what the front office says. I don't care if they fired me once before over this issue. I don't care if they fire me again. If you take drugs there is no place on this ball club for you."

Sometimes in my profession we make the things that managers do sound easy—but certainly, it was not easy for Whitey Herzog to do this. The Royals fired him for it. The press in St. Louis and New York, who regard Keith Hernandez as an icon, broiled him for it. The fans, both in KC and St. Louis, were incensed that he would get rid of star players and put unproven rookies in their place. Even I second-guessed the Hernandez trade, and I'm Whitey Herzog's biggest fan. His own players, his own peers must have questioned his fanaticism on this issue—yet he was to this crisis what Christy Mathewson was to the game-fixing scandal: the only man in baseball who stood up to the problem before it reached epidemic proportions.

So Hernandez got his act together. Great. The point was still made. No doubt all managers say their piece about drugs in spring training, or some time during the year. Uniquely among major league managers, Whitey could say his piece, and there couldn't be any doubt that he meant precisely what he said. Suppose that you were a young player on one of Whitey Herzog's teams, or perhaps an established regular trying to hold on to your job, and somebody offered you a little help. What's going to go through your head? "If Whitey did *that* to John Mayberry, what's he going to do to me? If Whitey told *Keith Hernandez* that his services would not be required in the future, what's he going to do to me if he finds out I'm using stuff?"

The Royals' organization decided, in 1979, that they didn't want to bite the bullet; they replaced Whitey with a much nicer man, Jim Frey. The forces that were trying to introduce drugs onto the roster had a heyday then; they fed the nice guy to the sharks. It didn't hurt the team for a year or so.

In the weight debate, Tanner stayed at home; when it came to drugs, Tanner stayed at home and hid under the bed. To hear Tanner tell it, he had never heard of cocaine until it came out in the papers that his players were using it. Of course, the pretense that Chuck Tanner didn't know that there were drug problems on his team is ludicrous; his press being so forgiving, it remained for the judge hearing the pandering trial to tear into Tanner in strong language for adopting this pose. I know a few people in baseball, but not very many or very well—yet I knew that the Pirate roster was riddled with drug problems. Didn't you? I remember in the summer of 1983 I almost got in trouble when I let it slip on KMOX radio, and somebody had to remind me off the air that it wasn't technically public. Everybody remotely connected with baseball knew that Rod Scurry had a serious problem; it understates the case to say that this was common knowledge. Anybody with an ounce of horse sense had to know that Dave Parker wasn't losing his batting eye by playing too much Trivial Pursuit. Tanner may claim he was unaware, but we all know that it is not physically possible to get your head stuck that far up your rectum.

I realized after the Pittsburgh drug trial was over that for the first time in years I was not aware of any major league player who had been involved with drugs whose name had not become public. It has been my observation, about insider information, that it exists only in passing. I remember one time about six years ago, when I first started dealing with player agents, I learned through one of them that a trade had been made a couple of hours earlier that had not yet been announced. The trade was announced about an hour later, but in that hour, as stupid as it sounds, I felt like such an important person, that I knew something which ordinary fans did not know.

Whereas fans tend to imagine that there is a standard type of information, insider information, which players and writers and a few others share about the game, I have learned that in fact insider status is just a stage that information goes through on its way to becoming public, that if the knowledge is of any interest it cannot help but escape. It may take an hour; it may take years, but the circle inside of which information is held grows inevitably larger and larger; it cannot grow smaller, and the boundaries of the circle are not firm enough to hold it in. Insiders use inside information to buy respect from those that they deal with, thus blurring to indefinable the line of the privy circle.

With something like the use of illegal drugs, the line is clearer—but the forces which draw it out are stronger, and its escape, while slower, is no less inevitable. By the use of hints and code words ("motivational problem," "lifestyle," "getting his act together," "getting straightened out," etc.) the information will get into the press. In time, the hints will become broader and the code words more obvious, until the line altogether disappears. The steps by which the background of the Hernandez trade gradually seeped out to the public, I think, is an excellent study in the process.

For this reason and others, journalism tends to have a lag time of about three years with respect to certain issues. Gary Gaetti, who emerged as an outstanding defensive player in 1983, should begin to receive credit for it in 1986 or 1987. And baseball's drug problem, which was quite serious from 1981 to 1983 but, I think, isn't anything like as serious now, has finally become the property of the public press. But unless I'm badly mistaken, we have seen the worst of it. If I think about it I guess I can recall a few people who got involved with drugs and got out clean, but for the most part, all the names are out now.

Incidentally, I remember writing an article about managers in 1983 in which I wrote that "A manager's job isn't to know when to hit and run. A manager's job is to know who is taking drugs so he can get rid of him before the rent on the habit comes due." The magazine wouldn't use the comment; they changed it to something more innocuous about knowing whether a player was over the hill or just in a slump. But think about that, and then think about the pathetic defense of Chuck Tanner: "I didn't know what was going on."

I'm not pretending to be shocked about drug usage. I have friends who used cocaine a few years ago; I don't think any less of them. Most of you do, too, and most of you know that you do. Many people truly, sincerely believed a few years ago that cocaine usage was really no big deal, that it was on its way toward becoming the social norm. Possibly Chuck Tanner is one of those people. That was *many people*, I said—but it wasn't most of us. It's kind of like the sexual revolution: I'm not the kind of person who has a strong desire to share my body with the masses, but I'm not going to pass judgment on those who do, or did. But the seventies are over, folks.

Comparisons are drawn between "Baseball's" drug problem and the gambling scandals of 1918–20, remembered now as the Black Sox scandal. There have been calls for players to be banned from baseball, as about two dozen players were then. Somehow the managers always get off clean. Black Sox manager Kid Gleason continued to work in baseball for several years, but doesn't it occur to anyone to ask what he was doing while the gamblers came into his clubhouse and seduced his players? According to the sworn testimony in a Federal court, Tanner knowingly let the drug traffickers into his clubhouse. According to the sworn testimony, he tried to warn his players that Curtis Strong was being watched, that they should avoid him for a while. Do we go that far in forgiving the excesses of an innocent, indulgent era?

Ueberroth didn't even choose to talk to him about it. There was a shocking psychological study a few years ago which showed that if the researchers created a moral climate in which torture was acceptable, most people were willing to torture another human being. Who is more culpable: the man who commits a crime, or the man who creates the moral climate in which the crime is acceptable? An impossible dilemma, I suppose. But I cannot understand how anyone can say, in essence, "Sure, he let the drug trade destroy his team, but he's a nice guy."

Sometimes I think that Chuck Tanner should be hung in effigy in every sporting place in the country. Other times, I think that his only offense was the cowardice of being nice. I think it is a twisted mind which places congeniality so high in the hierarchy of values.

What is rarely mentioned about the Black Sox scandal is that it was merely a part of its time, a time in which corruption was gaining rapidly in American society.

In society at large we use sports to express and defend our values, as well as to teach them. Strange as it seems, the reaction of the public in the period after the War to End All Wars was, in essence, that it was one thing when the police were corrupt, that it was one thing when juries were bribed and judges kept on retainer, that it was one thing when elections were rigged and politicians let contracts go to the highest briber, but when *baseball players* started fixing games, well that was just too much; something had to be done about it. And it was; the expulsion of the crooked players was a symbolic purging and cleansing of society which set the stage for the many other purgings and cleansings which are remembered now as the Teapot Dome scandal. It is so odd that this is remembered now not as the period when governors took bribes to free criminals, but as the time when a few baseball players threw the big game.

And in our time, what have we done? We have said that it is one thing when doctors and lawyers use illegal drugs. It is one thing when policemen and politicians use illegal drugs. It is one thing when talk show hosts use drugs, and actors and actresses and our musicians and our children, and drugs may run rampant in the military and who really cares, but when *baseball players* use drugs . . . well, gentlemen, something has got to be done. In time, will the 1980s be remembered as the period when *baseball* had a drug problem? And will it be forgotten that baseball shared this problem with the rest of the nation?

Very likely, yes. People say that it is hypocritical to judge baseball players more harshly than we judge others in society, that if school teachers and airline pilots and architects and engineers use drugs, that that is a lot more serious than a few baseball players. I say that it is not hypocritical in the least. We judge athletes more harshly even than we judge our friends, more harshly than we judge ourselves. Athletes are heroes. That is their job.

—1986

I wasn't kind to Chuck Tanner in the book a year ago, but I would never have believed what an awful job he would do as manager of the Braves. It is my belief that most people, as they age, become parodies of the things that they once believed in. I can't remember the exact quote, but Nathaniel Hawthorne said something to the effect that writers spend the last thirty years of their lives trying to figure out what it was they did so well when they were younger. In the context of life, confronted with an overwhelming array of options about what we should be and how we should make decisions, we choose to emphasize certain attributes that we find within ourselves. We select a philosophy of life as a man drifting in an infinite ocean selects a direction in which to sail his raft, because we are desperate to escape this bewildering ocean, youth. Life in the ocean becomes so much easier when you know where you are going and that there is land ahead.

But once we reach the land, then we begin to think that we really understand life. We start to feel superior to the young and to the lost at sea, drifting with the currents. We forget that we once could see truth lying at the horizon in every direction. Surrounded by others who have landed on the same earth or rock on which we ourselves found comfort, we begin to think that this is the only land there is, that all who do not sail in our direction are doomed never to escape the sea. We assert our values without respect to the complexity of real-life problems. Old soldiers, espousing patriotism and love of country over all other political virtues, become blind to the faults of their countries. Their courage, no longer demanded from them, withers into bravado. Young people who chose books and learning to help them make sense of the overpowering world become so enamored of the books that they lose interest in the world that those books were supposed to help them understand until, if they are historians, they are writing papers on where Napoleon went to the bathroom and, if they are psychologists, they are running rats through multicolored mazes and, if they are sabermetricians, they are trying to figure out whether or not strike-out-to-walk ratio is an indicator of growth potential in a rookie.

So it is with Chuck Tanner, a parody of positive thinking, representing positive thought chopped loose from life or the understanding of live, positive thought rescued from the sea of values and hailed supreme over all others, positive thinking lying on a great pedestal as dead as a beached tuna. The problem isn't with the idea that a team will play better if they keep a positive frame of mind. The problem is that this homily is Chuck Tanner's entire concept of how to manage a baseball team. He is completely out of touch with the talent. He is so out of touch with the talent that he gave 359 at bats to a player (Omar Morono) who has no positives—a .234 hitter with no power with a 4–1 strikeout to walk ratio who is a 52 percent base stealer. He has no concept of how it is, exactly, that he is going to win, except that he figures if everybody has a good year we'll win.

—1987

CHUCK TANNER'S FUNERAL HOME

Well, hello, hello and welcome, my friend, to Chuck's Happy Good-byes. Did you pet the puppy on your way in? Here, have a sunflower. Don't you look nice in dark colors?

Well, gee, I guess you probably know that most people in this line of work are just real serious and depressing most of the time, but we here at Chuck's Happy Good-byes have a philosophy. We want you to be able to say good-bye to your loved one with a smile on your face. We want you to come here and reflect on the *good* things about your loved one's life, and the great *joy* and *happiness* that Julie brought to you while she was with you. We want you to go out of here feeling that Julie is still with you, reminded that the bond between you has not been broken and will never be broken. We feel that if you take that approach you'll be better able to go on with your own life, while at the same time I'm sure that's what Julie would have wanted had she been here and had she been in her right mind.

With that philosophy, we do a few things differently here than you might find at some of the more traditional places. For example, we don't even let the people who conduct our services mention the D-word. Instead of using a minister, we use a warm-up comedian. You might ask your friends, rather than sending flowers, to send balloons. We had an organist who liked to play kind of depressing tunes once in a while, but I had the bitch banned from the chapel.

Well, let's talk about Julie a bit. As I understand it, she was a looker? Oh, that's very different. Well, gee, she sure brought happiness to a lot of strangers, didn't she? I'm sure she enjoyed her work, too; we'll have Ernie talk about that, how Julie was a person who liked to reach out and touch those around her. She wasn't living at home, then? What were some of her other pleasures? I mean, was she a gun collector or did she just happen to have that one around? Were all of her clothes as pretty as the ones she was wearing when she was brought in?

Borrowed the .32 from a friend, huh? Well, ordinarily we do like to stress the idea of the person going on to a better place, particularly in the case of an individual who has made his or her own decision about when the time has come, but if you don't feel that would be appropriate in this case we'll just skip it. My, you'll be amazed by how good she looks; she certainly does take to makeup like a duck to water. We've developed a special embalming process in which the top part of the cheeks is treated with a different chemical than the bottom part, and it causes the face to freeze into a permanent smile. It's lovely; I'm sure you'll be delighted.

Tuesday at 7:05. It's not a good idea to wear your best black clothes, because some people complain about the holes that are left by the smile buttons. Just wear a sports shirt or something; that's fine. Did you meet Willie Starfellow on your way in? Isn't he just a wonderful person? I'd think anyone would be proud to have a pallbearer like that. Wink at him on the way out and he'll give you a package of M&Ms for the road. Enjoy them. They're on the house.

—1987

Joe Torre

Did you ever notice how much Joe Torre looks like Rich Little? I keep expecting him to shake his jowls and do a little Trickie Dick for us.

Joe Torre was the National League manager of the year in 1982, or some of the National League managers of the year (I believe there are twenty-seven organizations which give AL and NL manager awards, and in any given season anybody is likely to win one or more of them. I think eventually it's going to wind up like the All-American teams; he's a *consensus* Manager of the Year). I am rather mystified by how these things are decided. There are some managers who are very good at winning these awards. If Bill Virdon gets through a season without being fired, he's an odds-on favorite to be the league manager of the year. Now, I guarantee you that if you poll Bill Virdon's players, they will not tell you that he is the best manager there is. If you poll the fans of his hometown team, they will as often as not be after his hide. There is just something about him, or about his teams, or about the relationship between his teams and their records, that habitually impresses some people. Maybe he learned it from Danny Murtaugh. Larry Shephard in 1969 led the Pirates to an 88–74 record, their best in three years, but took a terrible beating from the press and got fired. Danny Murtaugh took over the same team, went 89–73 and was a consensus manager of the year.

Joe Torre, for some reason, is in the same class. He is articulate and polite, but that does not really explain how he was able to take over a team (the 1977 Mets) which was forty-five games away from a season in which they had gone 86–76, manage them through consecutive seasons in which they finished 64–98, 66–96, 63–99, 67–95, and 41–62 and still emerge with his reputation untarnished. In New York, no less. Traded Tom Seaver, my butt; they shouldn't have declined by twenty games if they shot Tom Seaver. It wasn't just Seaver; everybody on the team went downhill. George Bamberger took over the team, posted the same kind of record and got catcalls.

Put it on record, anyway, that this is one bandwagon that I'm definitely not jumping onto. Torre managed the Atlanta Braves in 1982 very much the same way he managed the New York Mets for four years. He never did establish a starting rotation. He had a red-hot prospect in center field; the kid went into a slump and he gave up on him. He was indecisive, unreliable, continually trying to ride a hot hand. Maybe his style will fit the needs of the Atlanta organization. Casey Stengel never set up a starting rotation in his life; he won the pennant in '57 with no pitcher who started more than twenty-eight times. He never used a set lineup, either; he was always shifting from one guy to the other. He lost big with this style in Brooklyn and Boston, but he posted the greatest record that any manager ever had with the Yankees. Maybe Torre's style just needed the right circumstances to be successful. I'll believe it when I see a little more of it.

—1983

Ted Turner

Like Ray Kroc, Ted Turner seems never to have been tempted by moderation, by dignity or restraint. He is a man who plays hard at gentlemen's games, and whines when he loses that the victor was not a gentleman. No matter how hard he flees, he will always be pursued by an Awful Commonness, and that is what makes him a winner.

—1981

Sitting at a desk in Lawrence, Kansas, reading and stewing and trying to make sense of three men I have never met and no one has ever really understood. When I was looking through some things I have written over the years a pattern emerged which I was unaware of having created. It started with something I wrote in the 1978 *Baseball Abstract* while discussing the future of the Atlanta organization:

> The way that Ted Turner had gone about building his team reminds me a lot of when Charlie Finley first owned the A's. Finley made almost precisely the same mistakes, trading a package of talent for a slugging outfielder (Colavito) just as Turner did for Burroughs, giving money away to sign players like Lew Krausse and Dave Duncan just as Turner did with Messersmith and Mathews. But Finley, whatever his liabilities, learned from his mistakes on the field. He learned that most of his talent would have to be developed from within the system, because most organizations just will not let a winner get away from them. He learned to distinguish between a good ballplayer and a good batting record. And he learned, most importantly, what Gene Autry has never learned—that it just takes time, however painful. It seems to me that Turner has shown evidence of learning the same lessons, probably even a little faster. And I believe Turner will have a winner here in a few seasons.

In an article for *Esquire* in April, 1981, I compared Turner to another major league owner:

> Braves owner Ted Turner is in many ways quite uncannily like George Steinbrenner—except that Steinbrenner is a pale copy. Turner is the man Steinbrenner dreams of being.

The final element in this series was supplied in the 1981 *Abstract:*

> One should not assume that because Steinbrenner has not yet been done in by whatever disease is creating that foul

aroma, he never will be. In 1974, one would have had to say about Charlie Finley, just as now we hear about Steinbrenner, that "Sure, he's a heel, but he's a winner." It eventually proved to be more important that he was a heel than it was that he was a "winner"—just as it did to Spiro Agnew, to Richard Nixon. People who play the game too hard are characteristically unable to survive when the rules of the game change, as inevitably they do every few years. Steinbrenner plays *this* game very well, but when baseball turns a corner, as it will directly, Steinbrenner will be left whining, like Nixon in 1975, like Finley in 1978, that the rules were changed on him. And he will need the friendship of all the people he has systematically alienated.

A triangle, then: Turner is like Finley; Steinbrenner is like Turner; Finley is like Steinbrenner. I still believe everything I wrote above. I believe that Turner will have his champion, that Steinbrenner will come to a bad end, and fairly soon now.

And I am not the only one who sees these similarities. I remember when Ted Turner was new to the business, he reacted angrily when Furman Bisher made some sardonic remarks about wealthy men who buy teams to sit in the front row seats and cheer wildly and wear baseball caps with their business suits. Responded Bisher, "I did not say there was anything wrong with this, only that experience teaches us to be wary of the type."

The problem with the notion is that it could so easily encourage sack thinking: Turner is Steinbrenner is Finley, no need to watch the fine points. But, of course, they are not all the same man, and it is useful to stop and make ourselves recognize not only what it is that makes them different, but what it is that they have in common which makes us think of them as being the same.

A. *Similarities:*

1. *Flagrant disregard for the values of the group to which they belong.* One way of explaining why Turner paid the money he did to Claudell Washington would be to interpret it as a gesture of defiance directed at the other club owners, as a way of saying, "Pack it. I ain't listening. I'll pay whatever I want to pay."

2. *Intense desire to win.* Even if these men do care what

other people think of them, they care much more about having a winning team and thus behave as if they didn't.

3. *A neurotic need to be the center of attention,* which is the probable antecedent of that desire to win. These men are sophisticated emotional eight-year-olds, unable to accept the idea that there are other people around as interesting and as worthy of attention as themselves.

4. *All are shrewd.* Shrewdness is a one-dimensional form of intelligence, an intelligence which does not evaluate but merely pursues. All are intelligent enough to figure out how to gain the spotlight; none is intelligent enough to figure out why he has gained the spotlight.

B. *Differences:*

1. *Neither Finley nor Steinbrenner can abide the notion that he is imperfect.* In the case of any defeat or any frustration, both are compelled to find a scapegoat, turn on him and expose his failures to the public. If we lost, it can't be my fault. *I don't sense that Turner is like that,* at least to the same degree. He has some legitimate credentials as a sportsman and as such some understanding of his own limitations. Finley and Steinbrenner fire their managers at least once a year; Turner doesn't.

2. *Charles O. Finley lived to reduce people.* His great satisfaction in life was to (or is to; he is past only as far as baseball is concerned) force another man to kneel before him. When Jack Aker in 1966 stated publicly that he would never play for Finley again, he forced Aker to be the first member of the team to sign his contract for 1967. He invited confrontation with his players so that he could break their resistance to him, forced Reggie into a tearful home plate apology in 1970, forced Vida Blue to come back to play for less than he was worth in 1972 and forced Mike Andrews to sign a false affidavit to remove himself from the World Series in 1973. Some people think that Finley's failures after 1976 were due to his pocketbook. That's not it, at all. Finley could survive and even enjoy his cruddy habits in a situation in which the player had no options, in which his control over their careers was total. But regardless of how rich he had been, his team would never have stayed together after free agency.

Steinbrenner has the same sickness, but not to the same degree. If Turner has it, he hasn't made a display of it, that I've seen.

3. *Baseball is much more important to Finley and Stein-brenner than it is to Turner.* Without baseball, Finley and Steinbrenner would live in about total obscurity; Turner spreads his neurotic look-at-me-ism into several different fields. As such he probably thinks much less about baseball, schemes less and dreams less about it. I would guess Turner is probably as intelligent or more intelligent than either of them, but Finley eventually came to know a great deal about baseball himself, and Steinbrenner has had the judgment to hire good baseball people and *listen* to them, at least until the public begins to credit them with some of the Yankees' success, at which point it becomes necessary to fire them. I'm not at all impressed with the people Turner has running his organization.

Ask any politician; people have short memories. People talk about George Steinbrenner as if this were all new, as if no owner had ever been able to make himself the central figure of a ball club before, as if the constant bickering and endless petty crises of the New York Yankees were a thing without precedent. It is my perception, at least, that comparing the two:

1. The A's had more crises per minute than the Yankees do.
2. Finley was much more the center of attention on his club than Steinbrenner is.
3. The A's were a better ball club than these Yankees.

To me, Finley's ability to keep himself on the front page was even more remarkable than George's is. He did just as good a job of it without the advantage of being in New York. But it was new to me then, and therefore exciting, whereas it is familiar now and seems trite.

—1982

Earl Weaver

Earl Weaver may be the only manager in the majors today—Stengel was another—who uses complex platooning. What I mean by that is that in addition to simple platooning along the left-right axis, he alternates players according to several other variables, using home-run hitters more in home-run parks and against home-run–vulnerable pitchers, using defensive and offensive platoons when the circumstances call for it, putting more speed in the lineup when he thinks he can run, and, of course, batting Mark Belanger second against a pitcher he thinks Belanger can hit. This is what earns him his reputation as a genius: using excellent ballplayers in patterns that are more complex than those we are used to assimilating. That and the fact that he *is* a genius. But it's a technique that can backfire on you real easy, as, in fact, it did backfire on him in the sixth game of the 1979 World Series, and as it did on Stengel in 1960. I wouldn't recommend that anybody else try to manage this way, first of all because it can drive you nuts trying to figure out whether this edge is a little bigger tonight than that one. Earl can handle it. But when things start to go wrong, you can wind up with three regulars and thirteens guys who don't know what their job is, when they are going to play next or what you expect of them. The players get confused, and, to borrow from Stengel, the fifteen guys who are straddling the fence wind up on the side of the five guys who hate your guts.

But Weaver is uniquely able to deal with those two potential problems, with the complexity because he is smart and decisive, and with the personnel problems because he just doesn't care whether you like him or not. As I say, it's Earl's style and I wouldn't recommend it for anyone else, but he does make it work.

—1982

People who see things to which the rest of us are blind are called "mad" or "brilliant," "lunatics" or "geniuses," according to whether or not they are able to convince us that the things they see are real. Had any manager but Earl Weaver decided in the middle of the summer to make Cal Ripken, Jr., his shortstop, I would have written the guy off as a nut case. I was talking to John Walsh, the editor of *Inside Sports*, in late July. "What's Weaver up to with Ripken?" he wondered. "What's the idea of putting him at short?"

"I'm damned if I know," I replied. "I sure don't see any percentage in it. But I'm sure Earl Weaver knows more about what he is doing than I do." A couple of weeks later the Orioles came to Kansas City and wiped out in a four-game series, during which Ripken looked as much like a major-league shortstop as he does like Leon Spinks. Tom Evans called me from Baltimore.

"Why is our 'genius' manager playing this oaf at shortstop?" he wanted to know.

"Don't have an answer for you," I told him. "It looks just as silly to me as it does to you. I don't think that there has ever been a good six-foot four-inch, two-hundred-pound shortstop."

But Earl Weaver saw something that the rest of us did not see, and no fair person, in the end, could say that the move didn't work. He was so sure that he saw something out there that when the Orioles lost five straight games, he refused to recant and return Ripken to third, and when they continued to stumble around he refused to give it up, and when they fell flat on their face with seven more losses in a row and nine out of ten, he still refused to crack. What other manager can you name who ever showed such a commitment to an invisible advantage? But when the Orioles picked themselves up and somehow, miraculously, got back in the race, Cal Ripken was still at shortstop.

It is fair and accurate to point out that the DeCinces trade probably cost the Orioles the pennant. Dan Ford didn't do anything, and if the Orioles were going to play Ripken at short, they might as well have kept DeCinces at third. But Weaver didn't make that trade; reportedly, he didn't even like the trade. Indeed, that comment in one sense points out how unique and gutsy Weaver's handling of the situation was, because most organizations, having made that kind of commitment to Ripken at third, would rather die than switch him to short, effectively admitting that the first move was a mistake. Weaver didn't look at the move on the basis of how it reflected on what had been done before, and he didn't look at it on the basis of how well Ripken fits the image of a shortstop. He looked at it on the basis of how it would change the performance of the ball club. And he saw something the rest of us couldn't see.

—1983

Dick Williams

Sometimes in literature a hero forms a sort of bond, good or malignant, voluntary or involuntary, with some object or image (automobiles, freight trains, playing cards, locked doors) that is a part of everyone's life but which seems to haunt him and protrude inescapably into his fate. So it is with Dick Williams and second basemen. He has never, for one thing, stayed with the second baseman that he inherited. On every new managerial assignment, one of the first three things he has done has been to change his second baseman. There is nothing, perhaps, so odd about this, and sometimes the exchange has gone smoothly enough. Mike Andrews settled in smoothly in Boston, Jerry Remy in California. Sometimes it has not been so smooth, as in this case . . . more on that later. But looking back over Williams' career, now: He was fired in Montreal because he became locked in a struggle with his players and his front office that came about in large part because of his irrational insistence that a .211 hitter with no power who is none too swift on the double play and who frankly did not belong on a major-league roster was, believe it or not, the best player on his team. I find it a wonderful instruction on the usefulness of emotional attachments in decision making that this man who is ordinarily as canny a judge of talent as there is could form a blind spot so large that it would hide from him such monstrous ineptitude.

Yet having been finally released from this struggle, having been eventually and deservedly fired because of it, and having been directly and deservedly rehired by another team because when not dealing with Rodney Scott he is a wonderful manager, what does he do? He attempts—no, he *demands*, insists, sits in his office and throws a temper tantrum when his attempt is thwarted—to take his problem to San Diego with him!

Earlier in his career, do you remember how he left Oakland? He left in a dispute over Mike Andrews, a second baseman. This put an end to one of his noble experiments. Having no real second baseman in Oakland, he spent about a month in 1973 using three or four of them and pinch-hitting for each one when his turn came to bat. He used ten men at second in

Oakland in 1973 and an average of 1.7 second basemen a game for the whole year. An unfortunate side effect was that Williams was so busy with this clever nonsense that he never seemed to recognize that one of those second basemen was a twenty-two-year-old kid named Manny Trillo.

I am one of Dick Williams' biggest fans, but his conduct in the case of Tim Flannery is just bizarre, reprehensible, *sick*. He had a young kid who was struggling to make a place for himself in the major leagues, and he did everything he could to destroy that kid, shatter his confidence and tear him down. That is *not* what you hire a manager to do. And why did he do this? Because he was pouting. Because he wanted to bring his problem with him from Montreal, and Ballard Smith and Jack McKeon had the sense to tell him no, he couldn't. What I would have done, had I been Smith or McKeon, is lose my own temper and fire Williams. They handled it better than I would have; they stuck with him, and insisted that Williams stick with Flannery. Flannery might not make it—it is still an open question—but he deserves a chance. Rodney Scott has had quite enough chances, thank you.

—1983 Baseball Abstract

Weird events surrounding second basemen continued to dog Williams to the end of his managerial career. Williams' second baseman in 1983 was Juan Bonilla, a good defensive player (at that time) but a very poor hitter. In the spring of 1984 Bonilla popped off in spring training, and Williams immediately released him, bringing in Alan Wiggins from the outfield to play second base. This was an extraordinary turn of events for several reasons, not the least of which is that the move worked, or at least it worked for the year. Wiggins did well enough at second base and had a good year with the bat, and the Padres marched right into the World Series in 1984. In 1985, however, Wiggins had a relapse of his drug and personality problems, and (with the front office egging them on) the other members of the team voted to drive Wiggins from their doorway. There ensued an inevitable flurry of legal activity, but Wiggins was gone, and Williams was left (to his announced displeasure) with a platoon combination at second base. Again, the controversy involving the second baseman had become the focus of his season.

Dick Williams, after fighting for his job in the winter of

1985–86, resigned in the spring of 1986 and moved on to Seattle, where, guess what, a second base controversy was roar-
ing. The Mariners had released Jack Perconte, who was one of
their better players, for no apparent reason, and were playing
Danny Tartabull, an exceptional offensive prospect but marginal defensively, at second base. Williams immediately
moved Tartabull to the outfield and slid Harold Reynolds into
the second base slot. Reynolds was successful, and that, apparently, was the last second base maneuver of Williams'
stormy but distinguished career.

Section

IV

ESSAYS

On the $400,000 Rule

On June the fifteenth, 1976, Charles Oscar Finley announced that he had sold three star members of his world championship teams for a total of $3,500,000.00. That announcement set into motion a chain of events that led eventually to the establishment of the $400,000 rule, a commissioner's edict prohibiting teams from exchanging more than $400,000 in a player/cash transaction. As baseball now has a new commissioner, I would urge in the strongest possible terms that the policy be reconsidered and abolished in the best interest of baseball.

I have four points to make:

1. The action was originally taken in the context of a bitter personal battle between Bowie Kuhn and Charlie Finley, and like all things said in the heat of battle needs to be reconsidered before it is written in stone.
2. The decision was a key element in the series of events that sent baseball salaries skyrocketing in the mid-1970s.
3. The edict effectively abolished important rights of ownership in baseball, rights that had been exercised to help maintain economic stability throughout the history of the game, and did so at a time when those rights were most desperately needed by the owners.
4. The policy, set forth in the interests of the fans, has in fact proven to be in the worst possible interests of the fans that it was designed to protect.

Let us look at those one at a time.

1. *The context of the edict*

Charles O. Finley was an abrasive, frankly obnoxious individual who had been at odds with the power structure of the American League since 1963, thirteen years before the incident, when the league prevented him from moving his team to Louisville. The league attempted unsuccessfully in the mid sixties to enforce a clause in the league agreement that would have forced Finley to sell the team. He fought a bitter battle with the league in 1967 over his right to move the team to Oakland, during which his actions were widely perceived as threatening baseball's traditional exemption from the anti-trust laws. He embarrassed baseball in 1973 when he attempted to subvert the rules during the World Series by forcing a player to sign a false affidavit that he was injured so that he could be replaced on the roster; Kuhn ordered that the player remain on the roster. Finley publicly referred to Kuhn as the "village idiot."

With this background, at the time that Finley made the player sales they were perceived as being something that Charlie was doing with his usual public-be-damned attitude. When Kuhn voided the sales and Finley sued him, the discussion roared for a year about whether or not Kuhn had the *right* to do that. That was the issue in the lawsuit, whether or not Kuhn had the right to take the action that he took. The owners, whose distaste for Finley was as great as Kuhn's, rallied to Kuhn's defense and supported him in the lawsuit. There was very little discussion about whether the no-sales policy, not even then articulated, was needed or not needed; the discussion was whether he could do it. It could be argued that the owners had been looking for a way to get rid of Finley since 1963, and when they saw an opening, took it. It is not my purpose to argue that. It could be argued that Kuhn was responding to Finley's personal vendetta against him, and that the owners at that time did the right thing in supporting Kuhn. That's not the point either.

The point is that the action was taken and the policy was set in the context of a personal battle that no longer has any meaning, Kuhn and Finley both being gone now. The policy can be and should be looked at with fresh eyes.

2. *The economic impact of the rule*

This decision, in my opinion, did as much as the Messersmith decision itself to catapult baseball salaries upward, and has cost the owners millions and millions of dollars.

How? In several ways. In the absence of this decision, a team that was considering the acquisition of a free agent would have had an important option—to purchase a comparable player from another team. Would a team pay Player X1 $7 million for five years when they could purchase from another team Player X2, who was just as good, for $800,000? Or for $2 million? It seems unlikely. A team needing a first baseman would not have to have that free agent; they would have an option.

Second, many fewer players would have gotten into the free-agent market to begin with if the teams which were losing them could have sold them instead.

In this way, combining these two points, the absence of the $400,000 rule would have placed the owners in a cooperative arrangement, rather than a competitive arrangement, with respect to the players. Thus some portion of the money that was funneled from the owners to the players would have remained within a circle of the owners, money going from owner to owner rather than from owner to player. And with even a little bit less money going to the players, some fuel would have been removed from the inflationary fire; the rate of growth in salaries might have been twenty percent per year, instead of thirty percent per year.

Of course there would still be the Ted Turner, the George Steinbrenner who was throwing at the player however much money was required to impress him. But it would require then less money to impress him.

I am of course viewing it from the owner's perspective. In practice I've always been on the players' side in economic matters; I work with the agents. And I have mentioned this idea to two or three agents, and they have always grasped instantly what I meant. Because an agent's a negotiator, and the basic fact of a negotiator's life is that the strength of your position is wholly dependent on how many options you have. What an agent needs to get the salary he wants for a free agent is two teams that want the player. You can go to your boss and beg and grovel and plead for more money, and it won't mean a thing—but if his competitor offers you a fifty percent increase in salary, he'll offer a 60 percent increase.

Kuhn's edict removed from the owners a key option—the only other dollar option that an aggressive owner had. In so doing, he weakened greatly the position of the owners in salary negotiations.

3. *The rights of the owners*

At the time of the lawsuit, Finley claimed that he was merely doing something that owners had done repeatedly throughout the history of the game. Kuhn argued that those situations were different, and that what Finley was doing was unique and uniquely damaging to the fans.

Kuhn was dead wrong about that. It is difficult to imagine

how the parallels between Connie Mack's player sales of 1914 and the mid-1930s and Finley's attempted sales of 1976 could have been any stronger or any more perfect. Mack was faced in 1914 with a sudden increase in salary expectations, and with the prospect of losing his star players uncompensated if he did not sell them. From 1933 to 1935, he sold off a formidable list of talent because he could not meet his payroll. How is this different from what Finley was doing? What Finley was trying to do was exactly what an owner had always done to stay in the card game.

The owners reacted to that on a personal level; they said, "We don't want you to stay in the card game. We've been trying to get rid of you for thirteen years." I can see that, but did you also want to get rid of Bill Veeck and Ruly Carpenter and Mrs. Wrigley? Did you want to drive all of the old-line operators out of the game?

What I am saying is, even though it was not often used, the option of selling off players was an essential element in the long-term economic stability of the league. Kuhn removed that option from the members of the league at a time when they most desperately needed it. This contributed mightily to the economic destabilization of the game.

In addition to that, selling ballplayers in other situations was something that the owners had always had the right to do, and something which they had done on many other occasions —selling surplus talent, selling front-line talent to support a large farm system, as Branch Rickey did in St. Louis. Kuhn arbitrarily removed that privilege from the owners.

4. *The protection of the fans*

But, of course, he did it for the fans.

Look, suppose that you were the general manager of the Minnesota Twins. Kuhn removed from you two things: the right to buy talent and the right to sell it.

If I were the general manager of a ball club, the first thing I would want to do would be to try to acquire some more talent. I'd love to be able to go to the Kansas City Royals and say, "Look, if you don't want to play Onix Concepcion, we'd sure like to make you an offer for him." How does that hurt the fans? Talent that is considered surplus to Kansas City (Concepcion) or Milwaukee (Brouhard) or Boston (Nichols) could be very useful to Minnesota. The Yankees in the 1950s made those kind of sales; at the right price, you could still make them.

But what about going the other way? Ok, let's evaluate it. The Twins have (as I write this) a player of very real value in Gary Ward, a player that they could probably sell for a couple of million dollars. Only they can't sell him, and besides that they can't pay him, either. So what do they have to do? They have to get rid of him, but they have to get in return a package of young and unproven players, players who can't command a large salary.

And next year, they'll have to do the same thing with Kent Hrbek, or Gary Gaetti, or Tom Brunansky, or all three and why is this? Because they can't pay them. And why can't they pay them? Because they can't sell Gary Ward for money.

What Kuhn could not have anticipated in 1977 was the coming of arbitration awards that would force a team to pay $300,000 or $700,000 a year to a young player. The Twins are in a position in which they are forced to exchange large sums of money for talent, but they are prohibited from exchanging talent for large sums of money. Does that make any sense?

How does this help the fans of the Minnesota Twins? I defy anybody to give me a semi-cogent, quasi-rational explanation of how the no-sales policy protects the fans of a weak organization. Did it protect the Oakland A's under Finley? Did it protect Seattle when they were in danger of losing Floyd Bannister? Is it protecting the Twins? The no-sales policy in fact contributes to the further destruction of a weak team.

5. *Summary*

The selection of a new commissioner purges the leadership of baseball of their emotional commitment to an established policy. I urge the new commissioner to review that policy in the light of the current needs and goals of organized baseball. I urge him to consider his options, to consider perhaps the option of saying not that we will *prohibit* sales of players, but that we will review them, and retain our option to disallow them if they are damaging to the interest of the game.

I think he would find it difficult to find any logical basis for a continuation of the current policy.

—1984 *Baseball Abstract*

Originally published as an article about the Minnesota Twins.

On Artificial Turf

In the August 12, 1985 edition of *Sports Illustrated*, Ron Fimrite launched an attack upon artificial turf. I should say, to begin with, that a) Fimrite is a terrific writer, and I enjoy his work a great deal, usually, and b) I agree with him completely about the general idea that it would be best if artificial turf would pack up and move to South Yemen. I think, however, that a good cause is best served by the truth, and that in this particular case Fimrite has enlisted in the service of a good king a number of bad soldiers. The article quoted George Brett as saying that "The turf helped me when I was young and just learning to hit . . . but I'm a different hitter now—a line-drive hitter—and the turf just doesn't make that much difference." In 1984 George Brett hit .314 on the turf in Kansas City and .318 on the turf in other parks—but .242 on grass fields. In 1985 he hit .352 on turf and .306 on grass fields.

On the more substantial disagreement, Fimrite denies that artificial turf has made the game more exciting, and complains about cheap inside-the-park home runs and "a whole generation of mediocre and overrated fielders," whatever that means. At one moment, he complains about a ball that bounces away from Harold Baines, making a "laughable" hit—but in the next, argues that bad hops are a sacred part of the game. "The true hop is a sop to the mediocre, the unimaginative, the unresourceful." Apparently, they are a sacred part of the game only as long as they occur on grass fields, proving again that if you start with the assumption that the world was perfect twenty years ago, one can easily prove any change to be a change for the worse.

I think it is better not to deny that artificial turf has made baseball faster, more aggressive, and more exciting. I think it is better not to deny that artificial turf has given us some of the most exciting defensive play that we could ever hope to see. Artificial turf has made fielders confident enough to try some wonderful and innovative things; it's ludicrous to say that "On turf all you have to do is get your glove down." Artificial turf has helped immensely to open up a game that had become slow and methodical; I think we should acknowledge our gratitude for this.

But the fact that it was turf which brought the speed back into the game doesn't mean we have to keep the damned stuff. We can keep the speed in the game by doing a few simple things that ought to be done anyway, like limiting the number of times a pitcher can throw to first base to two. (Runner goes to second on third unsuccessful try to pick runner off first.)

I don't believe George Brett when he says that artificial turf has made careers shorter—but I do believe him, of course, when he says that it hurts his legs, and his ankles, and his back. To me, that's enough. It is not necessary that it shorten his career; it is enough that it makes a game painful, which is meant to played in a kind of controlled joy. Baseball is not football, which is supposed to hurt. George Brett and Frank White are among my heroes; I don't like to go to the game and see them ache and broil in insufferable heat. I think it is appalling to ask people to play football on artificial turf, but that's another story.

But when I think about artificial turf, I am most struck by this: that it has made so little progress in so much time. You know, I don't think that any successful innovation in baseball history has ever been adopted so slowly. Shin guards, face masks, the hit and run, the spitball . . . they all received intense criticism from the moment of their invention—but within a few years, all were in universal service throughout the game. The players of the dead-ball era had not a good word to say about Babe Ruth's bringing the home run back into baseball—but within eight years, every team in baseball had adapted its offense to the new reality. When lights came in there was intense controversy surrounding them—yet within a few years, every park except one had night ball, and within twenty years fixed lights had worked their way even into smalls towns in Kansas.

Yet here we are, more than twenty years after Astro-Turf, fifteen years after there seemed to be no doubt that the future of the game lay on artificial fields—and most major league teams still do not use it, the fans still have not accepted it, and the companies which pimp for it have long since given up trying to talk the caretakers of the older stadiums into converting. They are on the defensive; John Schuerholz is constantly forced to defend his decision not to convert Royals Stadium into a grass park. I wonder if the human body of baseball has not already rejected this foreign tissue, and if the transplant has not already failed?

What I think is that our values have changed. It's hard to remember this now, but in the sixties women who nursed their own babies were regarded as oddballs; it was so easy to buy formula, you know. That seems so stupid to us now; we don't think that way anymore. We are so much more suspicious of artificial things than we used to be, so much more protective of things which are natural. We don't buy aero-dynamic shaped toasters anymore. In the fifties and sixties we tore down shrines like Ebbetts Field, Forbes Field and Sportsman's Park with hardly a thought. Artificial turf, it survives from that time like a purple plastic dodo bird.

—1986

On Baseball Being 75 Percent Pitching

Let's take the statement that baseball is 75 percent pitching. First off, it is nearly impossible to know what is meant by this. "Baseball" is a lot of things—you got your games, you got your pennant races, your individual accomplishments, your personalities, your box scores, your anecdotes, your hot dogs; you've got your Hot Stove league and your televised games, your All-Star game and your World Series. Does this mean that 75 percent of all ball games are determined by who the pitcher is? Does it mean that 75 percent of ball games are determined by what the pitcher does? Does it refer to 75 percent of pennant races? Seventy-five percent of short series? Seventy-five percent of batter/pitcher confrontations? Does it mean that 75 percent of all tall tales are about pitchers? Does it mean that 75 percent of all hot dogs are eaten while the pitcher has the ball? What?

It doesn't mean any of those things; it's just a number picked out of midair and plunked down in the middle of a bunch of words in a way that seems to make sense, provided you don't think too hard about it. It's a bit like saying that "Philosophy is seventy-five percent God," "Movies are seventy-five percent acting," or "Sex is seventy-five percent physical." Or "That statement that baseball is seventy-five percent pitching is ninety percent nonsense."

However, to the extent that it is meaningful, it's false. We don't know what it *does* mean, but there are many things that it *might* mean. If pitching were the dominant part of the game, then there are many other, more specific statements which we would expect to be true. None of them are true. For example:

The teams which have the best pitching staffs would win the pennant 75 percent of the time. Doesn't happen. The team which has the best earned run average in the league wins the pennant just as often as the team which scores the most runs —but no more often. The correlation of team wins to runs allowed is virtually the same as the correlation of team wins to runs scored.

In a game, the team which has the better pitcher starting would win 75 percent of the time. Doesn't happen. On a very rare occasion, you might have a pitcher, like Dwight Gooden in 1985, who wins 75 percent of his starts—but it is a very rare occasion, indeed. If you're saying that "Pitching is 75 percent of baseball when Dwight Gooden is on the mound, so long as Babe Ruth isn't hitting," I might buy it.

In a free market economy, pitchers would make the most money, since they would be the most sought after players. Hasn't happened. In fact, on the average pitchers make less money than players at almost any other position.

Teams would never trade a regular pitcher for a regular player. Think about it—if you've got a twenty-five-man roster with nine pitchers, who represent 75 percent of the value, and sixteen other players who have 25 percent of the value, are you going to trade one pitcher for one hitter? Of course not— but teams do trade pitchers for hitters every winter.

The standard deviation of runs allowed would be larger than the standard deviation of runs scored. If pitching were 75 percent of the game, then one would expect the differences between teams created by pitching to be larger than those created by hitting. But they aren't; the standard deviations of runs scored and runs allowed are the same.

Pitchers would monopolize the award voting. If people really believed that baseball was 75 percent pitching, then one might expect 75 percent of the players in the Hall of Fame to be pitchers. They aren't. One might expect 75 percent of Most Valuable Players to be pitchers. They aren't. Even in the era before the Cy Young Award began to siphon off votes, pitchers pwon less than 40 percent of Most Valuable Player

Awards. Pitchers don't win 75 percent of Rookie of the Year Awards.

The most accurate formulas for predicting wins and losses from runs scored and runs allowed would have to give more weight to runs allowed—representing the team's pitching—than to runs scored. Again, it doesn't happen that way; in fact, the most accurate methods for predicting wins and losses from runs scored and runs allowed weight the two elements evenly —and no formula can be developed which retains a similar degree of accuracy while emphasizing one element over the other.

Teams would put most of their effort into developing strong pitching staffs. Managers would spend most of their time working with their pitchers. Clubs would employ more pitching coaches than any other kind of coaches. Indeed, if baseball were 75 percent pitching, then one would expect that most managers and most coaches would be former pitchers, since they would be best qualified to deal with the most important part of the game.

Doesn't happen. Managers spend as much time working with hitters as they do with pitchers. Teams employ as many hitting coaches as pitching coaches. Ex-pitchers are rarely hired as managers; most managers were infielders or catchers.

Almost all first-round draft picks would be pitchers. Less than half of first-round draft picks are pitchers.

Pitchers would be the dominant force in determining where and when each offensive event occurs. In fact, the identity of the pitcher is the recessive element of any such determination; the identity of the hitter is the dominant element.

What I mean by that is that the "spread of occurrence" for any offensive incident is greater for hitters than it is for pitchers:

No pitcher allows home runs as often as Dale Murphy hits home runs. No pitcher allows home runs as seldom as Bob Dernier hits home runs.

No pitcher allows hits as often as Wade Boggs gets hits. No pitcher, not even Dwight Gooden, allows hits as infrequently as Steve Jeltz will get a hit.

No pitcher strikes out hitters as often as Rob Deer strikes out. No pitcher strikes out hitters as rarely as Bill Buckner strikes out.

This is true of every significant area of performance, including those things like walks and hit batsmen which are usually considered to be controlled by the pitcher.

And what does that mean? It means that in order to create a working model or simulation of a baseball game, you must allow the hitter to be the dominant, shaping force in the game.

And if baseball were 75 percent pitching, one would not expect that to be true.

In short, none of it is true. We cannot say for certain that baseball is not 75 percent pitching, but we can say these two things: 1) that the statistical patterns which one would expect to manifest themselves in such an event do not occur, and 2) that while people may say that baseball is 75 percent pitching, no one acts in a manner consistent with this belief. The general manager who says that baseball is 75 percent pitching will turn around and trade his number-two starting pitcher to get an outfielder. The owner who says that baseball is 75 percent pitching will still pay out more money to keep the Gold Glove shortstop than he will to keep the relief ace. The manager who says that baseball is 75 percent pitching will spend an hour a day figuring out batting orders and an hour a week lining out his pitching plans. The reporter who says that baseball is 75 percent pitching will still vote for Willie McGee over Dwight Gooden as the Most Valuable Player. *No one in baseball acts as if he really believes that baseball is 75 percent pitching.*

In a sense, the argument that baseball is 75 percent pitching betrays the fundamental nature of the game, which is that it is circular. Every hit that a batter gets is a hit the pitcher allows. Every walk that the batter draws is a walk that the pitcher yields. Every run scored is also a run allowed. Whenever the offense succeeds, the defense fails at precisely the same moment and to precisely the same extent. The success of the hitter and the failure of the pitcher are not different things, but the same thing merely looked at from a different angle. So to say that baseball is 75 percent pitching is, in a sense, like saying that the head of a coin is worth more than the tail, or like saying that a room is bigger if you enter it from the left than from the right. A baseball game is created by the joining of the pitcher and the hitter into a single act. This problem with this old bromide is that it attempts to tear apart that which is in fact indissolvable.

—1986

On Baseball as a Business

Probably the stupidest thing that people say regularly about baseball is that of course baseball is not basically a sport. Baseball is basically a business.

Of course baseball is not basically a business; if it were it would have gone out of existence in the 1890s. Let us suppose that the economic structure of baseball were to collapse, that the "business" of baseball were to become untenable and go the way of all dinosaurs, while the public interest in the *sport* of baseball remained alive. Would baseball then cease to exist? Of course not. New economic structures would sprout from the ground like mushrooms. New businessmen would appear, anxious to make a buck by catering to the interest in the sport. There would be new contracts, new agreements, new logos, and perhaps a few new players along with the new "businessmen"—but there would be baseball just as before, as pervasive as ever, suffering no more than the jolt of an unexpected speed bump.

Suppose, however, that the *sporting* interest in baseball, the omnipresent public interest in who is winning and who is losing and why, were somehow to vanish. Would the business of baseball then carry on as before? Why, of course it could not; lacking the public dollars that follow the public interest, the business would immediately cease to exist. The businessmen, and even the athletes, are the mere servants of the craving for the sport.

So obviously, the game is essentially a sport. It must be a sport to survive. The business will survive precisely as long as it remains a sport.

What is so curious is that otherwise intelligent men can be tricked into failing to see this, and will say with earnest faces that of course baseball is basically a business. Why do they think this? Because *Peter O'Malley* sees it basically as a business? Because *Reggie Jackson* sees it as basically a way to make a living?

But this is merely a fault of perception, a disorientation in their habits of thought that results from their peculiar relationship to the enterprise. Consider the same argument as it might apply to anything else—let us say a can of O'Malley's Beef and Beans. Obviously, to Albert O'Malley, who owns the business, it is basically a business. To Roger Jackson, who drives a truck for O'Malley, Beef and Beans is basically a way to make a living.

But to the man who buys the Beef and Beans and takes it on his picnic, what is it? It is essentially a *food*, of course. No one but a jackass would argue that because Beef and Beans is basically a business to Albert O'Malley, because it is basically a business to Roger Jackson, it therefore is basically a business.

The unique thing about sports fans is that they have so much trouble understanding this. It would be stupid for Bill James to believe that because baseball is a business to Peter O'Malley and Reggie Jackson that therefore it must be basically a business to him, too. It would be stupid for Bill James to forget that it is not he who must accommodate the businessman, but the businessman who must accommodate him. In the Beef and Bean business, even Albert O'Malley and Roger Jackson would certainly recognize this. They would remind themselves daily that what they were dealing with here was essentially a food. They would regard such daily reminders as being essential to their being able to serve the public. They would never allow themselves to lapse into thinking that what was essential to the business was their getting their dollar.

The unique arrogance of the baseball businessmen is that, seeing themselves quoted in the paper every day, seeing their own distorted perspective on the undertaking reflected in the daily press, they have allowed themselves the luxury of forgetting this.

But what is far more remarkable is that baseball fans go along with it. Baseball fans have the ultimate victim mentality: they are actually willing to treat their own perceptions as merely an illusion. Baseball fans will swear up and down that what baseball really is is not what *they* see baseball as being, but what Reggie Jackson and Peter O'Malley see it as being.

Anybody who tells you that baseball is basically a business is either badly confused or a jackass. And you can tell her I said so.

—1987

On Clutch Hitting

Clutch hitting is supposed to be a whale of a matter, and if there is anything certain about it, it is that if you got a line on it it would turn out to be a goldfish. People are eternally poring over the statistics looking for evidence on the subject, yet if you provide any evidence they will reject every iota of it which does not agree with their preconceptions; this issue touches the gut, and we cannot have mere numbers telling us that our favorite players don't have it. And that is the gut of the matter, for what people want here is not a fact which is cold and brittle and unyielding, but justification and vindication for what they have always known, proof positive that that callow youth who shuffles in from left field and hits .300 is a .190 hitter in a clutch situation, an .070 hitter with the game on the line, while that scrappy little shortstop only hits when it means something. A racist will invariably tell you that blacks don't hit in the clutch.

At the same time, that lies may be told in the name of the Lord is a poor reason to be an atheist, and that exaggerations and rampant sloppiness are common in the name of clutch performance does not mean that there are no clutch situations or that it does not occasionally happen that a team will perform over its head or below par in those situations.

—1982

On Computers in Baseball

One of the people I interviewed last summer for the job as my assistant was a very nice young man named Paul Izzo. Paul hails from Providence, Rhode Island; he grew up, as it happens, just a few blocks from the boyhood home of Dave Lopes, soon to be designated a shrine. Paul showed me an article in an old *Baseball Digest* which talked about Davey Lopes growing up in an East Providence ghetto. The area in which he grew up is, in fact, not a ghetto at all. It's a very nice, turn-of-the-century neighborhood.

I thought about that a lot during the summer, a short essay on the minor irritations and insults of racism in America; a similar essay was what we might call the incident of Eddie Murray's family. David Earl Lopes is sort of black, and everybody knows that black people grow up in ghettos. So Dave Lopes has to live with that.

I am in the same article with the Oakland A's and their blessed computer in more newspaper stories than you can count. I am not complaining; it sells books. Only I haven't quite figured out what I am doing there. My work has nothing to do with computers. I don't know any computer languages and couldn't write the most basic program. I enrolled in a computer science course as a junior. I lasted about three weeks.

But my work, while it has nothing to do with computers, has something to do with numbers, and a lot of people who don't understand the one don't understand the other, either. And so as far as they are concerned, we are all living in the same ghetto.

That having been said, perhaps my thoughts on the future of the computer in baseball would be of as much interest as the next person's. As mentioned, I recently purchased a computer, and am still learning how to use the canned programs that come with it. The main thing that you are struck with in the process of learning about a computer is how incredibly stupid it is. The machine simulates intelligence so well that when you accidentally slip through a crack in its simulations and fall to the floor of its true intelligence, you are awed by the depth of the fall. You give it a series of a hundred or a thousand sensible commands, and it executes each of them in turn, and then you press a wrong key and accidentally give it a command which goes counter to everything that you have been trying to do, and it will execute that command in a millisecond, just as if you had accidentally hit the wrong button on your vacuum cleaner at the end of your cleaning and it had instantly and to your great surprise sprayed the dirt you had collected back into the room. And you feel like, "Jeez, machine, you ought to know I didn't mean that. What do you think I've been doing here for the last hour?" And then you realize that that machine has not the foggiest notion of what you are trying to do, any more than your vacuum cleaner does.

The machine, you see, is nothing; it is utterly, truly, totally nothing. And all of the fascination and the speculation about the computer, about "what *it* is going to do" and "how *it* will change things" in baseball and in other areas is completely misguided, because *it* is not going to do anything and *it* is not going to change anything.

We are going to do things with the computer. *You and I* are going to change the world, and we're going to change baseball, and we're going to use the computer to do it. Machines have no capabilities of their own. Your car cannot drive to Cleveland. What machines do is extend *our* capabilities.

What is unique (exciting, terrifying) about the computer is that it extends our capabilities to such an enormous extent and in so many different areas—in more different areas, I think, than any new invention since the tire iron. The reason for this is that almost everything which can be done on paper can be done easier and faster (some would say better, but I'm not convinced of that yet) on a computer. Since all of our lives revolve to a large extent around literacy, around words on paper and numbers on paper, our lives are in time going to revolve to the same extent around computers. Whether we like it or not.

Some terrible things, unimaginably terrible things, are going to be done with computers in the next thirty years. Do not kid yourself that it's not going to happen; deal frankly with the fact that it is going to happen. Some marvelous, wonderful things are going to be done with computers. I look forward to them. We are going to change our lives, using the computer, far more than we have changed our lives using the automobile, far more than we have changed our lives using the television machine. I have no doubt that that is true, because the computer expands our capabilities, for good or evil, in far more sweeping and comprehensive ways than the automobile, which in truth expands only our ability to move around, or the television, which expands only our ability to observe. I am not afraid on balance. It is only human nature that we are going to see a little more of, blown up larger than life by the new machine.

Before we approach any nearer to that point, I have a recommendation. Computers should be banned from the dugouts. Right now, before any of them are put in there to begin with, *Ban* them.

Computers aren't going to be bad for baseball; it's not anything like that. But they will, or would, put an unnecessary distance between the fans in the seats and the man in the dugout. Computers do not belong in the dugout for the same reason that bicycles do not belong on the basepaths: They would remove the game from a human level. Let them study their printouts before the game starts.

Some people have expressed to me a concern that what is being done in baseball with the computer is (ahem) not in the best interests of my profession, of sabermetrics. I am speaking here not only of the Oakland experiment, but of the computers that have been hauled into Comiskey, the Kingdome, and a couple of other places. I stress that I do not know any of these people. I have never met them, wouldn't recognize them if I passed them on the streets. I don't share many of their interests. They live in another part of the ghetto.

And from what I hear, I don't *want* to know some of them, either. I gather, frankly, that some of baseball's computer people are world-class oysters, dogmatic fellows who think they know more about baseball than anybody else on the planet, and consequently have no intention of listening to anyone. The concern that has been expressed to me is that some of these people may be doing us more harm than good.

If that's true, it's unfortunate. But I'm not all that concerned, and let me explain why. There is, you see, no such thing as "computer knowledge" or "computer information" or "computer data." Within a few years, everyone will understand that. The essential characteristics of information are that it is true or it is false, it is significant or it is trivial, it is relevant or it is irrelevant. In the early days of the automobile, people would say that they were going to take an "automobile trip." That lasted about ten years; after that, people went back to talking about trips as they had before. They were vacation trips, or they were business trips, or they were trips on personal matters, or they were trips to the coast or they were trips to the mountains. After the novelty wore off people still traveled in automobiles, but they ceased to identify the trip with the machine and returned to identifying it with its purpose. People stopped driving to Cleveland just to have some place to drive. That's what we're going through now with the computer; twenty years from now the term "computer information" will sound quaint and silly.

The main thing that is happening in computers now is that they are becoming much easier to use. As computers become easier to use, our dependence on "computer people" becomes less. Computer people are not going to be running baseball in a few years; indeed, computer people are not going to be running anything in a few years except computers. The rise of the computer age is not going to put computer specialists into positions of power any more than the rise of the auto age put auto mechanics and bus drivers into positions of power. Don't worry about it.

I am engaged in a search for understanding. That is my profession. It has nothing to do with computers. Computers are going to have an impact on my life that is similar to the impact that the coming of the automobile age must have had on the life of a professional traveler or adventurer. The car made it easier to get from place to place; the computer will make it easier to deal with information. But knowing how to drive an automobile does not make you an adventurer, and knowing how to run a computer does not make you an analytical student of the game.

—1984 *Baseball Abstract*
Originally published as an article about the Oakland A's.

The Defensive Spectrum

I'll teach you a trick for trying to get a line on what kind of a defensive player somebody out of the past was, somebody you didn't see play. I use a spectrum of defensive positions which reads, left to right, Designated Hitter, First Base, Left Field, Right Field, Third Base, Center Field, Second Base, Shortstop. (Catchers, for very good reasons, are not included.) There are diverse consequences of the spectrum, but what I wanted to point out at the moment is that if a player is good defensively at his primary position, then he will ordinarily put in some games or even a few seasons at the positions to the right of where he normally plays; if he is a poor defensive player, the tendency will be to shift him to the left of where he normally plays. Thus a good defensive third baseman, like Gary Gaetti or Mike Schmidt, will ordinarily have some games in which he plays shortstop. A third baseman who doesn't have very good range will ordinarily have some games where he is used at first base. Both Schmidt and Brett played some shortstop early in their careers, and have played some first base in their later years, a common pattern.

An outstanding defensive shortstop, since he cannot be shifted rightward, will usually play almost 100 percent of his career defensive games at short. Through 1987, for example, Ozzie Smith has never played an inning at any other position, or Ozzie Guillen either. Luis Aparicio never did. Wayne Tolleson, a marginal defensive shortstop, has played second, third and the outfield. The more exclusively a shortstop is used at shortstop, the better a defensive player he usually is, and this is a very useful thing to know when you are looking at the records of a player from the past, like George McBride or Roger Peckinpaugh, and wondering what kind of a defensive player he really was.

At first base, on the other hand, the rule is just the opposite; the better a defensive player is, the more likely it is that he will fill in from time to time at other defensive positions. George Scott, Ron Fairly, and Vic Power all played a significant portion of their careers at other positions. Gil Hodges played the outfield, catcher, third base and even a game at second base, while Willie Aikens never got off first base except to DH.

Sure, it's not a perfect rule; Keith Hernandez has played only seven games at positions other than first. But if I was evaluating a third baseman out of the past, and I could know one of two things, his fielding percentage or how many games he played at shortstop, I would a lot rather know how many games he played at short. Ignore this rule when dealing with the San Francisco Giants.

—1988 adaptation of comment from 1983 *Baseball Abstract*

On The Designated Hitter Rule

Before one can attempt to say anything intelligent about the effects of the designated hitter rule, it is necessary to stop and recall the climate of speculation near hysteria into which the rule was born. Volumes were written in the winter of 1972–73 about how this rule was going to change the game. People wrote that the DH rule would take the bunt out of the game. They wrote that it would keep old hitters around until they were fifty. They wrote that it would destroy competitive balance (because the good organizations would have an extra hitter to get in the lineup but the poor wouldn't). Some people argued that the DH rule would actually drive offensive totals downward (by keeping the good pitchers in the game longer). Some argued that it was a ruse to keep salaries down (I can't remember why). One of the loudest complaints was that beanball wars would get out of hand; an extension therefrom was that teams would divide into factions of hitters and pitchers. There was a general agreement that this was only a foot in the door, and that other gadgets were sure to follow.

In the climate of the times, it was inevitable that anything that happened in the American League was going to be laid at the door of the DH. If, in 1973, an American League hitter had hit .400, if a pitcher had won 30 games, if a team had won 112 games, if the American League had won the All-Star game, if a batter had been killed by a pitch; if Mark Belanger had won the batting title or the Cleveland Indians the pennant, it is absolutely certain that these effects would have been traced, somehow, to *that rule*. If there had been three separate incidents of chimpanzees getting loose on the field, if there had been an outbreak of diarrhea among second basemen, if a terrorist group had occupied Fenway Park, it is extremely likely that these things would have been attributed to the rule. That is not a joke; it is an absurd reality. Can you not see the editorial of, say, Dick U. Oldsportswriter, on the Monday morning after the Fenway terrorists surrendered:

> But what can the fuzzy-thinking old men who run baseball expect when they kidnap the game itself, subvert its rules to serve their own ends, but that desperate and fuzzy-thinking young men will do the same thing? Baseball does not belong to the men who have seized its rules and destroyed its traditions any more than Fenway belongs to the Petrocellites. I see the tragedy in Fenway and the DH rule as being two horrible symptoms of the same disease.

OK, OK, I'm pushing my luck. Anyway, what happened in

1973 was that the American League had thirteen twenty-game winners, and the National League had but one. Inevitably, a logical bridge was established between the two: The DH rule was making it vastly easier to win twenty games.

I am unsure whether this connection is 100 percent a fiction, or only 95. I know it is at least 95. Consider the following facts, or deny them:

1. The number of twenty-game winners in the American League immediately before the DH rule was adopted was already at historic highs. The 1971 total was eleven, the highest in fifty years; the 1972 total would have been in double figures had not a strike wiped out the first ten days of the schedule.
2. The National League level of twenty-game winners happened, by a coincidence clearly irrelevant to the DH rule, to be at a historic low in the period just after the rule was adopted.
3. In 1973, no National League pitcher started more than forty times, while fifteen AL pitchers *averaged* over forty starts apiece. This, again, is clearly irrelevant to the DH rule.

The myth that the DH rule was making it vastly easier to win twenty games took root because no one bothered to examine the facts.

—1983

On Drugs in Baseball

I know I'm probably going to get hung for suggesting this, but has anybody ever considered the possibility that cocaine and amphetamines really do enhance athletic performance in certain respects? One study that I've got to do sometime is to compare the before and after performance of players who turn themselves into treatment programs. If thirty percent come out better ballplayers than they were before, I'd be surprised.

One of the complications of such a study is that an improvement in performance, if it did occur, would probably be gradual, while a decline in performance would probably be immediate.

I don't really believe that drugs make anybody a better ball-player. I do believe this: that the physical and emotional construct which creates a successful athlete must be understood in its entirety, and not discussed piecemeal. That, I think, is the reason that players who go on weight-training programs or health-food kicks, or players who are helped by hypnotism or other psychological counseling, or players who make a sudden leap forward after working with a batting instructor, will almost always relapse in the next season. True excellence in any field is supported by an incredibly complex structure of habits, skills, knowledge, intelligence, confidence, courage, experience and diverse abilities which in athletics means diverse physical abilities. If a player's performance makes a sudden leap forward because of an improvement in one area, he reaches a level that the complete framework of the man will not support. If he has a great season because he gets on an emotional high and for half a season he thinks he's Ted Williams, then the next year he'll fall into a slump and remember that he isn't, or he will have a minor injury that will bring him crashing to earth, and he will not be able to get that feeling back; his deeper confidence will not support the level of performance to which he has soared on the wind of the streak. If a batting instructor corrects a flaw in his swing, then the pitching pattern to him will adjust, and in a year he'll be back where he was; his knowledge of hitting will not support the level of performance at which he has operated temporarily. A pitcher who develops a new pitch will often have a terrific year, hit a hot streak and wind up working more innings than he has worked in years, and a muscle will tear or a tendon snap because his body simply will not support the role into which the new pitch has projected him. A year ago a psychological counselor was being credited with playing a major role in lifting the White Sox to new heights by removing their doubts and helping them to visualize success, but where was he last summer?

When a player has been using a chemical substance for years, I think that it often happens that that substance becomes a part of the fabric of his life—and thus, however evil it is by itself, it becomes a part of the structure that supports his success. When it is removed, that fabric is torn, and it may be years before the tear can be stitched over.

—1985

On The Five-Man Rotation

I have it in my head that it was the Los Angeles Dodger organization which began the current movement toward five-man
pitching rotations. If this is not correct I will be happy to be
instructed on the subject, but as I understand it the Dodgers,
following the early retirements of Sandy Koufax and Don Drysdale, decided to go to a five-man pitching rotation while rebuilding the team, shifted briefly back to a four-man staff in
1974, lost Tommy John to an injury in half a season and then
didn't win the division in 1975 anyway, so decided to return
to the five-man plan. And, to kidnap a metaphor, when Walter
O'Malley sneezes, the National League catches a cold. Since
Walter has been dead for two or three years, this perhaps does
not bode well for the NL, but you know what I mean. From the
Dodgers using a five-man rotation to the NL using it is not a
long step.

Until I decided last spring to do a thorough study of the
issue, I really had not taken in the extent to which the four-
man pitching rotation had fallen out of favor. My view of the
subject, in short, was this:

1. If I have a four-man pitching rotation and you are trying to
   persuade me to switch to a five-man rotation, what you are
   saying is that I should take eight starts away from my best
   starting pitcher, eight away from my second-best starting
   pitcher, eight away from my third-best starting pitcher,
   eight away from my fourth-best, and give all thirty-two
   starts to my fifth-best starting pitcher.
2. Before I am going to do that, I want to see some real good
   evidence that I am going to get something back in exchange
   for it.
3. I have not seen any such evidence.
   Ergo,
4. I wouldn't do it.

I am aware, of course, that the fact that I have not seen any
such evidence does not prove that no such evidence exists.
The Dodgers usually know what they are doing, and for all I
know they may have conducted extensive testing before they
decided to do it this way.

There are a couple of anomalies in the adoption of the five-man rotation. The first anomaly is that although the American League has the designated hitter rule, the National League has almost universally adopted the five-man pitching rotation, while the American League has not. That seems backward; one would think the adjustment would occur first where there was the most strain on a pitcher's arm.

The second anomaly is that the organizations seem to have adopted a protectionist policy toward their players at a moment when they have just surrendered that which they are attempting to protect. Ten years ago, it was one thing to say that we are using a five-man rotation to protect our pitchers' futures, because that future really belonged to you. You either used it or you traded it; either way it was yours, to do what you would with it. It's not that way any more. What sense would it make for the Toronto Blue Jays to cut Dave Stieb back to 240 innings to protect his future, when it seems to be agreed that his future includes free agency? None at all. What sense does it make for the Dodgers to protect Valenzuela's arm so that four years from now Valenzuela can sell it to the highest bidder? I don't mean to sound callous, but when the economic structure is one that enables the player to say "You've got to give me every penny that I can get from anybody, and to hell with what happened in the past," that player has got to expect the team to say "You've got to give us every inning that you can pitch, and to hell with your future." The one is the logical complement of the other. I think that baseball management, grounded in economic paternalism for decades, has never been able to make the switch to modern business realism, the foundation of which is greed: That, indeed, is two-thirds of the problem, that management insists on the one hand in fighting hopeless battles to resurrect the old paternalism, and on the other hand in flinging fistfuls of money at the players, half of which is intended to purchase their services, the other half to purchase their affection and loyalty. I think that when baseball management grows up, the four-man rotation is going to make a comeback.

—1983 *Baseball Abstract*

Although the maturing of management has occurred—the old paternalism is dead—the comeback of the four-man rotation, anticipated here, has definitely not occurred. All major league teams now use a five-man pitching rotation most of the time.

On the Economics of Baseball

One of the unwritten laws of economics is that it is impossible, truly impossible, to prevent the values of society from manifesting themselves in dollars and cents. This is, ultimately, the reason why athletes are paid so much money: that it is very important to us to be represented by winning teams. The standard example is cancer research; letters pop up all the time saying that it is absurd for baseball players to make twenty times as much money as cancer researchers. But the unavoidable hard fact is that we are, as a nation, far more interested in having good baseball teams than we are in finding a cure for cancer.

Now look, both of my parents died of cancer, and I fully expect that it's going to get me too, in time. It would be very easy for me to say that cancer research is more important to me than baseball—except that I don't do anything which would be consistent with such a statement. I think about cancer research a few times a month; I think about baseball virtually every waking hour. I spend many times as much money on baseball in a year as I give to cancer research—and so do you, and so does almost every goddamned one of those guys who write the letters saying that it is ridiculous for baseball players to make more money than cancer researchers. You write it down on paper, the money you spend going to baseball games, the money you spend willingly on transportation to and from sporting events, the money you spend on overpriced beer and hot dogs and baseball games, and in buying books and magazines about baseball, and on baseball cards or other collectibles—and on the other hand, how much you spend on cancer research.

The pool of money which we pour into athletics makes it inevitable that athletes are going to be better paid than cancer researchers. *Dollars and cents are an incarnation of our values. Economic realities represent not what we should believe, not what we like to say that we believe, not what we might choose to believe in a more perfect world, but what our beliefs really are.* However much we complain about it, nobody can stop that truth from manifesting itself.

—1986

On Intentional Walks

What would you think of a rule allowing a player to turn down a walk if he wanted? Not just an intentional walk, but theoretically any walk.

This is probably the most major rule change that I could support. Think about it: Why was the walk rule adopted? The rule about four balls being a walk was adopted to force the pitcher to pitch to the batter, not to dodge him by throwing balls out of reach. The rule accomplishes this, ordinarily, by creating a penalty for not pitching to the hitter—the hitter gets a free pass.

The problem is that in some game situations the penalty is so weak that the rule does not work, and is actually stood on its head; the pitcher takes the very rule that was adopted to force him to pitch to the hitter, and uses it to avoid facing a tough hitter. This is directly contrary to the intent of the rule, and for that reason I think it is consistent with the rules for the hitter to be given an option as to whether or not he wants to walk.

The rule could be adopted in several forms, but the essential idea is that if you walk a hitter and he turns down the walk and you walk him again, he goes to second base, and everybody else advances by at least one base. The rule could be written so that if the walk was refused the count would revert to 0–0, or, in the weaker form, so that the strikes would carry over but the balls would revert to zero. In the latter case, it would be unlikely that anybody would turn down a walk to hit behind in the count (0–1 or 0–2), so what the rule would effectively mean is that if you wanted to intentionally walk a hitter, you would have to give him at least one strike in the process.

Some of my friends have objected that the rule would take strategy out of the game, but I think that's completely wrong. What it would do is create an option for a strategic response, and thus it would *create*, rather than destroy, strategy. It gives the offensive manager an option: Do I take this free pass and express my confidence in the next hitter as well as my opinion that the other manager's action is wrong, or do I invoke my right to make him pitch to Dale Murphy? Thus the rule would expose directly conflicts of opinion between managers. If one manager chooses to give an intentional walk and the other manager chooses to accept it, then clearly the two men disagree about the correctness of the strategy.

I'm not advocating this rule; just urging you to think about it. I think in general it is in the best interests of the game to allow the Dale Murphys and Tony Gwynns and George Bretts to hit with men on base. I know the rule seems radical now, but if it had been thought of in 1887 I think they'd have adopted it.

—1988

The Law of Competitive Balance

Several years ago I undertook a series of studies which were designed to enable me to predict the movement of a team upward or downward in one year based on an analysis of several factors from the year before—a subject, it happens, which no longer interests me. I was attempting, by finding the answers to a series of relevant questions, to develop a sort of "technical analysis" of the season to come. Those questions included:

What percentage of the time does a team improve in one season if its starting lineup in the previous season averages twenty-five years of age? Or twenty-six, twenty-seven, twenty-eight, . . . thirty-three?

If a team improves in one season, what percentage of the time will they also improve in the next?

What is the average win total in the next season of teams which win one hundred games in one season? Teams that win seventy games? Ninety?

Do teams which change managers usually improve?

I eventually concluded, to complete the digression, that while there was knowledge to be gained by answering the questions, the subject was. . . . how shall I say? Beyond the capacities of the research. A lot of fans feel that your ability to predict the pennant race is a test of your expertise as an analyst. My feeling is that nobody in the world can predict a pennant race, period, because the outcome is dependent on major variables of which no knowledge can exist at the time the prediction must be made. And to the very limited extent that a race is predictable, I think you'd have better luck with systematic fundamental analysis, as Pete Palmer has, than with the technical analysis that I was trying to develop.

But some of the answers to these questions remain interesting:

1. What I have since described as the Plexiglass Principle: If a team improves in one season, it will likely decline in the next.
2. Now called the Whirlpool Principle: All teams are drawn forcefully toward the center. Most of the teams which had winning records in 1982 will decline in 1983; most of the teams which had losing records in 1982 will improve in 1983.

Other studies later extended both of these principles to individuals. If a player's batting average improved in one season, I found, it would likely decline in the next, and vice versa. The players who hit for the highest averages in one season, I found, would reliably decline in the next season. Of those who hit for the lowest averages, most would not be playing regularly in the following season, but most of those who were playing regularly would raise their batting averages.

Why does this happen?

These were not things that I had expected to find. Weaned on the notion of "momentum" since childhood, I had expected a team which won eighty-three games one year and eighty-seven the next to continue to improve, to move on to ninety; instead, they consistently relapsed. Half-expecting to find that the rich grow richer and the poor grow poorer, I found instead that the rich and the poor converged on a common target at an alarming rate of speed. Sporting teams behave over a period of years as if a powerful magnetic center was drawing on them, tugging them toward it, defying them to stay up or to stay down or to drift away from it.

Why does this happen, and how does it happen? The Law of Competitive Balance: There develop over time separate and unequal strategies adopted by winners and losers; the balance of those strategies favors the losers, and thus serves constantly to narrow the difference between the two. There develop (in all sports and in life in general—it is merely that the orderliness and detailed record-keeping of the games of life enables us to trace its effects more clearly in the sporting world) over time (within a season, between seasons, within a game, between games) separate and unequal strategies which are adopted by winners and losers (and which logically *should* be adopted by winners and losers). The balance of those strategies always favors the team which is behind, and thus serves constantly to narrow the difference between the two (between the team which is behind in a game and the team which is ahead, between the team which has been strong and the team which has been weak).

The essence of that difference is in how the two teams view the need to make changes. If a team wins ninety-six games and its division, that team develops a self-satisfaction which colors all of the decisions that the team needs to face. The team looks over its roster and discovers, say, a thirty-one-year-old shortstop coming off a .238 season. If the team had finished out of contention, there is little doubt that they would replace that player. As a bad team, what they would likely do is look for a kid with ability, somebody who might play the position for ten or twelve years. As a near-miss contender, what they would do is look for a proven player who could help them get over the hump. But as a winner there is a tendency to say "Well, he's only thirty-one, he's had some good years, and he's still doing the job on defense. We won the pennant with him last year." And thus the winning team, because they are winners, does not address the problem.

In other sports more than in baseball this process of adaptation takes place inside the game. In a basketball game, if one team runs off a string of points, which team calls time? Review the situation in your mind: Notre Dame leads Grunt State 33–28 with eight minutes left in the half. Suddenly, Grunt State rips off nine quick points; it is 37–33 with five left in the half. Who calls time out? Obviously, Notre Dame. What does the announcer say? "Only a four point lead in the first half, but Grunt State really has the momentum going for them now." But what actually happens, in your experience, when the teams come out of the meeting? Does Grunt State go into the half with a ten-point lead? Never happen. Notre Dame will come out and restore order nine-and-a-half times in ten.

Why? Because, who changes his strategy? Who runs in a substitute? The Notre Dame coach says "Hey, they're beating us bad on the boards and killing us on the outlet. John, you've got to get up over the back of that Moose; I put Wilson in to get back and head off the break." But what can the Grunt State coach do? He is frozen by his success. The operating dynamic in the situation is not the "momentum" that the announcer will be talking about; it is the Law of Competitive Balance.

A beautiful example of the Law of Competitive Balance occurs in football, with respect to what is called the Nickel Defense. The Nickel Defense involves the use of an extra—a fifth—defensive back, a move which makes it easier to move the ball on the ground (the line is short a man) but more difficult to throw a long pass. Most fans hate the thing; the call-in shows are full of it. "Why do they use that thing? How often do you see a team hold its opponent in check all game, get a lead late and go to that Nickel Defense and allow the other team to march right down the field and get back into the game?" In a narrow sense, they're right—it does happen. A lot. But what people don't understand is that when a team gets behind, say twelve points behind in the middle of the fourth quarter, they become increasingly willing to gamble. They might have a long pass play in their book which they figure has maybe a 30 percent chance of being a long gainer, a 5 percent chance of being a touchdown, but a 15 percent chance of being intercepted. Now, in a close game you're not going to use that play except on third and long; it helps your opponent more than it helps you. But if you're two touchdowns behind with time running out, you go to it. It doesn't make any difference if you lose by two touchdowns or three; a play that improves your chances of winning from 15 percent to 18 percent is worth running. If your chances of winning are 50 percent, a 30 percent gamble looks bad; if they are 15 percent, it looks great.

It is worth running, and it is worth defending against. If you don't use the Nickel Defense, you're giving them the 15 percent to 18 percent improvement; if you do, you're letting them march downfield on the ground.

What the fan is observing when he sees the late rally is not the effect of the Nickel Defense, at all. It is the effect of the Law of Competitive Balance. Teams which have been held in check all game are going to score late sometimes, regardless of what defense you use, because they gain a strategic advantage from being behind.

There is a very similar defensive maneuver that takes place in baseball—except, being baseball, it happens in a much more subtle way. You know the saying about guarding the lines in the late innings of a close game? Why do they do that?

To move the third baseman nearer the line decreases the chance that a ball will be hit safely down the line, but increases the chance that a ball will be hit between third and short. Thus it *increases* the chance of a single, but *decreases* the chance of a double. The move generally allows more singles than it prevents doubles, thus it *increases* the chance that the opposition will be able to put together a big inning. But, because it prevents the double which would put the runner in scoring position, it *decreases* the chance of allowing a single run. Announcers like to puzzle over why you guard the lines in late innings when you don't early. You guard the lines in late innings when you wouldn't early for exactly the same reason that you bunt in the late innings or issue an intentional walk in the late innings. Baseball is a big-inning game; in the third inning, the key thing is not to give up those three- or four-run innings that will blow you out. But in the eighth inning, it doesn't matter whether you lose by one or three. The one-run inning becomes much more important, so you guard the line.

Plunging on into what is now a full-fledged digression . . .

I am convinced that the rule of thumb about guarding the lines in the late innings of a close game is on balance a good one. It has evolved through the Natural Selection of Strategies; it has stood the test of time. However, I am much less sure that it is a good one *in all parks*. It is very possible that there are parks, like Royals Stadium and Three Rivers and Busch, where the danger of a double down the line should *always* take precedence, from the first inning on, and it could well be that there are parks, like Dodger Stadium, where the grass slows the ball down to where it is never that grave a threat, and in which, therefore, one should not guard the lines in the late innings. How long would it take you to come to that realization just by watching? To get back to the subject . . .

In the first stages of free agency, many people believed that free agency would enable the rich to grow richer while the poor grew poorer. Of course, just the opposite happened. Competitive balance has become so strong that we are approaching parity. George Foster said last year, and was widely quoted as saying, that we would never again see super teams like the 1975–76 Reds; with free agency, he said, nobody could afford them. What people are saying about free agency now, we should note, is *exactly the opposite* of what they originally said. Then they said it would *destroy* competitive balance; now, it is going to *enforce* competitive balance.

Why has that happened? For a lot of reasons, but what it comes down to is, the Law of Competitive Balance. How many players have actually left weak teams to go join contenders? Damn few. A lot of the strong teams—the Dodgers, the Royals, the Reds—began by turning up their noses at free agency. They could afford to. The St. Louis Cardinals may have wanted Floyd Bannister, but when it comes right down to it, did they want him as much as the cities that didn't already *have* a World Champion? Of the four early big spenders in the free agent market, three—the Angels, Braves, and Padres—were poor teams trying to buy championships. The more help you need, the more seriously you look at the options that can help you. The more fluid talent is (the more free is its movement from team to team), the greater competitive balance there will be.

Incidentally, this song about the rich getting richer and the poor getting poorer in baseball has been sung many times before across the history of the game, while in fact the differences between the best teams and the worst teams have shrunk inexorably from the day professional baseball began. Strong teams early in this century would win 70 percent of their games, but the .700 teams have disappeared, the .650 teams have disappeared, and even the .600 teams are becoming much harder to find.

Another place where the Law of Competitive Balance can be observed statistically is in World Series' play, by breaking down the won/lost sequences. Who usually wins the second game of the World Series, the team which has won the first game, and thus leads, or the team which is behind a game? Historically, the team which lost the first game has won the second well over half the time—as have teams which trailed in the series two games to one or three games to two. The team which is behind tends to win the next game most often (unless they are too far behind).

Why? Because they adjust. In the 1982 World Series, who moved his infielders in a couple of steps after the first game? The Cardinals lost that first game, and so they adjusted. They moved their infielders in, and they changed their batting order and their lineup for the second game, while Milwaukee played the same eight men and batted them in the same order. Granted, Milwaukee switched from a left-hander to a right-hander, and granted, Herzog switches his lineup around a lot more than Kuenn, but I would bet you dollars to pesos that if you checked the history of the World Series, you would find that the team which loses the first game of the series makes far more lineup changes for the second game than does the team which wins the first game. You lose the first game, you start to wonder, do we have enough power to win in this park? Could we take more advantage of the bunt with their third baseman? Is our first baseman ever going to come out of his slump? You win the first game, and you make excuses for the first baseman.

A team which *loses* a pennant by three games or less is much more likely to win the race in the following season than is a team which wins by three or less. Again, an observable fact, which the Law of Competitive Balance explains.

The Law of Competitive Balance also applies to individuals. Who experiments with a new batting stroke, a .300 hitter or a guy who is fighting to keep his job? Who tries to develop a new slider, an eighteen-game winner or a guy fighting to stay in the big leagues? The less talent you have, the more you are forced to learn, to adapt, to adjust. Among the ten best managers in baseball today, who was more than a marginal player? This process constantly diminishes the distance between the best players and the worst; it draws the George Bretts and Dennis Eckersleys down and it lifts the Brian Downings and the Charlie Houghs up.

And finally, it defines greatness. It is true in all sports, but it is more true in baseball than in others: Greatness in an athlete is self-defined. Great pitchers in baseball are those who erect standards for themselves so that they redefine an 18–13 season as a failure and only a hard twenty as a success. Great ballplayers continue to learn *before* they are on the road to oblivion. What does Pete Rose talk about when he talks about hitting? Adjustments: move up in the box, move back in the box; choke up on the bat, go down to the knob. He is talking about not letting them drag you down. He is talking about what you have to do to defy the Law of Competitive Balance.

—*1983 Baseball Abstract*

The original article also contained reports on several studies which documented many of the statements herein. Because those reports were statistical in nature, they have been deleted from this version in keeping with the spirit of this book.

On Lou Gehrig's Streak

I've never believed that Lou Gehrig's record was as unbreakable as people would have you believe. You hear people say that Gehrig's record will never be broken because today's players don't have the kind of dedication that it would require to stay in the lineup for fourteen years. This is obviously a silly argument. First, I don't think that human nature changes very much from generation to generation. The sportswriters of Gehrig's time said most of the same things about players then that are often written now.

But even assuming that the attitude of the average player has changed, this has little to do with the chance that the streak will be broken. Why? Because *if* the streak were to be broken, it obviously would not be broken by an "average" or "typical" player, whose attitudes were characteristic of his time, but by an exceptional individual like Gehrig, Ripken, Dale Murphy or Billy Williams. I would tend to stand that argument on its head, and argue that the record is more vulnerable than it might appear, precisely because human characteristics like determination and the ability to play with pain can be applied to breaking it. I mean, DiMaggio's streak is going to be hard to break because determination is almost irrelevant to it; you can't manufacture a hit by being determined. I expect Gehrig's record to be broken in my lifetime.

—1988

A History of the Beanball

Incidents of players being hit with the pitch were probably the central story of the National League's Western division in 1984, directly involving five of the six teams:

On April 8, Houston's best player—and, indeed, one of the best players in baseball in 1983—was lost for the season and possibly irreparably damaged when hit by a pitch, thus largely ruining the season for the Astros.

On April 29, San Francisco's Mike Krukow was ejected from a game after hitting Cesar Cedeño of Cincinnati, who had homered off of him the last time up, with his first pitch.

On May 27, the best starting pitcher in baseball, Mario Soto of Cincinnati, was ejected from a game and suspended for his part in a brawl that developed after Soto whistled a pitch past the chin of Atlanta's Claudell Washington, who had been hitting home runs off of him.

On August 9, a brawl broke out after Mark Davis of San Francisco hit Enos Cabell with a pitch. Cabell had homered off of Davis in their last previous meeting, a couple of weeks earlier.

On August 12, San Diego and Atlanta engaged in the most famous on-field melee in years, involving three hit batsmen, two fights, nine fines or suspensions, ten thousand dollars, five arrests and at least three cover stories.

There were lesser portions of the controversy in the other three divisions, and in the wake of all this there was a great deal of discussion in the media about what it all means, as indeed there should have been. Are the pitchers getting meaner? Are the players becoming hypersensitive? What is the best way to control it? How common are serious injuries resulting from hit batsmen? What injuries are most common? Are there more of them than there were ten years ago? How often do they have an impact on the pennant race?

What is missing from these discussions is one of the things that is always missing from journalism, which is by definition concerned with what is happening right at this very moment: historical perspective. What I wanted to do with this article is to contribute that to the discussion.

PART I: THE TURN OF THE CENTURY UNTIL RAY CHAPMAN

Baseball in the 1890s was violent. It was violent in every respect, and as such it was natural for the ball itself to become a weapon.

It is apparent that, as we entered this century, the use of the ball as a weapon was not uncommon. Hit batsmen were first counted by the National League in 1899. The records in the 1900 *Spalding Guide* include only pitchers pitching in fifteen or more games. Those pitchers for whom records are available pitched in 1,592 games and hit 721 batters with pitches, a rate (remembering that there are at least two pitchers in every game) of about 91 hit batsmen per 100 games played.

The American League opened for business in 1901 on a pledge of clean baseball. They did not allow intimidation of the umpires, they did not allow physical or verbal abuse of opponents, they did not allow vulgar or unbecoming conduct on the field, and they did not allow pitchers to throw at hitters. Though the new league did not maintain records of the numbers of hit batsmen in their first years, it seems likely that their totals were never as high as those of the senior circuit.

The success of the American League forced the National League to follow suit, and hit-by-pitch totals dropped dramatically. By 1910, the rate of HBP/100 Games was down to 64; by 1916 it was down to 50, and by 1920 down to 46—about half of the 1899 count. Hit batsmen were declining at an annual rate of about 3 to 4 percent.

But at the same time as this successful effort was being made to clean up the game on the field, more and more pitchers were adopting the discoloration or soiling of the baseball as a tool of their trade. Introduced about 1902, the spitball became popular within a few years. There was an ongoing dispute about whether it should be or could be prohibited, but it wasn't, and so ever-increasing numbers of pitchers began to use the thing. By about 1910, a clean ball was never in play. When a ball was hit into the stands and the spectator refused to return it so that a new ball had to be put in play, the players in the field, who kept the palms of their gloves moist with tobacco and licorice juice for just such an occasion, would immediately discolor it rather than allow the opposition to get a few whacks at a clean ball.

This was dangerous. From the time that these pitches first appeared, some people argued for rules against the spitball and the "emery ball" on the grounds that a hitter could be hurt if he didn't see the pitch coming. Other people said that wasn't so, but deep down I think everybody knew that it was. Minor-league players were being killed with pitches on occasion; I don't know exactly how many, but there were at least five fatal beanings in the minor leagues between 1909 and 1920. A summary of the known instances of players in professional baseball being killed with pitches is given at the conclusion of this article—that is, those that I found. There must have been others prior to 1920 that I didn't find. The 1910 *Reach Guide* lists the death of a player named Leo Smith, who played for Kokomo in the Northern Indiana League and died as a result of injuries suffered in a game played May 23, 1909, but it doesn't say exactly what happened to him.

Anyway, as you probably know, in 1920 a major league player, Ray Chapman, was hit by a pitch from Carl Mays, who was sort of a combination of Dan Quisenberry and Nolan Ryan, and died. The death of Chapman, a popular player and an outstanding talent, was a shock to the baseball community. What then to do?

The 1921 *Spalding Guide*, reflecting on the Chapman tragedy, said that "a head helmet for the batter is not to be despised. There is nothing 'sissy' about it. The first time that a catcher wore a mask he was hooted. The first time that a catcher wore shin guards he was jeered. Both of these are accessories to the game now, and very useful." The batting helmet, nonetheless, would not receive a trial in professional baseball for another twenty years, and would not be adopted for more than thirty.

PART II: FROM THE DEATH OF RAY CHAPMAN
UNTIL 1948

What was done was to start keeping clean balls in play. In the winter of 1919–20 (that is, the winter before Chapman's death) a rule had been passed limiting the use of the spitball to two pitchers per team. League policy early in the 1920 season mandated that dirty balls be thrown out of play, but the pitchers (and managers) complained constantly about having to use the new, shiny baseballs, which they said were difficult to grip. As the season progressed the umpires relaxed their vigilance about dirty baseballs, and the league began to drift back toward the emery ball era of the previous years.

The death of Chapman halted that drift; in 1921 the league offices were adamant about the use of clean baseballs. The rule limiting the use of the spitball to two pitchers per team was changed to allow only a few specified pitchers to use the spitball—not two per team, but a list protecting only a few veteran pitchers. To allay complaints about the balls being difficult to grip, the practice of umpires rubbing down the baseballs with clay began early in the 1921 season. The practice continues today.

Following a brief aberration in the early twenties, the trend in totals of hit batsmen continued downward at an accelerated rate, dropping from 49 hit batsmen per 100 games in 1922 down to 29 per 100 in 1933. Although there may have been such an incident, I have found no record of any player in organized baseball being killed with a pitch in the 1920s, other than Chapman.

In spite of these declines, the 1933 *Reach Guide* reported that the American League had, on July 11, 1932, "adopted drastic measures to curb the growing use of the beanball by pitchers." They passed a rule saying that a pitcher throwing a beanball was to be removed from the game for the first offense. For the second offense he would receive ten days' suspension without pay, and for the third offense thirty days' suspension without pay.

The perception that the problem was getting worse in the face of the evidence that it was probably getting better is an interesting phenomenon. It was quite a bit, I should say, like what we saw in 1984. There seems to be a rule that the worse the problem is, the less you hear about it; for example, although most of the fussing about it was in the National League West, there are significantly more hit batsmen in the American League than the National, and there also seem to be quite a few more injuries resulting from them in the AL.

Anyway, the declines continued, though they were very small for a few years after that. In 1936 George Tkach, a player in a low minor league, was killed by a pitch; this incident attracted almost no public attention, and was not even mentioned in a seven-hundred-word summary of the league's season which appeared in the 1937 *Reach Guide*. But in 1937, major league baseball almost had its second fatality as a result of a pitched ball—and this time, the victim was a major star.

In late May, Mickey Cochrane, the superstar-manager of the Detroit Tigers, was hit in the head by a fastball from Bump Hadley, a hard-throwing veteran of the Yankees. The beaning came toward the end of a rough series, and there were rumors that Hadley was throwing at Cochrane; indeed, there were the same about Mays/Chapman, though not as many. Cochrane could well have died; doctors found it necessary to drill a hole in his skull to relieve the pressure.

I get the impression, though nobody exactly says so, that Cochrane's wits were permanently scattered by the beaning. He wanted to resume playing; Detroit owner Walter Briggs, knowing that another beaning could kill him, wisely forbade it.

There had been equally serious injuries in the majors in the twenties and thirties, but never to such a major star as Cochrane, a two-time Most Valuable Player. This touched off another round of soul-searching, and another round of proposals for how to prevent future incidents. No action was taken, but hit by pitch totals continued their downward drift.

PART III: FROM WYNN TO GIBSON

The old-timers in every generation will always tell you how much rougher the game used to be than it is now. The old guys used to play with pain; you didn't see them taking a day off with a hangnail like these modern sissies with their cushy contracts. No sir; they played with broken ankles, they slid harder than they do today, and they used to tag you so hard that they'd break your arm. The pitchers in the old days were real mean.

And it's been that way since baseball began; the old guys were always tougher. The players of Lefty Grove's era talked about him as if headhunting were his main pleasure in life, yet in his entire career he hit only 42 batters with pitches, and he had several years in which he hit only one batter in more than

200 innings. I guess the players then were more spry than they are now.

But the fifties really were a rough time in baseball. Ted Klusewski really did break a guy's arm in the process of applying a tag. There were a lot of brawls. The Giants and Dodgers fought every time they got together, and the number of players who got hurt in the middle of these does not suggest that they were just milling around looking bad. In June of 1957 the Yankees had three major on-field melees in one week, two of them triggered by hit batsmen. And they really did throw at each other.

The number of batters being hit with pitches shot upward in 1949. Why? I don't know, exactly. What I had always assumed happened—and I may have written that it did—was that HBP totals shot upward after batting helmets came into use in the mid-fifties. One can see why that would happen; the batting helmet would diminish both the pitcher's fear of killing someone, and the batter's fear of being killed, which would cause more players to crowd the plate and more pitchers to work inside.

Hit batsmen did increase after the batting helmet came in —but a more thorough review shows that the trend clearly began in the late forties, four years before batting helmets were introduced by the Pirates in 1952. One minor league player, Stormy Davis, was killed by a pitch in 1947; Ottis Johnson of Dothan was killed in 1951. I am fairly certain that Johnson was the last player in organized baseball to be killed by a pitch— clear proof of the value of the batting helmet.

Anyway, what happened in 1949 that caused hit by pitch totals, which had stayed between 309 and 361 every year from 1937 to 1948, to shoot up to 449 in one leap? The game was changing then, as it always is. Home run totals were going up rapidly at that time, which means more players crowding the plate. Walks and strikeouts were also going up rapidly, which means more pitches being thrown. Casey Stengel came to the Yankees, and Casey was a tough guy. The black players were coming into the game, which may or may not be relevant. A generation of players was in place now that didn't remember the sick feeling that baseball men shared when Cochrane was hurt. None of this seems an adequate explanation; whether all of it is or not, I can't say.

Once the corner was turned, the totals of hit batsmen went up steadily for twenty years. Early Wynn was famous for throwing at people, but in his career he hit only 65 batters with pitches. That was a lot for his generation (1939–63), and it is a substantial number compared to Whitey Ford (career total of 28), Sandy Koufax (18), or Warren Spahn (42). But Wynn was a piker compared to those who came along in the mid-fifties. Don Drysdale hit 154 batters with pitches. Jim Bunning hit 160. Bob Gibson hit 90, Jim Kaat 122, and Gaylord Perry 108.

There are all kinds of interrelated things that we are talking about here. We're talking about brushbacks, beanballs, and sheer accidents; we're talking about retaliation mixed up with control of the inside corner of the plate. But there can be no doubt that those pitchers who are aggressive in claiming the inside part of the plate wind up hitting more batters than those who aren't.

There were gradual signs that baseball was developing a problem. On September 8, 1952, a beanball war developed between the Giants and Dodgers that led to the suspension and fining of Leo Durocher. Players were hurt by pitches, but then there have always been some of those; it's hard to tell whether there were more or fewer. In the December, 1955 edition of the *Baseball Digest*, Dizzy Dean observed that it "used to be we'd throw at one hitter and it would be just like knocking 'em all down. I mean they would all get respect for you and not try to get too smart. Now . . . they have to throw at each one of 'em. Now they're even throwing at the seventh and eighth place hitters. Consarn it, we never used to bother with those kind."

After a series of beanball wars early in the 1958 season, the presidents of the two leagues, acting simultaneously, issued a new regulation (June 6) which called for an automatic fifty dollar fine on the first warning to any pitcher for throwing at the batter. By 1968 there were 48 batters per 100 games played being hit with pitches, up 91 percent from what it had been in 1947—and the pitchers were in complete control of the game.

With pitchers being allowed to pitch inside, batting averages were declining almost annually. Nobody liked this too much, particularly the fans. In the twenty years of increasing totals of hit batsmen (1949–68), average attendance per game played in the major leagues declined steadily, from a 1948 peak of 16,913 to a 1968 average of 14,217. (In view of the fact that the number of doubleheaders played decreased greatly, the per-date decline in attendance would have been even larger.)

PART IV: RE-ESTABLISHING ORDER

Don Drysdale was quoted last summer as saying that "It used to be that the pitcher took part of the plate and the hitter took part of it. Now it seems like the hitter wants the whole thing." Tony Kubek, respectful of Mike Schmidt, still discounts the claims for him as the greatest third baseman of all time, saying that a lot of things have changed, that "they've taken the inside corner away from the pitcher." It is inevitable, you see, that men think of the way that things were when they were young as being the natural order. What Drysdale and Kubek don't understand is that *their era*, in the context of baseball history as a whole, is far more abnormal in this respect than the game of today.

After the 1968 season, there was a consensus in baseball that the pitchers were too much in control of the game, and a series of actions were taken to turn things around:

- The mound was lowered.
- The strike zone was made smaller.
- Six teams (The White Sox, Braves, A's, Phillies, Dodgers, and Royals) either shortened their fences or made other park changes designed to help the hitters.
- The umpires decided to take the inside part of the plate away from the pitchers.

This final action was never publicly announced; nonetheless, I am fairly certain that it was done, and that if you talked to someone who lived through the era, like Tom Seaver or Ferguson Jenkins, he would tell you that it was. What I think the umpires decided to do was not to try to challenge the accepted practices of the veteran pitchers, but to start cracking down on the younger pitchers and those coming into the game —issuing warnings if need be, and just not giving them the pitch on the inside corner of the plate. The old guys, like Gibson and Drysdale and Bunning, they allowed to continue to work inside—in effect, creating a grandfather clause for them. That is probably the reason that this action was never announced to the public, as the idea that different standards were being used for different players would not have set well with many of the players or fans.

These actions had their effect. Hit batsmen began to decline in 1969, and batting averages, after almost half a century of going down, began to go up. The long-term effects of the actions of 1968–69 have probably worn out by now; indeed, it is quite possible that what we heard in 1984 was the noise that a trend makes when it executes a left turn.

PART V: WHAT THEN SHALL WE DO?

That, in fact, is exactly what it turned out to be—a trend making a left turn. The frequency of hit batsmen, which was at 30 per 100 games in 1981, shot up in the years 1984–87, reaching 40 per 100 games in 1987, about where it was in 1972.

All kinds of interrelated subjects . . . beanballs and brushbacks, control problems and control of the inside corner, accidents and retaliation, injuries and brawls and temper tantrums, rules and regulations and the unwritten ethics of the sport; it is all a lot more complex than the HBP column tells us.

In September of 1984, *The Sporting News* issued an editorial that reviewed the problem of beanballs, injuries and possible solutions, and concluded by throwing up its hands in despair, saying that none of the solutions would work and that the players should be allowed to sort things out for themselves. On hearing this, Charles Spink, co-founder of *The Sporting News*, rolled over in his grave and had a heart attack.

With all due respect, I think that that editorial was uncommonly misguided, and belies a massive ignorance of the history of the game as well as a failure to think through the argument. Charles Spink spent the better part of ten years (the 1890s) raging about the fact that the powers of baseball were doing exactly what *The Sporting News* now advocates that they go back to doing: letting the players sort it out. The results of this policy were catastrophic, and if the policy were adopted again they would be catastrophic again. Does a responsible policeman, on learning that there is a barroom brawl in progress, say, "Oh, let them sort it out themselves. They always have."? Does a responsible schoolteacher, on seeing a fistfight developing in the schoolyard, say, "Oh, let them sort it out themselves."? There are schoolteachers in every school and policemen in every precinct who think that that is the way it should be done—and any time one of these jungle-rules advocates gets into a position of authority, the community has got a real serious problem on its hands.

Violence, once begun, begets a cycle of violence that can roll across centuries and level cities. To intercede in that cycle of violence at the earliest possible moment—to put a firm and fast lid on the people who want to sort things out once and for all—is not only *a* proper function of authority, it is *the* proper function of authority. If the league offices and the umpires have no other proper function in a baseball game, that is the one thing that they must do. The suggestion that the powers of baseball should abdicate this function and allow baseball to develop some sort of wild west code of honor is just flat crazy.

Another thing that gets me about the attitude of a few journalists and a number of old ballplayers toward this problem is the obvious double standard that is applied to past and present performers. The aggressive pitchers of today, like Pascual Perez, Mario Soto and Mike Krukow, are presented as if they were some sort of hooligans because they blister one under somebody's chin and a fight breaks out—but Don Drysdale and Bob Gibson can say things like "If I was pitching today I'd lose half my salary to fines," and talk about the glories of keeping the batter from digging in, and that somehow is cute, or even noble. If Bob Gibson and Don Drysdale were pitching today, they would abide by the rules that are enforced today.

I am a fan. I am a cash customer. I think that I speak for 99 percent of the cash customers when I say that I do not go to baseball games to watch baseball players sort out their personal differences. Did you ever see anybody plunk down five dollars a head to take their kids to a rumble in the alley? Neither did I.

And if the problem does start to grow more serious, there are any number of workable alternatives for dealing with it:

1) *The Frank Robinson Solution.* Before he was a manager and known for having the league's most antagonistic pitching

staff, Frank Robinson had a solution that he liked to recommend: Forget all about the intent of the pitcher. If a pitcher comes inside two or three times, tell him to take the rest of the day off. The umpire doesn't need to make any judgment about what the pitcher has in mind; he just needs to say, "It looks like you're a little wild today, son, we'd better get another pitcher in here before somebody gets hurt."

2) *Increase the On-Field Penalty for a Hit Batsman.* Send the batter to second base, rather than first. Or if there is a runner on base, make the hit batsman a force advance, rather than just filling up an empty space. Or send the runner to first base on the first hit batsman of the game, to second base on the second one, and to third base on any subsequent one. Or put the runner on first base and give the next batter a 2–0 count. Or put him on first base and give his team four outs in the inning. There's a million ways you can make it unprofitable for a pitcher to throw at a hitter.

3) *Create a Financial Penalty for an Excessive Number of Hit Batsmen.* An extension of the Robinson Principle to off-field action: Create a rule that says that the first four hit batsmen of the season are free; after that each one costs one half of one percent of your salary.

Is that unreasonable? I don't think it is unreasonable at all. Consider:

a. To throw a pitch to the place where the batter is standing is prohibited by the rules of the game.
b. To throw a pitch to the place where the batter is standing is dangerous. People get hurt.
c. The pitcher has a professional responsibility to prevent that from happening.
d. If a pitcher repeatedly fails in his professional obligation to do his work in a safe and responsible manner, it is not at all unreasonable for him to suffer an economic penalty, regardless of his lack of ill intentions.

Again, these rules are suggested alternatives *if a problem does start to develop;* I don't think we have seen enough now to justify their adoption. The players have the right to approve rules changes, and that creates a question of whether they would accept the third proposal. My experience in dealing with players during salary negotiations leads me to believe that they would endorse it heartily, if a) there was clear evidence of a worsening problem, and b) it was offered to them in the right form. If the owners just tried to adopt the rule as they saw fit and then shove it down the players' throats, no, of course they wouldn't accept that.

But ballplayers, by and large, do not want baseball to be a violent game. They do not want to get hurt, and they do not want to see other players getting hurt. Only a few pitchers hit more than four batters with pitches in a season, and probably many of those could avoid doing so if they stood to lose money if they were careless, so that the people who stood to lose money on the deal would be a tiny minority, while all would benefit from playing a safer game. The rules should be reasonable. The money collected should go to a charity, or to the players' pension fund, or to a special fund for the emergency needs of minor leaguers, rather than simply returning to the pockets of the owners. The pitchers should not be asked to be the only ones at risk; non-pitchers could also be subject to penalties for such things as throwing bats or charging the mound. The entire proposal should be hammered out by a joint player/owner committee, rather than designed by one side and offered to the other. Given those conditions, and given that there were a clear need, I think the players would vote for the idea about five to one.

The problem of the beanball is not, I think, a critical issue at this time. But baseball players do get hurt, regularly, when hit by pitches. Batting helmet or no batting helmet, a baseball is a potentially lethal weapon. Some people would say that that's just part of the game, to which I say that human beings decide what is and is not a part of the game; injuries resulting from pitches are part of the game only if we decide that they are. The conflict over the pitcher's right to endanger the health of the batter has been a problem throughout the history of the game, and the day will quite surely come when we will face that problem again. I have not the foggiest idea when that will be. But if we think through the problem now, we will be ready for it then. It will be a disservice to the heroes of tomorrow if we choose instead to hide behind clichés and the hollow bravado of the heroes of yesterday.

—Edited from the 1985 *Baseball Abstract*

Record of Known Cases of Death
from a Pitched Ball in Professional Baseball

1900–87

September 24, 1909—Charles Tenhuy, second baseman of the Dayton club in the Central League, suffered a fractured skull and died after being hit by a pitch by a man named Hagerman, pitching for Grand Rapids.

July 14, 1910—Philip Forney, an umpire in the Western association, died as a result of paralysis that set in after he was hit over the left eye by a pitched ball.

September 16, 1913—Clarence Stearns, described in the *Reach Guide* as a "well-known minor league player," died at Winnebago, Minn., from a hemorrhage of the brain attributed to having been twice hit by pitches during the season.

February 16, 1914—Gardner Lowe, a minor league pitcher, died at Delmar, Del., "from an infection supposed to have been caused from being hit by a pitched ball the previous summer."

June 19, 1916—John Dodge, an infielder with Mobile in the Southern League, was killed by a pitch which struck him in the face.

August 16, 1920—Ray Chapman of the Indians hit in the head by Carl Mays, died the next day.

August 27, 1936—George Tkach, second baseman of Superior in the Northern League, hit by pitch; died September 2.

July 16, 1938—Linus (Skeeter) Ebnet, shortstop of the Winnipeg club in the Northern League, hit by pitch; died July 21. (A reader pointed this out to me after I omitted Ebnet from the original list. I have unfortunately lost the reader's name, but I thank him all the same.)

July 3, 1947—James (Stormy) Davis, twenty-year-old outfielder for Ballinger in the Longhorn League, was hit in the head by a pitch; died July 10.

June 2, 1951—Ottis Johnson, an outfielder for Dothan in the

Alabama-Florida League, was hit by a pitch from Jack Clifton, a pitcher for Headland; he died June 10.

—1985

A History of Being a Kansas City Baseball Fan

I am, and have been for as long as it is possible to remember, a fan of the Kansas City baseball teams. In my youth this required that I support the Kansas City Athletics, the only team in modern history which never had a .500 or better season. Well, that's not exactly true; the Milwaukee Brewers of 1901 and the Seattle Pilots of 1969 had losing records in the only seasons of their existence, but that hardly counts, and the Seattle Mariners have not yet had a winning record, but they will within a year or two.

Under current conditions it would be very difficult, if not impossible, for any baseball team to become as bad as the Kansas City Athletics were. In modern baseball, when a team gets to be bad they acquire the high picks in the draft of high school and college players. Unless they were to do an atrocious job of evaluating the talent, this gives them enough of an edge that, over a period of five or seven years, they will begin to move back toward the center of the league. Just as it takes time to reach the levels of greatness represented by such teams as the 1963 Yankees, the 1953 Dodgers and the 1970 Orioles, it takes time to reach the nadir of performance represented by the A's of the mid-sixties. With the draft, the calendar now is working against such a possibility.

Thirteen straight losing seasons . . . the mind reaches for a yardstick. If you are a fan of the San Francisco Giants, you certainly have encountered some rough sailing in recent years. But the longest span of consecutive losing seasons ever turned in by the Giants, either in San Francisco or New York, either in this century or the last, is four.

If you are a fan of the Detroit Tigers, you certainly can remember some tough times here and there between contenders—but again, the longest string of consecutive losing seasons that you could possibly recall would be four, because that's the most they've ever had.

Not many teams have ever had thirteen.

The Brooklyn Dodgers, da bums who suffered centuries of frustration before developing into a powerhouse in the forties, never exposed their fans to thirteen consecutive losing seasons.

The Pittsburgh Pirates were a joke from the early 1940s until the coming of Danny Murtaugh, a team so bad that computer analyst George Wiley says they should have finished ninth in an eight-team league. But the Pittsburgh Pirates have never had thirteen straight losing seasons.

The Mets of the sixties, the late seventies and early eighties were the most spectacular losers of the expansion era, losing one hundred twenty games in one season and becoming a campy favorite while making an annual event of last place. But even the Mets have never suffered thirteen straight losing seasons—nor, indeed, has any expansion team, not the Padres, not the Expos, not even the expansion Senators.

For as long as most of us can remember, the Chicago Cubs have been baseball's lovable losers, the team that went into a coma after World War II and did not emerge until 1984. But even the Chicago Cubs have never suffered through thirteen straight losing seasons.

First in War, First in Peace, Last in the American League ... remember the original Washington Senators? The Washington Senators never suffered through thirteen consecutive losing seasons.

The White Sox punted the World Series in 1919, and were condemned to a long, dark exile of forty years before they got a chance to redeem themselves. They missed that chance and have waited another quarter-century, to date, for another one. But the White Sox never went through thirteen consecutive losing seasons.

The Boston Braves, in their half century of going head to head with the Red Sox, rarely came out on top; they were the worst team in the National League in the first decade of this century, and were consistently among the worst teams in baseball in the twenties and thirties. But the Boston Braves never had thirteen consecutive losing seasons.

The Cleveland Indians, in our own time, are hardly a model

of a perennial powerhouse; it is tough to remember when the organization fielded a good team. But the Cleveland Indians have never had thirteen consecutive losing seasons. In fact, their longest two streaks added together only amount to thirteen seasons.

And *even the Browns*. Even the St. Louis Browns, the hapless Brownies . . . yes, even the Browns never suffered through thirteen consecutive losing seasons.

This one fact, however depressing, testifies only to the duration of the frustration; there was more to it than that. The A's not only never had a winning record, they never came close to having a winning record. They were never in any *danger* of having a winning record.

They very rarely had a winning *month*. Here; I'll list all the months in A's history when they won as many games as they lost (not including Octobers, and they never won more than two games in October):

1955—None
1956—None
1957—None
1958—April (8–4) and September (14–13)
1959—April (9–7) and July (19–11)
1960—None
1961—May (14–12)
1962—August (16–15)
1963—April (12–7) and May (13–12)
1964—None
1965—None
1966—September (13–9)
1967—None

Let's see . . . that makes nine months in which they played .500-or-better ball, which means they had losing records in sixty-nine months out of seventy-eight. The best month that the A's ever had in Kansas City was July of 1959; they started that month nine games out of first place, and finished nine and a half out. By the end of August, one month later, they would be twenty-one behind.

How bad were the A's? Well, consider this: The recent history of the Texas Rangers is not exactly ablaze in glory. *Over the last thirteen seasons the Rangers' won/lost record is 140½ games better than the A's record in Kansas City.* The A's record in Kansas City was 829 wins, 1,224 losses; the Rangers have beaten them by 136 wins, and taken 145 fewer losses. How bad is eleven games a year worse than the Rangers?

How bad can you get? The San Francisco Giants, now . . . there's another prize organization. Over the last thirteen years the Giants have beaten the record of the Kansas City A's by 145 games. Or how about using the Cleveland Indians as a standard? Some people have had the audacity to suggest that the Indians have the most dismal history of any major league franchise. Over the last thirteen years the Indians record is 942–1091, which is only 123½ games better than the A's.

The A's won/lost percentage for their years in Kansas City was .404. Only once in the last thirteen seasons—that being 1985, when the Indians lost 102 games—have the Indians had a winning percentage as low as .404, as low as the *average* winning percentage of the Kansas City A's.

The Cleveland Indians have been around for eighty-five years. In that time they have had six seasons with winning percentages below .400, three of which happened more than seventy years ago. The KC A's, in existence for only thirteen years, had seven seasons with winning percentages below .400. *The Cleveland Indians, in their long and largely dismal history, have had fewer truly dreadful teams than the Kansas City A's were able to pack into their brief thirteen-year life.*

That was my childhood.

In the A's thirteen years in Kansas City, the only pitcher to win as many as fifteen games in a season was a fellow named Bud Daley, who twice won sixteen. Only five pitchers ever won more than twelve in a season, and most of those still had losing records.

In the A's last three years in Kansas City, the most runs driven in by any player in a season was sixty-six. I would guess that no other team has ever gone three years without having a player drive in more than sixty-six runs.

In the same three years, the highest batting average by a regular was .270.

There have been worse teams. The thirteen consecutive losing seasons is not a record; the Red Sox and both Philadelphia franchises either matched or worsened it. The situation was not quite the same; the fans of the Red Sox and the Philadelphia Athletics could at least console themselves with the memories of the perennial champions who came just before the losing began, whereas the Kansas City fans, reflecting on the time before they were losers, could remember only the time when they were considered bush league.

But I couldn't remember that. I was only five years old when the A's arrived.

Though unified by the execrable quality of the teams, the A's passed through three distinct periods (three "building phases") between Philadelphia and Oakland, each one creating distinct riddles and emotions for me as a child fan. The first period was the Arnold Johnson years. Arnold Johnson, the first owner of the Kansas City Athletics, was a business associate and close friend of Del Webb, co-owner of the Yankees. Apparently believing that the way to make money in the outlands was as a supplier of talent to the wealthier organizations, Johnson funneled talent to the Yankees in a long series of three-for-one and five-for-two trades. Among the players acquired by the Yankees from Kansas City were Cletis Boyer, Roger Maris, Ryne Duren and Bobby Shantz. Ralph Terry was traded by the Yankees to the A's in 1957 after pitching ineffectively in trials in 1956 and early 1957; he was twenty-one at the time. When he got his feet on the ground as a major league pitcher, he was returned to the Yankees. When Enos Slaughter got off to a slow start with the Yankees in 1955 he was exiled to Kansas City; when he established that he could still hit and the Yankees needed him, he was sent back.

There was a bad smell about these trades, but much more irritating than the trades of prospects and the "loans" of other players in the development stage were the exchanges of the A's best players to the Yankees. Art Ditmar, the A's leading pitcher in their first two seasons (he won 12 games each year) was traded to the Yankees, where he pitched fairly well for four years, and was the Yankees' best starting pitcher in 1960. Harry (Suitcase) Simpson, after driving in 105 runs and hitting .293 for the A's in 1956, was in pinstripes by late 1957. Bob Cerv, after having the best offensive season that any KC A was ever to have in 1958 (he hit .305 with 38 homers, was elected to the All-Star team and batted cleanup for the American League), was returned to the Yankees in 1960. Bud Daley, after winning 16 games for the Athletics in 1959 and 1960, was traded to the Yankees in 1961. Hector Lopez, who seemed to be developing into a fine hitter, was traded to the Yankees in 1959. After Duke Maas pitched well in 1957 (219 innings with a 3.28 ERA), he was shipped on to New York, where he went 26–12 over the next two and a half seasons. If you look at the 1958 Kansas City team, which was the best A's team in the city (they finished 73–81), you might note that the top three home run and RBI men were Cerv, Maris, and Lopez; the team leader in strikeouts, innings and several other pitching categories was Ralph Terry. By 1960, all were with the Yankees.

Kansas City had been a minor league outpost for the Yankees for many years, and nobody minded too much so long as they weren't theoretically competing. But Kansas City is an extremely self-conscious town—we'll get into that later—and the pinstripe pipeline rubbed the city at a raw spot, the rawest spot Johnson could have found. With every KC/New York trade the protests grew louder, the bitterness in them grew sharper.

To a child, none of this quite made sense. I lived eighty miles from Kansas City, never went into the city and never saw them play in person. We didn't have a television, but I listened to them on the radio and studied the sports section of the Topeka paper. Why did so many people hate the Yankees? Why were so many people angry at the owner, when the radio broadcasters (of course) said that he was such a fine man and that what he was doing was in the best interests of Kansas City in the long run? Why did they root for the team if they didn't like them?

The notion of an inferiority complex is difficult for a child to figure out on his own in the best of circumstances. Having never visited either Kansas City or New York, I could have had no sense of the difference between one city and another. The history of the Yankees overlording of baseball meant nothing to me. A child has no way of understanding history because his concept of time is too limited; he can't imagine what is meant by a period of years. I could gather from it only that our team did not win very often, and that some people felt we were being taken advantage of. I rejected the idea that we were being taken advantage of because it seemed to me to be related in some way to self-pity.

In truth, how damaging these trades were is not absolutely clear. The group of players who had played well with the A's —Cerv, Simpson, Daley, etc.—were mostly players of marginal value who had one bright fling with the Athletics, and did very little to help the Yankees (or anybody else) after their trades. As for the trades of younger players like Maris, Boyer, and Terry, the A's also *received* some good young players from the Yankees, including their two best players of the early sixties, Norm Siebern and Jerry Lumpe, and two other players whom they gave up when they acquired Maris, Vic Power and Woodie Held. Terry was a big winner with the Yankees, but I doubt that he would have been much had he stayed in Kansas City.

The certain facts are that

1. The A's were a bad team.
2. They traded all of their best players to the Yankees, and
3. After that, they were a worse team.

That's enough to convict Arnold Johnson in almost any court, but it should be noted that the A's farm system in these years produced very little talent—maybe two or three players of quality. He had to try to come up with young players from somewhere. What he tried didn't work.

Arnold Johnson died on March 10, 1960; in the fullness of time his estate was able to sell the team to one Charles Oscar Finley. At first Finley's Athletics, perhaps influenced by holdover personnel in the front office, perhaps only by habit, continued to make sweetheart deals with the Yankees. The trade of Bud Daley, the A's most successful pitcher ever, was the last straw; the public was outraged. Finley and his new General Manager, Frank Lane, promised the Kansas City public that there would be no more Yankee trades.

The years beginning in 1961 could be described as the era of false promise. In 1961 and 1962 the A's were committed to youth; in 1963 this commitment wavered and in 1964 it collapsed. I was a full-fledged fanatic by now, rarely missing a game, often pacing a harrowed pattern around the front room as the A's wrestled to preserve a rare victory, more often sitting doggedly through the last out of a depressing rout. In my youth I believed the things that I was told by the announcers—that the A's were just a run here and a run there away from winning a lot more games, that they were just a player or two short of being a contender, that if they could just catch a break here and there they would get some momentum going and be over the hump. Every year we had different announcers in Kansas City, as Finley fired one after another, but each group reassured me about the banalities of the last. It was not merely that I began each spring full of promise, but that I arrived at the middle of August with the same expectation—that at any moment the breaks would change, the momentum would switch and the river would begin to flow uphill.

What seemed especially puzzling to me was the failure of the young players to develop. Annually the A's would spring upon us three or four unheard of youngsters. As the season evolved these kids would rush to the brink of stardom and retreat, looking for the consistency and gaining the experience which would put them among the best in the league at their positions. Yet while the other organizations would take young players and develop them, none of the Athletics' young performers would ever progress an inch from the point at which he entered the league. I couldn't understand how this could happen, how the A's could so consistently come up with the non-bloomers; it seemed to me that just by the law of averages, as it is familiarly known, it should be our turn to have one develop sooner or later. A few examples, in alphabetical order:

Jim Archer pitched 205 innings with a good 3.20 ERA as a rookie in 1961, but would start only one major league game after that season.

Norm Bass won eleven games as a rookie in 1961, but would win only two more games in his remaining major league career, and within a few seasons would give up baseball to concentrate on his football career.

Ed Charles hit .288 with 17 home runs, 54 walks and 20 stolen bases as a rookie third baseman in 1962, but never again had as good a season.

Dick Howser as a rookie shortstop in 1961 was the best lead-off man in baseball, hitting .280, drawing 92 walks, stealing 37 bases (second highest total in baseball), and scoring 108 runs. The only major league leadoff man to have a comparable season was Maury Wills, who hit .282, scored 105 runs and stole 35 bases. Compared to Wills, Howser was several years younger, drew 33 more walks with 12 less strikeouts, and hit for much more power (38 extra base hits against 23). Yet a year later Wills had developed into one of baseball's biggest stars—while Howser, after fracturing a leg in a collision at second base, never approached the same performance.

Manny Jiminez hit .301 in 139 games as a rookie in 1962, but never again played regularly in the majors.

Jose Tartabull, proclaimed by the announcers as the fastest man in baseball in 1962, hit a solid .277 in 107 games as a rookie—but never had as good a season again.

There were other examples. I was mystified by why this kept happening to us. Over the years, I have noted again this effect, that when a good organization comes up with a young player that young player will develop, but that when a weak organization comes up with a good young player he seems less likely to progress. From this distance, several things are apparent. One is the pressure that a bad organization puts on young players. Dick Howser was a fine young player—but he was expected to carry the ball club. Any time a young pitcher showed promise he would be given a heavy workload and the high expectations that came with it. That pressure complicated the learning process for each youngster.

Second, the players on the A's had no example to guide them. When the White Sox would come up with a young player, he would have the example of Luis Aparicio to go by, to see how he handled the daily pressures, what his work habits were and how he conducted himself getting ready for the game. When the Dodgers would come up with a young pitcher he would have the example of Don Drysdale or Koufax; when the Orioles had a young player he could study Brooks Robinson, while the Yankees, of course, were surrounded by such quality. The A's players were on their own.

Third, a few of the A's players—but, I would stress, only a few of them—were not really prospects of any particular quality, but rather were the rejects of other organizations, let go because of defensive skills or personal qualities that would manifest themselves after the player got a chance to play. Ed Charles, one of the rookie "finds" of 1962, had been kicking around the minor leagues for almost a decade before he got a chance to play. It is not surprising that he played well in his rookie season, and not surprising that he played less well after that. Jim Archer, too, was no prospect, a throw-in in a trade with the Orioles who surprised everybody and hurt his arm when he pitched well in 1961. While the radio announcers could fool me by extolling the virtues of young players like Jim Gosger, Roger Repoz, Dan Pfister and Haywood Sullivan, the reality was that they simply did not have quality skills.

But fourth and most importantly, the organization suffered from extreme instability, resulting in a truly remarkable lack of commitment to their best young players. In individual instances perhaps one can make excuses for the organization. Granted, Dick Howser did not play well in the first half of the 1962 season. Granted, he was injured badly and out for the second half of the 1962 season; granted, when he was ready to get back in the lineup Wayne Causey was playing very well at the position.

But that's three "granteds," and it only covers one player. One of the stranger cases was that of Manny Jimenez, the only player of his generation from San Pedro de Macoris. Acquired from the Braves' system in exchange for Bob Shaw, the big, strong left-handed hitter was among the league leaders in hitting for the first three months of the 1962 season, until Charlie Finley arranged a private conference with him and told him to stop concentrating on hitting for average and to try to hit more home runs. Finley not only did this, but he immediately went up to the press box and told everybody that he had done it, and why he had done it and how he had done it. Later, he would insist that he hadn't done it at all, and when that didn't work he said that he had done it, but only after his manager and his coaches had tried unsuccessfully to tell Jimenez the same thing.

Anyway, Jimenez went into a slump immediately thereafter and finished the season at .301, losing almost 30 points in the last two months. Jimenez was not a good outfielder or a good baserunner. Even so, .301's all right; .301 with medium-range power (11 homers, 69 RBI in 479 at bats) for a twenty-three-year-old rookie . . . that's a place to start something from.

When Manny Jimenez went to spring training the next year he found himself without a job. In a search for more power, the left field slot had been given to Chuck Essegian, a thirty-one-year-old veteran who had never before played regularly, but had hit 21 homers in 336 at bats with Cleveland in 1962. Finley felt that, playing regularly, he would hit 35 home runs. He hit 5. Jimenez spent a good part of the season in the minor leagues. While on the A's roster he pinch hit and filled in, hit .280 on the road to oblivion.

Why did the A's do this astonishingly stupid thing, to replace a twenty-four-year-old .300 hitter with a thirty-one-year-old nobody? The lack of commitment to the young players with talent reflects the extreme instability of the organization. As well as a different radio announcer every year, the organization had a different manager, usually different coaches, frequently a different general manager. It is my belief that men like Finley are compelled to change those who work for them in highly visible positions because their own low self-esteem and feelings of inadequacy cause them to project their own shortcomings and weaknesses onto those around them. When Finley saw his own flaws reflected in those who represented him to the public, he felt that he had been exposed, his carefully hidden failings laid bare. This terrified him, and compelled him to fire anyone around him who was anything less than perfect.

But every new manager, every new general manager and every new coach had new ideas about who could help the organization and how he should be used. The most games played by any A's player in their thirteen years in Kansas City was 726, by Ed Charles; in other words, not one player was able to last as long as five seasons as a regular. Emphasizing the instability, Finley was forever farting around with the fences, yanking them in as far as the rules would allow and then pushing them back. A pitcher would learn that he could get by with a particular pitch one year, and the next year the same ball would be in the seats, while a young hitter would learn to jerk the ball into the seats one year, only to see those same seats moved back by twenty-five or thirty feet the next season.

Yet the changes in personnel do not fully explain the organization's amazing lack of commitment to the young players with whom their fate rested. One of the recurrent themes of Bill James analysis of baseball: Bad organizations will tend to project their weaknesses onto their best players, and ultimately will dwell not on what the player *can* do, but on what he *can't*. And what better example of this can there be but Manny Jimenez? The kid's hitting .330, he's got a little power but *we're still losing*. If we're losing he must not be doing all that well. He's not a great outfielder or any kind of a base runner, so he's got to hit for more power.

At this vantage there is little doubt that, left alone, Jimenez in time would have developed some power, and would have been a quality major league hitter, the type of player who could help win some games. Another example was Jose Tartabull, the little center fielder. Here, in 1962, was a twenty-three-year-old kid who could fly, play center field and hit .277. Given a full shot, Tartabull would very likely have developed into a player who could help a team win. Instead, the A's saw him as a player who had no power and didn't throw very well; he too was out of a job in the spring of 1963. Bobby Del Greco, a thirty-year-old refugee from the National League with a career average of .229, was in center.

A year later the A's had another young center fielder whom I left off the list above, a guy named Nellie Mathews. If you're inclined to focus on the negatives, Mathews offered no challenge. He ran OK but not as well as you might want your center fielder to run, he struck out too much (143 times), hit .239, was too aggressive on the bases and didn't throw great. If you were inclined to focus on the positives, you'd see a twenty-two-year-old kid who hit some doubles (27), some triples (5), and some homers (14), drew a few walks (43) and, according to all reports, hustled from the beginning of the game to the end. The average wasn't much, but in 1964 there were a great many regulars who hit less. Even the best teams in baseball at that time had .220 hitters in their lineups.

Finley was like a man who plants a garden every spring with energy and enthusiasm, but who sees by mid-summer not the green, fresh produce he had envisioned, but a weedy, overgrown patch of dry vegetation. Embarrassed by this, he rips out the garden so that no one would see his weeds. Unlike Jimenez and Tartabull, I wouldn't hazard a guess as to whether or not Mathews would have developed into a ballplayer. I know for sure that in the A's situation—they lost 105 games that year—I'd have been happy to take the chance. I'd figure that here's a young kid, if he lifts his batting average 20 or 30 points, maybe improves the strikeout and walk data a little bit as he goes along, maybe edges up from 46 extra base hits to 60 . . . well, he's going to have a job. It is equally likely that his faults might have reached up and swallowed him, that the tendency to strike out might have gotten out of hand and choked off his production, as the weeds will choke a garden. But we will never know. When spring training opened in 1965, center field was patrolled by a thirty-one-year-old defensive specialist named Jim Landis. Career batting average, .247.

In the first four years of the Charlie Finley era of the A's (1960–63), some progress was being made. The team's records for those four years were 58–96, 61–100, 72–90, and 73–89. Though some traits of the man tended to retard the progress, Finley *did* care about winning—indeed, he may have cared more about winning than any other owner of his time. Losing did not reflect well on him. The 1963 team, still a fairly young team, had a very good infield and three or four decent pitchers, although the outfield had no punch and the catching was bush league.

This progress was too slow for Finley; he was tired of losing. He was tired of having the professionals in his organization tell him that you had to build with youth, that you had to build from within, that it just took time. He was very concerned about the team's lack of power—the same concern that had led to the Jimenez and Essegian debacles of earlier years. At some point in the 1963 season he had a conversation with his manager, Ed Lopat, which was to bring this era of progress to a close, and re-set the A's clock to the beginning of another building cycle.

Lopat had been a member of the formidable Yankee teams of the late forties and early fifties, and apparently he was trying to explain to Finley the Yankee formula. The Yankees, according to Lopat by way of Finley, had a simple trick for winning the pennant every year: it all had to do with the short dimensions down the lines—296 to right, 301 to left. With the short lines and deep center field area, all the Yankees had to do was keep around some power hitters to pull the ball in the seats, teach their own pitchers to keep the ball out away from the opponent's power hitters, and they'd have a big home run advantage.

No doubt Lopat did not intend to make it sound so simple; the odds are overwhelming that Ed Lopat at least had a clue that there was more to it than this. No doubt he would have explained this to Finley, had the conversation continued a few minutes longer. But Finley took this confession from the ex-Yankee very much to heart, and set out to replicate the conditions. To acquire one power hitter, Jim Gentile, he traded the best player on his team. To acquire another, Rocky Colavito, he traded the rest of the good players on his team. Then, blundering across the fine line between the stupid and the ridiculous, Finley ordered Municipal Stadium in Kansas City to be rebuilt to the exact field dimensions of Yankee Stadium.

To begin with, this was not physically possible; he would have had to rent center field from the city street department. Second, it was not permitted by the rules of the game, which, though protecting the existing parks, did not permit new fences to be constructed within 325 feet of home plate. And third, the whole idea was nuts.

Never to be deterred by such details, Finley constructed a pavilion in right field and called it his "Pennant Porch," boldly suggesting that what would win the pennant for New York would also win the pennant for Kansas City. The commissioner's office, which was more up on the rules of the game, insisted that Finley have the seats torn out to at least 325 feet. Finley, complaining bitterly of unequal treatment, eventually complied, after which it became the "one-half pennant porch," although a chalk line was painted across the outfield to show where the fence had been. Whenever a fly ball was hit over the line the public address announcer was instructed to announce that "That ball would have been a home run in Yankee Stadium." (It is said that the practice of making this announcement came to an end in the eleventh inning on May 2, when the Minnesota Twins became the third team in baseball history to hit four consecutive home runs. It is said that following the home runs by Oliva, Allison, Hall, and Killebrew, Earl Battey drove the ball to the wall in left, and the announcer dutifully intoned "That ball . . . would have been a home run . . . in Yankee Stadium." The announcement was discontinued the next day.)

The number of home runs hit in Kansas City increased from 139 to 239. Of the extra 100 home runs, the A's picked up 55, and their opponents 45. Those 45 were enough to enable the

Kansas City team to set an all-time record for home runs allowed in a season, with 220.

The 1964 season obliterated the steady progress of the previous years. Not until the rookie draft was instituted in 1965 was there any new evidence that the A's would ever escape the second division.

One should not depart from this subchapter of Kansas City's bleak baseball youth without a note about its lingering effect in the minds of those of us who witnessed it. You who are regular readers will know that one of the things that I look for in a manager and admire in a good manager is his willingness to commit himself to a young player, and that in particular I have cited Dick Williams, Whitey Herzog, and Dick Howser as being strong in this area. All three of those managers know what it is that they expect a young player to do, and all three are able to avoid being distracted or disoriented in those periods when the player's weaknesses manifest themselves more clearly than his strengths. Those three managers (and several others, as well) played for the Kansas City A's in this period. In the same way as nothing will teach a man self-discipline like an extreme example of profligacy, one wonders if perhaps the need to make a commitment to young players was not impressed deeply upon these gentlemen by this obscene example of their youth, a team with no ability to make a commitment to anything or anyone. I would bet that there was a time, about 1960, when Dick Williams and Whitey Herzog sat in the Kansas City dugout and chatted about why they were in last place, and one of them said to the other (or both said at the same time), "You know, there's a lot of guys here who could play the damn game if they would just leave them alone and let them do it."

I was half grown by the mid-sixties, and I got to see a game occasionally. To the credit of Charles O. Finley, he learned from his mistakes. Following the hard lesson of 1964, he accepted the professionals' wisdom, accepted that it just takes time, that a good team must be built of youth and time, and that only patience could combine the two. The willingness of the organization to let a young player develop improved dramatically after 1964. Finley never again fell for the idea that there was a magic formula that could convert his team into a winner overnight. The A's resumed their torturous crawl forward.

In 1968 the Athletics moved to Oakland. At first many of us were determined to keep rooting for the Athletics; I had no experience in loving any other baseball team, and didn't imagine that I ever could. But in truth, rooting for Charlie Finley was damned hard work when he was right in front of you, and all but impossible from halfway across the continent.

In addition to being ugly and smelling bad, the Kansas City A's had a bad personality. I say this, as Broadway Danny Rose said, with all due respect. Charles O. Finley considered himself to be a master showman, and the team fairly swarmed in cutesy promotions and special events. They had the usual stuff like home run hitting contests, fireworks and special days for people who were retiring—even people who weren't any good —as well as more adventurous stuff like cow milking contests and pre-game rodeos. Sheep grazed in the grass beyond the outfield; they were joined later by a mule. One year a cellar-bray-tion (a mule brays, get it?) was planned for the day that the A's got out of last place, but they never did. A mechanical rabbit popped out of the ground to deliver clean baseballs to the umpire. An automatic plate duster was installed. Finley put in a public picnic area (well, anybody can have a good idea once in awhile).

Finley would make a "day" out of anything. He once had a special day for an umpire who had been involved in some controversy, presenting him with a seeing-eye dog.

When Rocky Colavito got close to 300 home runs, he tried to generate public interest in the pursuit of this goal by scheduling an event and lining up a list of prizes to give him, headed by a plaque of 300 silver dollars.

He tried to give a "poison pen" award to KC writers who wrote disdainfully about these antics, but of course nobody would accept it.

He inaugurated the era of colored uniforms, and tried to inaugurate colored bases and colored baseballs as well.

There was a rule in the books requiring the pitcher, with no one on base, to deliver the pitch within twenty seconds of receiving the ball from the catcher. If he didn't do so, a ball could be called. Finley felt that this rule should be enforced, and put a clock on the scoreboard to count down the seconds;

when the time elapsed a horn would sound. This, of course, was designed to show up the umpires for not enforcing the rule, and the umpires appreciated the effort. In addition, a pitcher in the act of delivering a pitch was often not enthusiastic about hearing a horn go off, and Finley was told to shut the thing off. He shut off the horn, but kept the clock. One umpire actually did call the penalty ball, against Kansas City pitcher Diego Segui.

For a time we had a woman broadcaster, for a few games late in the season ("Was that a slow one?" she would inquire of her co-workers.) Don't get me wrong, I'm all for having a woman broadcaster, but it would help if she was a baseball fan —my wife, for example.

When the Beatles first toured the country, Charlie tried to get them to schedule a stop at Municipal Stadium on their tour. He tried this, however, after the tour was already booked, and when he was initially rebuffed he began throwing money at them to get them to re-schedule so as to accommodate. Eventually he paid them an amount of money to make a one-night Kansas City appearance that was reportedly more than he was paying his entire starting lineup for the season. In the weeks before the show, the game broadcasters hyped this event non-stop; Finley was hoping to fill the park, and thus recoup his investment. When the crowd was disappointing, the announcers sniffed that Kansas City wouldn't support Charlie after he had put out a lot of money to get the Beatles to come to town. His players were not particularly appreciative, either.

Finley would appear on his pre-game show once in awhile, but rather than talking about the outlook for the ball club, he would entertain us with his opinions about who should be in the Hall of Fame, how the rules should be changed and what a wonderful human being he was.

This junk was not the worst part of having Finley around. He feuded constantly not only with the press, but with his players, his staff, and the league office as well. Bitter holdouts were the order of the day in spring training. Public criticism of the players was commonplace. At times the team would come close to open revolt about some silly rule or about the mistreatment of a player.

He feuded with the city, which owned the park. But that wasn't the worst part, either.

Finley spent virtually his entire time in Kansas City threatening to move. First he tried to move to Dallas-Fort Worth. The league wouldn't let him. He tried to move to Louisville. He signed a lease on the Louisville park. The league wouldn't let him go. He sued the league. He wanted to move to Denver. He wanted to move to New Orleans. He talked about moving to Phoenix. He talked about moving to Seattle. He talked about moving to places that didn't even have ball parks.

He wanted to change cities for the same reason that he wanted to change managers. Once he had embarrassed himself in front of the city he wanted to wipe the slate clean, start all over with some people who didn't know anything about him.

At one point the league tried to kick him out. They had some sort of clause in their agreement—I never really did understand all this, to tell you the truth—that if you were bad enough, they could kick you out of the club. Finley was about as bad as you could be, and they tried to kick him out. Apparently the clause was not enforceable, because he refused to leave and they couldn't make him. Or maybe the attempt to expel him was merely intended to force him to agree to stay in Kansas City.

He was involved in constant lawsuits. He hired and fired Frank Lane within about a year; Lane had to sue him for the balance of his contract.

When the expansion Royals came to town, it was immediately obvious that this organization was different. In their first season they won sixty-nine games, which may not sound like much to you but it would have been a good season for the A's, and it is one of the best figures for a first-year expansion team. But more important than that, in the early years, were the small touches which put the signature of class on the organization. The circus atmosphere was gone; the emphasis was all on the ball team.

Whereas the A's, for announcers, had subjected us to a long succession of ex-network men on the way down, small-timers on the way nowhere and local announcers who had been fired by other teams, the Royals took the time and trouble to interview hundreds of people and locate a talented young man, Denny Matthews, who would come to represent the organization to Kansas City the way that Ernie Harwell represented the Tigers to Detroit or Vin Scully represented the Dodgers to LA.

Lou Piniella, after winning the American League Rookie of the Year Award in 1969, actually had a *better* season in 1970. Young players who did not succeed were given a respectable amount of time to be evaluated, and then were dismissed. No promotions were built around snake charmers, rock concerts, barnyard animals or attempts to embarrass the owner's enemies.

Whereas the A's organization was rather a grimy, dirty machine, grotesquely inefficient and with a personality nobody liked, the Royals tended to the other extreme; they seemed antiseptic, colorless, mechanically efficient and with not much personality to like or dislike. This was a very welcome change. We had moved from the slums to the suburbs.

In September, 1967, I moved away from home to attend Kansas University; a few days later the A's played their last game in Kansas City. I wonder sometimes how this sudden separation from my childhood affected the type of baseball fan that I became. From years of listening to the A's announcers, I had acquired the inevitable conviction that they had little idea of what they were talking about. I think, really, that this is one reason that so many intelligent people drift away from baseball at about that age, that if you care about it at all you have to realize, as soon as you acquire a taste for independent thought, that a great portion of the sport's traditional knowledge is ridiculous hokum. When baseball's explanations for things begin to look childish, the sport tends to get pushed back into childhood.

I was now, in addition to this, suddenly cut loose from my adolescent devotion, and forced to follow a new, different, and sharply contrasting team. My affection for the game as a whole was too much a part of me to be just cast aside, but my affection for the Royals was decidedly limited, and in fact it would be years before I would learn again to care blindly about my adopted heroes. It was not until Susie began to get involved in the game, ten years later, that I was able to recapture, through sharing her experience, the creative innocence required to abandon my emotions to the flight of the team.

The Royals seemed to me to be a product created for the public's consumption. This put a distance between me and the sport, and for a period of time, rather than simply following the team through the accepting eyes of a fan, I surveyed the game as coldly as if I had stumbled upon it as a foreigner— although, of course, I retained the enormous background of information about baseball that a fan develops. When Susie began following the game in the late seventies, the distinction between those teams which were manufactured in our own time and those which had simply always *been there* meant nothing to her; to her, as it will seem to our child, the Royals were simply there. Like all the other teams.

The accident of fate was that the period of my psychic separation from the emotional level of the sport corresponded to the period of my education, and so it happened that I began to borrow ways of looking at the game not from sportswriters, announcers, and other fans, but from the academic disciplines of history and the social sciences.

The Kansas City community had long regarded Charlie Finley's A's as an embarrassment. Given a new, professional team to represent them, the city rallied around the Royals, determined to avoid a repetition of the petty, unpleasant relationship between team and town. An organization of businessmen, known as the Royal Lancers, was formed with the explicit purpose of helping the team to succeed economically. Specifically, they sell season tickets. And they're *real* good at it. I don't really know a lot of the details, but I gather that a local businessman named Earl Smith was quite instrumental in providing the impetus and leadership for this coalescence of the business community.

The A's had no fair complaint as to the crowds they drew. The Braves were in Milwaukee for thirteen years and had winning records all thirteen years. The Athletics were in Kansas City for thirteen years and had losing records all thirteen years. In spite of this, the Athletics drew 1,500,568 fans in their last two seasons in KC—34,073 more than the Braves drew in their last two seasons in Milwaukee. However, this may be misleading because the Milwaukee fans were boycotting the Braves in their last half-season in Milwaukee, whereas the Kansas City fans were sort of doing the opposite. There was a clause in the contract between Finley and Kansas City that the agreement could be abrogated if attendance was below 850,000. There was always speculation that Finley, in his eagerness to move, was deliberately trying to keep attendance down so as to keep this clause in play. In his last years the KC fans obstinately tried to keep attendance up so as to reduce Finley's bargaining power. Besides that, there's always been a lot of people around here who like baseball.

But if the A's attendance was adequate, the attendance of the Royals was abundant. The team was built with astonishing speed—astonishing, at least, to a young man who had grown up thinking that to have a losing team was the normal way of life. I had been conditioned to believe that for a losing team to right itself and become a winning team was an immortal task, and certainly would not be accomplished in less than seven years.

In three years the Royals were in contention, and since then they have virtually never been out. They have been extraordinarily fortunate. In their fifth season they brought up George Brett. No matter how smart you are, no matter how good your system is, when you find a George Brett you're lucky. If you came up with one every five years, you'd never lose a pennant.

In their first four years, under the direction of Cedric Tallis, the Royals turned in a run of trades that ranks with those made by Frank Lane in Chicago about 1950 as the greatest series of exchanges in history, in every case giving up a player who was to do nothing or virtually nothing in the major leagues in exchange for a player who would play in the major leagues for many years, in most cases finishing high in the balloting for Most Valuable Player. In four years the Royals acquired Lou Piniella, Amos Otis, Cookie Rojas, Freddie Patek, John Mayberry, and Hal McRae, all for players who did essentially nothing in the major leagues. Later they added Darrell Porter to the list. Of course, as before, they were extremely fortunate in this era; nobody is *that* smart. An odd thing was that almost all of these trades were, at the time they were made, unpopular. The public's reaction to the Hal McRae trade was "Why are we giving up Roger Nelson for this guy?" Watching this unfold, in stark contrast to the patternless, turbulent experience of my earlier favorites, I was left with almost a superstitious awe of the Royals' organization. Until 1983 I reacted calmly to anything that the Royals could do. When they gave away John Mayberry I didn't second-guess them. When they fired Whitey Herzog I didn't second-guess them. I always said, "You gotta figure those guys know what they are doing."

We will assume that you know the history of the Kansas City team in the late seventies, and will pass over it with only one argument. That has to do with the quality of the team. The good fortune that had blessed the organization in the city, in the farm system, and in their trades abandoned them in post-season play, and they will forever be remembered as the second-best team in the league in the late seventies. There is no convincing evidence that they were not the best. True, they did lose three of four play-off matchups against the Yankees, but they missed winning three of four by only two innings.

To a baseball fan this may be convincing evidence, but if a coin lands on its head three times in four nobody is convinced that the coin is weighted. They were the type of team, like the 1985 Cardinals, that usually doesn't do well in a short, crucial series—too aggressive on the bases, too dependent on speed, too young and inexperienced. The Royals consistently beat all of the powerhouse teams in the American League East throughout those years; it was rare for any of those teams, including the Yankees, to win the season series against KC.

Having written those words, of course, I am compelled to get out the books and check the facts, and now that I do so I see that this occurrence was not rare; it was nonexistent. In *The Bronx Zoo*, Sparky Lyle wrote that "I hope to hell they realign the Divisions like they're talking about and put Kansas City in with us because it would be the last play-off spot they ever see. If they had been in the East this year, they would have been fourth." In fact, in that season the Royals had won outright their series against all of the tough teams in the Eastern Division, beating the Yankees six of eleven, Boston, Detroit, and Milwaukee six out of ten, and Baltimore eight out of ten.

In their four championship seasons, the Royals never lost the season series to any of those teams, and posted winning percentages against them of .656 in 1976, .627 in 1977, .627 in 1978, and .617 in 1980. It is much more likely that if they were to realign the divisions, it would be the last play-off spot that the Yankees would ever see. And more likely than that, the Royals would win their share, and so would the other good teams in that division.

But, of course, who had been a better team during the season was not what was at issue in post-season play. When I look at the great teams of history and try to compare one to another, one question that I like to ask about each is "How many players were there here who were really outstanding players, who were good enough players to play in a thousand or 1500 major league games or win 100 or 150 games, and who were at or near the peak of their game at this time?" Not "What were their stats in this particular year?" but "How good were they, really, and how many good players did they have?"

The Royals in those years had more than a dozen. Five key members of the 1977 Royals were still playing regularly in 1985, eight years and who knows how many games later; those five are Porter, White, Brett, Cowens, and McRae. Two of the *bench players* on that team are still around, those being Wathan and Buck Martinez. Three other regulars have retired after good careers, those being Otis, Mayberry, and Patek. The pitching staff included several men who won over a hundred games, including Splittorff, Leonard, Gura, and Pattin. Other members of those teams included Willie Wilson, Cookie Rojas, and Dan Quisenberry; Rojas was old but the others weren't. There are others that I haven't mentioned who played a thousand or more games. You check out the great teams of history, and you won't find many who can match that.

Following the World Series in 1980, the performance of the Royals' organization began to waver. In the malignant summer of 1981, the Royals finished under .500 for the first time since 1974. There was no apparent reason for the decline. The Royals had won 97 games in 1980 with a team that was actually *younger* than the champions of 1976–78, due to the development of Willie Wilson, Clint Hurdle, and Dan Quisenberry, as well as U.L. Washington's having taken the shortstop job.

In 1982 the Royals won ninety games, but there were many things about the team that concerned me. By now the team was being run by a different General Manager, John Schuerholz. Running short of proven pitchers, the organization had attempted to patch up the staff with burned-out vets like Vida Blue, Dave Frost, Don Hood and Grant Jackson. Clint Hurdle, after having a fine season as a twenty-two-year-old in 1980, encountered personal and health problems in 1981. The organization dumped him and gave the right field job to Jerry Martin, a thirty-three-year-old player of modest ability. This decision seemed to me to be strongly reminiscent of the A's of my childhood, and to be not at all consistent with the practices which had built the Royals into a fine team. Worse than *pitching* Vida Blue, which was all right, was the fact that the organization had given up three pitching prospects, including Atlee Hammaker, to do so.

In 1983 the team reached another low, finishing 79–83 and with a serious drug scandal. The habit of trying to solve the pitching problems with beat-up veterans had reached self-parody. Trying to plug the gaps as key pitchers like Splittorff, Gura, and Leonard got old and injured, the Royals had imported Gaylord Perry, Eric Rasmussen, Steve Renko, and Bill Castro—on the same staff with holdovers Blue, Hood, Gura, and Splittorff. Oh, it was ugly; I don't think anybody on that team could throw eighty-six miles an hour except Vida, and he couldn't get it over.

Fairly or unfairly, it seemed to me that the succession of trades that Schuerholz had made defined a philosophy about the sport and how to succeed in it. As a fan, I was aghast. I thought "I've seen this done before, and *it doesn't work*." The team roster had acquired players like Joe Simpson, Leon Roberts and Greg Pryor. I had taken pleasure in watching young role players like Frank White, U. L. Washington and Dan Quisenberry earn their spurs and grow into valued performers; I was not thrilled to see those positions on the team being filled by players that I knew had no chance to amount to anything.

At this point, in the 1984 *Baseball Abstract*, I abandoned my long-held belief that "those guys probably know what they're doing." John Schuerholz, I wrote, "has yet to try anything that worked." Schuerholz "doesn't want to put Ron Johnson in the lineup and find out why he hits .336 at Omaha; he wants to come up with a 'proven' player. Somebody like Bruce Bochte."

In view of the success of the Royals over the last two seasons, it is incumbent upon me to consider whether my remarks at that time were unfair to Schuerholz. I don't honestly know. It is clear that since then, while *some* of the importing of declining players has continued (i.e., the trades for Jim Sundberg and Lonnie Smith), there has in general been a return to the practices of earlier years. Like Amos Otis, Freddie Patek, and John Mayberry, Steve Balboni was a capable young player trapped in a bad situation; the Royals liberated him in exchange for very little, and he was one of the top home run hitters in baseball last season. In the spring of 1984 a commitment was made to the next generation of young pitchers, and those pitchers have turned out to be better than anyone would have dared hope.

The thing is, I really don't know what happened within the offices of Royals Stadium. Perhaps I inferred incorrectly what John Schuerholz was trying to do in the period 1981–83. Perhaps Schuerholz was confronted with a situation in which there simply were no good young players available to him, and he felt that the best thing he could do was to try to stabilize the team by bringing in some experienced players until the young ones were ready. If so, what I wrote then was unfair. Another possibility is that there was a time, about the same time that I wrote that article, that Ewing Kauffman held a meeting and said, "Look, John, you're a bright young man, you're a good negotiator and we're glad to have you here, but what you're doing with the team just isn't working. We didn't get where we are by dragging in ballplayers three-quarters of the way through their careers. We got here by giving young men a chance to play, letting them surprise people. Let's go back to that." If that's closer to what happened, then what I wrote was fair.

But John Schuerholz has to be given credit for what he has done. It's a simple game; if you win, you deserve credit for it. John Schuerholz has rebuilt the Royals into one of the best teams in baseball.

By August, it was fairly apparent that the 1985 Royals had a chance to be remembered. I try to recall . . . was there a specific game in there, about the tenth of August perhaps, when I suddenly looked down and realized how brutally resilient this team could be when the situation arose, how strong was their will to survive and how sure their instinct for the kill? Whether or not there was one moment, the hunger of the Royals had manifested itself quite suddenly, and seemed, far from being "intangible," to be as palpable as the August heat.

The 1984 team, though the best of a poor division, was not

too much of a ball club; there was little room for disappointment when the Tigers destroyed them in the Championship Series. If that team had been in the A.L. East, they *would* have finished fourth. At best. The pitching staff was a combination of rookies and reclamation projects, and that was the best part of the team.

In early 1985 the Royals looked a little better, while not winning any more consistently. The pitchers had done what second-year pitchers are supposed to do and reclamation projects are not supposed to be able to do; four of the five starters were throwing harder than they had in 1984. George Brett was playing as well as he has ever played, and not too many have ever played better. The offense was inconsistent.

In late July, the offense clicked and the Royals began methodically churning good opponents into mush. From July 19 through the end of the season the Royals played thirty-two games against teams who finished the season with winning records. They won twenty-three of those thirty-two games, a remarkable .719 winning percentage—against the good teams. Excepting a one-game makeup against the Tigers they won nine straight series against winning teams, beating the Yankees three straight games, the Tigers two out of three and two out of three, the Blue Jays two out of three and two out of three, the White Sox two out of three and then three straight, and the Angels two out of three and three out of four.

It is fortunate that no one was able to market an "Eau de Mariner" or "Essence of Ranger," or the Royals' post-season play would have been short and unmemorable. Through the same period, they played poorly against .500-or-less teams, winning twenty-two but losing twenty-one. The Red Sox were neither a good team nor a bad team, winning 81 and losing as many; in August the Royals beat them in Fenway Park, but lost to them in Kansas City, where the Red Sox have always played poorly. But they seemed to treat each challenge from a strong opponent as a dress rehearsal for post-season play.

They lost Jim Sundberg for a period, and this slowed them down a little; they lost Willie Wilson for a while, and felt his loss as much. But the pitching was there almost every day, and when they were good, they were very, very good. This ability to rise up and strike down the best of opponents was on my mind in the first days of September, when I was analyzing the things that might happen in post-season play for my newsletter. I recognized the weaknesses of the club, and concluded the newsletter with this paragraph:

But the Royals are hungry for a World Championship ring. Ewing Kauffman, who is selling off the team in stages, desperately wants to have a World Championship before he goes, and is probably applying pressure at the top of the organization to see that no effort is spared to bring it about (although if he is, it doesn't get into the papers). Frank White, George Brett, Jim Sundberg, Dan Quisenberry—these guys are past thirty and have never won it. They know that they're not going to get many more shots. To Willie Wilson and Lonnie Smith, the World Championship would be the ultimate triumph over their personal problems. For Wilson, another World Series would be an opportunity to remove the stigma of the 1980 series, when he was unjustly and inaccurately portrayed as the Royals' goat. My gut tells me that they're going to do it.

Earlier in the newsletter, I had written that, having seen almost every game between the Blue Jays and Royals either in person or on TV, I found it very difficult to believe that the Blue Jays could beat the Royals. When the playoff started, it didn't take them long to make a believer out of me. The Blue Jay team that I had seen was a superbly talented team, but a team which made exactly the kind of mistakes that lose playoffs, and plenty of them.

But in the first two games of the playoff, it was the veteran Royals who made the mistakes. They made so many mistakes in the first game that they wiped themselves out, losing 6–1. In the second game, they made just enough mistakes to lose, being charged with three errors and blowing the lead twice.

Two notes are in order about Game Three, which, even had it not been a play-off game, would rank among the most memorable contests that I've ever seen. I hope the sense of this came across in the TV version; I didn't see the broadcast, but I gather that Bob Costas did an excellent job:

#1—George Brett that night turned in one of the most brilliant individual performances in the annals of the sport. In the first inning he crushed a low pitch into a gentle breeze from right, the ball landing thirty to forty feet beyond the fence down the right field line. In the top of the third he turned in a spectacular defensive play, spearing a hard smash down the third base line and looping a perfect throw around Damaso Garcia, who was trying to score on the play; the play was, in essence, two very difficult plays—the stop and the throw—unified by a split-second decision. In the fourth, with the wind now howling in from right, he lined a pitch off the top of the fence in right-center for a double; the ball was hit much harder than the homer in the first. In the sixth, with a runner on first and the Royals down by two, he hit the ball a mile high toward center; it eventually came to earth just over the fence to the center field side of the 385 sign in left-center, tying the score. In the eighth he singled and scored the game-winning run.

For the game Brett hit 1.000, slugged 2.750, scored four runs and drove in three. And yet, you know, the Royals could very easily have lost that game. After George had put them ahead 2–0, the Blue Jays scored five runs in the fifth inning, then had the bases loaded with two out. Steve Farr came into the game and got the out that he had to get to keep the game within reach. Jim Sundberg homered in the bottom of the fifth to cut the margin to two and take some of the wind out of the Blue Jays' sails. Willie Wilson got on to start the sixth, doubling the value of Brett's second homer. After Brett reached in the eighth, McRae bunted him to second and Balboni singled him home.

I think that just shows how false, how truly silly, the idea is that one player "carries" a team, or that one player turns a team around, or that one player is, really, anything except one player. The man put on a one-game show that nobody could sustain, nobody could match, even for a period of two or three games—and yet without the key contributions of five other players, his team would have lost that one game.

#2—Also missed in the hugger-mugger surrounding Brett's historic game was the realization that the Blue Jays may have played their best game of the series on that night. Ernie Whitt gunned down Willie Wilson stealing in the first, saving a run. In the second Damasco Garcia made a lightning-quick backhand grab of a ball that Frank White floated in front of second. Following Brett's double in the fourth, Hal McRae drove the ball into the gap in right-center. While I was wondering if Mac had enough oats left to make a triple out of this, Jesse Barfield materialized and caught the ball on the dead run. On the very next pitch, Frank White slashed the ball along the same vector, but harder, farther and flatter than McRae's ball. Barfield added a 9.6 bellyflop to his act, and got to this one, too, a remarkable catch. Then, after making a routine catch for the third out, Jesse hit a two-run home run off the Cy Young winner in the top of the fifth, tying the score. Who's George Brett?

And those plays *almost* wound up taking a back seat. On Steve Balboni's game-winning single in the eighth, Tony Fernandez was that far away (hold up thumb and forefinger) from making the greatest defensive play that I have ever seen. Balboni swung hard and fisted the ball into left-center, I would guess 150 feet over the shortstop's head. The ball was not hit hard, but a ball hit with that trajectory in that direction is *always* a single for a power hitter; nobody had any chance to make the play. Fernandez broke into a full gallop at the crack of the bat, and missed by inches of catching it over his shoulder. You know I'm a great admirer of Ripken and Trammell and Yount—but friends, no other shortstop in the American League would have been within 50 feet of that ball when it landed.

In the fourth game the Royals lost when Al Oliver beat Dan Quisenberry for the second time in the series; in the fifth Danny Jackson pitched out of serious fourth-, fifth-, and sixth-inning jams en route to a shutout. In that game the Blue Jays made the first of the baserunning mistakes for which I had been waiting.

In the fourth inning the first two hitters, George Bell and Cliff Johnson, singled, with Johnson's ball landing in front of left fielder Lonnie Smith. Bell decided to challenge . . . let us say, Bell decided to *insult* Lonnie's throwing arm, and Lonnie made a fine throw to third. Brett decoyed as if there was no play, then grabbed the ball and slapped the tag on Bell; he argued, but he was out.

This incident became somewhat celebrated as the playoff wore on, as Bell lost his temper a number of times during the playoff, almost got into a fight after being hit with a pitch while, in general, playing magnificent baseball. The fans were on him.

But missed in the controversy (it was a close call) was what is so often missed about an over-aggressive baserunning decision: the damage that it might have done. Reconstruct for yourself what might have happened without that play:

Bell	singled to right
Johson	singled to left
Barfield	groundout (1–3), runner advancing
Upshaw	groundout (5–3)
Iorg	flared a single into right
Whitt	doubled into right field corner
Fernandez	groundout (5–3)

Iorg's single and Whitt's double came in the fifth inning, because of the extra out; Iorg didn't score but probably would have with two out. Bell's aggressiveness might, just *might* have cost the Blue Jays three runs. They lost the game, 2–0.

And what was the potential gain? The best estimate that I could make, which comes from page 153 of Pete Palmer's *The Hidden Game of Baseball*, is that the difference between having runners on first and second with no one out and having runners on first and third with no one out is 26/100 of a run.

An offense is a chain. The value of the chain depends upon its length, how far it will reach. Imagine that this chain is six feet long, but if you stretch out each link on the chain, maybe you can make the chain seven feet long instead of six. But if you stretch a link too hard and it breaks in the middle, then what?

Then what you've got is two worthless pieces of three-foot chain.

By what he had done in the first three games, Al Oliver had taken Dan Quisenberry out of the series. When they returned to Toronto, Dick Howser figured out a way to take Al Oliver out of the series. For four seasons Bobby Cox had followed a policy of strict platooning; when the opposition manager switched from a left-handed pitcher to a right-hander or vice versa, he would pinch hit for any of several players. This policy served him extremely well. With the complications of their profession cut in half, players like Rance Mulliniks, Garth Iorg, Ernie Whitt, Buck Martinez and others had developed into productive hitters. In addition, Cox was able to get the entire roster involved in the winning effort, contributing greatly to the development of a cohesive atmosphere in the Blue Jay clubhouse, plus the fact that, with about thirteen players having regular playing time, his bench was extremely strong and his ability to withstand an injury markedly improved.

With the American League pennant on the line, Dick Howser turned that policy around and pointed it at Bobby Cox's temple. The Blue Jays are much better against right-handed than left-handed pitchers, and Howser had begun the series with Mark Gubicza, a right-hander with a 14–10 record, in the bullpen, and so starting three left-handers. When Howser would bring in his right-handed relief ace, Cox could empty his bench and apply unrelenting pressure.

If, however, he empties his bench as soon as you switch pitchers, then what happens if you make that change in the middle of the game? Howser decided to find out. Gubicza started the fifth game, and, after allowing single runs in the first and third, cruised through the fourth and fifth. In the sixth he had allowed a single and a walk with only one out. There were eleven outs left in the game, but Al Oliver was at the plate. Howser brought Bud Black, a left-hander, into the game.

Cox pulled the trigger. Cliff Johnson, a right-handed hitter, was brought in to hit for Oliver. In the seventh inning, Garth Iorg was brought in to hit for Mulliniks, and in the eighth Cecil Fielder hit for Ernie Whitt, with Hearron coming in to catch. By the ninth inning the bench was empty—and Dan Quisenberry was able to get back into the series.

Right-hander Bret Saberhagen started the seventh game; he had not pitched well against Toronto either in the season or in the series. In the first inning Saberhagen took a shot off his hand—the second time in the series that the Blue Jays had pounded a safety off his person. The hand swelled up, and Saberhagen left after three innings.

Again, a left-hander came into the game.

Again, Cox pulled the trigger.

Iorg replaced Mulliniks.

Johnson replaced Oliver.

Jeff Burroughs replaced Ernie Whitt.

The left-handers were gone.

Quisenberry came in to finish up.

When Al Oliver was pulled out of the game, the camera showed him in the dugout. He was furious, slapping the seat and scowling. He knew that when he was out, the Royals would go to the right-hander, and the Blue Jays would have no response move.

His deportment was not what it should have been in the situation, and might well have hurt him when he was looking for a job over the winter. But he was right.

One of the great rules of life is that we all establish "policies," although we call them habits or preferences or beliefs or techniques, which are useful to us, but which we continue to use after the reason for them has evaporated. We have a hard time seeing things as they *are* because we can never get what they *were* out of our heads. There's a saying among military men that each war is fought by the lessons of the last one. Political decisions are made the same way; the political leaders of the late forties saw the Korean problem in terms of World War II. Those of the early sixties treated the Vietnam dilemma as if it were a re-run of Korea. We acted tentatively and indecisively with respect to Iran because after Vietnam, every potential involvement was viewed as another Vietnam, rather than being seen as its own complex problem. Now we look at the situation in the Philippines, and we wonder if we have another Iran on our hands. In each conflict, we have seen not the problem which existed, but the shadow of the last one.

What Dick Howser did to the Blue Jays, you couldn't do over a period of time. He used four starting pitchers in two nights; you can't do that all year. But Howser reacted to the unique situation, and Cox didn't. Had the series gone on one game longer, he would have figured out a response to it. He's a fine manager, and he did (on the whole) a super job in Toronto. But he let Dick Howser get one step ahead of him at exactly the wrong moment.

A WORLD SERIES NOTEBANK

Part 1: Prologue

Overlooking the paranoid protestations of Kansas City fans, hypersensitive after years of put-downs in comparisons with the Yankees, it is difficult to understand why the Cardinals were so heavily favored to win the series. There is no credible basis for the belief that the eastern media would favor St. Louis over Kansas City merely because they are 240 miles to the east.

The superiority of the Cardinals' won-lost record was certainly what started the snowball rolling. The habit of dismissing the American League West probably had something to do with it; it was largely ignored that in 1985 the AL West had two teams which won ninety games, three teams over .500 and three teams not very far under .500. The Royals' poor record in post-season play over the last ten years had something to do with it. The fact that the Cardinals had beaten two media darlings, the Mets and Dodgers, might possibly have had something to do with it. National League smugness certainly had a great deal to do with it. The tendency to focus on speed, at the expense of more valuable characteristics such as power and frontline pitching, certainly had much to do with it.

In any case, by the time the series was under way, it had reached the point of the preposterous. To an objective observer —one who had not had the opportunity to witness the Royals daily—the Cardinals should have been a slight favorite, perhaps a seven-to-six favorite. But nine to four? John Nelson, writing for the Associated Press in the last week of the season, wrote that "The Kansas City ball club of the American League would be woefully overmatched against St. Louis of the National League, and an I-70 Series might become something of a good, old-fashioned Western barbecue." Hal Bodley of *USA Today* wrote that "Versatility and flexibility should carry St. Louis to a World Series victory against cross-state rival Kansas City." The article was accompanied by a chart showing that St. Louis had an edge at every position except third base. Pete Rose said that the Cardinals would win in four straight.

With respect to the *USA Today* chart, let me raise three points:

1. The Cardinals' team earned run average in 1985 was 3.10, which was 49 points (or 13 percent) better than the National League average. The Royals staff ERA was 3.49, which was 66 points (or 16 percent) better than the American League average. In spite of this, Bodley rated the Cardinals superior in starting pitching, relief pitching, and defense. Now if you have worse starting pitching, worse relief pitching and worse defense, how can you have a better team earned run average?

2. In addition to the positions compared, *USA Today* gave the Cardinals pluses in all the peripheral areas considered—Team Speed, Defense, and Bench. But what was not mentioned here was the fact that the Royals had an enormous advantage in power, hitting 154 home runs to the Cardinals' 87. Even with adjustments for park and DH, that's an impressive difference; the Royals, playing in a poor home run park, were the only major league team with two players who hit 30 home runs. They also had other players with 14, 22 and 17 home runs, whereas the Cardinals had only one player with more than 13.

Over any period of time, power has been far, far more important in post-season play than has speed. Over any period of years, the team hitting more home runs has won the World Series more often than the team stealing more bases. It makes no sense to ignore power and focus on speed in an analysis of a World Series.

3. In comparing the catchers, St. Louis' Darrell Porter was rated the edge over Kansas City's Jim Sundberg. Darrell Porter was released after the season, and there was no perceptible rush to sign him. Jim Sundberg was *not* released after the season, and had he been so he would have received at least eight offers from other teams. This is the most inexplicable error in the analysis, and is difficult to ascribe to anything other than bias.

The Bodley article, actually, was paired with another; his was "Why the Cardinals Will Win the Series," and the other was "Why the Royals Will Win the Series." The problem is that, while the "Cardinal" half of the article gave the Cardinals a 10–1 edge in comparisons, the "Royal" half of it also gave the Cardinals a 6–4 edge with the bench being even, and the accompanying article, rather than saying that the Royals would win, argued that it was not impossible that the Royals might win. It concluded with this ringing endorsement:

Kansas City doesn't awe you; there are no less than six AL teams more difficult to contain.

But, the Royals can win, especially in a one-week series, if they can lull the opposition into a conservative game of baseball chess. Against a team as versatile and well-schooled as the Cardinals, it will not be easy.

To return to a familiar theme, I think that to a large extent these biases were fueled by *statistical* misunderstandings, misinterpretations of the statistics. For example:

1. The failure to recognize the Royals' pitching was as good as it is was created to a substantial degree by the failure to adjust for the ERA difference between the leagues, because of the designated hitter rule. It's funny—people would say that the Royals' offense would be hurt by the loss of designated hitter Hal McRae, but they would fail to pick up the obvious other half of the equation, that their pitchers would be aided by not having to face the other team's designated hitters. There's a difference of a little more than a half a run a game, but—until the series was played—few people seemed to take in that this meant the Royals were starting three pitchers with ERAs of 2.19, 2.37 and 2.92.

2. Another factor which was almost entirely overlooked due to a dysfunction of the statistical information services was the Royals' ability to stop the opposition's running game, particularly with Jim Sundberg catching. Information about a team's ability to steal bases is commonly available; it's in *The Sporting News* and *USA Today* every week, and is referred to often. But it's a two-way street; as important as the ability to *steal* bases is the ability to *prevent* stolen bases. The fact that the Royals were the third most-difficult team in baseball to steal bases against, allowing only ninety-two opposition steals on the season, was not published anywhere, and so was virtually a trade secret. The Cardinals, while a much better base-stealing team, were not nearly so strong in the prevention category.

3. With respect to certain head-to-head matchups, there was a tendency before the series to focus on the *season's statistics*, rather than focusing on the *abilities* which those statistics described. There are several examples, but the clearest is in center field, where the Cardinals were often afforded a huge edge for their MVP center fielder, Willie McGee.

If you look at the two players—McGee and Wilson—there is virtually no difference as to their skills and true level of ability. Both players are extremely fast, and have exceptional range in center field. Both are switch hitters, both hit a great many triples and show occasional home run power. Their strikeout and walk frequencies are virtually the same. Their skills as base stealers are virtually identical. Their throwing arms are about the same, fair to good. McGee won the batting championship in 1985, but Wilson also won the batting championship, in 1982. McGee's career average is .307; Wilson's is .301.

The 1985 season should not have convinced any thinking person that Willie McGee is a *significantly* better ballplayer than Willie Wilson. There was no reasonable basis for an expectation that McGee would outperform Wilson in the 1985 series.

The same can be said of the second basemen. Tommie Herr had a fine season—but it is very hard for me to see that he is distinctly superior to Frank White, or that there was any reasonable basis for the expectation that he would outperform him in the World Series.

But people didn't see that, because they focused on 1985 statistics, rather than on abilities. One of the fundamental things that I have tried to say to the baseball world in general is not that we need to look at new and different baseball statistics because baseball statistics are good and perfect ways of looking at baseball, but that we need to consider new and different baseball statistics, and new and different ways of looking at the ones we have, because we have many misconceptions which are based on our faulty impressions of what statistics mean.

Game One

It was something of a shock to the Cardinals, then, to get into the series and discover that the Royals knew in which direction to run the bases, that indeed they seemed to do this almost by second nature, as if they had long practice in it. The Cardinals were amazed to discover the Royals familiar with such nuances of the game as bunting, turning the double play, hitting curve balls and relaying throws back to the infield; they had not been led to expect that it would be this way, and felt rather betrayed by it. The Cardinals should have remembered that the people who said they couldn't lose in October were the same people who said they couldn't win in April. They didn't know what they were talking about in April, and they didn't know what they were talking about in October.

Before the first series game I went in to do a show on a

Kansas City television station. They asked me who would win. I have learned from experience that these gentlemen do not appreciate a straight answer—to wit, how the hell would I know—so I said that if it was a short series the Cardinals would win, but if it was a long series the Royals would win. The logic, worth repeating only because it worked out so well, was that the Cardinals were a good enough team that they were capable of blowing the Royals away before the Royals got their feet planted, but that if the Royals were to maneuver themselves into a position from which they could win, then they'd pull it out.

Susie and I attended the game with Craig Wright and his friends Sean and Cindy. I had never before been to a World Series game, and was surprised at how different the experience was. On the way in I grumbled about the thirty-dollar price of the ticket, but on arriving at the park was struck by the absurdity of this; you pay forty-five dollars for tickets to a Broadway show and don't think anything of it, and this is *the World Series*. No one has a divine right to attend the event, and if you're not willing to pay a good price for the ticket you shouldn't be there. The parking lot was abuzz with ticket scalpers (trying to buy, mostly), people hawking souvenirs, people winding up tailgate parties, people carrying signs saying "Came all the way from San Diego—Need Tickets." A few thousand standing-room only ducats had been sold, and in places it seemed that there was less room than this advertised. A small jazz band played at the entrance to the park; a marching band was on the field as we arrived. The bunting, the rows of people standing behind the seats and the special auxiliary press box changed the look of the familiar stadium.

Reba McIntire pitched "The Star-Spangled Banner," and Danny Jackson sang the first inning. I *love* to watch Danny Jackson pitch. The first time I saw Danny pitch in '83—it may have been his first major league outing—I wasn't impressed. We had heard a great deal about him as he shot through the farm system, going 17–3 in his first season in professional ball. My initial reaction to him was "What's with this kid? He doesn't throw very hard, although the fastball has good movement, and he doesn't seem to have a curve ball—uses that slider as his breaking pitch." His motion was awkward and he didn't have any kind of control. I saw him again a few days later and couldn't believe I was seeing the same pitcher. He still had the good movement on his fastball and he still didn't throw a curve, but the fastball now cracked into the mitt, he intimidated right-handed hitters with a slider that exploded on their fists, his motion was extraordinarily fluid—what it was was gorgeous—and his control was excellent.

I've seen him pitch many times since, and there has always been that dichotomy. Sometimes he shows up at the park with nothing; he's awkward, flails around out on the mound, doesn't have a clue as to where home plate is and doesn't throw hard enough to get by with pitching there if he did. When he doesn't have it, he's going to lose. Sometimes he'll struggle through two, three, four innings, and you almost think he's going to turn it around, but I've never seen him do it. On those days he mixes in 60 percent pitches that are OK with 40 percent pitches that are trouble—a deadly ratio.

But other times, you know he's going to win the game as soon as he takes the mound. He is basically a two-pitch pitcher, with a fastball and a slider, and the batter can put the bat on either pitch most of the time. But the fastball moves so much, and is thrown so hard, that the hitter rarely makes solid contact with it, while the slider snaps in on a right-hander's fist so sharply that a right-handed hitter's best shot is to try to bloop it over the infield, while a left-hander is lucky to avoid turning it into a GB5.

Jackson is very tough to run on and hardly ever allows a home run, so that one basically has to beat him by putting together long strings of singles and walks. He's going to walk a few people because his pitches move so much that they'll jump out of the strike zone, but when he has his stuff, Danny is a steamroller. He'll give up a single here, a walk and a run there without ever giving the sense that he is in any trouble. If he were consistent and had a strikeout pitch (either a curve or a good change-up), he would be the best pitcher in the American League.

Whenever I see Danny pitch I always tell whoever I'm with that I can tell in the first inning whether he's going to win. The fifth game of the AL playoff was the first time I've ever not been able to form an opinion in the first inning. The first game of the World Series was the first time I've ever formed the opinion, and been wrong. In the play-off game, I didn't know that he was going to win until the second inning. I gather that he must have been nervous or something, but in the first inning that night he threw some very good pitches but looked awkward at other times. I've never seen him do that before— look fluid for a couple of pitches and awkward for a couple of pitches in the same outing. He struck out the side in the second inning, and the steamroller was rolling.

In the first series game, Jackson definitely had his stuff, maybe better stuff than he had when he shut out Toronto. The Cardinals were the best team in the National League, and they managed to beat him anyway. In the second inning the Royals got two singles, two walks, and an error, but scored only one run because Buddy Biancalana missed the bunt on a suicide squeeze. Howser's strategy here, though never second-guessed, is uncharacteristically conservative and perhaps questionable. Here's the sequence of batters beginning with Frank White, leading off the second:

White	2–3
Sundberg	W
Motley	1B
Balboni	1B + E7
Biancalana	W
Jackson	K
L. Smith	1B

Tudor was struggling with his control, and seemed to have very little going for him. He walked Jim Sundberg, threw ball one to Motley and gave up a single on the 1–0 pitch, got behind Balboni and gave up a single on a 3–1 pitch, and had missed the strike zone with two out of three pitches to Biancalana before the abortive bunt attempt. He was eighteen pitches into the inning, and had thrown nine balls and two line drives to left.

Howser probably guessed that, trying to find the plate, Tudor would take something off and come in the pitch, since a walk to the weak-hitting Biancalana would have been, no pun intended, a Cardinal sin. Instead, Tudor threw a terrible pitch, and Biancalana missed connections on the bunt. But the price for this was not *simply* the lost runner from third base, but also that 1) the inning ended before Lonnie Smith's single, which would have scored two runs, and 2) batting with two

This Time Let's Not Eat the Bones   **322**

out, Jackson did not have the opportunity to attempt a sacrifice. Suppose we assume:

a. that Biancalana would have walked anyway,
b. that Jackson, bunting with only one out, might have been able to execute a sacrifice, and
c. that Smith would have gotten the same hit that he did.

(a) (Biancalana's walk) is extremely likely, (b) is problematic but not impossible, and (c) is entirely unknown but the only assumption for which we have a reasonable basis. If it had happened, the Royals score how many runs in the inning? 1-2-3-4; 4–0, KC, and the game is pretty much over. Even if Jackson strikes out, it's three runs. Dick Howser tried to play for a 2–0 lead, and it didn't work out, and I'm not faulting him for it. Incidentally, Howser ordinarily does not like to bunt.

Jackson tied the Cardinals in knots for two innings, then walked Pendleton leading off the third. Darrell Porter, batting eighth, hit a ground ball just out of the reach of Frank White, Pendleton scooting to third. With no one on base and a slow man at bat, Frank White takes his position out in short right field, and the ball would have been an easy play for him; playing for the double play, he had pulled in and edged toward second base, and the ball got into right field. With one out, Willie McGee got Pendleton home with a GB4, and the game was tied.

Things simply were not breaking the Royals' way. Lonnie Smith singled to lead off the third, then got picked off first, 3–6–3, *again* costing the Royals multiple runs (two) given a normal sequence of events. Look at the sequence of batters beginning with Smith:

L. Smith	1B
Wilson	PO4
Brett	1B
White	3–
Sundberg	2B

White's squib down the first base line would certainly have moved the runners up, and Sundberg's double would obviously have scored them.

Instead, it remained tied at 1–1. With one out, Landrum doubled. On a two-two pitch to Cesar Cedeño, Jackson busted the slider on Cedeño's knuckles and shattered his bat, the head of it helicoptering out to the shortstop position. The ball blooped over Brett's head up the left field line, and the Cardinals had a 2–1 lead. It was all the runs they would need.

All season, whenever Susie and I had gone into games we had been extremely fortunate as to the people seated around us; we made it through almost the entire season without being in earshot of an obnoxious drunk. On this memorable occasion, the law of averages caught up with us. We were seated three rows behind the last human being in the Western Hemisphere that I would ever want to marry into my family; she is to this day known in our house only as The Dreadful Woman. The Dreadful Woman combined the virtues of a coquettish southern belle, the kind that during a Tennessee Williams play you always want to rush onstage and strangle to speed up the plot, with those of your ordinary garden-variety obnoxious drunken fan. She had a voice that would remind you of a clarinet with a broken reed, set to the volume of an air horn, and I suppose that she had been a cheerleader two or three years ago, for she was determined to lead the section in cheers. She was a Cardinals fan, which was not the problem; in fact, the ingrained hospitality with which midwesterners receive guests is probably all that kept her alive as the game progressed. Whenever anything happened . . . no, that's not right; whether anything happened or not she would leap to her feet almost with every pitch and, turning around and gesturing with her arms as if tossing an invisible baby into the air, imploring the section to screech along with her and give her some sort of reassurance about how cute she was. After about a half-inning of this, every time she got up she would, naturally, be greeted with a chorus of people yelling encouraging things like "Sit down," "Shut up," "Watch the game," "Lady, pleeeease," and "Will you get your ass out of the way?" However, being apparently none too swift even when sober, she could not take in that it was not anyone in particular who was yelling these things, but everyone in the entire area taking turns. Having focused on someone who was abusing her, she would fasten onto the luckless soul—several, I am sure, will never go back to a baseball game so long as they live—and begin to whimper accusingly about how she didn't mean to do any wrong and she was just trying to enjoy the game and didn't they want to enjoy the game and didn't Royals fans like to have fun and what had she done except cheer for her team and couldn't they be friends? Eventually she would shake hands with whoever it was; this was, after all, the only way to get her to stop whining in your face. Then she would grab her camera and put her arm around her new friend and have her husband (or boyfriend, or whoever the poor bastard was) take a picture of the event.

She had other uses for the camera—for example, she would try on a funny hat, stand up on her seat, hand off the camera to a stranger and have him take a picture of her. She would do this, mind you, with the inning in progress.

The rest of the fans in the right field bleachers were not exactly a prize aggregation, either. There was a crowd camera near us, and scattered around were several dozen children and nitwits whose attention was entirely focused on it. Whenever this camera panned near us they would leap to their feet and hold up banners, requiring the people sitting behind them, which was all of us except the front row, to jump up and down constantly in an attempt to follow the game. There were several beach balls bouncing around, enough that it took the baseball fans in the area two or three innings to capture each one and neutralize it with a pocket knife. It was easily the worst Kansas City baseball crowd that I've seen.

Also seated around us were a number of die-hard, lifelong Cardinal fans who had driven over from St. Louis (five-hour drive) to see the game. By the fifth inning, the Dreadful Woman had most of them discussing whether they should continue to support the Cardinals or perhaps should switch to the Royals. Several people offered to buy the Dreadful Woman a beer if she would just go stand in line to buy it. She took one guy up on his offer, apparently not understanding the purpose of it— she warn't easy to insult, this girl—and as she was leaving a guy about ten rows behind us shouted "Remember where your seat is—section 342." Needless to say, Section 342 was in an entirely different part of the ball park, but it didn't work. When this happened, the wavering Cardinal fan beside me turned around and said "God, does she go all the way back there? I would have assumed he was safe." We enjoyed the game for a half-inning until she returned.

John Tudor may be a great pitcher—he looked like a great

pitcher in Game Four, and you can't argue with 21–8—but he sure as hell didn't show it that evening. In the fourth inning, after Jim Sundberg's double, Darryl Motley flied to right field deep enough that Sundberg, not exactly a speed merchant, was able to move to third base. Steve Balboni popped softly down the left field line, apparently out of play, but Terry Pendleton made a wondrous effort on the ball, racing top-speed down the line to catch the ball near the seats, over his shoulder, then whirling to throw out Sundberg at the plate. In the sixth inning, Willie Wilson led off with a single, Frank White hit a line drive to the warning track in left field, and Jim Sundberg made Tudor throw ten pitches before getting him out for the first time. In the seventh inning Motley drove the ball into the left field corner (caught), Lynn Jones hit a pinch-hit triple and Hal McRae was hit by a pitch before Tudor departed, a winning pitcher by the grace of God and his defense.

Danny Jackson was magnificent. After Cedeño's bloop double he faced the minimum number of batters, eleven.

After the game Bob Gibson was on the radio. The fact that the Cardinals' victory was little short of a miracle had, apparently, not come across on television. The Cardinals had hit only three balls hard—well, two hard and one reasonably hard —in the game; the three were the doubles by McGee and Clark, both thrown out at third, and the ground single by Herr off of Quisenberry. The Royals had blistered the ball all over the park—in fact, I think they hit the ball harder off Tudor in Game One than they did in Game Seven, when they beat him 11–0. The Royals had twelve balls that were crunched. Each team had lost two runners on the bases; the walks and hit batsmen were even at four apiece. Dave Nightingale of *The Sporting News* had seen the game much the same way I had:

> You might conclude from such a script that the National League champion Cardinals were getting the living bejabbers kicked out of them by the American League champion Royals.
>
> Conclude differently.

But many other people had completely missed the fact that the Cardinals' victory was a stone fluke, and on the radio Gibson was certain that the Cardinals would win the series in four straight. He spared no details in explaining why. He acknowledged that Jackson had pitched well—he was quite amazed by this—but even so the Royals had not been able to take the game. So from now on they were going to be easy pickings. We drove home in a dark mood, remembering The Dreadful Woman, and remembering how the season had ended in so many other autumns.

Game Two

In the 1913 World Series, Chief Meyers, the star catcher of the New York Giants, split his hand open making a catch in pre-game drills before the second game of the series. He was not able to play in the rest of the games, but his replacement, Larry McLean, filled in sensationally, hitting .500 (6 for 12), making no errors and even doing a good job containing the Philadelphia running game; he was by far the Giants' best player in the series. Still, the Giants lost the series, and the Giants' supporters felt sure that they would have had a better chance had Meyers been healthy. As John Foster wrote in the 1914 Spalding Guide, "How much this turn of misfortune had to do with the ultimate outcome, no one can tell. An opinion would be merely the estimate of a critic who endeavors to analyze the possibilities of chance. If the New York team had been at its best, it might still have been defeated. It certainly was not at its best."

A neighbor had asked me to pick up and take to the second game a man who lives in my town who had a ticket but no way to get to the stadium. He turned out to be a very agreeable older man, about seventy-five to eighty, and a big baseball fan. We drove through Leavenworth on the way, and he remembered seeing Del Crandall play for Leavenworth in 1948 or 1949, he wasn't sure which. I didn't know that Leavenworth had a minor league team then, and we talked about it. I asked if he had ever seen a World Series game before; he said "Oh, no," and added that it had always been a dream of his to see one. I arrived at the stadium thinking how little the winning and losing mattered. Later I got out a book and checked; Del Crandall hit .304 for Leavenworth in 1948.

As Susie and I were walking down the aisle toward our seats the man in front of us yelled gleefully "I don't think she's here!" We broke out laughing; we were looking for the same thing. We had the same seats for all four games in Kansas City, if there were to be four games in Kansas City, and the thought of spending three more games trying to get *her* to shut up had considerably dampened our enthusiasm for the event. We never saw her again, but it was easy to spot the people who had been in the same seats the day before. They were distinguished by the wary looks that they cast around until the offending seat was occupied.

Melba Moore sang the National Anthem, and Coretta Scott King threw out the first pitch. Nothing happened through three innings. The Royals got their leadoff man on in each of the three, but lost two of them to quick double plays, and Cox struck out the side the other time. The Cardinals through four innings had only three balls hit out of the infield, mounting one threat on a walk and Tito Landrum's two-out single.

In the fourth the Royals scored two runs before anyone was out. Wilson led off with a single, and Brett and White followed with doubles to right. Mike Roarke visited the mound, and Cox, who had not made a good pitch since taking the mound at the start of the inning, immediately stiffened. But the Royals had a 2–0 lead.

For some reason Craig and I got to talking about pitchers' motions. Cox throws across his body; at the moment of release he is not squared away toward home plate, so that he throws his arm across his chest, his forearm slapping hard into his chest at the completion of the delivery. It looks to me like there must be tremendous pressure on the muscles just below the joint in his shoulder. I guess it will probably be a little while before it catches up with him, but I'd say there's about an 80 percent chance that his productive years as a pitcher will be ended by shoulder trouble within three to five years. Be sure to write and remind me if it doesn't happen.

Anyway, we got to talking about motions in general, and Craig had some intriguing ideas about the subject, related to things he has learned from talking to Ranger pitching coaches, evaluated with his own research. He has become a recent convert to the importance of the pitcher's getting the glove out in front of him while throwing the hard pitches, thus 1) hiding the ball, and 2) facilitating the act of throwing the glove hand back as the ball is released, maximizing the forward thrust of the other hand and balancing the body. I told him he should write a book about this stuff. He said he was thinking about it, which is a step forward from what he said the last time I told him that, which was that he *wasn't* thinking about it.

My theory about motions is that most managers don't have a very good sense of when a pitcher is tired, and that this is probably the one thing in baseball that a fan at home watching the game on TV can see *better*, if he pays attention, than the manager can. The fact that managers don't, in general, have any idea when their pitchers are tired is supported, I feel, by the things they say about it—for example, that the pitcher's readings on the radar gun have not dropped, or that what they look for when a pitcher is tired is when he starts dropping down, not coming over the top. I argued that this is an extremely late and unreliable indicator of when a pitcher is tired, and . . . well, I'll get to that in the pitcher's comments, or some place. Craig was unconvinced. I told him to put it in his book.

No one reached in the Cardinal fifth, the Royal fifth, or the Cardinal sixth. In the Cardinal innings, Brett made the two best defensive plays of the game, fielding a big hop behind third and gunning down Pendleton, then diving for a ball in the hole, stopping it, getting up and throwing out Tommie Herr. In the sixth the Royals got a single, a stolen base and a walk, but didn't score; Brett again drove the ball to the wall, this time in left, but was short. In the seventh the Royals got a walk from Balboni, a bunt from Leibrandt, and a single from Lonnie Smith, but Tito Landrum, emerging as the star of the series, nailed Balboni at the plate.

In the eighth Frank White hit a two-out double off the wall in left. A left-hander, Ken Dayley, was on the mound. In my scorebook I had written in "PH—Motley for Sheridan," but had to scratch it out as Sheridan came to the plate. The switch would have been consistent with what Howser had done late in the year, but on reflection I could see why he had not made the move. If he had gone to Motley, Herzog would very likely have switched to a right-hander; then, with his other right fielder out of the game, Motley would have had to stay in, and Howser would have taken his best defensive right fielder out of the game, for no gain, with a 2–0 lead. I decided Howser was right; better to save the pinch hitter in case he was needed in the ninth. Sheridan grounded to second.

We have arrived at The Blunder. It had been a fast game up to this point; the first pitch was thrown at 7:31, and at 9:42 the

Cardinals began what seemed, until the following Saturday, as if it would be the pivotal inning of the 1985 World Series. Charlie Leibrandt had retired thirteen consecutive hitters entering the inning, and it required a real pessimist to note that the last two had hit the ball hard.

What is a managerial blunder, to begin with? Is it a decision about the odds in the game that is wrong on the percentages? No, it can't be, because *none of us knows exactly what the true odds are* in any given game situation. None of us knows, and none of us will ever know, not a hundred years from now when they have computers that will fit on your fingernail and spit out the history of the universe at a billion words a second, none of us will know for sure what the odds are because each unique situation contains a thousand variables, at least a hundred of which will not have had enough trials to be evaluated. In short, no one can ever know how this pitcher will pitch this batter under these exact lighting conditions when this pitcher is this tired. We will know much more about it later than we know now, but we will never *know*.

But we do know what the book says. What we know is *how an ordinary manager would handle this situation* in an ordinary case, and we know *why* he would do it that way. There are three elements of a managerial blunder:

1. It is a move which goes against the conventional practice,
2. It occurs at a key moment of the game, and
3. It doesn't work.

Those three elements are always present when a manager is accused of blundering, and whenever those three elements are present, the manager will be accused of blundering.

Willie McGee, batting leadoff due to the injury of Vince Coleman, was up first. McGee hacked at a pitch inside, then got around late and fouled a pitch into the Kansas City dugout. It was 0–2. Leibrandt fired, and gestured in excitement as if he had struck out McGee. The replay seemed to show that he had, but the National League umpire called it a ball. McGee doubled into the left field corner on the next pitch.

The first pitch to Ozzie Smith came in tight; Ozzie tried to turn his back into it, so as to get on base, but the ball scooted by him into the catcher's glove. Ozzie fouled off two pitches, took ball two to even the count and then grounded out to third. 2–0, tying run still at the plate.

Tommie Herr took ball one, then swung and missed at two pitches before popping out to right field. Leibrandt had retired fifteen of sixteen. Just for a little excitement Pat Sheridan fired to third base, the throw being completely unnecessary and fifteen feet off target. No damage; it was still 2–0.

At 9:48, six minutes into the inning, Gary Blaylock visited the mound.

Just days earlier, Jack Clark had effectively ended the National League season with a monstrous home run on the first pitch from Tom Niedenfuer. With that home run, the message finally began to get through to the American public: Jack Clark is the National League's Eddie Murray. He's not as durable as Eddie, but his dossier of game-breaking batting accomplishments is hardly any less impressive than is Eddie's. He led the National League in "game-winning hits" twice despite playing for the Giants, and one year I did a breakdown of them and showed that almost all were legitimate, late-inning blockbusters. In 1984, according to Elias, he hit .415 in late-inning pressure situations. In 1985, according to my subjective reading of Cardinal scoresheets, he was wall-to-wall deadly.

"So," asked Craig Wright as Blaylock stood at the mound, "Would you bring in Quiz here?" "No," I said, "I'd let him have the tying run." What he did with the tying run was not impressive. He threw three straight balls, two of them almost in the dirt, and then gave up an RBI single on the 3–0 pitch.

That was it for me; if it was my game Quisenberry was in. That was the way Dick has played it for years: when the game is on the line, Quiz is on the mound. When he was *really* good, a couple of years ago, Quisenberry became a major factor in the game in the fifth inning. The logic was this: Let's say that the Royals were one ahead in the fifth inning, but the other team had a man on and Babe Ruth at the plate. You'd be thinking "Well, if he gets the Babe out here he's got the bottom of the order up in the sixth. That means that Babe and Lou and company don't come up again until the seventh at worst, and if it gets *really* tough in the seventh inning, Quiz can come in and the Royals will still win. So *if he just gets Babe out here in the fifth inning, then the Royals win.*"

It wasn't just the Royals who thought this way, either; managers would use their pinch hitters in the fifth or sixth innings, trying to keep Quisenberry out of the game. In a sense, every Royals game revolved around trying to get to Quisenberry, and it was something that you started thinking about, really, as soon as you got to the park.

Quiz wasn't nearly that sharp last year; even so, one generally regarded having him in the game as preferable to *not* having him in the game. Here's the situation: The Cardinals have the tying run at first and two out, so it takes either a home run or a string of hits/walks for the Cardinals to go ahead. Quisenberry doesn't allow many home runs—fewer than Leibrandt even last year, when Leibrandt was having his best year and Quiz wasn't. That's an indication for Quisenberry. Quiz is a right-hander; the next two hitters were right-handers. That's an indication for Quisenberry. True, Herzog could have pinch-hit Van Slyke, but *after one hitter* he would either have to let the right-hander hit, or substitute a lesser hitter. Van Slyke would have been coming in cold, which is preferable to having a hitter at the plate who has been in the game. Van Slyke is no reason not to bring in Quisenberry. In fact, Quisenberry did face Van Slyke later in the inning, and got him out on one pitch to end the nightmare.

Leibrandt had thrown four straight unsuccessful pitches to Clark; that's an indication for Quisenberry. Leibrandt had thrown seventeen pitches in the inning; that's an indication for Quisenberry. Leibrandt had thrown 123 pitches in the game; that's an indication for Quisenberry.

In Leibrandt's last previous start, in the Toronto series, he had pitched eight shutout innings, and entered the ninth with 110 pitches behind him and the top of the order up. He lost that game, 2–1. That's an indication for Quisenberry.

In the 1984 season, according to the *Elias Baseball Analyst*, hitters facing Charlie Leibrandt in his third, fourth, and fifth innings of work had hit an overall .258 with virtually no power —a .328 slugging percentage. Hitters facing Leibrandt from his sixth inning on hit .297 and had a slugging percentage of .471. Ouch.

Tito Landrum came to the plate, facing Leibrandt. He fouled off the first two pitches, then refused to bite as Charlie nibbled for a corner; it was 2–2. He popped up the next pitch, a pop up drifting softly down the right field into fair territory. Pat Sheridan, pulled around to center, couldn't get there.

It was 9:54; the Royals were still ahead. Quisenberry was still warm. The lead run was on second, but the Royals were still ahead. Leibrandt had now thrown 22 pitches in the inning.

Then came the decision that I really, sincerely, seriously can't understand. By this time, we in the right field bleachers were tearing our teeth out, wondering why Quisenberry was not in the game, wondering why, if Howser had lost faith in Quisenberry, Joe Beckwith was not in the game, or if not Beckwith then Gubicza, or if not Gubicza then almost anybody would do. Not only did Howser *not* bring in Quisenberry, but *he walked Cedeño.*

Now think about this, first of all, as if it were a table game —a re-creation of the basic percentages of the situation. If this were a table game, you would never walk the man intentionally to load the bases, because if you do that, then that means that another walk drives in the tying run. Since Pendleton's *on base percentage* is obviously higher than Cedeño's *batting average,* it certainly would not be profitable to walk Cedeño in a table game.

This, however, is not a table game—this is far worse. The real situation has an additional damned good reason not to walk Cedeño. If you walk Cedeño, then the hitter *knows* that you can't afford to walk him, too. He *knows* that if he is patient you have got to come into him. The pressure on the pitcher goes up, and the batting average of the man at the plate goes up.

Leibrandt got behind Pendleton 1–0. After Pendleton took a called strike, he got behind him again, 2–1. Finally Terry Pendleton swung. He lofted the ball into the gap in left-center. Cedeño scored from first. It was 4–2, St. Louis—and at the time, the World Series seemed to be over.

I have great respect and admiration for Dick Howser—but I have run that inning through my head again and again, and I just don't get it. Maybe we overreacted, emotionally, because we all expected Quisenberry to come in after Clark, so that it seemed like not one mistake, but three mistakes. What Howser said was that they had made a decision before the inning that Charlie still had his good stuff—his readings on the radar gun were good—and that it was his game to win or lose. To me, that sounds like saying you let the house burn down because you'd made a prior decision to ignore the smoke alarm.

Of all the reasons to get Dan Quisenberry into that game, the most important was the number of pitches that Leibrandt had thrown. After a pitcher has thrown 15 pitches in an inning —any inning—his effectiveness diminishes. Any time a pitcher throws more than 15 pitches from the seventh inning on, you've got to start thinking about getting him out of there. But the pitch that beat Leibrandt was (not counting the four on the intentional walk) his 26th pitch of the ninth inning, and his 132nd pitch of the game. Twenty-six pitches in the ninth inning of a close game? I don't think I've ever heard of that before.

Dan Quisenberry came into the game at 10:01.

Games Three Through Five

At the end of Game Two, a delegation of Cardinal fans in the right field bleachers stood and conducted organized cheers for several minutes in the midst of the stunned and dismayed Royals fans. When Leibrandt was rolling along in the seventh and eighth, a chant of "Char-lee, Char-lee, Char-lee" had filled the stadium; afterwards, the men in the Red hats picked up the chant, changing the rhythm just enough to make it recognizable as the derisive, taunting singsong of one child tormenting another. It was an extraordinarily rude, boorish performance, a chorus of men who, guests in our park and in our city, in the thrill of victory had chosen to savor not their own victory, but the anguish of the opponent.

When the series moved to St. Louis, Susie and I went home to watch it on the TV with the rest of you, and so began to be exposed to the World Series as it was being seen through the eyes of the media. We learned then that one of the recurring themes of this coverage was the generally oafish behavior of the Cardinals. In the main I tended to attribute this to the poorly managed crush of the bloated series media, which was no doubt suffocating the Cardinals, making it difficult for them to do what they were trying to accomplish, and impossible to enjoy the doing of it. Still, I wondered about the rudeness reported of the Cardinal players, and the rudeness I had witnessed in their fans. Al Michaels reported Cardinal fans shouting into the press box at the New York writers, "Hey, how about your Mets now?" I wondered whether, after a winter of put-downs and a summer of redemption, vindication had not passed into vindictiveness, and self-justification into self-righteousness. It has been my experience that the Lord rarely wastes much time in punishing those particular transgressions.

The third contest was no contest. Both teams threatened in the first but didn't score. In the fourth, Lonnie Smith slashed a two-run double just out of the reach of Van Slyke. In the fifth, Brett singled and White hit a tremendous home run, knocking Andujar out of the game. Bret Saberhagen, who has probably never blown a four-run lead in his life, began throwing 90 percent strikes. In the sixth the Cardinals got a run on three straight singles—the only time after the first inning that they were to get a runner as far as second base, prompting Herzog to remark that the Clydesdales, who got a little out of hand in a pregame show, had spent more time at second base than his players had. The Royals added two more in the seventh on a walk to Brett, a double by White and a single by Biancalana.

In the fourth game, John Tudor was superb. Through six innings Tudor looked like a pitcher who would never allow a run again. In the seventh inning, the Royals could as easily as not have won the game. Brett led off with a single, and White drove the ball to deep center field, but out. Sundberg singled with one out, but Motley popped out. Balboni walked to load the bases with two out. Hal McRae, strapped to the sidelines by the National League rules, pinch hit for Biancalana. A graphic showed that McRae had ground Tudor into pulp when the two went head-to-head in the American League—but, obviously pressing, Mac lunged at the first pitch, which was inches off the ground. The threat ended. It was the only game of the series in which the Cardinals would outplay the Royals.

Tito Landrum started the scoring for the Cardinals with an opposite-field home run in the second. It was Tito's third extra-base hit of the series—all of them, incidentally, hit to right field. By this time Tito was becoming a folk hero. Tito, who turned thirty-one on an off day during the series, was noted before this only for his home run which gave Baltimore the American League championship in 1983. He proved to be a capable outfielder and, apparently, the only player on the Cardinal team that the Royals didn't know how to pitch to. The predictable signs appeared—Tito for President, How about our General Tito, Tito, I don't believe we're in Kansas anymore. They were bleak, but they provided a relief from the war of the Fat Lady signs. Cardinal fans had jumped the gun with signs like "The Fat Lady is warming up," "Meet me in St. Louis, Fat Lady," and, on Thursday (of course), "The Fat Lady Sings Tonight." Back in KC, Royals fans responded with "The Fat Lady is Choking," "Fat Lady, Go Home," and "Shove it, Fatso." But I'm getting ahead of my story.

Unspoken but apparent in all this is the somewhat local and fraternal nature of the confrontation. Like many Royals fans, I root for the Cardinals in the National League; it's a habit from long ago, when Cardinal broadcasts came into this area. Susie and I went to St. Louis in September to see the Cardinals play a couple of games, and were delighted to see them again in October. But to the outside media, this tended to create the impression that the story of the World Series was not the story of one team against another, but the story of the region in which all of the games were played.

I live in Kansas. Eastern Kansas is not flat; it rolls gently, much like Massachusetts, so that in driving through the country one has the experience of passing through a series of vistas, each covering a quarter of a mile to three quarters of a mile of road time. It is a very beautiful area, so much so that when I am required to drive through it daily I grow to enjoy the experience more and more, watching the subtle and sudden changings of the colors in each landscape. The grainfields leap from dark black to brilliant green in days when the crop first appears, fade day by day into a more muted green, then suddenly turn brown or gold or a mixture of colors when the crop ripens. Then that crop will be gone and a patch of dull gray/black earth may set there for a few days before it begins to become something else. The farms are all small and much of the land is unworkable, so that a wooded area provides a backdrop for almost every field, and each field is divided by one or another kind of fence and small road for the farming equipment. A hundred kinds of wildflowers grow beside the roads, and the colors of the trees change, and the houses change, and the skies change, and the earth changes, and the cows and the sheep and the horses grow up and move around, and the creeks come up and settle back down so that the landscape each day seems different and more graceful than it did the day before.

In spite of this, by some bizarre trick of fate, this area has been chosen in the nation's consciousness to represent No-where—an ugly, barren, empty, square space from which people come but do not return. In movies, people who come from nowhere come from Kansas. This preconception is so strong that people who come here often see nothing except what they have been taught to expect, and learn no more of the area around them than a man driving across an Apache reservation picks up of the Apache language.

When I was starting my newsletter, I had a meeting in New York with a man who was interested in investing money or advice or something. He began the meeting by telling me that he had been to Kansas, several times, and regaled me with a few stories about what an awful place it was. It seems he was quite offended by the fact that we don't have any buildings higher than twenty-eight stories. Another time, just before going on national television, a network sports personality asked me where I was from, and upon learning that I was from near Lawrence, Kansas, informed me that he had once spent an evening in Lawrence and that there was nothing to do there.

Of course, it isn't every New Yorker who will do this, but a small number who make a deep impression. I always wonder, when this happens, whether if I was black or Jewish these people would take the same opportunity to make use of a few ethnic slurs, or if I was from Bophutswana if they would tell me how insufferably hot and fly-infested it was in Bophut-swana. I know that they would not, and I wonder why I am not entitled to the same courtesy. I reflect upon my own episodes of extreme tactlessness, which are frequent and therefore easy to recall, and let the occasion go forward without incident. Usually.

The impressions that we have of a people or place stem largely from the images of artists (in all fields); the way that people see Mississippi largely originates in the work of Faulk-ner, Eudora Welty, and a few other creative people. It is an unfortunate fact that this area has not been well or honestly served by the nation's artistic community. To give you just a couple of examples, you might remember a song that was made popular by Art Garfunkel a few years ago. . . . I think it was called "My Little Town":

And after it rains, there's a rainbow,
And all of the colors are black,
It's not that the colors aren't there,
It's just imagination they lack,
And everything's the same back
In my little town.

That song was written by Paul Simon, a great artist, an enormously talented and intelligent man, who incidentally was born and raised in Brooklyn, New York, still lives in New York City and frankly knows as much about people who live in small towns as a meadowlark knows about the feast of the epiphany. If, in fact, he were to live in a small town, he would discover that one of the great pleasures in living there is that small-town people have wonderful imaginations, probably because they don't live under the minute-to-minute pressures that city life puts on a body, occupying the mind so fully that it cramps the imagination.

Then, too, you might remember the vivid, and depressing, portrayal of small-town life in the movie *The Last Picture Show*, which won a number of Academy Awards in 1971. The movie presented small-town life as a dismal, frustrating series of misdirected ambitions and failed relationships. This cinematic masterpiece was directed by Peter Bogdanovich, another very bright and talented artist—and another Brooklyn boy, who, to be honest about it, doesn't have an eggplant's notion about what small-town people do before and after the basketball game. Through carelessness, callousness, indifference to the truth, these people adopt, repeat and perpetuate a set of images about small-time life that is nothing but a stack of filthy lies.

L. Frank Baum, who wrote *The Wizard of Oz* and used Kansas as the gray, bleak Nowhere from which Dorothy escapes, based the portrait upon his experiences—in South Dakota.

If you're illiterate, don't go to movies and never leave the state, I suppose that all of this doesn't get to you, but if you're an active, reading person, the naked prejudice directed at you begins to lose its charm after a while. You encounter it virtually every week; let me give you just two examples of things that I was reading during the World Series. In *The Village*

Voice of October 22, there was an article by James Ridgeway detailing a murder which was committed by some white-supremacist nut case not far from where I live. "During the 1920s, the Ku Klux Klan was powerful in Kansas," writes Ridgeway, by way of helping explain this murder which happened in Nebraska in 1985, "running entire counties. And today in this region where life is never easy, the farm depression is taking an especially harsh toll." Well, tell me, Mr. Ridgeway, is life easy in New York City? Does the depression take no harsh toll in the ghettos of the east? The allegation about the Ku Klux Klan running entire counties in Kansas is admirably creative, but let us suppose that this was turned around, and that a small-town Kansas newspaper was doing a special on a murder in the Village. In the course of explaining why Tom shot Ralph, they would drag in by-the-by the power of the mob in Little Italy in the twenties, and throw in a few gratuitous comments about how tough life is in the big cities of the East. Would this not strike you as hopelessly provincial, irrelevant, and more than a little stupid? Can you imagine the hysterical laughter that it would provoke in the offices of *The Village Voice*? Yet it would be far more fair and relevant, for the KKK, so far as I know, has not existed in Kansas for many years, while the same cannot be said of the mob in New York City.

A few days later, reading a fine biography of W. C. Fields written in 1949 by Robert Lewis Taylor, I encounter the theme again:

(Fields) pondered the bleak plains of Kansas, the arid habits of its people, the high voltage of its divinity . . .

All of which, and most particularly the latter, are entirely fictitious.

With enough repetition this becomes profoundly irritating, but it is also profoundly trivial; the only real cost of it is that at an impressionable age, young Kansans or young Missourians will sometimes believe the lies that are told about them—just as young black people or young Jewish people will develop negative self-images if the slanders directed at them are not effectively countered.

Anyway, comes a World Series, or a National Convention in town, or what have you. Because of this treatment, Kansas

City is somewhat of a self-conscious city. This is to put it mildly. They are . . . well, *anxious* to see how they will be reflected in the press attention. They are *so* anxious about this that they make fools of themselves. It is acutely embarrassing at times; visiting press people are shanghaied into television interviews to reveal their feelings about being in Kansas City. "How do you feel about Kansas City? Tell us that you love us. Tell us why you love us. Tell us what you love most about us. Wouldn't you really rather be here than in Los Angeles?"

There is a tendency to attribute the negative image of the area to "the media," which is massively unfair; the media, in general, merely reflect the images which are current in the society, and will bend over backward to avoid reflecting them unfairly. There are a few people who will come out from the east for the Series and tell us what an ugly place we have, but this is not common. Yet Kansas Citians are so insecure—so paranoid, really—that Al Michaels came under attack merely because he said a number of nice things about St. Louis.

For the benefit of anybody who is not familiar with the cities, St. Louis is a much nicer city than Kansas City, and I'll tell you why in a moment. Yet at every insurgence of the national media, Kansas City press packets are handed out repeating a number of overworked boasts about the place. "Kansas City has more fountains than Rome." Well, I suppose so; the only problem is that about two-thirds of Kansas City's fountains are just jets of water shooting up in front of a branch bank in the middle of a bunch of Burger Kings and stuff, and have the esthetic impact of large lawn sprinklers. "Kansas City has more miles of boulevards than any city except Paris." This one always conjures up images of the International Board of Boulevard Certification, walking along saying "No, I'm afraid this one is just an 'avenue' unless you widen the curb space by four more inches and plant six more trees per half-mile." Another favorite is "Kansas City is the Christmas Card capital of the Midwest." Can you imagine going into New York City for a World Series and having a press person come out to Shea and tell you how many Christmas cards are printed in New York City?

There are about seven reasons why St. Louis is a much nicer city than Kansas City. Number one, it is older, and has a much richer architectural heritage. Number two, its neighborhoods are much stronger. As Kansas City has grown, it has absorbed and neutralized the small cities around it, none of which retains a distinct flavor to contribute to the city. This hasn't happened in St. Louis. Number three, the downtown area is much more pleasant—you can walk around it, there's shopping there, the ball park is there. Kansas City's downtown area is basically a business area. Number four, St. Louis has integrated the river into the city, adding a great deal to the city esthetically; Kansas City has buried its river underneath a heap of train tracks, access roads and dirty bridges. Number five, St. Louis probably has more good restaurants. If it doesn't have more of them, they're easier to find. Number six, St. Louis has many more areas that one can walk around and enjoy. Kansas City is all built to accommodate the automobile. And number seven, you can drive around St. Louis without getting lost. Unless you stay on the interstate system, Kansas City has got to be the most confusing, frustrating city to drive around in the United States, with the possible exception of Atlanta, and Atlanta only because all of the streets are named "Peachtree." The Kansas City street department renames their streets about every three blocks so that it is all but impossible to keep track of where you are and how to get where you want to go. Drive you nuts.

That being said, there are things to like about Kansas City. It's reasonably clean. The best restaurants in Kansas City generally don't have any kind of expectations about dress; requesting a jacket or tie is considered rather pretentious. I like that. I'm more comfortable eating out in KC than I am in New York—but anybody who suggested that the third-best restaurant in KC would crack the top fifty in New York would be out of his skull. The city's image would improve a lot if they would just accept themselves for what they are, and stop handing out malarkey about how many miles of boulevard they have.

Kansas City has a world class inferiority complex, but they also have a world class ball club. On the evening of October 24, 1985, that ball club was one game away from being eliminated. Fortunately, the man with the nuclear slider was on the mound for Kansas City. The Royals made Bob Forsch throw twenty-six pitches in the first inning, scoring a run on two singles and two outs. The Cards tied it in the bottom of the first on doubles by Herr and Clark, both hit very hard. I wasn't worried; fifteen of the seventeen pitches that Danny Jackson threw in the first were strikes.

The Royals scored three runs in the top of the second, the big hit being a two-run triple by Willie Wilson. Forsch left the game a loser, having thrown fifty-four pitches and gotten only five men out. The Cards didn't get the ball out of the infield in the second. In the third they loaded the bases with two out, but Jackson got Landrum to pop out on a slider.

With one out in the fifth inning, Willie McGee reached base but was picked off first by Jackson. All season long, Steve Balboni had had a great deal of trouble making the throw to second after this happened; he had thrown the ball into left field God knows how many times. All season long, we (Royals fans) were kind of afraid that the other teams would catch onto it, and begin to exploit it. Late in the year, they did, particularly the Rangers; when a runner was picked off first he would simply head for second, figuring that Balboni would probably throw the ball away.

Against the Cardinals, this was a major concern. But in the fourth game of the series, Bud Black picked off Ozzie Smith, and Balboni did one of the things that he had not been doing all year. Instead of trying to throw over Ozzie, he chased Smith most of the way to second, then made the short flip over his head.

Now, in the fifth inning of the fifth game, Jackson had picked off McGee, and Balboni did the other thing that he hadn't been doing all summer. Racing two or three steps into the infield, he cut McGee out of his line of fire, squared up toward second base and made a nice throw. Maybe he just happened to make those plays when it counted—but it seems much more likely that someone (Lee May, perhaps?) had worked with him in late September to solve the problem. We never did hear. No one commented on the change.

One of the inexplicable things that happened in the mumbo-jumbo chemistry of the nine million soft-core sports media at the series was that it was determined, somehow, that Steve Balboni was to be the goat of the event. Balboni had had a rather poor playoff, and the idea that he was not contributing was preserved by a sort of intuitive logical paradigm which went:

a. Steve Balboni doesn't do anything except hit home runs.
b. Steve Balboni hasn't hit any home runs.
c. Steve Balboni isn't doing anything.

Steve Balboni was, in fact, having a very good series, from the beginning. He hit .320 for the series, had an on base percentage of .433, struck out only four times, handled far more chances than any other player in the series and committed no errors, and made several fine defensive plays. While he had only four hits (all singles) in the first five games, his hits in the first two games had been very important ones at the time they occurred, the first one driving in the first run of the series (and the Royals' only run of the game), and the second hit bringing the tying run to the plate with one out in the ninth inning. Between singles and walks, he had made significant offensive contributions in every contest.

Jackson was never challenged again. In the seventh inning, Brett slid into the dugout in a spectacular, but unsuccessful, attempt to catch a pop up; that failing it became strike one, and Jackson struck out the side on nine pitches. (I wonder if that's ever happened before in a World Series game? I'd be very surprised if it has.) The Royals added a run in the eighth and one in the ninth, and had their second easy victory of the series.

Game Six

The second game of the 1985 World Series was only the eighth such dramatic ninth-inning reversal in the history of the fall classic—that is, the eighth time that a team had gone into the ninth inning behind and had won the game without extra innings. Most of the first seven games are well remembered.

In the first game of the 1908 series, Chicago blew a 5–1 lead and trailed 6–5 entering the ninth, then scored five runs to send the Tigers of Cobb and Crawford down to a 10–6 defeat, triggering a 5-game rout for the Cubs.

Twenty-one years later, the Cubs were the victims. In the next game after the fabled contest in which the Athletics scored ten runs in the seventh to overcome an 8–0 lead (which Fred Lieb called the most exciting game he ever saw), the Cubs entered the ninth with a 2–0 lead and got the first man out, only to lose the game on a two-run homer by Mule Haas and a run-scoring double by Bing Miller. (All this happened just days before the stock market crash of 1929, incidentally. Any Cub fan who had invested in the market must have thought we were nearing the end of the world.)

Twelve years later, in the fourth game of the 1941 World Series, came the infamous Mickey Owen passed ball. The Brooklyn catcher failed to catch a third strike which would have ended the ball game. The Yankees scored four runs before the third out was finally recorded, and turned a 4–3 defeat into a 7–4 victory.

Six years later, Brooklyn got even in an even more famous game. Yankee pitcher Floyd Bevens had a no-hitter and a 2–1 lead with two out in the bottom of the ninth, but with a runner on second due to a walk and a stolen base. Yankee manager Bucky Harris then flew in the face of the book, intentionally walking Pete Reiser to put the potential winning run on second base, and suddenly lost the game, the no-hitter and probably his job (a year later) when Cookie Lavagetto doubled off the right field wall, scoring two for a 3–2 Brooklyn win.

It was twenty-five years before this would happen again. In the fourth game of the 1972 series, the Cincinnati Reds had a 2–1 lead and a man out, needing two more outs to tie the series at two games apiece. The A's hit five consecutive singles to score two runs and win the game.

Three years later, in the second game of the memorable 1975 series, the Red Sox held a 2–1 lead with two out in the ninth inning, when Dave Concepcion singled to tie the score off of Dick Drago, then scored on a double by Ken Griffey.

Kansas City was the victim of the next two incidents. In the fifth game of the 1980 series, the Phillies entered the ninth trailing 3–2, but rallied on a single by Schmidt, a double by Unser and a single by Trillo. In that game, Philadelphia was looking at Dan Quisenberry for the fifth straight game and for the third inning of that game, and it was widely felt that Jim Frey had let the Phillies see too much of Quisenberry.

The came the second game of the 1985 series, in which it was widely felt that Dick Howser waited too long to let the Cardinals see Dan Quisenberry. Needless to say, it had never before happened twice in one series.

Through eight innings, the sixth game of the 1985 World Series seemed almost like a rerun, combining used parts from the first two contests. As in the second game, Charlie Leibrandt was pitching . . . well, near perfect. Leibrandt retired the Cardinals in order in the first, second, third, fourth, fifth, and seventh; only three balls, all routine flies, were hit out of the infield in those innings. In the sixth the Cardinals had two singles, but the Royals got out of it with a double play.

As in the first game, the Royals were pounding the ball all over the park, but were denied by the determined Cardinals.

In the first inning Lonnie Smith doubled to lead off and moved to third with nobody out, but failed to score when Danny Cox struck out George Brett.

In the second inning, the Royals got one hit and lost another on a superb play by Ozzie Smith, diving for a ball behind second and flipping it backhand to Herr for an inning-ending force-out.

In the third inning, Willie McGee made a fine over-the-shoulder catch of a liner scorched by Lonnie Smith.

Leading off the fourth, George Brett hit another mammoth, mile-high drive caught by Cedeño inches from the top of the wall. (If this series had been played in Yankee Stadium, Babe Ruth and Reggie Jackson would have become second-class legends by the time it was over.) Frank White then bunted for a single, but was called out at second base trying to steal. The call at second was questionable, and cost the Royals a run, as Sheridan singled to right two pitches later, but in truth the Royals could blame themselves for that one as much as anybody, for had White simply stayed at first he would have scored, given the same sequence, on a single by Sundberg that was adjourned into the fifth inning. They didn't try to blame anybody. Balboni plastered the third out on a line right at McGee.

In the fifth inning, Sundberg singled leading off and was sacrificed to second, but died on base.

In the sixth inning, Wilson singled leading off, but Brett hit into an easy 4–6–3 double play.

In the seventh inning, the Royals got a walk from Balboni and a single from Biancalana.

At that point, the game began in earnest to repeat the essential points of the painful second game. This was a scoreless game, a complete pitcher's duel, now late in the game. Due up after Biancalana's single was Leibrandt. To allow Leibrandt to hit in this situation was tantamount to abandoning an excellent scoring chance, and for that reason it made no sense to me. If the Royals had used a good left-handed pinch hitter here —say, Iorg, Orta, or Quirk—their chance of scoring a big run would go from about .030 to about .250. Offsetting this, you had the difference between Charlie Leibrandt on the mound, magnificent but with seven innings already gone, or having Dan Quisenberry. Leibrandt stayed in to hit, but it seemed to me (and still does) quite unlikely that a tiring Leibrandt was *that much* better than a fresh Dan Quisenberry. I felt that Howser had punched the wrong button.

Immediately, it began to come back at him. As a hitter, Leibrandt struck out. As a pitcher, he suddenly lost it. Pendleton drove the ball to deep center field, although Wilson got there. Tito Landrum singled (to right field, as always). Cesar Cedeño walked, putting two on with one out, but Darrell Porter struck out on three pitches. With two out, runners on first and second and the pitcher coming up—the exact same situation that Howser had just faced, except a half-inning later in the game—Herzog used his pinch hitter, a journeyman named Brian Harper.

Harper ripped a two-strike pitch into center field. The Cardinals had the lead.

Quisenberry came into the game. He was outstanding, retiring four of the five hitters he faced (McGee, Herr, Clark—people like that) and allowing a scratch single on a ball tapped in front of the plate. But in their turn between those four outs, the Royals didn't score, and the Cardinals still had the lead going into the bottom of the ninth.

At that point, I almost left the ball park. I *never* leave the park with a ball game in progress. The last time I left the park before the last out was on opening day at Yankee Stadium, 1983, when the Tigers beat the Yankees 13–2, and it was cold and raining and we had a dinner appointment. But I almost left this one. I remembered that the Cardinals were 88–0 when they held a lead going into the ninth inning. I remembered that the ninth-inning turnaround in the second game was only the eighth in the history of the series. Most of all, sitting there in a pool of wasted enthusiasm, I remembered the last game we had seen here. I remembered the Cardinal fans jeering "Charlee, Char-lee, Char-lee" after it was over. The air felt as heavy as lead, and I felt almost compelled to run away from it, to escape before the last ray of hope was used and the gloom that hung over us like a zeppelin would land on our shoulders. Three outs, and the season was over. I didn't want to see those three outs. I did not want to be there when the 1985 Royals, a team of such determination and dogged resourcefulness that they had escaped brushes with death a dozen times, finally bit the dust.

I can't understand what happened then. The Royals mounted another challenge—as they had all game—and the Cardinals this time simply fell apart; there is no other way to put it. Jorge Orta beat out an infield single, and Clark argued briefly about the call, and in the nine and one-half innings remaining in the 1985 World Series the Cardinals did absolutely nothing that would remind one of a contending team. Jack Clark misplayed a pop-up, and Steve Balboni drilled a single, putting the winning run on base. Darrell Porter, finally helping to pay the Royals back for the World Championship he cost them in 1980, let a ball get by him, putting the tying run in scoring position. Whitey Herzog decided that Hal McRae was to be intentionally walked, giving the Royals a chance to tie the game with a walk, and giving Howser two chances to win it with the left-handed pinch hitters he had saved from the seventh inning.

The zeppelin struggled away from our shoulders; hope rose in every throat. Dane Iorg flared a pitch over first base. As it left the bat there was no doubt that it would end the game. Andy Van Slyke almost managed to create some doubt; Van Slyke made one terrific play to cut the ball off and fire home, but the game was over.

No one in the park was sober.

The sudden emotional lurch, from severe communal depression to sudden shared ecstasy, was as intoxicating as rum. It is impossible to describe the feeling of the crowd minutes later, but it is possible to describe briefly their actions, which may give you some clue. People jumped up and down until the stadium shook. Strange men hugged each other and wept with joy. A co-ed a few rows in front of us wet her pants. A continuous roar sailed into the air for nearly twenty minutes, until every pair of lungs in the county was too hoarse to contribute any more to it, and then those in the stadium sat and stared at the empty playing field. A half hour after the game hardly a seat was empty. I'm told that some people didn't leave the parking lot until almost dawn the next morning.

Game Seven

The Cardinals, you see, were the Team of Destiny. By late October we had been hearing this for two solid months. The team was supposed to lose at the start of the season—they were an excellent team, but few people seemed to realize this, so they were supposed to lose—and then one thing broke right for them and then another and another, and when Jack Clark went out in late August and *even this* worked out well for the Cardinals, due to the superb play of Cedeño, then the Cardinals had become destined to win the championship. I don't know what the Cardinal *players* were thinking, but the Cardinal *fans* had been 100 percent convinced that the 1985 Cardinals were touched by the hand of God, and could not be dissuaded from adding another World Title to the long St. Louis list.

If the Cardinals were the team of destiny, the Royals were the team of determination. Few people outside their clubhouse believed that they could win—but they obviously did. I say that this is obvious not merely from the fact that they *did* win, but from the things they did on the field. Frank White, who earlier in his career was a terrific bunter but doesn't bunt much anymore, began picking out key moments of the game and dropping down bunt singles—I think he must have done this about six or eight times after September 25. Willie Wilson, never a particularly disciplined hitter and a hitter who for that reason sees a lot of pitches a foot out of the strike zone, began at key moments letting those pitches go by, putting him ahead in the count. Their defensive concentration and execution was tremendous—the best I've ever seen. Their individual defensive skills were good to excellent (four regulars have won Gold Gloves, and any of the four could have won the award in 1985), but on the defensive plays that require two or three or four players to work together, they were extraordinary—as a team of past-thirty stars should expect to be if they're going to win. There were several examples of this in the World Series, but the easiest to remember is the remarkable Wilson-to-White-to-Brett relay which caught Willie McGee at third on what everyone assumed was a triple in the fifth inning of the first game. Combining these skills, they would maneuver themselves into a position from which they had a chance to win—and then they would win. The only team that I ever saw that seemed really similar was the 1980 Phillies, which, with Rose, Boone, Schmidt and Bowa (among others) had the same kind of tenacity.

As the teams arrived at the park for Game Seven, the series was literally even. Each team had won three games, and each team had their Cy Young candidate rested and ready to go. The Royals were at home, but that seemed to mean little because of a) the closeness and similarity of the two cities (nobody was really far away from home), b) the extreme similarity of the parks themselves—both turf parks with long power alleys, pretty good visibility, and c) the fact that the *visiting* team had won three of the first six games. The series was as even as it could be.

In the 1975 World Series the Red Sox ace starter was Luis Tiant. By the age of thirty-four, Luis Tiant didn't throw particularly hard or lay claim to a spectacular breaking pitch, but he held his innings together by deception and control and a superior defense. He started the first game of the series, and pitched a five-hit shutout. Four days later he faced the Reds again, and emerged with a complete-game victory.

But when the Reds saw him the third time, the jig was up. Deception is a limited resource; no con man ever made a living very long in one town. Before Tiant departed his third start he had surrendered eleven hits and six runs.

The series was literally even—but the core element of Cardinal magic had been shattered. Maybe I'm completely wrong, but that's the only way I can understand it: the Cardinals thought that they were *supposed to win*, that this was their destiny and that nothing could derail it. When the Royals scratched and clawed their way back into the series, and then a break or two went against the Cardinals, they were suddenly alarmed, flooded with self-doubt. They reacted angrily, as if "What is this? I thought we were supposed to win this thing? We won more games than they did, didn't we? *Everybody told us we were going to win.*" Whitey Herzog actually pointed out angrily after the seventh game that the Cardinals had won 108 games to the Royals' 99—as if teams had not been winning the World Series with fewer wins than the opponent for more than eighty years.

For the seventh game of the series, Don Denkinger was behind home plate, and it couldn't have mattered less if it was Ray Charles. John Tudor had nothing. In the first inning George Brett ripped a single to right and Frank White drove the ball to the track. No damage.

In the second inning Steve Balboni had home run depth on a foul ball. Craig and I tried to remember times we had seen a batter hit a foul homer and a fair homer in the same at bat. I've seen Balboni do it a couple of times. He didn't see another pitch anywhere near home plate. Darryl Motley, up next, ripped another foul home run, this one just missing the left field line. And then we saw it. We'll remember this one. Motley put the Royals two runs ahead on the next pitch. The crowd went wild and the ball was gone before Motley was out of the batter's box.

In the third inning, the Royals lined foul shots all over the park. Lonnie Smith saw three balls in the dirt and swung at one of them. Among the fifty-five pitches John Tudor threw that day, this was the only one a Royal batter swung at and missed. With one out and Brett at the plate, Tudor began to stall. While delivering one pitch to the plate, he threw to first base six times; Brett eventually got an infield single. Then, unaccountably, Tudor seemed to forget about the base runners, and Brett and Smith pulled a double steal on a 1–2 pitch to Frank White. White fouled off five pitches in the process of drawing a walk. Jim Sundberg also walked, forcing in a run. John Tudor left the game. It was 3–0.

Bill Campbell came into the game. Steve Balboni fouled off his first pitch, took two pitches outside and ripped a single between Smith and Pendleton. It was 5–0.

The first pitch of the Royals' third had been thrown at 8:04 P.M. The inning ended at 8:29.

St. Louis had the heart of their order up in the fourth, McGee, Herr and Clark. The first pitch of the St. Louis fourth was thrown at 8:31. The last was thrown at 8:35.

The Royals had two singles and a stolen base in the fourth, but lost the inning to a 5–4–3 double play. The game was still alive; it was still 5–0.

The first pitch of the St. Louis fifth was thrown at 8:45. The last was thrown at 8:49.

The Detroit Tigers in 1934 led the series three games to two and were coming home to Bennett Park for the last two games. With Schoolboy Rowe pitching the sixth game, they felt the series was theirs. But after a heartbreaking 4–3 loss on Monday afternoon, the Tigers came to the seventh game having to beat Dizzy Dean, the best pitcher in the league, although Diz was working with only one day of rest.

The Cardinals blew the game open in the third inning, scoring seven runs. Stunned, the Tiger fans were silent for a while, but then began to get surly. In the sixth inning, Tiger third baseman Marv Owen made an unnecessary phantom tag of Joe Medwick after Medwick tripled (the ball had been cut off), and so Medwick slid hard into third, expecting the tag. The two exchanged words, but it came to nothing. But when Medwick tried to take the field in the bottom of the sixth . . .

The Cardinals won the seventh game, 11–0.

The top half of the fifth inning of the seventh game of the 1985 World Series lasted thirty-seven minutes, was one of the wildest half-innings ever played in a World Series, and radically changed the image of the St. Louis Cardinal baseball club throughout the nation. I will give you a decoded version of my notes exactly as I took them down at the time, then we'll discuss it later. This was the inning (X means the ball was put in play):

        Fifth vs. Campbell
1st Pitch:
8:51
Sundberg   BX
              Single in front of Van Slyke
8:52 Herzog out/Jeff Lahti into game   8:55
Bones   SBBX
              Ground single between third/short
              Runner to second
Motley   SBFFX
              Single to right-center (opposite field)
              Sundberg scores, Balboni to second

Biancalana   ScCBX
Strikeout swinging
(Sc means attempted to check swing)

Saberhagen   X
Bad Bunt; 3–6 force-out
Saberhagen just beat 3–6–1 double play
Balboni to third (No sac awarded)

Smith   BCsFBF
(Smoke appears in stadium . . . where is it
from?)
X
Ground double up third base line
Two runs score
Batter to third on throw

Wilson   SX
Grounded up middle; Herr made nice effort but
Wilson beat 4–3 play
Smith scores

9:04 Herzog out/Ricky Horton in game   9:06

Brett   X
Line single to right-center
Wilson to third
NO THROW TO THIRD!
CARDINALS GIVE UP!

White   BB

9:09 Herzog out/ Andujar in game
  Double switch with Jorgensen entering to play left/batting
  ninth, Andujar in seventh spot   9:12
  (White still batting with 2–0 count)
         CFFFFFFBX
         Single in front of Jorgensen
         Wilson scores, Brett to third

Sundberg   BBFBFB
      Joaquin argues about call
      Herzog comes out to argue

9:19 Herzog thrown out of game! . . . Herzog now livid . . .
really lights into Denkinger (last night's call?)
9:22   X (Ball four)
      Andujar argues again . . . thrown out of game . . .
charges Denkinger . . . four Cardinals hold him off (Cedeño
leading?) . . . did he bump ump? Suspended?
9:23 Forsch to mound 9:26

Bones   B
                Wild pitch; all three runners advance
                BCX
                Drive to center
                Well hit in right/center but McGee got it
9:28/ 6 runs/ 7 hits/ 0 errors/ 2 left/ 11–0 Kansas City
Would you believe?

Not fully described here is the Cardinals' behavior on the field, for which they were torn apart by the nation's press. If you ever get the time to walk through these notes in your mind, visualizing what's happening, what you will get is a picture of a team falling apart as their chances of winning evaporate.

I wrote the words "No throw to third . . . Cardinals give up!" just minutes before all hell broke loose, and in view of that I was trying to remember why I had written this. I think what happened was that the Cardinal defense did not move into position after Brett's single. With a runner scoring on the play and another runner going to third, there should have been people scurrying around getting in position to back up throws, etc. The Cardinals, competing up to that point, suddenly just stopped doing those things; they stood and watched the play flat-footed. Which, in view of the fact that the score was now 8–0, is understandable.

And immediately, Herzog brought Andujar into the game. Now, this is the decision that is *really* hard to explain. The situation is all but out of hand, teetering precariously on the brink of chaos. A calm head is needed, and you're going to bring in . . . Joaquin? I mean, I *like* Joaquin Andujar; I think he's great. But this is like calling in Don Rickles to arbitrate a touchy labor dispute. This is like sending James Watt to deliver a message of condolence. This is like calling Jerry Lewis in to assist in a tricky brain operation. And apart from that, Andujar hadn't done anything right in a month.

Herzog used five pitchers in the inning (Campbell, Lahti, Horton, Andujar, and Forsch). I remember one other time when he used five pitchers in an inning, in the sixth inning of the third game of the AL playoff in 1976. In 1977 he used six pitchers in the last two innings of the fifth and deciding game, trying unsuccessfully to protect a lead.

Most managers won't use five pitchers in an inning because they believe that the more pitchers you use, the more chances you have to find out who doesn't have his stuff on that particular day. Herzog will because he doesn't put much stock in what you have on a given day; he believes that it's the manager's job to get the best possible matchup of pitcher's abilities against hitter's abilities. I admire him for that, because I agree with him and because he is willing to take the criticism and do what he thinks is right.

But I thought this day what I thought the other two times: Whitey, it sure looks bad when it doesn't work.

Too much has been said about the Cardinals' bad behavior in that inning, but since it is too late to undo this, let me get in my two cents' worth. Ozzie Smith was quoted as defending the Cardinals' behavior, saying, "We're competitors. Any time you feel you've been cheated, you should react that way." That's the John McEnroe defense; this doesn't count as making an ass of myself because I *really believe* that ball was out. Gee, Oz, I never thought of it that way, but since you mention it, I kind of wonder if maybe the Cardinals' reactions were too modest. Who's John Tudor trying to fool, anyway, punching out an electric fan? If he *really* felt like he was cheated, I'd be thinking he'd look for bigger game, like maybe a batting practice machine, a helicopter . . . he should have been willing to drop-kick an air conditioner, at the very least. And Andujar, he's pretending to be so upset . . . why, he took the mound unarmed, didn't he? I can't understand that. The man had twenty-four hours to stew about it, and you know it's not that hard to pick up a piece in our society, yet he took the mound with murder in his heart but not a damn thing up his sleeve. Felt cheated, indeed.

No, seriously, the Cardinals' behavior wasn't *all* that bad. Managers get thrown out of games all year; I don't see what the big deal is if it happens in the seventh game of a World Series. We might remember that while it is, to us, the climax of the show, it is, *to the participants*, like witnessing a death in the family, the death of a dream which they have nurtured for months or years, have fought hard and worked hard to bring to the edge of reality. We've never been through anything like it, most of us, but we must imagine the situation as a firestorm of hope, fear, dismay, pressure, hope against hope and hope against the stark terror of the scoreboard. I imagine it's quite a bit like being gathered around your grandmother's deathbed with 40,000 ecstatic strangers yelling, "CROAK! CROAK! CROAK!"

I am not saying that the Cardinals' behavior was laudable, but that the media might have done well to remember that old saw about walking a mile in a pair of used moccasins, or whatever it is. I would point out to you that the only other team which has ever gone through the same thing, the 1934 Tigers, didn't handle it a whole lot better. Just a week earlier, the Royals had done a similar number on the Blue Jays, beaten them decisively in a game that the Jays never expected to have to play to begin with. The Blue Jays handled it well, but their fans didn't. Objects were thrown on the field, and the game was stopped at least three times by fans running out of the stands, including one unfortunate heavyweight who performed so badly that the Toronto broadcaster designated him an American. Which, by the way, I'm not real crazy about. I mean, the Canadians were quite miffed because a half-dozen jerks were quoted as saying they didn't want the World Series played in Canada, and I'll be happy to say that anybody who feels that way—I personally have never encountered anybody who does—should consider having a brain implant. But how would the Canadians react if an American announcer assumed that because a given fan did something stupid, he must be a Canadian? This is not cute, guys, this is bigotry.

With a 11–0 lead, Bret Saberhagen more or less junked his curveball, change and slider and began throwing fastballs. The Cardinals hit them hard, and drove a number of them to the track. Had they been content to take singles, they likely would have gotten on the board—but had they threatened to get on the board, Bret Saberhagen would likely have started mixing in a few breaking pitches.

It took him six minutes and 17 pitches to retire the Cardinals in the sixth.

It took him four minutes and 8 pitches—8 fastballs—to do the job in the seventh.

It took him three minutes and 9 pitches to retire the Cardinals in the eighth.

He threw his first pitch in the ninth at 10:09.

At 10:10, thirty years of frustration had ended.

The Royals were champions of the world.

Epilogue

It's funny, you know. I've been as big a baseball fan as you can be all my life, but *I never knew a baseball game could make you feel so good.* The celebration at the stadium lasted for twenty or thirty minutes before the Royals, showing the inimical corporate taste for which they have long been noted, began trying to clear the stadium. "Thank you for your support. We'll see you next year." More cheering, yelling and random running around. "Thank you for coming. Tickets will be on sale for the 1986 season at . . ." Still no cessation. "Thank you all for coming. We're going to start turning off the lights now." Lights go out. More lights go out. More announcements. All right, we can take a hint. I suppose they were worried about paying overtime to the cleanup crew.

It took us another thirty minutes to get back to the car, and forty to escape the parking lots. Susie and I drove to an area of Kansas City called Westport. Thousands, maybe tens of thousands of people swarmed the streets, in many places packed in so tight that it was difficult to move. It was past midnight on Sunday; the bars were closed in self-defense, and people wandered around the crowd trying to buy beer or sell it. There were many more buyers than sellers, and the area was dry as the Sahara in a half hour. Virtually the entire crowd wore blue, but absurdity is in the eye of the beholder, and there were no eyes there to sense the absurdity of us as we meandered in circles, slapping high fives with passing strangers (including, when street conditions permitted, those riding by in convertibles and dune buggies), grinning and singing and yelling in the air phrases without meaning or spelling or distinguishable syllables, hugging and holding onto loved ones, catching an occasional spray of Budweiser in the face from a colleague in revelry, joining in war chants scarcely more intelligible than the random shouts, climbing fire escapes to hang hastily designed banners from the windows of cooperating samaritans, wandering around and around until the faces of the others became familiar landmarks of the scene, seeing others dance and weep with joy and sharing the feeling with them and wanting for the evening not to end and for sleep not to come and divide us from what had happened that night.

I thought about Charlie Finley and the "cellar-bray-tion" he had planned twenty-one years earlier. At length we headed home, into streets alive with the singing of horns. Whenever two cars met arms would reach out and wave and horns would sound. We stopped at a fast food place for a burger; a carload of young black men behind us tooted and smiled at us, and we honked and waved and smiled back, and repeated the exercise as we drove out. People tingled for days. 104 percent of the Kansas City population became baseball fans; everyone I know called to say how much he had enjoyed the series and how amazed he had been at the afterglow of the series; the phone companies made a fortune from the reunions of old friends. Office workers who didn't even like each other smiled at one another until they became self-conscious and began to giggle. It was two weeks before anyone had a thought about anything else.

The Cardinal fans did not universally accept the fact that their team had been fairly beaten, and to help them gain this acceptance, let me point out a number of facts:

1. The Royals hit .288 in the World Series, the highest batting average by a series team since 1980, when the Phillies hit .294 and the Royals .290.

The Cardinals hit .185 in the series, the lowest batting average by a series team since 1969.

The 103 points by which KC outhit St. Louis barely misses being the largest difference ever, and is by far the largest ever for a seven-game series. Even before the seventh game, the Royals had out-hit the Cardinals by a huge margin, .270–.190. And there is no area of play which a Cardinal fan could point to up against this, since the Royals also bettered the Cardinals as base runners (seven stolen bases for the Royals, two for the Cardinals) and there was no appreciable difference in terms of power or defense. Cardinal pitchers issued 28 walks in the series; Royal pitchers issued only 18.

The Cardinals' only argument is that, because of the way things worked out, they deserved to win despite being badly outplayed in most phases of the game. The argument is, giving it every advantage, that the Cardinals are a superior team, but merely disintegrated in the face of a bad call. Hell of a defense.

2. The Royals won three games in the series by five runs or more, winning 6–1, 6–1, and 11–0. They were the first team in twenty-five years to do that. The 1984 Tigers did not win any game so decisively (they had victory margins of one, two,

three, and four.) The 1983 Orioles won one game by five runs, and the 1982 Cardinals won one by more than five (twelve). The last team to win *two* games by decisive margins was the 1978 Yankees, who routed the Dodgers 12–2 and 7–2 (but also lost one 11–5). The Oakland A's, while winning three straight World Championships, never won a World Series game by more than three runs. The 1927 Yankees outscored the Pirates by five runs only once (8–1, third game). Only three other teams in the history of the sport have won three World Series games by margins of five runs or more, and one of those was the 1919 Reds—in an eight-game series, with the cooperation of the opposition.

I don't want to get too deeply into this, but the ability to win games *decisively* is one of the best quick indicators of relative quality. Whereas one-run games involve a lot of luck, a bad team very rarely beats a good team by a decisive margin. If you take the 1986 Guide when it comes out and check the games in which the first-place teams played the last-place teams (that is, Toronto against Cleveland, Toronto against Texas, etc.) I would guess that you would find that the first-place teams would win about 70 percent of the time overall, but 85 percent or more of the time when the game was decided by five runs or more. That's why blowouts are one of the most interesting things to watch in the early season. If the Seattle Mariners, for example, were to win several games by big margins in the first few weeks of the season, then you should look for them to be in contention all the way—whereas if they win all of their close games early, it doesn't really mean that much.

3. The team which scores more runs in the series wins about 80 percent of the time. The last time the team which scored more runs did not win was 1977, when the Dodgers outscored the Yankees 28–26, but lost the series in six games.

The Royals in 1985 outscored the Cardinals by fifteen runs, 28–13. This was the largest run advantage in the series in twenty-five years, and the largest run advantage for a non-Yankee team since 1919, when the Sox threw the series.

Let me list below all of the series in which the runs scored and allowed were similar to those in 1985, and following that some samples of the press reaction to those series. If you read carefully, you might notice that one example is somewhat out of line with the others. First the series:

1910	Philadelphia (A)	35	Chicago (N)	15
1911	Philadelphia (A)	27	Giants	13
1927	Yankees	23	Pittsburgh	10
1937	Yankees	28	Giants	12
1938	Yankees	22	Chicago (N)	9
1939	Yankees	20	Cincinnati	8
1954	Giants	21	Cleveland	9
1961	Yankees	27	Cincinnati	13
1985	Kansas City	28	St. Louis	13

Now the reactions:

1910 Series:

"[The Athletics] fairly overwhelmed the hitherto almost invincible Cubs, and won with such ease as to leave no doubt as to their superiority, and nothing for even the most rabid National League partisan to cavil at. The Athletics out-ranked the Cubs in every department of the game, batting, fielding, running, pitching . . . to leave absolutely no doubt that as a team, or individually, they are not only superior to their defeated opponents, but that they are by long odds the greatest base ball team in the World today."

Francis Richter, 1911 *Reach Guide*

1911 Series:

The Athletics as a team excelled the Giants in the mechanical points of pitching, batting, and fielding; and also in the matter of resourcefulness, perception, co-operation, and steadiness under stress. They were also more adept in the finer points of the game . . . the Athletics showed superior defense, heavier batting power, more resourcefulness and reserve power than the Giants.

Francis Richter, 1912 *Reach Guide*

1927 Series:

The Series was over before it began as awed Pirate players sat on the top step of their dugout watching Babe Ruth, Lou Gehrig, Tony Lazzeri, and company, considered baseball's finest team ever, pop dozens of balls over the outfield fences in batting practice.

The display of power destroyed the Pirates' confidence and they went down easily in four straight games.

Maury Allen, *Baseball's 100*

1937 Series:

Not many were betting on the Giants, who were three-to-one underdogs. The wise money was right. The Yankee hitting demolished the Giant pitching with such methodical force that [Giant manager] Terry got a telegram from a Giant fan who informed him, tongue in cheek, to "change your signals. The Yankees know them."

John Devaney and Burt Goldblatt
The World Series: A Complete Pictorial History

1938 Series:

Mightier than ever, the New York Yankees retained their title as the No. 1 base ball team of the majors by scoring a grand slam over the Chicago Cubs, National League pennant winners.

Jimmy Isaminger, 1939 *Reach Guide*

1939 Series:

Quite all base ball-minded people seemingly had picked the Yankees to win the American League pennant before the 1939 race began. With that task accomplished the fans were inclined to the belief that the Yankees also would win the world series . . . (at the end) many critics considered the club the strongest ever organized in base ball . . . Like other clubs before them [Cincinnati] found out that the New York team of 1939 had too much offensive power for their kind of base ball.

John B. Foster, 1940 *Spalding and Reach Guide*

1954 Series:

The surprising New York Giants sent the Cleveland Indians down to a stunning defeat in the 1954 blue-ribbon classic. The Indians . . . amazed both friend and foe by failing to win a single game as the relentless Giants rolled on to . . . a one-sided victory.

"The Giants, who arose to every occasion during the league season, played the same aggressive, alert, heads-up ball which enabled them to nose out Brooklyn and Milwaukee."

Fred Lieb, 1955 Official Baseball Guide

1961 Series:

This mightiest of all home run teams continued its hard hitting in the World Series against Cincinnati, taking the Reds easily in five games, hitting seven home runs along the way.

The 1961 New York Yankees had [reached] heights never scaled before, and never equaled since.

Donald Honig, Baseball's 10 Greatest Teams

1985 Series:

[The Cardinals] should have been home in St. Louis, nursing their hangovers and picking confetti out of their hair from the joyous parade downtown. They were not undone by the precocity of 21-year-old Bret Saberhagen or the singing sword of George Brett (but by) American League umpire Don Denkinger.

Bill Conlin in The Sporting News

No, Mr. Conlin, I'm afraid not. The truth is that the Kansas City Royals kicked the holy crap out of the overmatched National League representatives. By a run of extremely good fortune in the close games, the Cardinals were able to keep the result in doubt for six games and three innings; they should be quite grateful for this.

Also in *The Sporting News*, Jack Craig wrote that the "Series, in all candor, offered relatively little excitement." While "excitement" is a subjective term, and I wouldn't question Craig's right to see it that way if he wants, I sure can't agree with him, either. In addition to the two dramatic ninth-inning rallies, an unprecedented thing, the first game of the series was extremely tense, and the seventh game, while not close, was certainly exciting. The series offered human interest angles (Wonder if it's the first time anybody ever had a baby in the middle of winning the series MVP award?), expected heroes

(Brett, Saberhagen, Tudor) and unexpected heroes (Iorg, Landrum). The series had a clearly defined story line, developing from the moment it began, in the regional nature of the combatants and the return of Herzog to Kansas City, along with several other players (Porter, Iorg, Lonnie Smith, Braun) going up against old teammates. The series had controversy with a capital C; it was distinguished by a good deal of classy behavior and a few low-rent antics. The fielding, headed by the play on which a million-dollar athlete heaved his body into the dugout trying to catch a pop-up, was excellent throughout, and offered a number of memorable moments. The chess game of the series was a second-guesser's delight, with questionable managerial decisions on both sides. The series featured a team that was the heaviest underdog in several years rallying to win from a position which no team had ever escaped before (losing the first two games at home). There were no see-saw contests, due to the inability of the Cardinals to score runs, but I think, honestly, that it was the best World Series in ten years. And I think the performance of the TV ratings, gaining strength almost every night, will bear that out.

The National League representative in the 1911 World Series, the New York Giants, was the greatest base-stealing team of all time, stealing 347 bases, a record which still stands. The leader of the larcenous brigade was their twenty-three-year-old left fielder and leadoff man, Josh Devore. The pitching staff was headed by two twenty-game winners, one right-handed and one left-handed. The National League partisans felt sure that their running game could break through against their series opponents.

Answering for the American League was the Philadelphia Athletics, a team with a mediocre outfield but an exceptional starting rotation and a fine infield, led by third baseman Frank Baker, who hit .334, led the American League in slugging percentage and drove in 115 runs. The editor of the 1912 Reach Guide, Francis Richter, wrote that the National League manager, John McGraw, "was handicapped by the fact that with but two star pitchers against [Connie] Mack's three stars the latter always had an 'ace in the hole' against him."

The first game was a pitcher's duel, and the Giants pulled ahead in the series with a 2–1 victory. Later the Jints added another one-run victory, rallying from a 3–0 deficit with one in the seventh, two in the ninth and one in the tenth for a 4–3 win. But in time, the batting of Baker, the star third baseman, and the superior pitching depth of the American League representative began to imbalance the series in the favor of the AL club. The Athletics won the final and deciding contest in an eleven-run blowout, the score being 13–2.

For the series as a whole, the Athletics outscored the Giants twenty-seven to thirteen, and limited the NL club to a puny .189 batting average. John McGraw was given a public reprimand for abusive language on the field, though, as Richter wrote, this incident "was made far too much of by the newspapers." Richter also reported that "The Athletics throughout the series accepted every decision without question and lived in every way up to their reputation as the most gentlemanly team in the arena."

In later years, the editors of baseball guides would become faceless company men, concerned only with compiling the standard elements of the form and giving no one cause for offense, but at this time guides were still personal, fun and informative; editors would digress into amusing sidelights or challenge the reader with original ideas, as they saw fit. Summarizing the series for the 1912 Reach Guide, Francis Richter wrote these words:

> There could hardly have been any special excellence manifested in the base-stealing line . . . in view of the fact that for both teams grand masters in the art of pitching, catching, throwing and watching the bases were handling the ball in each and every game. In the six games only eight bases were stolen . . . and the Giants' unquestionable excellence in this department had little or no chance to assert itself, for the reason that they seldom reached first base, owing to light batting, and when they did get there they found it impossible to secure the good start so indispensable to successful base stealing . . . .
>
> In nearly all forecasts of the 1911 World Series the base-stealing ability of the Giants was regarded by the critics as a great factor in their favor. In commenting on this the editor of this guide, in an editorial forecast of the World's Series pointed out the fact that "invariably in World's Series

'straight base ball' was the rule; that all series were settled by the pitchers and batters . . . the matter of superior speed on the base paths cutting little or no ice."

On "Inside" Baseball

Inside stuff is very big in sportswriting today. TV shows, newspaper columns and sometimes whole books are dubbed "Inside Baseball" and "Inside Football"; magazines run features called "Inside Pitch" and "Inside Corner" and promote "Inside Scouting Reports." A book appears called *High Inside*, and months later another follows called *High and Inside*. The Society for American Baseball Research, an aggregation of dedicated outsiders outside of whom one can scarcely get, compiles a collection of research pieces into a book; this is called, of course, *Insiders' Baseball*.

Inside looks, inside glimpses, inside locker rooms and inside blimpses; within months we shall have seen the inside of everything that one can get inside of without a doctor's help, and now that I think about that I remember seeing a sample copy of a Las Vegas tout sheet that featured an "Inside Medical Report." In the collapse of the original "Inside Sports," perhaps the nickname shattered and the shards landed across the horizon.

What has really happened, of course, is that the walls between the public and the participants of sports are growing higher and higher and thicker and darker, and the media are developing a sense of desperation about the whole thing. It is easier to ape Steve Carlton's example in how to deal with a reporter than it is to effectively mimic his dedication to excellence, so every day more players become unapproachable; the simple expectation of being able to communicate with the inside is decaying.

Silence, though, is but the ultimate weapon, the last line of defense. The first line of defense is the cliché: How do you feel today Jim I'm optimistic I've always had good luck against Lefty Grove what did he throw you that you hit into the seats I think it was a breaking pitch that didn't break is this the biggest day of your life no this is just the first step we still have to win the series has Willie helped the team Willie has added a dimension to the team that we didn't have before and how about Frank Frank has adapted to his role well and hasn't complained at all about not being used more why did you fire Charlie I've the greatest respect for Charlie but sometimes a change just has to be made and we were just happy that Billy was available why did you sign this yoyo he's a winner and a gamer and you can throw away his batting average when the game is on the line.

Clichés are the soldiers of ignorance, and an army of sentries encircles the game, guarding every situation from which a glimmer of fresh truth might be allowed to escape. An occasional player—a George Hendrick here, an Amos Otis there—can never learn to command the cliché, thus is forced to keep silent, unless he chooses to see embarrassing revelations about himself splattered in ink. Players used to have public nicknames, wild things like Circus Solly and affectionate names like Sunny Jim and Unser Choe (Our Joe) and media handles like the Commerce Comet and the Donora Greyhound. Now the big thing is to have *private* nicknames. The players invent them and use them and then the reporters make a game out of trying to overhear them and find out where they come from and reveal them to the public; once revealed, they evaporate, for their only purpose is to separate us from them, to designate in code the speaker and the one spoken to as true insiders.

This is *outside* baseball. This is a book about what baseball looks like if you step back from it and study it intensely, but from a distance.

You know the expression about not being able to see the forest for the trees? Let's use that. What are the differences between the way a forest looks when you are inside the forest and the way it looks from the outside?

The first thing is, the insider has a much better view of the details. He knows what the moss looks like, how high it grows around the base of an oak and how thickly it will cling to a sycamore. He knows the smells in the air and the tracks on the ground; he can guess the age of a redbud by peeling off a layer of bark. The outsider doesn't know any of that.

To a person who sees the image of anything as being only the sum of its details, to a person who can conceive of the whole of anything only by remembering this event and that event and piecing them together in a succession of images... such a person is likely to look at the *Baseball Abstract* and say, "What is this? This isn't *baseball*. This guy James doesn't know anything about the chatter bouncing off of the dugout walls, nor about the glint in the eye of a superstar, nor about the routines and integral boredom of baseball's lifestyle, with which each player great and small must contend."

No sir, indeed I don't. There will be in this book no new tales about the things that happen on a team flight, no sudden revelations about the way that drugs and sex and money can ruin a championship team. I can't tell you what a locker room smells like, praise the Lord.

But perspective can be gained only when details are lost. A sense of the size of everything and the relationships between everything—this can never be put together from details. For the most essential fact of a forest is this: The forest itself is immensely larger than anything inside of it. That is why, of course, you can't see the forest for the trees; each detail, in proportion to its size and your proximity to it, obscures a thousand or a million other details.

But is it not obvious that that is also the one most essential fact about a pennant race—the size of it, the enormity of it, the fact that no one, no matter how hard he tries, can take in an appreciable portion of the details of any one race? Consider a single moment in a pennant race, a July moment in a minor game against a meaningless team, but a moment in which a ball is hit very hard but caught by an outfielder who is standing in the right place, but before it is caught it must be hit, and before it is hit it must be thrown, and before it is thrown this pitch must be selected, and this pitcher must be selected, and this batter must be selected, and there are reasons why he was selected to throw and why he was selected to hit, and there are reasons why this pitch was selected and why it was thrown this way and why it was swung at and why it was hit and why, finally, the outfielder chanced to be in the right place, so that in this single moment, the simplest moment of a pennant race, there is a complexity that surpasses any understanding.

A game consists of dozens of batters and hundreds of pitches, and a season for one team consists of hundreds of games, and the league consists of a dozen or more teams. And how many details can you think about, to add up to a pennant race in your mind?

Is it not obvious, then, that it is only in stepping *away* from the pennant race that we can develop a vision of it? No one could remember at any one time a significant portion of the at bats that Mike Fischlin has in a season—not even Mike Fischlin's wife. How then, remember the season?

That is why statistics have such a place in baseball. Statistics look at games by the hundreds, and without the details. And that is why everyone who is a baseball fan—everyone, everyone, *everyone*—reads the statistics, studies the statistics, and believes what he sees in the statistics. Without them, it is impossible to have any concept of the game, save for meaningless details floating in space.

Let's talk specifics. What, specifically, can you see from outside the forest that you could never see from inside of it?

For one thing, you can map the terrain. Let us consider the players, the main component of the game, to be as the trees are to the forest. These are cognitive trees, able to see and think and answer questions if they take the notion. Suppose that there is a place in the forest where the ground is a little higher than it is in another place. Insiders, surely, would become aware of this as they trekked from one place to another.

But when it came time to measure the heights of the trees, how could they ever adjust for this? Can you tell the height of a tree by standing beside it and looking up? No, of course not; it's too big. And can you tell how good a hitter someone is by watching him hit? No, of course not; his season is too big. You could tell the biggest trees from the smallest; you could say in many cases that this tree was definitely bigger than that one. You could watch Dale Murphy and see quickly that he was a better hitter than Jerry Royster. But you couldn't guess the height of a tall tree when standing beside it within a twenty-foot range, and you couldn't guess the batting average of a hitter within a twenty-point range by watching him hit, even if you watched him hit for a year.

To get an idea of how tall the tree is, you must stand back and look at it from a distance. And to get a clear notion of how good a hitter someone is, you must look at him from a distance —in the records.

So now you stand back from these trees, get out of the

forest, and you see that one of them *appears* to be the tallest one. But then you remember: Isn't that where the high ground is? Maybe it only appears to be taller because the ground is higher over there.

Do you see where I'm heading? Let's talk Wade Boggs. Now he appears to be the best hitter in the league. But wait a minute —isn't that ground a little higher over there? Didn't Fred Lynn *appear* to be the best hitter in the league when he was playing over there? And when they traded him for Carney Lansford, didn't Lansford *appear* to be the best hitter in the league in 1981? How much higher is the ground? What *is* the tallest tree? Who *is* the best hitter?

Now if you are a dedicated student of inside baseball, what you do next is, you ask Wade Boggs about it. Or if you don't ask Wade Boggs, then you ask Rod Carew, or you ask Freddie Lynn, or you ask one of the other trees. And they naturally are going to give you different opinions on how much difference there is between the ground over here and the ground over there, depending to a large extent on where it is that they are positioned.

But if you are a student of *outside* baseball, you take a somewhat different approach. You say, "Damn, this doesn't seem to be that hard to figure out. The average height of a four-year-old walnut tree over here is this, and the average height of a four-year-old walnut over there is that. Do I really have to be a tree in order to figure this out?"

It is not only that the trees have a vested interest in the subject, and thus that they might lie to you or believe what it is in their best interests to believe. The trees really are not, when you think about it, in a very good position to evaluate the issue. I remember when Freddie Lynn went to California, he said he thought he'd hit better out there because he'd be close to his home. Now, he wasn't lying to us. He really thought that. The accommodation that he had made to Fenway Park was so subtle that it was subconscious. Remember this: All hitting takes place in the four-tenths of a second between the time the pitcher throws the ball and the time it reaches the plate. There isn't an awful lot of thinking going on there; it's mostly reflex.

As a tree grows its roots in one particular place in the forest, Freddie Lynn grew his roots in Fenway Park. And he learned something there. He learned that when they threw him a fastball on the outside part of the plate, he could slap it to left field and the result of that would often be something positive. Success. People would cheer for him.

To him, this has nothing to do with Fenway Park; it has to do with that pitch and that reflex. Only when you get him out of Fenway Park, you can throw him the same pitch and he can execute the same reflexive action (he has, by this time, no choice: He *must* execute that same reflexive action. He is conditioned to do it).

Only the result now is failure.

He was, you see, the ultimate insider of a forest, the tree itself. If he had looked at the question as an outsider, he could not possibly have been surprised by that failure. I mean, you take a guy who hits .380 in Fenway Park in some years and .260 on the road, you've got to figure that if you move him out of Fenway Park he's going to lose some points off the batting average. If you take a 300-foot elm tree and you move it to where the ground is forty feet lower, you've got to figure it's not going to stick up into the air quite as far—something more like 260 feet. But Freddie Lynn was surprised by it.

Another thing about forests is that they are awfully dark sometimes. There are shadows that reach halfway to the moon, there's a lot of underbrush, and there are many strange creatures who live in the forest, or who at the least are reported to live in the forest. Another important difference between inside and outside baseball is that baseball insiders see and report on lots of strange creatures there that we can't really see from out where we are. Clutch hitters are a big favorite.

Several people who have studied the issue from the outside have concluded—I hesitate to mention this—have concluded that clutch hitters don't exist. Dick Cramer was the first of those, and at the time I didn't think he had much of a point. What are they, then? We say, "The shadows of possums and squirrels, blown up to the size of a bear by poor light." They say, "You idiot, of course they exist. We see them all the time; see their tracks every day." I am much more modest than Cramer; I say merely that I have no idea whether they exist or not.

You do notice, though, that clutch hitters are *always* spotted briefly and in poor light. "There's really no way to measure clutch performance," insiders like to say; occasionally some statistics will leak out about batting averages with runners in scoring position, usually based on 100 or 150 at-bats, and never systematically available for scrutiny. Brief film clips of clutch hitters blazing through crucial October games are much treasured by the advocates, but then the guy probably doesn't play thirty games in October in his career, or if he does he starts going two-for-seventeen in the playoffs, and when you see these clutch hitters in clutch situations during the year, they never seem quite so terrifying. "Bring me the carcass of a single member of the species," we say. "Show me the evidence that there is a single player in all of baseball who consistently and predictably performs over his head in 'game' situations. Name in advance a single player who this year, 1984, will hit just thirty points over his average in the late innings of close games." But when no such evidence is forthcoming, they say, "The forest is dark and deep, and there are many places for a body to decay without being found. We don't need that kind of evidence. We don't need to see statistics on them. We live in the forest with them; we know that they exist."

Ah well; when Project Scoresheet is in place, we will answer this once and for all. No need to judge the issue until then.

So I go to look at the trees, as close as I can get from the outside. I go to baseball games, and (unlike sportswriters, who are there under deadline and thus not free to enjoy the occasion) I love going to baseball games. I go with my wife and friends and stay sober and get as wrapped up in it as I can.

But this book is not about the things that I see at baseball games with my own eyes, at least not mostly. This book has a breadth and scope in its vision of the game that requires a perspective that comes only with distance. It has an honesty in facing certain questions that a reporter, that anyone who is inside the game or even near it, could never afford. It has a sense of balance about all the parts of the game that could not come from any point within the forest.

It also has blind spots the size of the World Trade Center with an oak tree growing in every window. There are a lot of things that you just can't see from out here, folks. Dedication and leadership and desire and commitment; I see glimpses of all that, but you just can't see those things clearly from the outside, and it's silly to pretend you can.

I've never said, never thought, that it was *better* to be an outsider than it was to be an insider, that my view of the game was better than anyone else's. It's different; better in some ways, worse in some ways. What I have said is, *since* we are outsiders, since the players are going to put up walls to keep us out here, let us use our position as outsiders to what advantage we can. Let us back off from the trees, look at the forest as a whole, and see what we can learn from that. Let us stop pretending to be insiders if we're not. Let us fly over the forest, you and I, and look down; let us measure every tract of land and map out all the groves, and draw in every path that connects each living thing. Let us drive around the edges and photograph each and every tree from a variety of angles and with a variety of lenses; the insiders will be amazed at what we can help them to see. Or maybe they won't; who knows. But anyway, we'll have some fun. Snake oil, $1.95.

—1984

On Managers

Reading comments about managers a couple of summers ago, I decided two things: 1) that the consideration of managers was one of the most backward, most cliché-ridden, and least valuable discussions within the sports forum, and 2) that I wasn't helping.

The discussion of managers had gotten bogged down in the muck of opinion, I decided, because there was no established process to help distinguish the characteristics of one manager from those of another. We as sports fans possess a remarkable amount of knowledge about the characteristics of hundreds of players—who runs well, who hits for power, who strikes out and who has a good throwing arm—because we have extremely good established practices for helping us keep track of them. Many a man who works in an office with nine secretaries has not the faintest idea which of them is a better typist, which has a better attendance record or even what their educational backgrounds might be, but he knows which outfielder on a team across the continent hits for a higher average, how many games they played last year and where they played triple A ball. The information that we have is often dictated not by the information that we need, but by the information systems that we use.

The information systems concerning managers are backward; our knowledge of them is correspondingly limited. Nobody knows what to put on the back of a manager's baseball card. The *Baseball Register* doesn't know what to do with a manager, so they give his batting record; you look up Ralph Houk and it tells you that he hit .286 at Neosho in the Arkansas-Missouri League in 1939. This is a fine thing to know, but it really doesn't do much to help you understand how he manages or what he brings to a team.

And why are our information systems about managers so backward? Because we have gotten trapped in an unresolvable issue about whether a manager is "good" or is "bad." The fan, beginning with a position on the goodness or badness of the manager in question, interprets each action in the light of that reference and makes every question about him an extension of the first principle. Beginning with the premise that Bill Virdon stinks, every other question becomes a subheading of why Bill Virdon stinks. In the end no manager can be a combination of good and bad, of strengths and weaknesses, or of abilities and liabilities. In short, no manager can be seen as being what every manager is.

—1985

A manager's job can be divided into three levels of responsibility. The most visible level, and the one which draws the most comment from fans, is what might be called the *game-level decisions*. These are the day-to-day operational questions, such as who should play left field against this pitcher, whether we should bunt now, how long the pitcher should stay in the game, when to pull in the infield, when to pinch hit and who to pinch hit with, how to set up the lineup, etc.

The second level of responsibility, which we will call the *team-level* decisions, involves much larger questions which are much fewer in number. Team-level decisions involve quandaries for the manager like who should be the team's relief ace, whether a young pitcher is ready to start or should be kept in long relief or sent to the minors, whether to choose a regular or use a platoon combination in left field, whether to use a four-man or five-man rotation in April, whether to abandon a player in a slump or stick with him, etc.

The third level of responsibility is that of *personnel management*. Personnel management, in baseball as in everything else, does not revolve around decision making per se, but around characteristics such as courage, honesty, fairness, consistency, maturity, judgment, personality, flexibility, etc.

In this article I want to examine the interplay among these levels of responsibility, focus on a few specific issues, and try to distinguish what I perceive as the critical differences among major-league managers. I have talked for several years about trying to learn to see managers as being not simply "good" or "bad," arranged along a one-dimensional spectrum, but as talents each making a unique contribution to his team. This article is part of the attempt to do that.

A. GAME-LEVEL DECISION MAKING

As best I can estimate, a manager makes about seventy game-level decisions in an average day, or about eleven thousand a year. The number obviously can never be determined with any accuracy, for in theory there are many times that many options presented to a manager, while in practice the number of viable options for some managers in some games may be less than ten.

The first decision for each manager each day is who will be the starting pitcher. Because of its importance, this decision is worked out for several days at a time and announced long in advance of the game. No other game-level decision has the same importance, but there are eight (or nine) other starters to be selected each day. As a practical matter, every manager probably has at least three of those decisions preplanned for the season depending only upon availability, but for most teams there are three or four decisions to be made each day. When should the catcher be given a day off? Do we want to use a left-handed hitter at first base to get the platoon advantage, or a right-hander to get his defense?

Many managers (and I don't particularly endorse this) try to plan out as many of these decisions as possible so as to minimize the number of decisions they will have to make each day. This includes not only managers like John McNamara, Billy Gardner, Don Zimmer, Leo Durocher, and Ralph Houk, who prefer to use a regular at each position whenever possible, but also rigid platoon managers, like Bobby Cox, who may use two players at a position rather than one, but who still define the roles so firmly that a fan of the team, knowing who was starting for the opposition, could write out the lineup card. All of the managers that I named have had some success, but I feel that the most successful managers, like Earl Weaver, Whitey Herzog, and Sparky Anderson, tend to deliberately keep at least one or two positions open to allow them to make day-to-day realignments. Probably no manager since World War II kept open as many day-to-day options as Casey Stengel.

I think in general that I am suspicious of any manager who tries to eliminate decisions. I always suspect that a manager who reacts in an absolutely predictable way, regardless of the question, is not really thinking about the problem, and may be feeling intimidated by his responsibilities. Managers who use a regular at each position are only using about half of the roster, and often wear out their frontline players, only to find themselves with no bench. Rigid platooning is not as bad, because it does rest half of the roster and tends to create in-game options for the other half.

Once the starting lineup is selected, there arises the question of how to set the batting order. A nine-man batting order can be arranged in 362,880 different ways, but again, at least half of the players are normally fixed in advance. You usually know who your leadoff man is, who your cleanup hitter is; obviously you bat the pitcher ninth. These fixed points are necessary to cut the three hundred sixty thousand alternatives to a manageable number. A manager who prefers to use a set regular lineup will ordinarily also prefer to lock in as much of the batting order as possible.

There are maybe eight or ten moments during an average game in which it is debatable whether the pitcher should come out or stay to face another batter. If you lift the pitcher you have to face the decision of who to bring in. Before you can bring in a reliever you have to make a decision to have him warming up. These decisions are critical in many ball games.

In some games there are no viable pinch-hitting options; in

other games there might be ten or twelve moments at which a pinch-hitting decision has to be made. Non-obvious decisions about moving the infield in or playing it halfway have to be made two or three times a game, as well as more minor positioning decisions which are probably left to coaches. Decisions about starting or holding the runner or calling for a hit and run are almost continuous throughout the game, requiring response decisions about pitching out, putting on a play, etc. A team averages about thirteen base runners a game, many of whom never run or always run and some of whom will be on in situations where nothing really can be done, but if there is an option the decision has to be made and remade and remade throughout a sequence of pitches, so you can count that at anywhere from five to thirty decisions a game.

Reasonable opportunities for a sacrifice bunt probably occur less often than once a game. Hitters who are 3–0 must be told to take or hit away. There are opportunities for defensive substitutes and pinch runners; however, a manager in an average game only makes about three actual substitutions other than pitchers, so it seems to me that one must conclude either that the opportunities for these changes are not numerous, or that most of such opportunities can be easily rejected.

Recognizing, then, that someone else could argue that it was actually five hundred decisions a game if he wanted to, I get a reasonable estimate of about seventy decisions a game in which a manager has multiple viable options. That is more work-related decisions than many of us face in a month. It is, of course, upon this mass of evidence that the merits of various managers are most often debated.

I have always taken the position that I would not try to evaluate managers on this basis. The lifeblood of my work is the attempt to build toward absolute knowledge on specific issues. It has always been my belief that with the very rare exception of a case in which a manager does something just really, really stupid, it is impossible to prove objectively that any game-level decision was correct or incorrect.

A lot of people like to pretend that they have analyzed these decisions and know how to make them, but what they have really done is weighed out very carefully three or four factors influencing the decision, and ignored the other fifteen or twenty factors about which they could not obtain reliable evidence. Statisticians often forget that percentages represent not the complexities of a single at bat, but the probabilities in a large number of at bats, which tend to balance distortions and create a neutral mix. A player who is a .238 hitter overall may be a .310 hitter with four times as much power in a given situation, if he has a number of advantages working for him, such as the platoon edge and a short fence in the ball park. A hitter who cannot hit a curve ball may improve dramatically if he is facing a pitcher who does not throw a curve ball. He may hit a high pitch much better than a low pitch.

I am not saying that it is not useful to measure and evaluate as many factors of performance as we can. By all means; let us measure. Let us know what each batter hits against right-handed and left-handed pitchers and high-ball and low-ball pitchers. But the interplay among these distortions and non-random factors is incalculable; the real player will always be more complex than the data set which represents him. And for that reason we can never know what the real probabilities in an individual situation are; I don't and you don't and in truth the manager doesn't either. He chooses certain biases by which to make his selection, and he throws his fate to the wind.

If we cannot, then, evaluate objectively a single one of the eleven thousand decisions that a manager makes in a year, how must we feel in confronting the entire unrecorded mass of them? Humble, I say, very humble.

People will tell you that the manager doesn't really have any impact, that he can decide anything he wants but if the players don't execute it isn't going to matter. I can't understand that kind of thinking. There are many systematic differences in the ways that managers resolve these problems. Some managers pinch hit four times as often as other managers. Some managers bunt eight times as often as other managers. Some managers start the runner much more often, or issue intentional walks much more often. Managers differ radically in how they approach the question of when to bring in a reliever. If one man is right 51 percent of the time and another man is right 49 percent of the time, that's an advantage of two-hundred-twenty decisions a year for the man who is right (2 percent of eleven thousand is two-hundred-twenty). You mean to tell me that's not going to show up in the won-lost column? I don't care how much of a knee-jerk manager somebody is; making that many decisions, he has to make a differ- ence. Nobody could be so much by-the-book that he could make eleven thousand decisions without having an impact on the team.

But as important as they might be, these decisions are be- yond the reach of sabermetrics. As a fan, I think that John McNamara is a dolt. As an analyst, I try to steer clear of talking about game-level decisions.

B. TEAM-LEVEL DECISION MAKING

Team-level decisions for a manager are few in number but large in impact. A manager probably makes about ten major and thirty minor team-level decisions in a season. While of course the front office has a great deal of input into team level decisions, I think there are at least seven systematic differ- ences among managers in how they make team level decisions. Those are in:

1. Willingness to take a chance on a young player,
2. Decisiveness,
3. Preference for using a regular or a platoon combination,
4. Roster composition,
5. Tendency to prefer offense or defense in selecting a regular,
6. Type of offensive player preferred, and
7. Judgment.

There used to be a group of managers who used four-man pitching rotations and a group which used five-man rotations, but I don't think anybody uses a four-man rotation anymore.

Some of these categories are self-explanatory. I'll try to de- fine "roster composition" by pointing to a couple of strange managerial markers of the last two years. In 1987 Pat Corrales opened the season without a utility infielder on the Cleveland roster; he had four regular infielders and Cory Snyder, who would be pulled in from the outfield if need be. In 1988, Sparky Anderson opened the season with four right-handed hitting third basemen on his roster (Ray Knight, Jim Morrison, Tom Brookens, and Luis Salazar). Obviously, Corrales didn't make up his roster the way he did because he couldn't find a utility infielder (anybody can find a utility fielder), and Anderson didn't start out the way he did because all four players were indispensable. They had options. As such, the fact that they would make these odd choices tells us something about how they manage and what they feel is essential to their team.

Earl Weaver used to say that the biggest decision that he had to make in a year was who was the twenty-fifth man on the roster out of spring training. He would turn his roster over and over in his head, comparing it to every game situation that he could imagine. If I have Gary Roenicke in left field to start the game and I have to pinch hit for my shortstop early in the game, will I still have an option later in the game with a left-hander on the mound? If it's a 7–4 game in the second inning and we've knocked out their starter but we're still three runs behind and they switch to a left-hander, can I change to a right-handed lineup without ruining my defense? Earl used to drive himself crazy trying to think through all of those things.

John Wathan in Kansas City last July made an odd decision which defines his skills in a similar way, when he shipped Mike Macfarlane to Omaha and recalled Larry Owen to be his catcher. Macfarlane had overcome an early season slump to rank as one of the better-hitting catchers in the league by the time of his demotion, while Owen had long since established that he would battle the Mendoza line; still, Wathan wanted defense at the position. Wathan took a good deal of heat for the move, and to tell you the truth I wasn't too thrilled about it myself as a Royals fan—but the move did work out, as the Royals played better ball the second half of the year. The pitching staff did improve, and the team's record with Owen in the lineup was better than with Macfarlane.

It is these decisions, few in number but large in impact, that I think we have a fair opportunity to evaluate. The final category, judgment, may sound subjective by the title, but what I'm trying to point you to is something that is in fact rather easy to evaluate. What you're looking at is simple: When this manager made a decision about a player, was he proven right? Did it work out?

C. PERSONNEL MANAGEMENT AND INSTRUCTION

To evaluate a manager's ability to deal with players, obviously, is the role of a journalist or an insider; what I have as an outsider is only the ability to make a judgment about the information which is relayed to me by those people.

Now, to get to what I was really trying to say. In my opinion, to be successful over a period of time, a manager must do two things. First, he must contribute to the team on all three levels. A manager who contributes on any level can be successful for a short period of time, provided that that which he contributes is that which the team needs—but a failure on any level will ultimately undermine his career.

And second, he must integrate the three levels into a consistent whole. The manager must make decisions on all three levels not separately, but all at the same time.

On the first point, take Dick Williams. Williams's record as a judge of ballplayers was brilliant. He built a twenty-year record of making judgments about young players, who could play and who couldn't, which was just extraordinarily good, and as a consequence of that his teams almost always improved substantially when he took over. Williams was also a competent game manager—not a brilliant manager, I suppose, but as good as the next guy. But time and again, Williams fell down on the third point. His inability to hold the respect of his players led to grumbling and dissatisfaction, and thus ultimately to the failure of the team sufficient to bring dismissal.

Or take Chuck Tanner, please. Tanner's strength, in the short run, is his ability to motivate young players and create a positive clubhouse atmosphere. If you give Tanner a team which has a good deal of talent and which has no incipient attitude problems, Tanner for a couple of years is a heck of a manager. The problem is that Tanner's record as a judge of horseflesh is just awful. Time and again, Tanner has smiled broadly and complimented generously and thrust a player into a job, only to discover that the player didn't have anything like the abilities needed to do the job. So when personnel changes have to be made, Tanner is lost; he just keeps saying that if everybody has a good year we'll win, and the team just keeps losing. Tanner becomes indecisive, sticking people into slots and pulling them out, until ultimately the losing will destroy the atmosphere in the clubhouse. His inability to make team-level decisions consistently gives him few decent options within the game, which undermines his game-level management. The team loses, and the attitude, despite Tanner, will turn sour.

Or take Jim Frey. Frey, like Tanner, is a positive thinker. Unlike Tanner, his record as a judge of ballplayers is pretty decent. The problem with Jim Frey is that he is the worst game manager you can imagine. And ultimately, his players will lose confidence in him and confidence in their ability to win, simply because they know that everything that happens in a close game is going to come as a complete surprise to Jim Frey. Then they'll start backbiting, and it isn't long until the party is over.

Whenever that happens, of course, you know what the local columnist is going to write. He's going to write that the manager (Jim Frey, or Chuck Tanner, or whoever) has become the scapegoat for problems which were beyond his control. "If he was such a good manager a year ago," they will always ask, "why isn't he a good manager now? Has he gotten suddenly stupid in the last year?"

My opinion is that most managers are hired for good reasons, and are fired for good reasons. It's not that they get stupid after a couple of years. It is that most managers contribute on one level, or on two levels. By making that contribution, they change the needs of the organization. Once the needs of the organization change, in most cases they are no longer able to contribute.

Whitey Herzog has been a successful manager for a lot of years, I believe, primarily because more than any other manager of our time, he contributes to the team on all three levels, and successfully integrates the three sometimes warring needs of a manager into a consistent whole. That doesn't mean that he can win without talent; no manager can.

But if I've said it once, I've said it a hundred times: A manager is not an innocent bystander. Any manager who is an innocent bystander should be fired for being an innocent bystander. Any manager who is a victim of circumstances should be fired for allowing himself to become a victim of circumstances. Sure, it's a tough job, and sometimes it's an impossible job. But to say that a manager has been an innocent bystander to the collapse of his team is like saying that an engineer is an innocent bystander to a train wreck. That, to me, is the ultimate insult to a manager, to "defend" him by saying that he wasn't doing his job.

—Edited/Revised from the 1988 *Baseball Abstract*

On Official Scorers

Do you enjoy having opinions about issues that are beyond the realm of your experience? When you go to ball games, do you like to try to anticipate whether a play will be scored a hit or an error? Do you often fantasize about being the one who gets to decide whether or not a pitcher gets to keep his no-hitter? Do people ever tell you that you look stupid and could carry a pencil behind your ear without ruining your image? Would you do *anything* to be involved in professional baseball? If so, you might have a future as an OFFICIAL SCORER in the AMERICAN LEAGUE CHAMPIONSHIP SERIES or possibly even the WORLD SERIES.

Yes, OFFICIAL SCORERS are often just ordinary, none-too-bright people such as yourself, who were caught hanging around the press box without a deadline and were put to work making vital decisions that have nothing to do with who wins or loses the game. And, best of all, with three OFFICIAL SCORERS now used for each game of post-season play, and virtually all major newspapers refusing to allow their writers to handle the task, opportunities in this exciting field are opening up at an explosive rate. If you would like to enter the glamorous, fast-paced, highly paid world of the OFFICIAL SCORER, and if you could accept being second-guessed on national TV and in publications like the *Baseball Abstract*, just fill out this examination and return it to to Urbane Pickering's School of OFFICIAL SCORING, Valentine Design, and Toilet Training; P.O. Box E-5; Cotton Balls, Iowa. You could be eligible for valuable scholarship assistance while you study to become an OFFICIAL SCORER.

OFFICIAL SCORER'S APTITUDE TEST

Name _____

Address _____

Education (if any) _____

Favorite Official Scorer _____

This test will be self-scored, so we ask that you not look at the answer before making your selection.

1. In the seventh inning of the second game of the American League Playoff, the bases are loaded with one out when the batter grounds to second. The out is recorded at second, but on the relay to first Schofield's throw is about four feet wide of the bag and first baseman Wally Joyner, rather than catching the ball, attempts to keep his foot on the bag and reach. In so doing he falls down and the ball gets loose. Joyner picks up the ball but throws wildly toward home plate, thirty feet up the line, allowing a second run to score. Should you score this:

A. An Error on Joyner,
B. An Error on Schofield,
C. Just One of Those Things,
D. No Harm, No Foul, or
E. Let's Blame It on Gene Mauch.

(The answer is B, an error on Schofield. While it is true that the rules do say that you can't assume a double play, the rules don't specifically tell you what to rule when the first baseman tries to create a double play that isn't there and compounds the consequences of this by making a bad throw to another base. We advise you to blame it all on the shortstop. As to rules 10.13(e) and 10.14(c), we never heard of either of them.)

2. In the sixth inning of the third game of the American League Playoff, there is a runner on first and one out. The batter hits a chopper down the third base line, and Wade Boggs has an easy play at first base. Instead, he attempts to make the play at second base, and the throw pulls the second baseman off the bag, would you score this:

A. An Error,
B. A Fielder's Choice,
C. An Infield Fly, or
D. A Homicide.

(The correct answer is B, a fielder's choice. The fielder had an easy play, and he chose not to make it. The rules don't specify whether it's a good choice or a bad choice; they just say it's a choice.)

3. In the seventh game of the American League Playoff,

Gary Pettis is playing in left center field when a drive is slashed to deep right-center. Pettis runs six miles and comes within an eyelash of making the play, but the ball bounces off the tip of his glove and the batter reaches third. Should you score this:

A. A Triple,
B. An Error on Pettis,
C. A Double and an Error,
D. An Intentional Walk, or
E. Guilty but Insane.

(The correct answer is B, an error on Pettis. The key question here is, "Ordinary effort for whom?" While it's true that there isn't a center fielder in the world today who would have made the play, Willie Mays and Tris Speaker would have had it easily if they'd been playing in straightaway center.)

4. In the seventh inning of the fifth game of the World Series, the batter hits a high pop foul within five feet of first base. Bill Buckner overruns it, tries to recover by leaning backward, loses his balance and falls down, the ball bouncing off the thumb of his glove. Would you score this:

A. An Error,
B. A Sacrifice Fly,
C. Normal for Bill Buckner, or
D. No Play.

(The correct answer is D, no play. While this of course would be an error for Dave Kingman or Steve Balboni, the key words in this case are "Bill Buckner." Playing with bad knees and cauliflower ankles, Bill Buckner has been an example of courage and determination for us all. He's good copy.)

—1987

On Range Factors

This article was originally published in the 1982 Baseball Abstract. The statistics and references given throughout the article are for the 1981 season or the period before 1981.

A rude essay, this is; quarrelsome, nasty. It has been seven years now since I wrote an article for the *Baseball Digest* entitled, overoptimistically, "Fielding Statistics *Do* Make Sense." That article put forth, in essence, a simple truth: that the most important piece of raw statistical information about a fielder is the number of plays per game he makes. Not the number of plays that he doesn't make but somebody thinks that he should have, which is what an error is, but the number he does succeed in making.

Since that time I have argued for the recognition of range factors as the basic defensive indicator. And I do mean argued. Why this particular issue always seems to upset the teapot so I don't know; people seem so enamored of that odd and marginally meaningful concept, the error, that they will pitch the most desperate arguments in an attempt to avoid the inevitable recognition that it has little importance in modern baseball. Let us review the course of the discussion.

When I wrote the original range factor article in 1975, it was assailed by readers who were upset about the "rating" given to their favorite ballplayers. "Through the use of this method," one wrote, "Bobby Murcer, who has long been recognized as a defensive standout in right field, was given the lowest rating in the league in his position." Another wrote, "A player is penalized simply because fewer people hit the ball in his direction. This is like charging a batter who has just received an intentional walk with a time at bat." And also, "A player who enters the game in the late innings . . . will be penalized by being charged with a full game played." "If Bill James wants to do away with fielding averages, he will have to do better than his range factor method," wrote another *Digest* reader. Another *Abstract* reader wrote that he "didn't think too much of range factors, because there [are] too many things that aren't counted, such as two players being involved in one play, an outfielder saving an extra base by a strong throw, etc." I believe that every amateur sabermetrician in the country has written to inform me that some teams' pitchers strike out more batters than other teams' pitchers, and that this could alter the range factors of the fielders who play behind them. Others have pointed out that range factors tend to be team contained, each team having twenty-seven outs a game to be divided up, regardless of how well or poorly they field as a group.

A few of these arguments have merit. Most of them, to be blunt about it, are useful mostly to illustrate what a horrible intellectual stew men can serve up and swallow when they decide not to let careful analysis intrude on their prejudices. I am being too harsh; baseball exists to be enjoyed, and if you need your prejudices to enjoy it, why not? It is not fair to expect people to spend their lives studying sabermetrics before they can comment on the subject. But people fail to distinguish between ratings and records. They fail to distinguish between methods and raw data. They never give a thought to *definition* and *purpose*, to what is being measured. They dress up their prejudices with asinine analogies and irrelevant objections and then expect me to ignore these things so that we can have a dialogue as equals. And that is why I am being so harsh; I am just tired. I am tired of the argument. I am tired of trying to put this argument behind me, once and for all. And I am tired of the intellectual standards of the field being what they are. But, one more time:

1. "Through the use of *this method*. Bobby Murcer, long recognized as a defensive standout in right field, *was given* the lowest rating in the league in his position."

A. There is no method. Range factor is a raw statistic.

B. Bobby Murcer was not given anything. Bobby Murcer in 1975 made fewer plays per game than any other right fielder in the National League. That is an absolute fact that does not change depending on how one feels about it.

C. Range factor is not a rating.

D. As to the general point, so what? In the same year, Carl Yastrzemski drove in fewer runs per bat than any other regular first baseman in baseball. Did anyone write in that that couldn't be right because Yaz was long recognized as one of the top run-producers in baseball? In the same year, Ralph Garr, long recognized as one of the top singles hitters in baseball, hit .278. Bob Gibson, long recognized as one of the top pitchers in the game, went 3–10. This doesn't invalidate RBIs, it doesn't invalidate batting average, it doesn't invalidate won-lost records, and it doesn't invalidate range factors.

When people have no way of monitoring something, no way of watching it day to day, they tend to think about it in simplistic terms. If a player has good range, he should *always* have good range; if a good throwing arm, he should *always* have a good throwing arm. The ultimate in this line is Tony Kubek's statement that hitting and pitching are "variables," and that it is the "constants" which win pennant races. There are no constants in baseball. There are no players who *always* throw to the right base or *always* back up the base that they are supposed to back up or *always* hit behind the runner whom they are supposed to hit behind. People forget that fielding performance is subject to all of the same vagaries of small pains, nagging distractions, snap judgments which sometimes don't look too good on the replay, pulled muscles and lapses of concentration that play on the more visible aspects of performance. All that one can expect of a meaningful statistic is that it have a strong degree of internal consistency.

2. "A player is *penalized* simply because fewer people hit the ball *in his direction*. This is like charging a player who has just received an intentional walk with a time at bat."

A. Penalized? Don't you own a dictionary? Range factor contains no penalties for anything.

B. Garry Maddox led all National League outfielders in range factor every year between 1974 and 1979. Would anyone seriously suggest that this represents nothing more substantial than a preference on the part of the opponents' hitters for hitting the ball in the direction of Garry Maddox? Larry Bowa made between 4.2 and 4.8 plays per game every season between 1972 and 1981. At the same time, Ozzie Smith has made over 5 plays per game in every season since he came up. How is it possible that, year in and year out, opposition hitters hit 5.2 or 5.5 baseballs per game in the direction of Ozzie Smith and 4.6 in the direction of Larry Bowa? Wouldn't the most trusting Larry Bowa fan begin to find that a bit suspicious after a while?

C. Baseballs are not hit *to* fielders. Baseballs are not hit in the direction of fielders, at all. Baseballs are simply hit, and fielders run them down. Range factor is the statement of how well they run them down, or at least how often.

D. Well, it is quite a bit like charging an intentionally passed hitter with an at bat, yes, but it really reminds me more of the servant woman who was guillotined in 1792 because her employers thought she might have lifted some silver. As Polonius said, "Very like a whale."

3. "A player who enters the game in the late innings . . . will be penalized by being *charged* with a full game played."

A. He is credited, not charged, with a game played, not a full game played, but we'll overlook that because the reader has a point. In some cases, yes, this is a problem; in 1978 it caused Willie Wilson to have a lower range factor than Lou Piniella. "Willie Wilson has less range than Lou Piniella?" asked a reader, rhetorically.

This is a much more common concern in basketball and football statistics, where per-game averages are the rule rather than the exception. It is not a difficult thing to deal with; if a basketball team has a zone-breaking guard who comes off the bench to score a quick eight points, everybody knows that this is not the same as having a starting center who averages eight points a game. In baseball, most averages are figured on the basis of opportunities, because offensive opportunities are easily discovered. It is an attempt to apply the same concept of per-opportunity success to the evaluation in fielding records which has led fielding stats to be the ill-conceived lot that they are. Relying on percentage success figures has blinded many people to an obvious flaw, which is that, unlike true percentage measures, a fielder's total chances are by no means his total chances. Fielders do not take turns. Any time a baseball is hit to center field, the center fielder is presumably trying to catch it—yet only if he succeeds or narrowly fails does he receive credit for a chance.

Since meaningful ratios cannot be based on opportunities, they have to be based on the context in which those opportunities occur. Games are what we have, perfectly adequate to the task in 80 percent of the cases. If we had defensive innings, that would be better. We don't. But most players are not late-inning defensive replacements and who cares what Luis Gomez' range factor is anyway?

B. Please don't write and ask me why I don't base range factors on at bats. I don't do it because it doesn't work.

4. "Willie Wilson has less range than Lou Piniella?"

The reason Willie Wilson had a low range factor in 1978 is perfectly obvious. He had a low range factor because he was a late-inning defensive replacement who had a lot of games of two innings. If your purpose is to not learn from the records, you can draw any number of damn fool conclusions from perfectly respectable data. Bruce Sutter has a lifetime won-lost percentage of .500. Rickey Henderson in 1981 was caught stealing twenty-two times as often as Bucky Dent. Henry Aaron holds the career record for grounding into double plays; the guy must have run like Gus Triandos' mother.

To destroy a statistic, by those standards, requires only that one focus on some player for whom the statistic is, for good and obvious reasons, misleading in one way or another, and then ignore the good and obvious reasons. The problem with the logic is that it leaves you poorer for believing in it; you wind up knowing less than you started with, and that is not the purpose of logic or the purpose of statistics.

5. "If Bill James wants to *do away with fielding average*, he will have to come up with something better than his range factor method."

The person who invented runs batted in, well after major league baseball began, did not do so to eliminate batting average. The development of new information to measure a different facet of a player's skill does not imply the elimination of the earlier data.

6. "There are too *many things* that aren't *counted*, such as two players being involved in one play, an outfielder saving an extra base by a strong throw, etc."

Again, what does that have to do with anything? It's like saying that triples totals are irrelevant because they don't tell you how many doubles the player has hit or the batting average is not to be trusted because it doesn't adjust for speed. Statistics measure one thing at a time. *Then* you put the things you have measured together to reach conclusions. This is true of range factor as it is of every other statistic.

I warned you that I was not in the warm mood; I wonder if I'm becoming crotchety in middle age?

There is no category of statistical information extant which some sabermetrician has not examined in depth, found wanting in one way or another, and so declared to be meaningless. I write a lot about the limitations of statistics, about the illusions incorporated in runs batted in totals and the massive effect that Fenway Park has on the statistics of the people who play there. Because of the way that statistics are often handled, with these crude "meaningful" and "meaningless" categories, people sometimes think that I am trying to move the traditional range of performance indicators—RBIs and ERAs and won-lost records and fielding percentage—over to the "meaningless" category and trying to put some esoteric stuff that you never heard of into the "meaningful" group. And then they feel compelled to tell me that the other stuff is subject to all sorts of limitations and therefore is meaningless.

But that is not what I am saying at all. I am saying: *The same standards of evidence should apply to them all.* All baseball statistics are meaningful; all incorporate illusions. Yes, range factors are subject to outside influences of a variety of types. They have this in common with every other statistical category of the game, bar none. All individual statistics in baseball are subject to a wide variety of outside and irrelevant influences. There is a great difference between hitting forty home runs in Atlanta and hitting forty home runs in the Astrodome, but that does not make home run totals meaningless. There is a great difference between winning sixteen games for the Yankees and winning sixteen for Seattle, but that does not make won-lost records meaningless. There is a great difference between hitting .300 in Fenway Park and hitting .300 in Anaheim, but that does not make batting averages meaningless. We can sort through all of these things and still see clearly who is and is not a good pitcher or hitter. We can do the same with fielding statistics; it all begins with accepting that there is a difference between being subject to illusions and being meaningless.

The fact is that a player's range factor, with all of the problems that people can dream up for it, is substantially a creation not of the player's circumstances, but of his range afield. That range factors are meaningful can be shown in a ridiculous variety of ways. For example:

1. When a player is traded or when he moves from one team to another, all of the illusions change. He has a different pitching staff, different people playing beside him, a different playing surface. If range factor were substantially a creation of these conditions, then he would also have a new range factor. But, generally speaking, he does not.

Buddy Bell had the highest range factor among American League third basemen in 1977 and 1978, when he played for Cleveland. Toby Harrah, third baseman for Texas, had range factors at or near the bottom of the league. Bell posted range factors of 3.08 and 3.45 (very high); Harrah posted range of 2.43 and 2.45, which is low. In the winter of 1978–79 the two players were traded for each other in a rare straight-up swap of players at the same position. Thus, all of Buddy Bell's extraneous influences shifted to Harrah, and all of Harrah's shifted to Bell.

What happened to their range factors in 1979? Nothing. Bell's range factor remained at or near the top of the league, and Harrah's remained at the bottom. How can one possibly interpret that, except to say that it shows that Bell had very good range and Harrah very poor?

2. Virtually all players' range factors decline gradually over time. They usually increase for two or three years after the player comes into the league as he learns to play the hitters, then hold steady or increase slightly until age twenty-seven or twenty-eight, then decline.

This is not a surprise. It is exactly what one would expect to happen to a player's range afield as he grows older. But if, instead, range factor is essentially a product of circumstances and not of range, why does this happen?

3. Particularly among outfielders, players who have speed, reflected in the offensive columns 3B and SB (triples and stolen bases), will usually have high range factors. Willie Wilson and Rickey Henderson have outstanding range factors, every year. The highest range factors among National League outfielders were posted by Andre Dawson and Omar Moreno. There are exceptions, of course, but if you look at the group of outfielders who have high range factors you will find that, as a group, they also have high totals of triples and stolen bases; if you look at the outfielders who have very low range factors, you will find that they hit few triples and stolen bases.

This isn't as true among infielders as among outfielders, because a larger part of range in the infield is based on reaction time and positioning skill and less from pure speed. But, again, why is this so, if it is not because range factors indicate range afield?

4. Players who lead the league in range factor are very rarely moved to a less demanding fielding position; good hitters who have low range factors are very commonly moved leftward along the defensive spectrum. (I can't cite studies to prove these things, but nonetheless they are true, and you can see that they are true if you look.) If range factor does not indicate good range afield, then why does this happen?

And if you can explain any of these things, how can you possibly hope to explain all of them? And why are you trying?

Range factors are not beyond error. They must be used carefully, but all statistics must be used carefully. But unlike fielding percentages, which distinguish among fielders by ones and twos and occasionally twenties, range factors distinguish among fielders by dozens and scores and occasionally hundreds. If one second baseman is making two hundred plays a year that another is not making, and if that is a true measure of the difference in range between the two, do you know what that means? It means that if the one with good range is a .150 hitter and the one with poor range is a .400 hitter, you're better off with the .150 hitter. You just don't ignore a thing like that. There are very few raw statistical categories which are more important than a player's range factor.

Generally speaking, players who are recognized as good fielders will also be players who have high range factors. I would say that the statistics agree with visual observation at least 85 percent of the time; that is, indeed, another way of validating the statistic. The Gold Glove winners—Maddox, Dawson, Wilson, Moreno, Schmidt, Ozzie Smith, Burleson, Nettles, Brooks Robinson, Buddy Bell—throughout most of their careers they have had very high range factors.

But a significant portion of the defense is what I call *invisible range*. Most of invisible range is accounted for by positioning skill. The key is that nobody watches a third baseman until the ball is hit. If a third baseman makes a diving, rolling grab at a ball after it is hit and snares it in his fingertips, then that is a great play, and the fielder receives a nice round of applause. But if the third baseman moves two steps to his left before the ball is hit, then the same play is routine, and the fielder gets nothing.

In addition to positioning skill, there is also *form*. As I observed before, batters are judged by what they produce, but fielders are judged by how they look in producing it. George Brett has never received public recognition for tremendous range, but until 1981 he had always had a tremendous range factor, and having watched him for many years I am absolutely convinced that he covers a tremendous area afield. But he makes all the plays standing up; he rarely dives for a ball. If he makes a play at all, he makes it look routine. The other extreme is Carney Lansford of Boston. Lansford absolutely will not make a play standing up unless he has to. On any hard-hit baseball, his first instinct is to dive toward it. Since the area over which one can dive to make a play is very limited, Lansford in fact has very limited range afield. Yet, since he makes a great many diving catches, many people think that Lansford is covering a lot of ground. He is young enough to outgrow this habit, and I hope he does, but you watch: There are balls going by Lansford that he should be getting to.

A few other exceptions to the rule: Darrell Evans of San Francisco was a brilliant third baseman for many years (great range factors in both Atlanta and SF) but received no recognition for it, mostly because he played on bad teams. Roy Smalley of Minnesota has had consistently high range factors, but is not recognized as a good shortstop. Alan Trammell of Detroit is a Gold Glover with low range factors. Robin Yount of Milwaukee's range is surprisingly good; teammate Gorman Thomas' range factor as a center fielder was exceptionally low. Bump Wills of Texas and Doug DeCinces of Baltimore make a lot of plays but have poor defensive reps.

And, of course, Larry Bowa. When *Sports Illustrated* was preparing their article about my work a year ago, they wanted to say something about range factors. I had written about Larry Bowa something to the effect that he covers about as much area as a string bikini, a judgment based in part on his range factors and in part on observation. But, wondered Dan Okrent, who was writing the article, couldn't Mike Schmidt's exceptional range right beside Bowa be cutting into Bowa's range factor? Sure, I said, it's just like if a player has a low RBI count and the man batting in front of him has a high one. You can always say that there weren't that many runners left on base for him to drive in. But that's a "factor," an "influence"—it's not an explanation. Then Bob Creamer, articles editor at *SI*, asked mo, "Well, just for my own personal understanding, couldn't Schmidt's range be causing there to be less plays left for Bowa?" Sure, I replied. Then Bob Sullivan, who was checking out the facts in the piece, asked me "But couldn't Schmidt's range. . ." Then after the article appeared, they ran a letter to the editor from a fan who wanted to explain that the reason Larry Bowa had a low range factor was that Schmidt was cutting off all those balls before they got to Bowa.

Well, OK, let's take a look at that. First of all, there are obviously balls which go through the Philadelphia infield, or any infield, in pretty good numbers, so if there are very many plays for which two players are positioned, it seems to me that somebody should seriously consider moving. But that's the kind of logic that can be right or wrong just about as easily. But look:

1. This is not the first time in the history of baseball that players recognized as outstanding have played beside one another at third and short. When Brooks Robinson, Mark Belanger, and Bobby Grich played for Baltimore in 1974, all three led the American League in range factor without getting in each other's way. Both Robinson and Belanger had consistently good range factors for several years, even though Belanger was such a bad hitter that he had to be pinch hit for. His range factors were still much better than Bowa's, and Bowa hasn't been pinch hit for. Tony Kubek led the AL in range factor one year while playing beside Clete Boyer, and Boyer covered more ground than anybody. Ron Santo and Ernie Banks, Dick Groat and Don Hoak, Gil McDougald and Phil Rizzuto—all of these combinations and many others have had third basemen and shortstops both leading the league in range factors. History shows hundreds of cases where both had very good range factors. Why didn't the Schmidt factor operate in these cases?

Editorial update: In 1984 the Cardinals replaced Ken Oberkfell, a third baseman with extremely limited range, with Terry Pendleton, one of the most brilliant defensive third basemen of our time. Oberkfell's range factors were 2.44 in 1983, 2.59 in 1984; Pendleton's were 3.24 in 1984 and 3.29 in 1985. In spite of this change, Ozzie Smith's range factor actually increased slightly from 1983 to 1984, and remained the highest in the league in 1985.

2. The proportion is all wrong. Suppose that you add together all plays made by both Bowa and Schmidt, and compare that to the other third-short combinations around the league. We all agree, do we not, that Schmidt has great range? That seems to be the common agreement among us. Yet when Bowa and Schmidt are taken together, they rank third to sixth annually in the National League. Doesn't that look much more like one fielder with outstanding range and one with average range or less, than like two fielders with outstanding range? It just doesn't add. There aren't enough plays there for two outstanding fielders.

3. One can study systematically the relationship between the range factor of a third baseman, and the range factor of his shortstop. That is, one can ask this question: What is the average range factor for a shortstop playing next to a third baseman with good range, and what is the average range factor for a shortstop playing next to a third baseman with poor range?

There is no inverse relationship. As was shown in a chart which accompanied the original version of this article, the average range factor of a shortstop is completely independent of the range of the third baseman.

As I said, range factor, like any other statistic, is subject to extraneous influences. It can be artificially lowered by playing less than nine innings a game, but that has nothing to do with Larry Bowa. It can be fractionally lowered by playing behind a pitching staff which strikes out a lot of people, but again, this has nothing to do with Larry Bowa. There is, when you get right down to it, an excruciatingly simple reason why Larry Bowa doesn't make very many plays afield.

He doesn't cover the ground.

—1982

On Rating Ballplayers by Statistics

The idea of rating ballplayers is an arrogant bit of nonsense, incurring inherent intellectual costs which can lead, if unchecked, to intellectual bankruptcy. There are many reasons for believing that and a few reasons for rating players even though I believe it, and I wanted to try to explain what those reasons are.

I am very leery of "great statistics," of statistics which consider everything and provide the once and final answer to great baseball questions, questions like "Who was the greatest player ever?" or "Who should have won the MVP award?" or "Who really belongs in the Hall of Fame?" or even, "Who is better, Dawson or Murphy?" It is my considered opinion that we have no business answering these questions by formula.

Great statistics exist about the fringes of all areas of research; meteorology has yielded up a "comfort index," Jimmy Carter in the 1976 campaign introduced to economics a "misery index," and psychology has the best-known great statistic of all, the "Intelligence Quotient," or IQ. I was much impressed by something that a psychology teacher once said to me about IQ testing. Suppose, he said, that we turn the same assumptions to the evaluation of a person's *physical* attributes. We all have parts which are attractive (even beautiful) and parts which are ugly (even grotesque). We have parts which are strong and parts which are weak. We have parts which are healthy and parts which are diseased. We have parts which are quick and parts which are slow, parts functional and non-functional, parts calloused and parts sensitive, parts agile and awkward and most of us, by the middle of life, are missing a piece or two. We are old and young, male and female, scarred and blemished. To sum up all of these, and rate them along a linear scale . . . ? To ask each of us to perform (old men and young women, the crawling and the doddering, the sick and the healthy) two hundred or three hundred physical tasks and evaluative mechanisms, and to score each just right so as to wind up with a "BQ" (Body Quotient) and say "OK, you're a 104, you're a 117, but you're a 76" would be preposterous. It would be a stupid waste of time.

Well, if it is preposterous for a person's body, it is not a bit less preposterous for his mind. It not only does not contribute to an understanding of a person's abilities, it gets in the way of it. It is not the proper function of a psychologist to herd people into straight lines and slap numbers on them. While we are talking about mental capacities, what about the capacity to love and the capacity to hate, the capacity to endure and the willingness to falter, the capacity to overcome obstacles, the capacity to recognize one's own good. Do we not all remember "intelligent" men who can remember their high school Spanish but forget to be kind to those who love them? If Hitler had an IQ of 126, must we say that he "had a good mind," far above average? Where does one draw the line between a refusal to learn and a lack of intelligence? The truth is that we all have parts which are weak, parts healthy and parts diseased, parts quick and slow and all the others.

And yet, we are stuck with it. Some Frankenstein or Rappaccini invented it in the innocent adolescence of psychology, and try as we might we cannot get rid of the damn thing, because it has become a part of the way that people think. It is the first concept that children are given with which to think about what goes on inside their heads, and when they are grown up to be psychologists they cannot conceive of themselves without their peg, and so set out to find more complicated ways of pegging others, when they should be about the task of developing broader, more realistic ways to think about human mental capacities. (Saul Bellow: *"We have a word for everything except what we really think and feel."*) The one-dimensional measurement of intelligence has given rise to an entire generation of people who have a one-dimensional concept of intelligence, of the one thing on earth which is most clearly not one-dimensional.

Sabermetrics is to baseball as psychology is to human nature, and I wish to perform no such disservice to baseball. The search for great statistics—and any ranking of a player must be done, if it is objective, by a great statistic—is not and cannot be a scientific undertaking. The "comfort index" is not exactly something a meteorologist would use to try to develop a better explanation of where and when tornadoes develop; it is something TV weathermen use to try to explain meteorology to the largest common denominator. A sophomore economics student would get an "F" for coming up with a "misery index"; it's something that a politician uses to enchant a particularly slow voter.

Great statistics have no clear idea of what it is that they are measuring. Some psychologists—the ones who are hung up on IQ testing—would claim that they were an exception, that they search for intelligence with scientific methods. But is it only the *methods* you use which decide whether what you are doing is science? What seems so odd to me is that while the search for intelligence measures progresses unabated, the question of "What is intelligence?" remains unanswered. How can you make a scientific measurement of how much of something somebody has, when you don't even know what it is that they are supposed to have? Can't you see a couple of chemists confronting the same problem:

"Dr. Durler, could you tell me how much derillium is in this alloy?"

"What's derillium?"

"I'm damned if I know, but we need to know how much of it there is in there, anyway."

Psychologists solve this problem by saying that intelligence is the thing that IQ tests measure, which is the scientific equivalent of taking your ball and going home.

I have a copy of a 1920 *Spalding Guide* which presents an "All-American Team" picked by something called "Total Average." This version of Total Average added together fielding percentage and batting percentage, plus won/lost percentage if you were a pitcher. Great statistics compress together unlike information into a common shape. Inflation percentage points are added in with percentages of people unemployed, degrees of temperature with humidity figures (maybe somebody should find a way to mix together the heat, humidity, wind, unemployment rate, inflation rate, Dow Jones average, price of gold in Zurich . . . call it the "total financial and economic life enjoyment factor"). They can do this because, like IQ, they have no clear idea of exactly what it is that they are measuring.

Great statistics consume information rather than produce it. When a meteorologist measures barometric pressure, humidity, heat, wind, or cloud height, he can make use of that information in many ways. If the barometric pressure is significantly different here than it is fifty miles from here, we can safely say that some air is going to be moving. If it is 37 degrees in Kansas but 67 degrees in Denver, then it probably is not going to stay 37 degrees in Kansas very long. Similarly, in economics there are unstable combinations of circumstances; if the rate of unemployment is high but the rate of new construction is also high, something has got to happen. If the tax rates are changed, that will change the economy in vaguely predictable ways. In sabermetrics, there are similarly impossible and unstable combinations of occurrences. A team does not hit .250 with little power in a .265 league and win the division. If a team loses a star outfielder to injury, that will change the team's ability to score runs in vaguely predictable ways (we can predict very accurately the impact of the loss; we cannot predict accurately the impact of the adjustments to the loss).

But great statistics are of little use in studying other issues; they consume knowledge but don't yield it. They are not a part of a discussion, they are the end of a discussion. I feel that it is the proper place of sabermetrics not to *answer* questions—not to say for you that A is a better ballplayer than B—but to develop a broad range of tools and measures that you or I or anyone else could use in developing our own answers. *Bad sabermetrics attempts to end the discussion by saying that I have studied the issue and this is the answer. Good sabermetrics attempts to contribute to the discussion in such a way as to enable it to move forward on a ground of shared understanding.*

Since great statistics attempt to tell you everything that you need to know about the subject in three easy digits, they must define out of existence everything that is not included in their measurement. We do not know how many times each player was thrown out attempting to take an extra base. We do not know how many times each player gave away a base by throwing to the wrong one. We do not know how many hits Ozzie Smith takes away from the opposition, nor how many doubles Dan Ford gives away in the corner. We do not know how many runs Jesse Barfield prevents by keeping runners on third base. We couldn't even guess now many runs Carlton Fisk saves for a team by his ability to call pitches or his ability to spot a problem with the pitcher's delivery. We do not know which or whether players are especially good in the clutch. And this is only the shadow of the monster; our whole ignorance is much larger than we can conceive of.

The work of sabermetrics is not to ignore all of these considerations or to deny them, but to find ways to deal with them. Given enough good sabermetricians, those ways can and will be found. Bad sabermetricians characteristically insist that those things which cannot be measured are not important, that they do not even exist. They run from the monster in terror, and insist that he does not really exist, that there is only That Shadow.

—1984

Revolution

I am writing this in the fall of 1987, and there is a football strike. At this moment the strike is not over, but the outcome has pulled into view like a dragon along the roadside. As each week of the strike passes, more players cross the picket lines to go back to work. The attendance in the second week of the strike was up substantially from the first week. The television ratings, though low, will head up as soon as the World Series is over. In one of the most crucial variables, the news media, which absolutely has to have something to write and talk about, has begun to write and talk about the players who are on the field as well as those who are on the picket lines. As time passes they will have more to say about those players who are playing, and less to say about those who are not. The public interest in those who are playing will grow; the interest in those who are not will wane.

In short, then, the players, having sacrificed several very nice paychecks, are as a reward going to gain absolutely nothing and will lose a great deal of bargaining strength as well. The owners' tactic of filling up the uniforms with available bodies and carrying on as if nothing really had happened has succeeded, which brings up an obvious question of why this has never been tried or really even been discussed in our own sport. Why it is that what works in one sport cannot work in another?

In the baseball strikes, the very short strike we had in 1985 and the much longer strike in 1981, there were no strikebreakers used, and there was no serious talk about so doing. If there is another strike next year there will be no talk about it again. The crucial difference between football and baseball in this respect is what I am going to call the players' insulation: the minor leagues. In football, there is only a fine line distinguishing those who are good enough to have jobs from those who are out scrounging for regular work. Players come out of college trained, ready to play, many of them good enough to leap right into the league and contribute. Others are not quite good enough, barely, and so they are let go—free. Sometimes teams make mistakes in judging, and those who are really good enough to play are let go. Sometimes a player who is let go by one team in August will be a star by December.

In baseball, this doesn't happen. Occasionally, a player will be released by one team and turn out to be a good player, but even so generally there is an interim of several years between the time of the release and the time of stardom.

The difference, of course, is the minor leagues. The raw talent distribution of the two sports is exactly the same: Talent in all sports is a pyramid. For every player who is this good, there are several times as many who are half as good, and hundreds who are half as good as that. In baseball those players are playing minor league baseball. Because they are playing in the minor leagues, they see themselves as standing in line, waiting for a chance which they know will come if they play well enough. They are within the structure that contains their eventual success. They will not violate that structure. The free football players know that their chance will never come within the existing structure.

So the second-level baseball players are not going to cross the picket lines, nor the third-level players either. That means that in order to play replacement games, you would have to dip way, way down into the talent pool, and what you would lose is what we might call The Prospect of Eventual Credibility. What replacement players have in football is the prospect of eventual credibility. In the first week of the replacement games, there were some players who played so well that they established pretty clearly that they should have been there all along. As each week passes, another one or two players per team is going to establish that he is better than one of the forty-five guys who isn't there. Further, as each week passes the players who are playing, competing as they are at the best level of football available, benefiting from the level of training, benefiting from the coaching and the weight rooms, benefiting from the experience, get a little bit better—while the players who aren't playing, week after week, get a little bit worse, their skills deteriorating from age, from the lack of training, from the lack of competition, until after a period of time that fine line that distinguished those who were in from those who were out just disappears.

Suppose that the players were to stay on strike for, let us say, two years. At the end of that time, if the union were to say "OK, we give up, go back to work," there wouldn't be any jobs for them to go back to, simply because they would, for the most part, no longer be good enough to play.

In baseball, that can't happen. In baseball, there is that gap, that insulation provided by the players in the minor leagues, which separates the best players from those who are out of work by a gap so great that there is no prospect that the players who could be called in to replace the strikers would ever rise to the level represented by the Mark McGwires, the Ryne Sand-bergs, the best young players around today.

So then, if the baseball owners were even to hint that they were thinking of using scabs, what do you think would happen? In a flash, the baseball players would start talking about forming a new league. We would see a repeat of what happened almost a century ago with the Players League of 1890, although most likely the players would not now attempt to finance the league themselves. It would take a year to organize it, but after that year the critical question would be "Who has the credibility here: the established leagues, or the players' league?" And the answer is obvious. Unlike in football, where the uniforms and the names recognized from college stardom provide a measure of instant credibility, in baseball all of the credibility would belong to the players.

And that is why, no matter what the situation is, you will never hear baseball owners whispering about using scabs to break a strike—because to do so would invite the possibility of a rival league, and a rival league could cause a $50 million investment to crumble in the owners' hands. No other outcome of a strike could be as disastrous for ownership, no matter what they have to surrender.

In football, you see, the owners have options because there exists a form of live football outside the existing structure, outside of their control. In baseball, *the existence of the minor leagues* forces the owners to deal with the players on generous terms, and forces them to pass on to the players a great deal of the income that in football the owners are able to keep for themselves.

Now, let's back off and run at this from a completely different direction.

The minor leagues were not created by the major leagues. The minor leagues originally formed on the same basis as the major leagues, only in smaller cities and even that caveat is limited, since there were moments in the early history of what is now the National League at which it played in places like Troy, New York, and Fort Wayne, Indiana, while minor leagues were left to thrash around in places like New York City and Detroit. In any case, the National League successfully established itself in the nation's largest cities, while other leagues, competitor leagues, foraged for what was left.

At first there was no reserve clause. This was a sort of primordial soup for baseball, an original chaos in which the land itself was liquid, and the players would just drift from team to team as suited themselves. So the owners said "We've got to get organized here. We can have competition between different leagues, yes, but we can't let these players move around from team to team just however they want. Let's construct a reserve arrangement." Organized baseball began, then, in an attempt to deprive the players of negotiating power.

In a few years the National League and the American Association began to pull ahead of the other leagues, and the best players began to become concentrated in these leagues. The owners of these "major league" teams would go to the owners of the minor league teams and say, "Hey, you've got a player there that we think is pretty good. I'll tell you what: We'll respect your reserve clause, but why don't you sell us this player for, say, a thousand dollars." The minor league team owner, who might be making eight hundred dollars on the year (this was a century ago), would sell the player to the big city team, and so the gap between the minor league and the major league teams would grow wider.

Well, it didn't take too long until the owners of some of the minor league teams began to realize that it was in their interest, when they had a player of quality, to hold onto him a while and let the interest grow, and then sell him to the highest bidder. So the major league owners got together and said, "Hey, we need to get more organized here. This situation is too . . . chaotic. We need to establish some arrangements whereby, when there is a player for sale, we'll have a way of claiming him, so we won't have this wild bidding for minor league players anymore. We'll meet with the minor league owners, and we'll establish a system where if they have a player to sell they can just list him, and then we'll see who picks up the option. To get them to go along with it, we'll fix a good price that they'll be happy to get for the player." And so they did, and then even more of the best players were all concentrated in the major leagues, and the gap was wider than before, and as inflation came along the amount of money that they actually had to pay for these young players began to reduce the cost of the talent.

Generous as this system was, there were some of the minor

league owners who weren't happy with it. Early in the twentieth century some minor league teams still refused to list their best players on waivers and sell them to the major leagues. You would have owners like Jack Dunn in Baltimore who would figure that "I'm in a pretty good sized city here. I can draw as many fans here as the Browns can in St. Louis. Why should I sell my best players to anybody?"

So the major league teams came back to the minor league teams and said "We've got to get better organized here. Let's set up a structure with different levels of minor league teams, and each level can buy whoever they want from the lower levels. We'll fix a good price, and we'll even let you keep the player for two or three years before you have to move him on up the line, and that way everybody will have a steady supply of talent—the major league teams from the top minors, the top minors from the B Leagues, the B Leagues from the C Leagues, etc. When the player is sold from a C League to a B League it'll be one price, and when he goes from a B League to an A League it will be more, so as you buy a player and pass him along you'll always make a profit. It's more fair to the player that way, if he has a structure that he can move up through. If we don't do this, you see, then the teams that keep all their best players are going to get so strong that they'll walk all over the rest of the league."

Well, that seemed fair enough to the minor league owners, and indeed the Baltimore team did walk all over the other teams, and so in time the minor league owners went along with it, and forced everyone in their leagues to go along with it, and so by the early 1920s every minor league team was required, by the rules of organized baseball, to sell its best players to the major leagues. As part of the deal, the major leagues agreed not to sign players straight out of high school. That way, each minor league team would have its own territory, and could sign the players out of high school and make a profit by selling them up the line.

So the gap between the major leagues and the minor leagues got a little wider, and in a few years the major leagues kind of forgot about their guarantees not to sign players out of high school. The minor league teams, mind you, are still at this point in the business of running baseball teams. They're not in business to develop ballplayers. They're in business to develop teams, get into pennant races, draw crowds and make money. Selling ballplayers is just one of the ways that they make money. So then the major league owners begin to pick out some of the weaker minor league teams and say, "Hey, why don't you go to work for us? Rather than just selling ballplayers to whoever claims them on waivers or negotiating a deal to sell them before the waiver claim hits, why don't you have an arrangement just with us? We'll pay you money up front—I'll tell you what, we'll pay you so much money up front that we'll guarantee you a profit for the season. Besides that, we'll provide players for you, guys we've got from other teams. You'll be like a farm, growing players for us and growing money for yourself."

Well, to a guy struggling to make ends meet in Mt. Vernon, Illinois or Decatur, Georgia, that sounded like a pretty good deal, so they'd go along with it. Those minor league teams, then, would get stronger and their opponents would get weaker, so then the major league teams would make arrangements with their opponents, too, or sometimes they would just flat buy them out. This went on for about thirty years or so, and then there weren't any free minor leagues left. Everybody worked for somebody.

Well, once everybody worked for somebody, the major league teams had the minor league teams over a barrel. There wasn't any negotiating, now; the major league teams just wrote the rules, and if the minor league teams didn't like it they could suck eggs. If the minor league team was in a pennant race and the major league team needed their best ballplayer, they'd just take him; hey, we don't care about your damned little pennant race. At first they were apologetic about this, and they would try not to do too much of it; when they took a star player from a contending team they would make every effort to replace him with a player off the major league roster or a potential star from a lower level, and they would try not to lift a player unless he really made a difference to them. In about ten years, however, that too went by the boards, and if a player was hitting .385 at AAA ball and the minor league team was a half game ahead with two weeks to play and the major league team needed him to pinch run once a week, they'd just take him anyway.

Historian Dee Brown has written that probably at no point

in our history did white Americans intend to do to American Indians what we actually did. It was a process, extending over a couple of centuries: One generation would make treaties, and the next generation would amend them, cut them back a little bit, claim a little more land, and the generation after that would forget about the treaties altogether, so that, looking at the entire pattern over a period of generations, one would swear that there was a conscious decision to drive the American Indian into the ground. The history of the relationship between the minors and the majors is very similar: One generation would make agreements, and the next generation would amend those agreements, and the third generation would renege on them entirely or forget that they had ever been made. The minor leagues, originally independent competitors of the major leagues, were by tiny degrees and yearly increments reduced into mere servants, living on crumbs, sustained by the major leagues for their own uses like a farmer keeps chickens, just for the eggs.

This process of driving down the minor leagues continues to this day. Just a couple of years ago, the owner of a minor league team told me that "Every year, they do something that makes it more impossible for us to operate. Every year, the major league teams change the rules a little bit to make it harder for us."

The minor league system as it exists today is an abomination in the sight of the Lord. Players are assigned to the minor league team at the last minute without the team having any say in who wears their uniform, players spend two weeks at a city and then are moved around like checkers, anonymous young men playing to develop skills rather than playing to win, teams in great cities drawing a couple of hundred fans a game, pennant races with no meaning, no connection between city and player, player and fan, fan and city. They have really, truly reached the point at which they don't care about winning.

If you're selling a sport and the players don't care about winning, that's not a sport. That's a fraud. Minor league baseball today is exactly what the 1919 World Series was: a charade, a rip-off, an exhibition masquerading as a contest. Earl Weaver in one of his books tells about one time when he was managing in the minor leagues and had a slugging first baseman that the major league team was trying to make into a third baseman. The guy couldn't play third base, and Weaver knew if he put him there he would cost him the pennant race. Earl wanted to *win*. In desperation, he finally started sending the major league team phony box scores, showing the guy playing third base when he was actually playing first, living in terror that a scout would catch him and he would get fired—for trying to win.

That's a disgraceful situation. Baseball, for most of the cities in the nation, has been reduced to the level of professional wrestling. By this horrible system, then, most of the nation is deprived of having real baseball. Look at a map— how many great cities do we have in this country? We've got twenty-three cities that have "real" teams; everything else is an imitation. Miami, Washington, Memphis, Phoenix, San Antonio, Indianapolis, New Orleans, Denver, Nashville, Oklahoma City, Portland—why do these cities have no real baseball? The Memphis team works for my team, the Kansas City Royals—but why should Memphis have nothing, so that Kansas City can have everything? Why should Memphis not be allowed to keep a good ballplayer, so that Kansas City can have them all? It's not right. It's unethical, it's immoral, it is corrupt. We have no right, as Kansas City fans, to use Omaha, Memphis, and Fort Myers as our servants. Every city, whether a great city like those listed above or a small city like Mobile or Bakersfield, should have its own proud team, the best team that it can support. There should be leagues, and there should be pennant races, and there should be civic pride invested in them. And they should serve no master except the urgency of competition.

And yet you see the wonderful irony of the situation, as for whose benefit was this greedy system established, and for whom is it maintained? For the major league owners, of course; they've got the whole $80 million TV contract to themselves (or is it more than that now?), and they don't want to split it eighty ways, they want to split it twenty-six ways. And yet, they can't really keep the TV money, being essentially merely caretakers who pass it on to the players, and why is that? Because of the minor leagues! If the system existed that should exist, there would be dozens of leagues, hundreds of teams, and, in one way or another, an inevitable supply of talent as there is in football, inasmuch as it would be impossible for the union to lock up the entire sprawling independent system.

Having struggled for a century to create this system, having tightened the organization of baseball tighter and tauter and sounder, having wrestled all of professional baseball into their ironclad structure, the owners now find themselves the victims of that system, their options eliminated by the fact that nothing exists for them to draw from outside their own ironclad structure. Like a tyrant suffocated in bed by his own hired thugs, major league baseball has choked nearly to death all of the other leagues, and now finds itself kneeling before its own hired help. It is, like the sorry life of Howard Hughes, a marvelous lesson on the end products of greed.

Another of the ugly features of the current system is the abuse of their monopolistic position by club owners in negotiation with cities. Although major league baseball has a relatively good record on this point in the last fifteen years, an example of what can happen is what has happened to the football St. Louis Cardinals. The Cardinals, who may be the Phoenix Asholes or something by the time you read this, are owned by an oversized wart named Bidwell. The Cardinals have a perfectly good stadium, Busch Stadium, a major league facility in every way; nonetheless, Mr. Bidwell is not satisfied. He wants a new stadium, all his own, and he wants the city of St. Louis to tax its $18,000-a-year citizens to build it for him, and if he can't have that at the very least he feels he is entitled to have several hundred luxury boxes constructed for him at taxpayer expense so he can sell them to rich people for $150 a game. In effect, Bidwell is telling the people of St. Louis that if they don't give him millions of dollars he will deprive them of their status as a major league football city—while Phoenix stands by, anxious to give him millions of dollars to acquire that status. It's an appalling situation, the most blatant abuse of monopolistic power.

In a setting of competing leagues, you see, the city of St. Louis would not have a great deal of interest in whether or not Mr. Bidwell threatened to move to Phoenix. St. Louis has proven itself to be a viable major league market. In a competitive environment, if one league abandoned the city, another league would immediately move in. The "owner" would have no power to force the city to dance to his tune. Building and maintaining a stadium would be strictly a matter of civic pride, as it should be.

It is all well to say that Lincoln, Nebraska, should have the best baseball team that Lincoln, Nebraska, can support, you might ask, but is baseball really viable there? Would Lincoln, Nebraska, really support a team, at all?

Answer: You bet your ass. A well-managed, free minor league team in Lincoln, Nebraska would draw 200,000 to 300,000 fans in a season. In 1949, in a system that wasn't very good but wasn't as oppressive as the one existing now, the team in Lincoln drew 149,000 fans. That's plenty to support an eighteen-man roster. The Nebraska Cornhuskers football team plays six home games a year in Lincoln and draws more than that, about 70,000 a game. We all understand that they're "minor league," that although they represent the best at their level of competition they couldn't stay on the field with the Kansas City Chiefs, a poor professional team. People will try to tell you that that's different because they're a college so the alumni support them, but anybody who has lived around here knows that's not the way it is. At least half the people who support the Cornhuskers never had any connection with Nebraska University. When you're growing up around here you just pick out a college team and root for them; whether or not you wind up going to that college is a completely unrelated issue. People will root for that team, and will invest their regional pride in that team *because that team is free to try to win.* They would do the same for a baseball team if that team was really trying to win. A Lincoln baseball team wouldn't get quite the same size of crowds because they'd have to split the audience with Omaha and Council Bluffs, Iowa, but they'd still draw real well.

People will tell you that television killed the minor leagues, but that brings us back to the same issue: If television killed minor league baseball, why did college football and college basketball boom at the same time? If the Boston Celtics and the Kansas Jayhawks are on television in this area on the same night, virtually nobody will watch the Celtics, although they are a vastly better team. Why? Television temporarily gripped the interest of the public and had a temporary effect on minor league attendance, just as it had a temporary effect on attendance at the movies, but those periodic recessions will happen. The problem here was that after this periodic recession passed there were no free minor leagues left to recover.

What would be the economic effects of freeing the minors? First of all, total attendance at professional baseball games nationwide would increase tremendously. Total professional attendance in 1987 will be around 70 million fans—a little over 50 million for the majors, but less than 20 million for the rest of the country. That figure would increase probably to the range of 170–200 million fans. There would be a great deal more interest in local teams. At present, most of the people in this nation do not live within easy driving range of real baseball. The Kansas City area has about 1.5 million people, yet it regularly draws 2.2 million fans or more—one and a half fans per person. If competitive teams were accessible to the fans, a figure of 200 million attendance for a nation of more than 240 million people is extremely realistic.

The TV money, however, probably would not increase. The national networks, rather than dealing with a monopoly, would have options; if the National League tried to hold them up, they'd start dickering with the Continental League, or the Pacific Coast League, or the Southwest Conference. The result: the same amount of TV money, cut up many more ways, meaning less TV and radio income per team.

Which would mean, of course, the end of the $2 million salaries. Many more baseball players would make a living, but none would reach the levels of tremendous wealth attained today.

"But what about the quality of play?," you might ask; "Aren't you really talking about an expansion of the current twenty-six teams to maybe eighty or a hundred teams, and isn't the talent already thinned out something terrible by expansion?"

Now there is a truly preposterous argument. This nation could support, without any detectable loss of player quality, at a very, very minimum, two hundred major league teams.

Think about it. If we had 240 major league teams, each team would represent about a million people. Do you have any idea how many people a million people are? Start counting people that you meet on the street sometime. If you live in New York and ride the subway, start counting the people on the subway. It will take you years and years of counting people that you meet on the street and in the subway to reach a million. You trying to tell me that's not enough people to pick twenty-five ballplayers out of?

Or look at it this way: start with a group of 250 people, and choose a baseball team from them. Let's see, with 250 people you should have about sixty men between the ages of eighteen and forty-five, at a guess, so choose the best eighteen athletes out of those sixty and make them a baseball team. (At this level, obviously some of the best athletes would be women, but never mind.)

Then put that team in a four-team league of such teams, and at the end of the year choose an All-Star team, the best player at each position. This will be the first generation All-Star team.

Put the All-Star team in a league of four All-Star teams, and at the end of the year choose an All-Star team of the All-Star teams; this will be the second-generation All-Star team.

Put that team in a league of four such teams and play a season and choose the best player at each position. At this point I'd say you should have a pretty fair team, wouldn't you? That would be the third-generation All-Star team.

Put four of those pretty fair teams in a league, and play a season with them, and choose the best players. That would be the fourth-generation All-Star team.

Put four of those together and play a season and choose a team of the best of them.

That team, the fifth-generation All-Star team, would represent about 250,000 people.

The team representing a million people would be the All-Star team that you would get if you repeated the process again, again choosing the best players. With 240 million people we'd have 240 teams, not counting the players imported from Puerto Rico, Jamaica, the Dominican Republic, Canada, Venezuela, Mexico or wherever. I'm not suggesting that we should have anything like 240 major league teams; I'm suggesting something like sixty major league and 150 free minor league teams.

To say that that level of talent, the seventh-generation All-Star team, is not good enough to be called major league talent, that we have to move another half-generation beyond that, so that each major league team represents 8 million fans rather than 4 million . . . well, it's absurd. It's making a distinction in talent which is unimaginably trivial. If you timed every man in the country in a hundred yard dash, the difference between the 650th-fastest man (completing the twenty-sixth team) and the 2000th-fastest probably would not be a hundredth of a second. It certainly would not be a tenth of a second.

Of course, if you instantly expanded from twenty-six teams to the number that should exist you would have a decline in the talent level. You'd have inexperienced players, a great loss in knowledge along with a minimal loss in athletic ability. It would take time for the knowledge of how to play the game and the acquisition of the developed skills to spread throughout the enlarged baseball population. But a gradual expansion of the number of teams? It wouldn't do a thing to the talent.

I'm not saying that we should not allow the best players to be concentrated in the best leagues. That will happen naturally. In college football or basketball, there is no rule that automatically, inflexibly railroads all of the best players to the biggest and best leagues—and yet that's where they are. You don't get too many NBA stars coming out of small colleges in Arizona. The best players will gravitate toward the biggest cities and the best leagues because that's where the money is. The small teams should be able to sell the rights to players while they are under contract, and the contracts should run out at regular intervals because men are not chattel to be moved around without their consent. It's one thing if it happens naturally, and quite another if it happens by force—the difference between rape and chemistry.

But is it really possible for this world to exist? Is this just an air-castle article?

It is, in theory, quite simple to see how the sports world could be changed to get rid of this peculiar closed structure in which we have lived all our lives. It requires only one action. It requires the Anti-Trust division of the Justice Department to order major league baseball (and football and basketball) to stop acting as a monopoly. That given, everything else I have outlined here will follow in time. It could be done either by the Justice Department or by Congress, or by the one at the behest of the other. As a practical matter, they could do this in either of two ways. They could order the existing major leagues to split into four competing entities (six to eight teams each), and instruct those four leagues that they must compete;

they must not coordinate their activities in any way whatsoever except to organize a National Championship. They can't get together to negotiate a TV contract. They can't get together to form reserve arrangements and inhibit the movement of players. They especially can't make collective decisions about which cities will have teams and which won't. Very quickly, at least one of those leagues would become aggressive, would expand to perhaps ten or twelve teams, and there would be a team in Washington and a team in Phoenix and a team in Miami within a few years.

The other alternative would be much slower and somewhat less certain, but is probably sounder in the long run: Order major league baseball teams to divest themselves of their minor league affiliates, and prohibit them from continuing to engage in predatory and monopolistic practices with regard to teams in other leagues—as they have done for a hundred years. Prohibit teams from forming alliances with teams in other leagues.

In time, since leagues would not be able to enter into the kind of unequal agreements with stronger teams that they have so long lived with—agreements which forced them to act in the interest of other teams—what would they do? The leagues would act in their selfish interest. It would be in the best interests of each league to move into the biggest cities that it could control. You would get a league, like maybe the Pacific Coast League, which might put a team in Los Angeles, snarf up San Jose and Sacramento, and move in the direction of being a West Coast major league. The Los Angeles team, trying to compete with the two established teams, might blow its wad on George Brett or Eric Davis.

If the first approach was selected, the major leagues should also be required to divest themselves of their minor league affiliates, or at least most of them. If the second approach was selected, the regulation should prohibit the existing majors from expanding for a period of fifteen to twenty years. At first, some minor league owners would complain that they were being cut off from their main source of support, which was their major league "partner." In the short run, of course, that's exactly what it would do: It would snip the lifeline, and force the team to scramble for survival on its own, by doing novel things like promoting, putting together a good ball team, getting into a pennant race and trying to win. Looking at the Phoenix team, for example, somebody would have to invest some money to build that team up toward a more competitive level. If there was the danger that an established league would expand into the Phoenix area, it would be difficult to get anybody interested in investing in the upstart team. But if the Phoenix prospects could be assured that there would be no expansion for the next fifteen years, then the Phoenix people could turn their attention toward building the best team they could put together.

Well, I hope I've made you think, anyway. I hope I have made you realize that the world in which we live is not the only possible world, nor even the best of all possible worlds. I am not arguing for these changes because I want to be provocative; I am arguing for these changes because I believe they would make baseball healthier, more exciting, and more fun.

Competition isn't always pretty. Teams would fold, go bankrupt sometimes, use nearly-naked usherettes in a cheap attempt to boost attendance, pull out in the middle of the night without paying their debts—all of the things that businesses do. Baseball would be less stable. It would change more rapidly than it ever has, in part because each league would be learning from the experiences of the other leagues. But it would be changing because it would be growing, and it would be growing toward a baseball world which is larger, stronger, smarter, richer, more diverse, and more fair to the fans. It can happen.

Hey, buddy, I love tradition, too.

—1988

On Salary Arbitration Cases

My off-season job is working in salary arbitration cases. The picture of a salary arbitration case which has filtered through to the public bears almost no resemblance to the real thing, for a simple reason: The press doesn't attend. Since reporters are not allowed in arbitration cases, they tend, understandably, to process what information they receive through the prism of their imagination, and to present to the public an image of arbitration cases as bitter, bloody liars' contests with the contestants pounding on the table and shouting insults. Real arbitration cases are polite, reserved, extraordinarily orderly, and involve as a rule almost no bitterness or anger. Of course, underneath the veneer of good manners, egos are straining at the leash and hearts are swinging in the wind, for a great deal is truly at stake—reputations, clients, futures, and usually a couple hundred thousand dollars.

The first thing I suppose I should say is that salary arbitration cases do not revolve primarily around how good the player is. I'll start there because that is the fundamental misunderstanding from which most others flow, the idea that in an arbitration case the goal of the player's representatives is to make the player look as good as possible, and the goal of the team is to make the player look as bad as possible. That's not what it's about. It's not an argument about how good the player is; it's an argument about what he should be paid.

Salaries in baseball are determined the same way that the value of your house is determined: by comparisons. A salary arbitration hearing is a condensed, pressurized imitation of the normal salary-negotiating procedure, and thus revolves around the question of who are the most comparable players to the man involved. If the player is asking for six hundred thousand dollars, he does not argue that he should get six hundred thousand dollars because he is a great player, and the team does not argue that he should get only four hundred thousand dollars because he is a terrible player. The player argues that he should get six hundred thousand dollars because that is what the salary scale dictates, meaning that the other major league players who have done the same things that he has done are getting paid about that amount. The team argues that the player should receive only four hundred thousand dollars for the same reason: because that is what the other players who have comparable skills and accomplishments are getting paid.

As players are never perfect, so comparisons are never perfect. If the player involved is a third baseman, then every other third baseman is a comparable player—to some degree. If the player involved is a leadoff man, then every other leadoff man is a comparable player—to some degree. If the player involved has hit three hundred, then every other three hundred hitter is comparable—to some degree. If the player involved has four-plus years of experience (has been in the major leagues four full years and less than five), then every other four-plus player is comparable—to some degree. If the player involved has had an injury during the season, then every other player who has had an injury during the season is comparable in that respect. If the player has had a bad year one year ago, then every player who had a bad year at the same time is comparable to some extent. If the player has stolen a good number of bases, then every base stealer is potentially comparable. If the player has a big platoon differential (if he hits left-handers dramatically better than right-handers), then every other player who has a big platoon differential is comparable to some extent. If the player's team has finished in last place, then every other player who plays for a last-place team is comparable to some extent.

What everyone is attempting to do in an arbitration case (player and team alike) is search for the comps (comparable players) which work to their benefit, and to distinguish the player from those which work to their disadvantage. If the man you are representing is a three-hundred-hitting, four-plus player who is a base stealer and plays third base and bats leadoff for a last place team and missed forty games with an injury and had a bad year a year ago and has a big platoon differential, and if there is another player somewhere in the major leagues who is a three-hundred hitting, four-plus player who is a base stealer and plays third base and bats leadoff for a last place team and missed forty games with an injury and had a bad year a year ago and has a big platoon differential, then you're stuck with him as a comp, and the next time this happens will be the first time. Short of that, players can always be distinguished; various ways can always be found to argue that the other player, though comparable in these six respects, is not a valid comparison for purposes of establishing a salary. And that argument, over and over again, is the essence of a salary negotiation, and therefore the essence of a salary arbitration. Arbitration hearings tend to occur for players for whom there are few good comps, because those are the cases in which a difference of opinion about where the player fits is most likely to occur.

Within those narrow guidelines, the question of quality becomes an important consideration; after all, one of the differences between six-hundred-thousand-dollar players and four-hundred-thousand-dollar players is that the six-hundred-thousand-dollar players are better players. But it's an important peripheral issue; it's not a central issue. In fact, because of the structure of an arbitration case, it is actually rather dangerous for the player's representatives to push the issue of quality too hard. The structure of a case is this: The player presents first, for one hour. The club presents its case for one hour, and then the player has a half hour to rebut the club's argument, and then the club has a half hour to rebut the player's argument. Theoretically, a case lasts three hours beginning to end, and it may actually be over in three hours if the arbitrator has another case scheduled in the afternoon or his daughter is having her debutante ball that night or something. In the more usual case, there are also coffee breaks, delays for procedural arguments which are not counted against anyone's time, additional time for summation, and people who run over their allotted hour or half hour. Occasionally there are "negotiating delays" in which the representatives of the two sides go into another room without the arbitrator and try to reach a compromise. A case usually runs four to five hours; the longest I have ever attended was the Joaquin Andujar case in 1980, which ran at least eight, maybe ten. That was some time ago and I've forgotten a few details, but it was a long damn thing, I know that.

Anyway, what I was saying—the player goes first for an hour, and then the team speaks for an hour. If you build your case around puffing up the quality of the player's contribution, the team can tear you down in about three sentences. You spend an hour explaining why Jonah Goldman is the greatest shortstop in the history of baseball, and the team's representative if he is smart (some are, some aren't) will say, "Yes, sir, we agree with all that. Jonah Goldman is a terrific shortstop, a great clutch hitter despite his .242 batting average, an important leader in the clubhouse and the best base runner on our team. *That's why we're offering to pay him four hundred thousand dollars.*"

See? Three sentences, and you just wasted your hour. That approach is, to me as a representative of the player, the scariest line of attack from the team, the most difficult attack to beat. Because the team can buy your assumptions and still win, you see; everything is relative. In absolute terms all of the money is staggering; no one can quite comprehend it. Four hundred, six hundred thousand—it's a hell of a lot of money no matter who wins. The issue is not whether the team's offer is fair in absolute terms, but whether it is fair relative to the salary structure. The team, if it is smart, wants to characterize its offer as being generous—and for that reason, it is not normally in the best interests of the team for its agents to portray the team as small, petty and intent on grinding down the player.

Of course, there are people who don't see it that way; there are lawyers and general managers (what a general manager is, really, is the agent for the corporation) who will come in and hammer on your player. But that doesn't worry us; if they do that, I'll guarantee you we'll beat them if the case can be won.

Let me back off a little bit from what I said before; the quality of a player's performance *should be* a peripheral issue, and in most cases is. I've certainly seen cases where it became the central issue. There are times when it is appropriate for the team to hammer on the player, if you have a player who is in arbitration at an unrealistic figure because he has a distorted idea of his contribution to the team. More often than that, I have been in cases in which, on behalf of the player, we successfully turned the quality of play into the central issue because that was the strongest line of approach that we had.

See, most people don't arbitrate on a bad season. Most players who are in arbitration are fairly good players to begin with, and generally coming off a decent season, although there are exceptions. If you're representing a real quality player, a player like Tim Raines or Roger Clemens or even a player like Kevin Bass, you're very happy to argue about whether or not he is a good player. There are times when the team's agents will try to put down the player as a kind of knee-jerk reaction, and will introduce negative material even about a great player. But from our standpoint as representatives of the player, that's a sucker play; if we can turn the hearing into an argument about whether or not Tim Raines is a good player . . . well, hey, we'd be fools to pass it up, wouldn't we? If a team is foolish enough to try to put down Roger Clemens, you can bet that our side will be prepared to pick up on the relevant material and show the arbitrator the other side of it, because if I get to argue that Roger Clemens is a good pitcher and you trap yourself into arguing that he isn't a good pitcher, buddy, you don't have a prayer.

But if the team is paying attention, they shouldn't allow that to happen—and, conversely, if we are representing Jonah Goldman, we shouldn't allow it to happen. When representing a marginal player, the introduction of any material designed to put a better face on his season is dangerous, for the same reason: that you are in danger of turning the arbitration hearing into an argument over whether or not Jonah Goldman is a good shortstop. And you can't win that argument.

Even assuming that you could convince the arbitrator to begin with. You have to understand—arbitrators are not idiots. That's another distortion of the press, this idea that arbitrators are sort of naive outsiders who will believe whatever you tell them. First of all, arbitrators are professional skeptics; they take everything you tell them with a grain or two of salt. The arbitrators of these disputes are members of the American Arbitration Association, men who make a profession out of getting in the middle of disputes, normally disputes between individuals and corporations. Every time he works a case the arbitrator hears two versions of everything. The longshoreman was fired for no reason, or he was fired only after six warning letters, eleven unexplained absences and four instances of being drunk on the job. The metal worker's loss of limb resulted entirely from his own carelessness, or it resulted from inadequate supervision of maintenance so gross and evident that it had been reported to management by dozens of employees. The arbitrator searches instinctively for the edges of the evidence presented to him and the implication of what goes unsaid. The arbitrators are lawyers, often college law professors, sometimes retired judges.

Second, *these* arbitrators are baseball fans. I don't know the details, but there is some sort of signup procedure within the AAA by which these people make it known that they are available, and the teams and the Player's Association agree upon those arbitrators who are acceptable. Neither side wants somebody who is so involved in the issue that he is going to come in with a preconceived idea of the player's value—but neither side wants somebody who is not going to understand what he is being told, either. Nobody wants somebody who doesn't know what ERA is. Occasionally somebody who doesn't know much might slip through the cracks and arbitrate a couple of cases before he gets axed, and those instances of course will be relayed to the public, but that is certainly a rare situation. I have never seen or worked with an arbitrator who didn't know what the discussion was about, and several have told me that they enjoy my books. My books are written for hard-core baseball fans.

So what you're dealing with, in the ordinary case, is a fifty-five-year-old law school professor who rooted for the Washington Senators in the time of Ed Yost and thinks Don Mattingly got robbed in the MVP voting in '86 and isn't going to tell you any of this. He has the player's stats in front of him. If you come into the case and you try to tell the man that Steve Balboni is Babe Ruth, what's he going to think?

Well, to be blunt, he's going to think you're full of shit. He won't tell you, but that's what he's going to think. So right off the bat, there are very distinct limits on your ability to stretch the player's credentials. You do, of course, try to cast the player in a favorable light; if he's a C player, you try to present him as a C+, and the club tries to present him as a C−. But that's the absolute limit; if you try to present a C player as a B− player or (God forbid) an A− player, you are guaranteed to lose the case. Because when that arbitrator gets back to his hotel room and pulls out the *Baseball Register*, there is no way that he is going to believe that that player is substantially better than what he sees in the book.

Arbitration cases revolve around credibility. That's the other big misunderstanding about arbitration, the idea that agents and teams will say anything to win a case. What an arbitration case is, in a sense, is a battle for credibility: Who does the arbitrator believe? Does he believe the agent for the team, who says that the men who are comparable to this man are paid about four hundred thousand, or does he believe the agent for the player, who says that the salary structure dictates a figure of six hundred thousand? He sits there, looking you over, studying your voice, your eyes, your exhibits, your mannerisms, your body language, running over and over through the back of his head "Who do I believe? Who do I believe?"

So you don't want to do anything which dirties your credibility—anything, a little white lie, an exaggeration, a misstatement, a wrong statistic, an error in your stat work. Anything like that can cost you the case in a twinkle of an eye, and once you lose the faith of the arbitrator you cannot get it back.

Beyond which, it is a two-sided process; after you present your case, the team presents theirs. And you know what that means? It means that every little lie, every exaggeration, every misstatement, every wrong statistic, and every error in your stat work will be called to the attention of the arbitrator. The team has (for all practical purposes) the same access to information that you have; every stat you have, they have. If you say that the player has hit .309 with runners in scoring position when it was actually .307, this will certainly be pointed out to the arbitrator.

So you stay so, so close to the truth—not only to what the truth is, but to what you can *prove* that it is. *You can't get by with anything.* Every statement must be nailed down with a statistic or some other piece of objective evidence.

OK, again, let me retreat a little bit. *My* rule, for *me* and the people I work with, is that you keep one foot on the truth at all times. But have I ever seen people lie in an arbitration case? Sure, many times; in fact, in most cases. The club's representatives have access to all the facts, but sometimes they don't have command of all the facts. Sometimes they don't realize that you can prove something and think they can get by with giving an opinion as if it were a fact. Some people simply don't know what they're doing, don't understand the process. And often, late in the case, the side which is losing will get desperate and begin telling little fibs, the arbitration equivalent of throwing deep on every play. Often, that's how you know that the case is really over and you start mentally packing up your briefcase, when the team starts saying things that they know aren't true.

One of the most stunning illustrations of the principle that you don't lie in an arbitration case, as well as of the dangers of using negative material about a good ballplayer, came in the Tony Pena case. . . . I think it was 1983. To be honest, we had a terrible day; I was working with Tom Reich's group, and we couldn't get anything to come out in the hearing the way we had planned it. We decided to have Tony speak in his own behalf, and that took three times longer than it should have and didn't accomplish what it was supposed to, and then we were short on time and trying to hurry the case along, and things got bollixed up pretty good. It was the worst job of presenting an arbitration that I have ever been a part of and we had a tough figure to defend, and just as we were about to hang our heads and ready our apologies, wonder of wonders, the stumblebums who were presenting the case for the Pirates decided to argue that Tony was a poor defensive catcher. I don't know what they were thinking of—Tony had been close to the league lead in errors, and I guess they thought we couldn't prove any different or they didn't know they had the case won or something; anyway, the lawyer the Pirates had hired decided to slander Pena as a defensive player. We perked right up after that; Sam Reich, presenting the case for Tony, asked for and received permission to cross-examine a Pirates' club official who was there. Pena had finished second in the voting for the Gold Glove Award, so Sam asked the team official if he thought the voters had made a mistake in their voting. The guy didn't know what to say, which is understandable because there wasn't anything he could have said; at length the lawyer, who had created this situation with his own silly mistake, had to ask for a time-out and take the guy in another room where he was obviously instructed that like it or not he had to lie and savage Tony's defense, and by the time this was over they were in worse shape than we were. Pena got his money.

Incidentally, in that case one of our best comps for Pena was Leon Durham. The lawyer for the Pirates, to distinguish Durham from Pena, said that Durham was "virtually a young Mickey Mantle." A couple of years later he was presenting the case for the Cubs against Durham, and he reportedly attacked Durham viciously, including the famous trick of showing a videotape of the ground ball going through Durham's legs in the 1984 Championship series. Same guy. I wish I'd known he was presenting that case; I'd of paid my own plane fare to get there.

There are several law firms around the country which have tried to build a trade in representing teams in arbitration cases. As a lawyer friend of mine says, a baseball arbitration is a lawyer's dream—hundreds of thousands of dollars on the table in one afternoon, with no appeals, no pre-trial discovery, no depositions, no maneuvering through the court's schedule. You just go in there one afternoon and battle it out, although it does take a few hundred hours of preparation.

But in general, and this is only speaking from my own experience, outside lawyers do not do a good job of representing the club. I'm not exactly sure why, but almost all of the lawyers I have seen working cases have fallen into one trap or another. They tend to rely on negative information to an unhealthy extent, and in many cases they're not as familiar with the nuances of baseball players as they need to be. For example, in one case I worked we used Wally Backman as a comp for our player, as an example of a well-paid platoon player; the lawyer for the club tried to put distance between Backman and our man (Denny Walling) by arguing that the Mets had given Backman a good contract because they intended to make him a full-time regular, an argument which looked pretty stupid when we pointed out that Backman's lifetime batting average against left-handed pitching was one-forty-something. A baseball man would have known that; he would have chosen some other way to try to distinguish Backman from Walling. And that was a terribly crucial point of that hearing, because Backman was probably our best comp; if they had been able to successfully distinguish Backman from Walling, we would probably have lost the case. A lot of times I don't think that outside lawyers completely understand the process of fixing salaries in baseball, and thus don't understand the way that an arbitration imitates that process.

Another thing that happens is that lawyers will often use little tricks that may work fine in front of a jury, but which are likely to backfire in an arbitration hearing. There's some yoyo that Dick Wagner hired in both Cincinnati and Houston whose central strategy is to obfuscate, obfuscate, obfuscate. What he tries to do, in essence, is confuse the issues of the case to such an extent that nobody can clearly prove anything, and then leave the arbitrator with some simple reason to rule in the club's favor. It's frustrating, and you want to jump over the table and wring his scrawny little neck, but you know that it's got to be as frustrating for the arbitrators as it is for us. The arbitrator is a lawyer, too, and if he's trying to clarify the issues in his own mind and somebody else is trying to keep them confused, don't you reckon he's going to notice? He beat us once, too, but I'd be happy to face that guy seven days a week.

Outside experts have a kind of credibility in any organization, and one can see why a general manager might feel more comfortable placing his case in the hands of a slick downtown lawyer, rather than some guy who works in his office. But with the exception of John McAdams of Texas, who has enough experience to understand the nature of an arbitration, I've never seen an outside lawyer do a good job of presenting an arbitration case, and I think most teams would be better off even putting the case in the hands of a scout or a low-level researcher than in the hands of somebody outside the organization.

Thinking about the Walling case, another limitation on the principle of absolute truth is what might be called a "characterization" of an ability. Randy Hendricks did a clever thing in the Walling case, when he asserted blankly that Walling had the best throwing arm of any National League third baseman. Now Walling has a good throwing arm, but I don't absolutely know that it's a hard fact that he has the best arm in the league. But when we said that he did, what do you think happened? They said that he didn't. They were using Eddie Robinson as an expert witness, so this lawyer asked him does Walling have the best throwing arm in the league? Eddie said he didn't know if it was the best arm in the league; he has a good arm but I don't know if it's the best in the league. We were thrilled. If Randy had said he had an above-average arm, Eddie would have said it was below-average, and then we'd have been arguing about whether or not his arm was above average. Instead we were arguing about whether or not it was the best in the league.

On something like that which is essentially subjective, you can take the initiative by characterizing it in the most favorable way, and then let them deny it. But even there, you've got to be careful. Suppose that you say that somebody is the best base runner on the team, and the guy on the other side pulls out a videotape and rolls in a VCR and says, "Here, let's take a quick look at this great base runner." If he can damage your credibility you can lose the case over some innocuous little statement like that; you can lose twenty-five points while trying to pick up one. So as I say, you keep one foot on the truth.

Not only can you not exaggerate your player's positives, but there are times when you are forced to introduce negative information about your own player, about something he doesn't do well. If a player has a big weakness—let's say he has led the league in errors, or he has hit .042 in the pennant race, or he has the worst strikeout to walk ratio in the history of creation or he couldn't hit a left-hander throwing beach balls. Something like that is going to be a part of the case come hell or high water; if you hide from it in your case, the team will introduce it with a great flourish. If you talk frankly about the weakness, you have a chance to present it in the best possible light. If there is no good light, at least you deny the team the opportunity of trumpeting it as fresh news.

The client won't like it, though; he'll always ask you why you had to talk about that. One thing I am asked a lot about arbitration cases is whether or not I use "my methods." They're not in this book, but in my other books I have introduced a lot of complicated, technical ways of evaluating and analyzing ballplayers. The answer is that while the approach which creates them has everything to do with an arbitration case, the methods themselves have almost nothing to do with arbitration cases, for a simple reason: time. You've got an hour to present your case, and you have a tremendous number of points that you need to make in that hour. You probably have twenty-five, thirty comps that you want to introduce and support, plus a handful of points to make about the player's ability, about the team that he plays for or some other peripheral issue. My methods for things like runs created and defensive efficiency are complex, not that easy to grasp. To spend even five or ten minutes explaining an analytical method is really out of the question.

It might be something you'd consider, if you knew for sure that he'd get it, and if you had a good idea that he'd buy it. But first, some people just don't understand complex mathematical systems, and we might be wasting our time trying to explain them. And second, remember that the arbitrator is a professional skeptic. What's the arbitrator going to think? In a partisan procedure, any complicated method is going to tend to strike an arbitrator as having been made up for the purpose of making the player look good. You know, you can always do that; you can always find some way of multiplying and dividing things which focus on this player's particular strengths and make him look good. Even if that's not what it is, even if it's a method that I've used for years because I think it's the best method available, it's going to strike an arbitrator as being something that you just made up. Occasionally I'll use something; for example, I've used the Pythagorean method to estimate what a pitcher's won-lost record would have been had he received average offensive support. But as a rule, I have to leave those guns at home.

The same applies to any "newfangled" statistic; in general, the arbitrator's not going to buy it. I've read a lot of times that the reason for game-winning RBI is that the players like to use them to put something over in an arbitration case. But again, remember who arbitrators are, fifty-five-year-old guys who have been baseball fans for forty years or more. To say that arbitrators regard game-winning RBI with disdain is like saying that a chicken regards a coyote with distrust. If a guy leads his team in game-winning RBI we'll mention it, but never in a million years would I put any weight on the stat. Older baseball fans tend to regard the concept of GWRBI as a personal affront, and on several occasions I have heard arbitrators launch into unsolicited tirades on the subject. You'd sure feel stupid if you based your case on game-winning RBI and then found out the arbitrator hated them.

The general heading of "there isn't time for that" covers a lot of things that people imagine that you might do in an arbitration case. For example, you never say that a player "might" do something, or "has the potential" to do something; you never say that a player is a potential MVP, even if it's true. For one thing, it invites an obvious response from the team: When he does that, he'll get paid for it. Beyond that, there isn't time for it.

Not that all arbitrators are fifty-five years old. Some of them are younger than I am. Some arbitrators sit and watch the hearing like a sphinx, one eye on their watch and staring at you out of the corner of their eye; others are very active, pressing you for more details on exhibits, comparing the team's exhibits to the player's, almost cross-examining you on your case. There's one guy who lets you know exactly how he reacts to everything you say, challenges the weaknesses of your case head-on. That's great; I'd love to have him every case. More often the arbitrator sits there with a noncomittal expression on his face, masking his reactions and trying to reflect an image of judicial impartiality.

Still, you usually have a pretty good idea by the time the

case is over whether you've won or lost. The ruling doesn't officially come in for a day or two, but usually you have an inkling. If an arbitrator is close to buying your position but can't quite, he will usually ask you one pointed, challenging question to give you an opportunity to cover your weakness. If you get asked that question, obviously you're in trouble. If the arbitrator has decided against the club early in the case (or against the player), sometimes he'll go over and swap jolly stories with the GM during a break, trying to soften him up so that the team doesn't take it personally when they lose and maybe won't have the arbitrator shot (dropped from the eligibles list). If one side starts to say things that they know are not true late in the case, as I said, that's a real clear sign that they've lost. Sometimes a case is lopsided; one side doesn't have an argument. Sometimes an agent for one side or the other will make a critical mistake and give away a central comp or something.

And sometimes you're positive you know who won, and the arbitrator will say different; there's a famous story about a 1983 hearing in which, after the case, the team offered to give the player 15 percent of the difference to settle. That's an insult, of course; if you thought it was an even case you'd offer 50 percent to settle, so 15 percent is a token, a way of saying that "we know we kicked your butt but we'll give you a little bit just on the theory that you never know." The player's reps thought about it all night and called the Player's Association the next morning to say that they were going to take the 15 percent. The Player's Association said "It's too late; the arbitrator already called—and you won."

Sometimes you suspect that arbitrators have made their decision based not on what is said during the hearing, but on their own knowledge of the player and of the salary structure. That's very frustrating when it happens, but it isn't necessarily an evil. It is a bad situation if the arbitrator makes a leap of faith based on his failure to understand the material he's been given, but what happens more often is that the arbitrator adds to the material he is given some of his own knowledge, knowledge he has gathered perhaps as a baseball fan, perhaps from studying basic research materials on his own. The knowledge the arbitrator has gathered from other cases he has heard is often tremendously important—for example, in the Walling case the arbitrator knew that the Mets had no intention of using Backman as an everyday player because he had heard the Tim Teufel case the week before.

Another case in which the arbitrator's prior hearings were crucial was the Andujar case in 1980. Although the case was hard fought and lasted forever, we realized later that we probably had the thing won before it ever began, because of a coincidence of scheduling. The day before that hearing, the arbitrator had heard a case for Dave Lemanczyk of Toronto. Lemanczyk's record was quite comparable to Andujar's, so that every comp introduced in our case probably could have been used in Lemanczyk's as well. But there were two crucial differences. First, Andujar's record was a little bit better; Andujar was 12–12 in 1979 and 37–37 lifetime, whereas Lemanczyk was 8–10 in 1979 and 33–54 lifetime, with higher ERAs. Both pitchers had been token All-Stars the year before, but Andujar had pitched in the All-Star game and Lemanczyk had not. And second, the Blue Jays had offered Lemanczyk five thousand dollars more than Andujar was asking for! We sweated it like any other case—but in retrospect, we probably would have had a hard time losing that one.

Which is extreme but not all that unusual; for all that the arbitration war is fascinating to me and I hope at least tolerably interesting to you, the fact is that most cases are probably 80 percent decided before the hearing. The cases are pretty much decided, most of the time, when the figures are filed at the start of the arbitration season.

Start with the position that there is a "true market value" for every player, which falls somewhere between the player's value as it will be seen by the team, and his value as it will be seen by the player's agent. However hard we work (and we work very hard indeed), however clever we think we are, the fact remains that whoever files closer to the true market value is going to win the case the vast majority of the time. What I hope I have been describing here is a process which is brutally honest, a process which forces you to recognize all of the player's weaknesses and forces the teams to recognize all of his assets. In an arbitration case, you can't hide from anything; it is all going to come out. Both sides talk, and the arbitrator reviews the exhibits. No matter what you do, you simply cannot make a player look substantially better than he is. You cannot make the existing salary structure look any different than it really is. And for that reason, if the player's true value is $450,000 and you ask for $600,000, there really isn't anything you can do to win the case.

The best case I've ever been a part of, purely on the basis of the preparation and presentation of the argument, was the Len Barker case in 1983 (following the 1982 season). Barker was a fine pitcher at that time—had led the league in strikeouts a couple of times, had winning records with a bad team three straight years, had pitched the perfect game. We had a lot of things to talk about, and Randy Hendricks outdid himself, put on a hell of a show. But the fact was, we were asking for too damn much money; the figure we had filed at, in retrospect, simply was not justified by the salary structure that applied to Barker. We thought it was when we filed, but we were wrong; we read the structure with our own bias.

By contrast, Tal Smith (presenting for Cleveland) was absolutely sleepwalking that day. There were a couple of individual comps that would completely have wiped us out, and he failed to mention their names; probably because he knew that he didn't have a lot to worry about. I have always thought that if that arbitrator had made his decision based on what he heard in the hearing, as he is supposed to do according to the rules, we would have won it hands down. But we lost.

And frustrating as that is, or was at the time, it's not wrong. We can't complain. A player shouldn't earn his money at the arbitration table. He should get what he earns on the field; nothing more and nothing less. As representatives of the player it is our responsibility to be as sharp as we can, to work as hard as we can, to present the case as professionally as we can—but that doesn't change the fact that a player shouldn't win the case because his agents are smart, hard-working, and professional. He should get the money only if his performance justifies it. At the time it seemed like a case of the system not working, but in retrospect I realize that what really happened is that the system worked even though by the rules it shouldn't have.

There is another way in which the arbitration game as it is actually played is, in my opinion, different from the way in which the rules are written. In theory, the burden of proof is shared equally by the two parties. If the player is at $600,000 and the team is at $400,000 and the true market value is $510,000, then in theory the player should win, because the preponderance of the evidence will be on his side. The true value is above what is called the "breakpoint," which is $500,001. You hear a lot about breakpoints in an arbitration case, but I don't know if most arbitrators pay any attention to them.

In practice, I've always felt that the burden of proof is on the player. If the player wants $600,000, I think he has to prove that the market value is somewhere over $575,000. If the team offers $400,000, they may be way off the market value, but they'll still win if they can show that the player's figure is too high.

That's one explanation (my explanation) of why the teams win over half the time. Another explanation is that the teams, being corporations, are less prone to emotional readings of the market. Many times you have to try an arbitration case because the player himself won't accept that he is what he is; the player thinks he's better than he is, won't accept a fair offer, and forces you into a case that you can't win. That may only account for 10 percent of the cases, but they're all losses for the players; there's no real counterpart for the teams. Another advantage for the teams is the structure of the cases, in which the team presents last, and thus has a better chance to get by with telling a few whoppers. If you think about the structure of the case, which I explained before, you'll realize that the player's side must rebut the team's arguments immediately after they are presented, while the teams have an hour and a half after the player presents his case to analyze it and tear it apart before their rebuttal period. That's another edge for management.

The other reason the teams win over half the time is that Tal Smith pushes the teams that he works for to file good figures. Believe it or not, Tal Smith isn't all that good at presenting an arbitration case; he should be half as good as his reputation. The first two arbitration cases I participated in were both against Tal Smith, when Smith was the general manager of the Astros. We won both cases decisively, but later that year Smith was forced out as Astro GM, and started his business as a consultant. One year later, we viewed with considerable amusement the emergence of Tal Smith as an arbitration genius, as he stormed to (as I recall) seven victories in eight cases in his first year as a consultant, a run of victories that he has since milked for a fortune.

We've faced Smith in arbitration Christ knows how many times since then, and we don't quake at the thought. Tal is boring, pompous, and uses a fixed methodology which makes his presentations predictable in every detail. It's a bullshit methodology to begin with, based on group averages rather than specific comps, and I'm not convinced that anybody buys into it. He also takes on so many cases that he doesn't have time to prepare properly for all of them. He has a team of experts who work with him; there's a guy named Chris Knepp who is very good, but the rest of them will put you to sleep and are prone to innocently kicking away key points of the argument.

With all of that, Smith wins more often than he loses, for the simple reason that, like me, he knows that in most cases the only thing that really counts is the figures that are filed. He gets the teams that he works for to file good figures, and that puts him way ahead.

There are all kinds of different ways to pick a figure. Essentially, the player can file high, file low, or file at the last offer; the team can respond from the same options. I assume this is self-explanatory; if the team's last offer is 400, then they can "file high" at 425–450, "file low" at 350–375, or file their last offer, 400.

Remember that the great majority of cases are settled between the time they are filed and the time they are scheduled to be heard, so you don't necessarily file a figure that you can win; you may file to improve your negotiating position. With three basic options for the team and three for the player, that makes nine possible combinations, and each one sets up a different scenario for subsequent negotiations. I'm not going to run them all down, but suppose that both team and player file high. That means that the team is probably filing closer to the player's real value, which means that in all likelihood the team will win the case if it has to be heard, which in turn means that the player has little leverage in interim negotiations. But it also means that the player has already won a substantial victory. If the negotiating positions are 400/600 and the figures are filed at 450/650, then the player has already won a substantial portion of what he wanted. He can compromise at 25 percent and still get a fair deal, and if he should happen to win at

650—well, that's just gravy. The team knows that it probably will win but is somewhat afraid of an upset; they also face the possibility of paying the player much more than he is worth.

If the player files low and the team files high, then the case won't be heard; they'll whittle away at the remaining difference. If the opposite happens you'll have a very hairy case, with the player winding up either overpaid or underpaid.

Anyway, I'm like Smith; I always want the agents I'm working with to file a figure that they can win if they have to—in other words, to file low. The agents often don't like to file low because if you file low you're giving away part of the difference; if you file at 575 you've given away 25,000 to start with. As an economics student (when I was in college), I've always wanted to design a "game" or a "simulation" to determine what the best strategy is. Any of you economists out there— has there ever been a study of this done? There are a lot of books written about negotiation, but I don't read them. The agents sometimes refer to filing high as "filing to negotiate" and filing low as "filing to win," but I always argue that if you file low your negotiating position is stronger, because both sides will know that you have a realistic chance of winning; if you file high you weaken your chances of winning the case, and thus wind up with less money even though you asked for more. But whether that is accurate or whether it's just my bias, I don't know. I'm biased because I just want to win the cases that I'm involved with; I don't have any vested interest in how much money the player gets.

Which brings up the next question that I am often asked: Don't you feel guilty helping ballplayers make all that money?

Baseball is an industry which generates millions of dollars, and which has generated millions of dollars for a long time. In an arbitration case, only one thing is at stake: whether a baseball player will get some of that money, or whether the owner will keep it. Take a look at who the owners are. They are people of extraordinary wealth and extremely questionable moral worth: Charles Bronfman of the Seagram's family, Gussie Busch of Budweiser, Peter O'Malley, Ted Turner, George Steinbrenner, Ewing Kaufman, John McMullen, Nelson Doubleday, Joan Kroc of McDonald's. I have never been able to understand why it was in the best interests of society for these people to keep the money that baseball generates.

I can understand people thinking that increases in baseball

players' salaries will force increases in ticket prices. I can understand people believing that, but it isn't true. A team sets its ticket prices at that point at which they believe they can maximize their income. The team estimates how many tickets they can sell at six dollars a ticket and how many they can sell at five dollars each and how many they can sell at seven dollars each and what the impact of each would be on concessions and parking, and they fix their prices at that point at which they will take in the most money. That point is precisely the same if their team payroll is one dollar or a hundred million dollars. If you believe they're going to give you a break on a ticket because their costs are low, I recommend that you keep current on your prayers.

I know it's a common belief that the clubs can simply pass along their additional costs "just as they do with every other product," but that argument doesn't prove anything except that economic ignorance is rampant. If you're honest, you'll have to admit that in the years of extreme salary inflation, there was no corresponding increase in ticket prices, which in fact declined over those years in real dollars (meaning that they increased more slowly than the prices of other products in the economy).

When a company's costs rise rapidly, what happens most often is not that they raise their prices, but that they are forced out of existence. The danger of skyrocketing salaries is not that they will increase consumer prices, but that they could force baseball teams into bankruptcy. That hasn't happened, and it won't happen, because a) baseball teams take in an enormous amount of money, and b) agents aren't that stupid. I'm not going to work through the math with you, but the next time you go to a baseball game, keep track of how much money you spend at the park. Three dollars for parking, six dollars apiece for two tickets, one beer and one hot dog apiece, a bucket of popcorn and you're in the neighborhood of twenty-five dollars. If there are thirty thousand people at that game, how much is the team taking in? Multiply that times eighty-one, and then figure about an equal amount for television and radio revenue and merchandising of the logo, and you realize that the players are being paid from a pool of a hell of a lot of money.

In 1962 Don Drysdale went 25–9 for the Dodgers; he was paid $35,000 for the season. Walter O'Malley for the year made $4.35 million from the Dodgers. $4.35 million in 1962 dollars is what . . . 12 to 15 million now? Something like that. Since that time, in addition to inflation, attendance has increased enormously, and radio and television revenue has increased astronomically. If salaries had stayed low, how much of a profit would the Dodger owners be taking home now? Twenty million? Thirty million? More? You tell me what the social good is in O'Malley and Gussie Busch pocketing that kind of a profit.

This used to be an emotional issue. When I started working with agents in the late seventies we had this tremendous feeling that we were working on the side of right and honor. That feeling was fueled by the hypocrisy of owners and their agents, who carried out a pretense that they were acting not in the interests of their own pocketbooks, but in the interests of the fans. Tal Smith actually said in the Joe Sambito hearing (1980) that he was there representing the fans. The arbitrator didn't tell him that he was full of beans, but he doesn't make that argument any more.

Now, of course, it's all different; if there is no social value in Marge Schott and associates keeping an extra million, there is also little social value in the young athletes being paid the incredible sums that they receive. Occasionally you still get some of that old feeling, when you're working with a young player and trying to help him get his first big paycheck after several years in the minor leagues. For the most part, it's all business now; you're just finding the player's slot in the existing structure. But I sure as hell don't feel guilty about helping the players, either.

You know why I work in arbitration cases? Because I love it. I don't make any real money doing this; in fact, one of my problems is that I forget to keep track of my time and often forget to send the agents a bill for my work, which makes them uncomfortable. I love the work; it sends adrenaline pumping through my system like nothing else I do all year. I can work on this stuff for twenty hours, sleep four and get up and go right back to work, alert as can be. I usually work at it so hard it damages my health, and I wind up the arbitration period with a fever, cough and runny nose, but while I'm doing it I just can't stop. One argument leads into the next, one exhibit suggests another, one line of approach points to another one, and I just keep at it.

The reason I love it is not difficult to understand. In the

years when my work was sabermetrics, the principal frustration of the job was simply getting people to look at the evidence. My job was to pick up issue after issue, and ask two questions about each issue: What is the evidence, and what does it mean? Some people believe one thing, some people believe the other, but what does the evidence say? What conclusions can you draw from the statistics? What are the biases and illusions inside the statistics?

When people are arguing about some baseball-related issue, one might think that they would be very anxious to know what the evidence is trying to tell them, and a few people are. But baseball is an insular world in which there is a great deal of thinly veiled anti-intellectualism. Baseball is a world in which BS is often exalted as holy writ while hard evidence is treated with contempt, in which all true knowledge is considered to be derived from experience, and therefore the value of what you have to say is determined by how good a ballplayer you were. An assortment of half-wits, nincompoops, and Neanderthals like Don Drysdale and Don Zimmer are not only allowed to pontificate on whatever strikes them, but are actually solicited and employed to do this, although of course there are also many intelligent men who occupy similar positions. The academic discipline required to sort through statistical evidence and learn what it has to tell you is not only not regarded as admirable, but is seen as a sure sign of a failure to understand baseball's finer points. Reasons are invented to dismiss studies before they are even examined, and if no specific reason comes to mind anything you say can be rejected out of hand because you don't understand baseball, only statistics. All the evidence that is needed to prove that you don't understand baseball is the fact that you do understand statistical methodology.

Baseball lives literally in the dark ages; baseball men have not yet reached the revelation of Sir Francis Bacon, which was in essence that since all men live in darkness, who believes something is not a test of whether it is true or false. I have spent years trying to get people to ask simple questions: What is the evidence, and what does it mean? This is a condition of the world and no one but a fool gets angry with the world because it is what it is, but there are profound frustrations in living in a world which awaits the Enlightenment.

But when the arbitrator comes into the case, what does he ask? *What is the evidence, and what does it mean?* One side says this, and the other side says that, so where do we look? To the evidence, of course.

An arbitrator views the baseball world almost exactly the way that I view it; he wants to know not what you believe or what he believes or what the prevailing "wisdom" is, but what the facts are. And so all of a sudden, everybody else is trying to play my game. All of a sudden, nobody says that there are lies, damn lies, and statistics. All of a sudden nobody says that statistics don't lie but liars can't figure. All of a sudden nobody tells you patronizing little anecdotes about when they were playing in the Three-I League or quotes to you the advice given them by Leo Durocher or the ghost of John McGraw.

It is, in short, suddenly very apparent how ridiculous all of that looks under the brutal light of an honest, give-and-take search for the truth. For one day, general managers, agents, ballplayers, and executives are desperately attempting to look at the baseball world the same way that I look at it 365 days a year. And I wouldn't give that day up for anything.

How much do I really have to do with determining the outcome of a case? Maybe 1 percent, something like that. I think I'm very good at what I do. In fact, I think I'm the best there is. If a player would have a 70-percent chance of winning a case without me, he probably has a 71 percent shot with my help.

I get asked many times what my record is in arbitration cases. In truth, I have no idea. A statistician or a researcher doesn't "win" or "lose" an arbitration case. The man who presents the case—the agent or the lawyer for the agent's team—can maintain and boast of his record if he wants to. The researcher may contribute to victory or defeat, but he does not play a central enough role to make it credible for him to trumpet "his" record; it would be sort of like a left fielder saying that he had won sixty-two games and lost forty-six. A pitcher can say that if he wants to; the left fielder can't.

In addition to that, there are all different levels of involvement in a case. I work with several agents, and I play a different role in each case. Sometimes I may take a phone call from an agent, write up an exhibit and put it in the mail, and never hear from anybody again, not even to say whether the exhibit was used or not. If I counted all the times I've done that, I could claim credit for a lot of wins without knowing whether I really had played any role in the case. Other times I may decide on the comps to be used, plan the attack, write all the exhibits, explain it to the agent on the plane and participate in its presentation. If I only counted those times, I wouldn't have many losses. So any self-edited won—lost record would be meaningless even if I gave it to you.

I'll say this: I think I work with the best arbitration teams in the world. I work with Tom Reich's group and with the Hendricks brothers in Houston, and I don't think anybody in the world presents a case better than we do. We win a lot more often than we lose. But it ain't my place to claim credit for the wins.

Nor is it likely that I will ever be the man who sits in the lead chair and presents the case. Again, whether this is true or whether it is just my ego, I believe that I could present an arbitration as well as, if not better than, anybody else. I think that I am closer to being on the same wavelength as the arbitrator than anybody else is, and I think that would be a tremendous asset to the presentation. But I also recognize that I am not following a career path which leads in that direction. It's like being a general manager; sure, I think I could run a baseball organization. But I'm not following a career path that leads in that direction. I'm not an agent; I'm not going to be one. It's very unlikely that any agent is going to ask me to present a case on his behalf, because their own egos would not allow that.

Salary arbitration has never driven salary inflation. Randy Hendricks told me something in 1979 which I have found to be a profound truth, which was that "Salaries in baseball string down from the top. If Dave Parker was getting one hundred thousand dollars a year, the average player would be very happy to play for thirty thousand dollars to fifty thousand dollars." I have found, in looking at baseball salaries over the last century, as well as in looking at salaries in other industries, that this is an absolute rule; the top figure in each group sets the salaries for that group.

Baseball owners for many years indulged the self-destructive belief that they could pay the best players incredible amounts of money without following through by paying the lesser players. This theory is still popular with fans, the idea that it isn't the salaries of the superstars which have gotten out of hand, but the salaries of the average players. But you have to understand that in any sport, differences between players which seem dramatic in the statistics are very narrow in fact, and that the players know this and for that reason will never accept inequitability in salaries. If the top player on the team is paid a million dollars, then the next-best player on that team is going to be paid $800,000 and the next-best player is going to be paid $600,000 and the average player is going to be paid $400,000 and the young players and subs are going to be paid $200,000, and there isn't anything that anybody can do to stop that from happening. Each group within the team will fix its sights on the group ahead of it, and will fight and scrape and scream and hold out and do whatever they have to do to get up close to the level of that other group.

Arbitration is the way that that gets resolved; arbitration is the process that fixes the interims between the groups. The idea that the salary scale can be slowed down by holding down the lesser players while the top end runs unchecked is like believing that a train can be stopped by pulling brakes on the caboose while the engine roars along. It is not only a false belief, but a destructive belief, one which creates incredible pressures within a team, pitting one player against another. Arbitration is the "hitch" which holds the train together—and thus it is also the force which prevents teams from being torn apart.

Which brings up the final point that I wanted to make. Of all the things which are said about arbitration cases, the most false is that arbitration cases create bitterness between the team and the player. This is such a bizarre distortion of the real situation that it absolutely makes my heart ache to hear people say this, although I know from where it comes; general managers sometimes say that to explain why players should not have the right to arbitrate.

The reality, of course, is that arbitration cases make a tremendous, tremendous contribution toward avoiding bitterness and preventing hard feelings between the team and the player, as well as among players on a team. You have to understand that bitter contract negotiations have been a part of baseball for more than a century. If you are thirty or over you should remember the acrimonious, and destructive, battle between Charlie Finley and Vida Blue, which followed Blue's MVP season in 1971; a little older and you should remember the bloody "joint holdout" of Sandy Koufax and Don Drysdale in 1966. If you read anything about baseball history, you will find similar battles have been waged by most of the game's greatest stars. Joe DiMaggio fought tooth and nail with the Yankees every spring from 1938 until near the end of his career, battles in which the most ugly tactics imaginable were used against him. Ty Cobb engaged in vicious feuds with the Tiger front office in 1914 and in several other seasons. Almost every great player held out at one time or another—before arbitration.

Historically, the majority of the most famous contract battles in baseball have occurred following the first or second outstanding season by a young player. Salaries of baseball players "climb a ladder"; if a player has a season of solid quality he may earn a salary of $175,000; if he has the same season again his salary may jump to $400,000, and if he has it again it may go to $600,000, etc. Although the numbers are bigger now, that has always been true; a player's salary doesn't "mature" until he has been around for five to eight years, after which the raises tend to be token or merely riding along with inflation.

A young player often doesn't understand this or accept it. A player who is new to us—a rookie—has usually spent several seasons (no, several *years*, as in years of his life) in the minor leagues, earning almost no money. During those years he is very aware of the discrepancy between his income and those of the major league stars. So when a young player storms the major leagues and has a season which puts him among the best in the game, he expects his salary to match those that he has been reading about—and it just doesn't work that way. In an ideal world the agent would help the athlete understand the system, but in the real world that is often impossible, because a) the relationship between a young player and his agent is usually a new relationship, not grounded in years of shared experience, and b) the agent fears that he will lose the client if the client senses a lack of support or a lack of enthusiasm for the player's cause. The club expects the young player to climb the ladder, and the player expects to jump to the top of the scale, and the result often is—or was, before arbitration—an explosion.

With arbitration, that doesn't happen anymore (or at least didn't happen, when players got arbitration rights after two years. Now, without arbitration rights until the third year, we are beginning to see some holdouts and increased bitterness for players in the first two years). Arbitration is a method of resolving the dispute; the player goes into the arbitration and says his piece, and he gets an answer. Before, these battles often went on into the beginning of play in April; now, one way or another, the battle is over on February 15. Before, the bitterness engendered by the battle often lingered for years, if the young player felt that he was mistreated; now, the fact that the player does get the opportunity to plead his case gives him the feeling that he has had recourse to justice, even if he has not been pleased with the result.

The clearest example of the salutary effect of arbitration cases in avoiding bitterness is the contrast between the case of Vida Blue and that of Fernando Valenzuela ten years later. The parallels between the players are strong. In each case, a young left-handed pitcher jumped out of the gate in April and dominated the league, drawing huge crowds and going on to a marvelous season. Each player started the All-Star game, led the league in most pitching categories, led his team to a divisional championship and won the Cy Young Award in his first full season. Each player then became embroiled in a salary dispute with his team, which in each case led to a holdout.

But there the parallel ends. Valenzuela, knowing that he would have recourse to an arbitrator one year later, settled his dispute in time to open the season with the Dodgers; Blue, without that opportunity, was left with no way to end his battle other than for one or the other (Blue or Finley) to surrender. Blue held out until May 2, pitched poorly at first, won only six games in his second season and, in the opinion of many, was permanently scarred by the battle. There is no doubt in my mind that had there not been an arbitration system, much the same thing would have happened to Valenzuela. His battle would have been longer, more bitter, and more damaging to both the player and the team than it was.

So it is very odd to hear people say that arbitration cases "create" bitterness. A salary arbitration case can become a place in which bitter feelings are vented—but not in any conceivable way is it the cause of those feelings. The cause of those feelings is that the player wants more money than the team wants to pay him.

In a way, it's like saying that the battle at Gettysburg created hard feelings between the North and South. But really, it's better than that; an arbitration case is war at its best, war fought with the weapons of civility and politesse. All wars should be decided by arbitrators; we'd save a lot of money and a lot of young men. The *best* thing that you can say about arbitration cases is that they prevent bitterness and ill will between player and team from festering. And, as often as not, you all go out to dinner together afterward.

—New Material

On "Saves"

The save rule has finally stopped changing. For about ten years the powers that be couldn't decide what a "save" was; they kept redefining it every two years, which kept the debate about its efficacy and fairness alive. They have settled on a definition now, which has made it possible for the save to become accepted, which gradually it is being. And I, for one, am glad.

There are two basic arguments against the save. One is the "Pitchers are awarded saves in situations in which they are not deserved" argument. Once in awhile somebody will get a save in a 17–3 ball game, and the people who write letters to the editors and call into talk shows will seize on such an occasion and work it for years. "Look at this. Don Hood got a save in a game the Yankees won 14–2! How can the statistic mean anything when somebody 'saves' a 14–2 game?" But you can pick up the paper any Monday morning during the season and find a case where some pitcher "won" a game when what he really did was allow San Diego or Seattle to score five runs off of him in six innings, while meanwhile some other pitcher was being charged with a loss for allowing the New York Yankees four hits and one unearned run while John was pitching a shutout. Where are the letters to the editors saying "Look at this! Dick Ruthven was credited with a win in a game the

Phillies won 17–12. How can the statistic mean anything when a pitcher gets a 'win' for a game like that?" The truth is that saves are far *better* defined than wins and losses are, that the description is far *more* carefully tailored to avoid rewarding an undeserving pitcher than is the description of the "win," which requires of a starter only that he last five. People seize on the occasional undeserved save *because it is uncommon*, whereas they simply accept the large numbers of undeserved wins and losses because they are commonplace. And by the way, why *shouldn't* Don Hood get a save in a 14–2 game? Why should the starter in that game be eligible for a "win" and the reliever not be eligible for a "save"?

The other objection is that saves are imbalanced; there should be a "failure to save" to balance the books. Well, great, count them. It is quite a different thing to say that saves are meaningless without being balanced. People actually say that saves are the only category in baseball where the positive is not balanced by any potential negative, where the player has a possibility of gaining something without any chance of losing something. This is riotous nonsense. Did you ever see a record for runners not driven in? How about double plays not turned? Sacrifice hits not delivered? The record books are full of uncounted negatives.

Not that saves are perfect. They're not, but neither is any other category. People make demands of a "new" statistic that they would never think of making of the traditional data. They demand that the statistic be pure wheat and no chaff. They demand that it tell them all there is to know about the subject. By those standards, all statistics would be found wanting.

—1982

The Split Season of '81

I did not cry out in protest in the summer of 1981 when it was decided to rupture the schedule, and for that omission I feel now (knowing full well that organized baseball would have paid not the slightest attention had I decided to starve myself to death over the issue) that I should apologize to somebody. Unlike most of my readers, I am not a baseball purist or traditionalist. The purist opposes any and all changes in the game, usually on specific grounds but, absent those, on principle. I do not dislike free agency; indeed, I think it has been great for baseball. Esthetically I don't like artificial turf, but I do think the effects of artificial turf on the game have been marvelous. I don't dislike the designated hitter rule. When they came I had no antipathy toward expansion, divisional play or doubleknit uniforms with gaudy colors.

In its own time every change of any significance has been heralded as baseball's doom: night baseball, televised baseball, air travel, the movement of teams to where the population had gone and therefore away from their old fans, the draft of players entering the game, the decline of the minors—each and every one has been proclaimed by purists a tragic and fatal blunder. And yes, you can add the breaking of the color line.

Yet baseball survives. Looking backward, I think you can see that for baseball to have been laced into the past would, in truth, have been much more dangerous than any of these changes. Teams locked into decaying stadiums in areas fast becoming slums, games played on Thursday afternoons with the world at work, half of the population not within driving distance of a team and no televised games for them to follow it with—such are not my notions of remedies for baseball's well-being. The tramp tramp tramp of history is not a death march. I have never written about anything, and please Jehovah, will never write about anything, that it is going to kill baseball. To adapt to an unknown future is treacherous, but to refuse to adapt is suicide.

And so, I said last summer, well, let's give it a try. The state of Missouri was split like the season itself on the issue, the St. Louis side bewailing it, the Kansas City side grateful. "But why should the Royals be given another chance after stumbling around in a daze for two months?" asked Peter Gammons, a question which, if you think about it, has a perfectly good answer: That's one of the rules of the game. You can stumble around in a daze for two months and still win. It happens every year. The purists in our area liked to say that it was unfair for the Royals to be given another chance after having put themselves in an impossible position. But the Royals did *not* put themselves in a position from which they could not recover. The Royals were twelve games behind with 110 to play, and a whole lot of teams have come back from that position to win. *The strike* put them in a position from which they could not recover. I'm not saying that it was fair, only that it seems to me that the sword of fairness was about as jagged on one edge as it was on the other.

OK, we tried it. It was a disaster. Bad teams in the race, good teams out of the race; winners losing out and losers lucking out, people threatening to lose on purpose, one team having to fly halfway across the country the day after the season ended to play a game that nobody was the least interested in to gain an advantage of dubious value, confusing standings and bewildering matrices of possibilities . . . It was the worst of all summers, and it was the worst of all summers.

The best arguments against the ruptured season, it turns out, had nothing to do with fairness. The whole issue of fairness was a red herring that prevented us from sniffing out the real rottenness in the format. The psychological pattern of the game, the gradual build-up day by day, unit by unit from 0–0 to 92–70, was utterly wiped out. It killed my interest in the race. I should have been and wanted to be glad that the Royals were back in it, but in truth I really didn't give a damn. The race for a pennant acquires its significance only from the things which are done in its pursuit, and the great charm of a baseball pennant is that *so much* is done in its pursuit. Detached from the things which had gone before it, the race seemed trivial.

—1982

The 1982 Season

Baseball, 1982. In dry moments in the dead of winter, one could not escape the feeling that baseball in the 1980s is a coda to a symphony finished, a few last notes being sounded to give a sense of finality to something which is in reality already over, its story already told and the audience, being baseball fans, already in the parking lot, gunning the engines and counting the children. But in the cushion-soft cruelty of April, pitches are being thrown, and by this simple act memories are being accommodated, desires fulfilled, and trespasses forgiven. The box scores have begun their familiar march. It doesn't take much to stir the loins of a loving fan.

Not that it was a dull winter. On the contrary, it may have been the first time in history that the off-season was more enjoyable than the season. "It was a fascinating winter," Bowie Kuhn must have thought. "I was on the edge of my seat the whole time." The Toronto Blue Jays took the Boston Celtics to court for tampering with a .187 hitter. Reggie Jackson and Graig Nettles wrestled in a restaurant; George Steinbrenner went three rounds with an elevator. The new general manager of the Chicago Cubs announced that he would lift a thirty-six-year-old ban prohibiting a Cub fan from bringing a goat into Wrigley Field. The new GM of the Kansas City Royals confessed in an interview that he had named his oldest son after Jonathan Livingston Seagull. It beats hell out of listening to Ray Grebey chew on his pipe.

The first prediction for the coming season, then, is an easy one: It has got to be a much better summer than last year's . . . .

—*Esquire* magazine
May, 1982

One of the unique and wonderful things about the 1982 baseball season was that the season of every team worthy of discussion, save Montreal, resolved itself into a very few games in which the team either did it or didn't. Some teams leapt from the starting blocks as if they were on fire ("When you are on fire," Richard Pryor has observed, "people will get out of your way"); others sprang from the blocks and fell immediately to their faces. Teams blew very hot and very cold for 145 games, and when they had done so they saw what they had wrought, which was to put about a dozen teams behind them and a short, happy pennant race ahead. Was ever a year so rich in diamond streaks and onyx implosions? Changes that usually evolve over the course of months were compressed into rock-hard crystal moments. My own team, the Royals, had the pennant race in control on September 15, and then lost ten of eleven games, six to bad teams and the rest to the Angels. In any normal season a collapse of such proportions would have drawn the baleful stares of the nation's press, but in 1982 we were allowed to suffer it alone. In wartime, one ceases to wonder at each report of a rifle.

Do not be too quick to suppose that it would be a wonderful world if every season, every pennant race, turned out the way it was in '82, one week to go and all four races still open for business. The NBA has naively supposed that it would be wonderful if every game was decided in the last two minutes. The problem with a seventeen-game pennant race is that if you know in advance that you're going to wind up with that, it leaves you with 145 games that don't mean a damn thing. Every season isn't like 1982; many pennant races are over by Labor Day, and most are over before the last week of the season. If that wasn't so, if there wasn't the constant danger of being put to sleep by a sudden slump, then the games of May and August would become meaningless, and baseball would atrophy, unable to regain its enthusiasm when the occasion demanded. The 1982 season needed its uniqueness to be so delightful, just as the 1981 season needed its uniqueness to be so painful.

—1983

Obviously, there is a considerable degree of overlap between the two following articles, which were originally written and published three years apart. I could have combined them into one article, I suppose, but decided to re-publish them in their original form, there being distinct elements as well as common ones.

On Statistics

The way in which baseball statistics are understood widely is as a form of language. Suppose that you see the number 48 in a player's home run column. Do you think about 48 of something? Do you think about 48 cents or 48 soldiers or 48 sheep jumping over a fence? Absolutely not. You think about Harmon Killebrew, about Mike Schmidt, about Ted Kluszewski, about Jose Canseco. You think about *power*.

In this way, the number 48 functions not as a number, as a

count of something, but as a word, to suggest meaning. The existence of universally recognized standards—a three hundred average, a hundred RBIs, twenty wins, thirty homers —plus the daily lists of league leaders and the weekly summary of everybody, transmogrifies the lines of statistics into a peculiar, precise form of language. We all know what .312 *means*. We all know what 12 triples means, and what zero triples means. We know what zero triples means when it is combined with zero home runs (slap hitter, chokes up and punches), and we know what it means when it is combined with 41 home runs (uppercuts, holds the bat at the knob, can't run and doesn't need to). Each number in each column draws on its relationship to the millions of others which any baseball fan has sometime seen in the same column and in the other columns as well to evoke an image of . . . to create a sense of . . .

I struggle for words, because that which it evokes and that which it creates a sense of is defined only by the other numbers and other columns. But it is not just baseball which these numbers describe. It is character. It is . . . what?

Let us start with the number 191 in the hit column, and with the assertion that it is not possible for a flake (I would hope that no one is reading this book who doesn't know what a flake is) to get 191 hits in a season. It is possible for a bastard to do this. It is possible for a warthog to do this. It is possible for many people whom you would not want to marry your sister to do this. But to get 191 hits in a season demands (or seems to demand, which is as good for the drama) a consistency, a day-in, day-out devotion, a self-discipline, a willingness to play with pain and (to some degree) a predisposition toward the team game which is wholly inconsistent with flakiness.

It is entirely possible, on the other hand, for a flake to hit 48 homers. Hitting 48 homers is a thing done by large, slow men three-quarters thespian and their egomaniac roommates and reckless men who swing from their reckless heels and sometimes hit and usually don't. But to get back to the 191 hits, is there not someone in your head, reader, when I say "191 hits"? In mine it is Bill White, that coil of graceful tension from the Gibson Cardinals. Whether White ever had exactly 191 hits in a season I don't recall. If he didn't he should have.

But in no case does that imagenumber stand alone, because standing beside it are those other nine columns, and they cannot be empty, unless they signify emptiness. And every combination between columns forms a unique chemistry; 191 hits with 27 home runs suggest one set of images (Bill White, Al Kaline), 191 hits with 12 home runs an entirely different set of images, 191 hits with two homers or 41 homers yet entirely different images. They have different origins: 191 hits with 2 homers results from shortening up on the bat and punching the ball through the middle and suggests an image of a gritty little guy with a quick bat who reads Harry the Hat on hitting. One hundred nincty-one hits with 41 homers results from a hyperpituitary talent and suggests a swagger. It suggests these images far more effectively and precisely and with more depth and complexity than do the words that I have used to recall them.

I have dealt with only two columns and with only one year. When the numbers melt into the language, they acquire the power to do all of the things which language can do, to become fiction and drama and poetry. One hundred ninety-one hits with 27 homers is one thing—it tells one story—when that season comes at the end of a struggle, but it is greatly different, and tells a different story, when it is turned in by a twenty-one-year-old kid who then fades gradually away.

And thus it is not just baseball that these numbers, through a fractured mirror, describe. It is character. It is psychology, it is history, it is power, it is grace, glory, consistency, sacrifice, courage, it is success and failure, it is frustration and bad luck, it is ambition, it is overreaching, it is discipline. And it is victory and defeat, which is all that the idiot unconscious really understands.

So it is that I (and not only I, but millions of others, I believe: lawyers who secrete *Who's Who in Baseball* in their attaché cases and puzzle their secretaries with pages of discarded numbers; actuaries and accountants who swear at numbers all day but caress them in the evening when they return dressed up as league leaders; students who study nothing so assiduously as *The Sporting News*) and the box-score reading legions could cheerfully spend the rest of our days reading numbers that were before discrete acts upon a baseball field. I work very long and very hard at sabermetrics, but my wife cannot tell whether I am working or playing, because the things that I do when I can sneak a minute from my work look so much like the work itself. Both consist in large part of sitting down with a Macmillan *Baseball Encyclopedia* and copying down charts of numbers in fathomless inexhaustible patterns. I used to think I was alone. Now I know that I am unusual only in the extent to which my occupation allows me to indulge myself.

Am I imagining things?

Do not the numbers of Ted Williams detail a story of fierce talent and, by the char of their ugly gaps, the ravages of exquisite frustration that ever accompany imperfect times? Do not the numbers of Roberto Clemente spell out a novella of irritable determination straining toward higher and higher peaks until snapped suddenly by an arbitrary, but now inevitable, *machina*? Do not the stressed and unstressed syllables of Willie Davis' prime suggest an iambic indifference? Is there not a *cavalcata* in Pete Rose's charge? Is there no union of thrill and agony in Roger Maris' numbers? How else can one explain the phenomenon of baseball cards, which is that a chart of numbers that would put an actuary to sleep can be made to dance if you put it on one side of a card and Bombo Rivera's picture on the other.

In my childhood I knew a master storyteller who had lived his life as a rodeo cowboy. A professional athlete, a man who did his work in front of the cheering or indifferent crowds, exactly at the same time as did Bob Meusel and Gene Robertson and Alex Ferguson, he retired and did rope tricks at rodeos and retired and delivered milk to us and retired and committed suicide at eighty-two, two years ago, and nobody knows or cares anything about him *because he has no numbers*. When I am dead, Wade will be forgotten because he has no autobiography in Macmillan, and Alex Ferguson will be remembered as long as there is baseball because he is a part of it.

The variety of stories that can be told is infinite. It is not that the numbers fill out a story which is known from other sources, but that the bits and pieces of knowledge which we have about the ballplayers flesh out the numbers *which are the true story*. There is no other fiction so absorbing and no other poetry so hypnotic.

—1982

On the Fascination of Baseball Statistics

Even before I got into sabermetrics I had always been fascinated by baseball statistics. No one could ever figure out why
this was, and I remember way back when I was in the sixth
grade my teacher used to take me aside and try to talk me out
of wasting all of my time this way. "William," he would say,
"you're a bright enough little kid. You've got lots of charm and
poise, and you're regarded as a leader around here. You hold
your liquor fairly well, and you haven't wet your pants during
school hours all week. So what's all this crappola about baseball statistics?"

As the years went by, I've thought a lot about that. When I
was in high school, Notre Dame contacted me to see if maybe
I wouldn't like to play quarterback for South North Dakota
State, who they had scheduled games against for the next
six seasons and were planning to mash into chinchilla food;
they were quite surprised when I demurred their generous
offer, and insisted instead on playing stupid games with
old box scores that nobody else even understood. My friends
would all get interested in drugs and penal reform; the boys
started to show an interest in the girls and the girls started
to show an interest in fine Corinthian leather and how
they did the special effects in commercials for Ty D Bol
and stuff, but me, I was always mostly interested in baseball
statistics.

Eventually I figured out what it was. I didn't care about the
statistics in anything else. I didn't, and don't, pay any attention
to statistics on the stock market, the weather, the crime rate,
the gross national product, the circulation of magazines, the
ebb and flow of literacy among football fans, or how many
people are going to starve to death before the year 2050 if I
don't start adopting them for $3.69 a month; just baseball. Now
why is that?

It is because baseball statistics, unlike the statistics in any
other area, have acquired the powers of language.

1) *Baseball statistics have the ability to conjure images.*

Suppose that I write down lines of statistics for two players
who do not exist:

	G	AB	R	H	2B	3B	HR	RBI	SB	Avg.
Stan	157	618	119	213	51	19	12	78	29	.345
Freddie	138	484	61	123	17	0	34	84	1	.254

Now let me ask you a few questions about those two players. Which one runs faster? Which one is stronger? Which one is older? If I told you that one of those players was twenty-three years old and the other was thirty-six, would you have any doubt about which was which? Which player strikes out more? Which player plays first base, and which one plays center field? Which one has a twenty-seven inch waist, and which one has thirty-four-inch thighs?

You know the answers to those questions—and yet I told you in advance that the players do not even exist. How can that be? You probably have an image of those players that goes far beyond that level, an image of grace and beauty for the one, an image of a lumbering old right-handed first baseman playing out the string with a bad ball club for the other. You may have decided subconsciously that one is black and the other is blond; you probably have a hazy idea of their histories. What twenty words could conjure up two images of such detail?

2) *Baseball statistics can tell stories.*

This player does not exist; I just made these numbers up:

Year	G	AB	Run	Hits	2B	3B	HR	RBI	BB	Avg.
1964	15	47	6	10	2	1	0	9	4	.213
1965	29	96	12	23	2	1	3	14	3	.240
1966	38	128	20	29	4	2	7	21	9	.227
1967	11	38	6	10	1	0	1	4	4	.263
1968	51	170	26	42	5	2	6	22	14	.247
1969	129	393	59	106	13	4	19	62	44	.270
1970	111	363	39	85	11	3	13	45	37	.234
1971	60	166	20	42	5	1	6	22	18	.253
1972	87	242	25	58	7	2	8	29	25	.240
1973	128	371	60	104	14	3	24	70	40	.280
1974	142	514	51	118	15	3	20	67	47	.230
1975	36	88	10	22	3	0	4	13	9	.250
1976	24	60	6	14	2	0	2	8	6	.233
1977	4	7	1	1	0	0	0	1	1	.143
Total	865	2683	341	664	84	22	113	387	261	.247

Yet you know who this player is, and what his history has been; you can see so many things that these numbers do not directly tell you. He was a minor league power hitter who kept missing his chances to establish himself in the big time. He was called up in September in '64 but didn't hit a home run in 15 games; he got a chance to play during an injury in '65; he started the season with the major league team in '66 but was shipped out after hitting .227 in thirty-eight games. By the time he finally proved himself as a major league player he was pushing thirty, and confined to a platoon role; he was well into his thirties when he had an outstanding season as a platoon player in 1973, and finally became a regular the next year. He hit twenty homers in '74 but his average was a disappointment, and an early-season injury the next year pretty much finished his career. He belongs in a class with Ken Phelps, with Bill Robinson, with Mike Easler; they are players who missed five years out of their careers because they didn't get hot at the right time, and the job wasn't there and waiting for them.

The lines below tell a far different story, a story of a player who was supposed to be one of the greatest ever, but wasn't:

Year	G	AB	Run	Hits	2B	3B	HR	RBI	BB	Avg.
1950	16	52	13	17	5	0	3	7	6	.327
1951	145	546	107	175	46	3	13	41	52	.321
1952	153	597	137	192	42	11	35	113	46	.322
1953	162	615	121	201	48	8	28	110	56	.327
1954	152	573	105	187	39	8	26	101	51	.326
1955	157	590	107	192	37	8	29	107	49	.325
1956	37	138	31	51	10	2	12	36	13	.370
1957	116	428	57	133	23	2	21	74	32	.311
1958	141	534	74	167	30	3	29	106	44	.313
1959	135	498	55	149	26	1	20	76	35	.299
1960	148	523	52	147	29	3	17	68	46	.281
1961	138	490	43	134	25	2	15	64	36	.273
1962	145	506	40	142	26	2	14	65	42	.281
1963	78	104	9	27	5	0	3	12	8	.260
1964	124	335	25	85	16	1	7	37	28	.254
1965	27	44	4	12	2	0	1	5	4	.273
1966	10	17	1	4	1	0	0	2	1	.235
1967	2	3	0	1	0	0	0	2	0	.333
Total	1886	6593	987	2016	410	54	273	1026	549	.306

This player came up late in the season at age twenty, maybe twenty-one, and burned across the sky for sixteen games. After having a great year as a leadoff man in 1951, he began to hit home runs early in the season in 1952, and emerged as one of the bright young stars in the game. He was an outstanding player for three years after that, seemingly destined for the Hall of Fame, yet he also began to have his critics; people began to say that he wasn't as good as he ought to be, and he wasn't growing. In late May of 1956 he was headed toward a season that would remove all doubts and silence all the critics when he suffered a severe injury and was out for the year. Likely it was a knee injury, for when he returned his speed was gone, and though he could still hit he was not the same player. By 1963 he was reduced to the role of a pinch hitter; he was traded that winter to a lower outpost in the second division, where he could get back into the lineup in 1964, but he wasn't up to it. He returned to his old team as a pinch hitter-coach for a couple of seasons after that, and wound up his career there, and not until he was retired a few years did people begin to remember what a heck of a player he had been.

Baseball statistics, quite unlike the statistics pertaining to anything else, can narrate stories of promise and frustration, of opportunities taken and opportunities missed, can tell of speed and grace, of wasted talent and determination overcoming misfortune. They can peg a thousand degrees of success and detail the nature of a thousand failures. Of course they do not tell the whole story; what paragraph of words could tell you all there is to say about the life and times of another man?

Baseball statistics, then, form a kind of primordial literature that is enacted in front of us each day. When supplemented by human details from the sports pages of daily newspapers, by the obituaries of heroes past, when fleshed out by personal glimpses of players actually performing the feats described, this literature acquires a measure of the depth and texture of Dostoevski or Updike. While it is in some respects inferior to other forms of theatrical experience, the baseball career has the advantage of a real tension created by the knowledge that the end of the story lies not in the designs of some calculating and manipulative story master, but is yet to be determined day by day and box score by box score. The impetus that causes men to consume box scores is not very different from the impetus that causes them to enjoy fiction or drama or film or gossip.

3) *Baseball statistics acquire from these other properties a powerful ability to delude us.*

When I speak of the power of statistics to delude us, I am not saying that figures don't lie but liars can figure, or that there are lies, damn lies, and statistics, or any of that ridiculous bullcrap. I get asked on talk shows a lot whether one can lie with statistics, which is a really, really stupid question; of course one can lie with statistics, exactly as one can lie in English, or in German, or in French, or in any other form. There is nothing about the use of a number to make a point that makes a man any more or less honest than he was before.

To go backward on that one for a moment, there was a time when Americans, being an honest, trusting people with a heavy streak of rationalism and an instinctive trust of science, had an unhealthy faith in the validity of statistical evidence. Advertisers sometimes took advantage of this, and when the advertising industry exploded after World War II, this abuse became rampant for a few years. Simultaneously, Americans' belief in science began gradually to wane, and by the late fifties a robust skepticism about statistics and their value had permeated American life. Several books were written (and became quite popular) encouraging Americans not to be so trusting of statistical evidence, books which were good and useful at the time, but which now seem as dated and silly as the naive faith in statistics which they cautioned against.

This reaction was nowhere more felt than in American sportswriting. A superb sportswriter named Jim Murray wrote an article in 1957 for *Sports Illustrated* about "Phony Hall of Famers." By phony Hall of Famers he had in mind people like Ty Cobb—I am not joking—and Rogers Hornsby, who had great statistics but, to hear Murray tell it, never did anything to help a team win a ball game. When Murray wrote about Ted Williams, whom he hated and probably still does, he was absolutely convinced that there was no connection between good statistics and winning teams; when campaigning to get Roberto Clemente the MVP award, he lapsed into a more traditional position.

The evolution of statistical information about baseball, progressing nicely from 1869 to 1955, was frozen solid for a generation afterward. When new statistics have been added, they have most often been well-meaning but sloppily defined attempts to get at the essence of the game by measuring things like "saves" and "game-winning RBIs," rather than modest attempts to generate specific information (like how often a player goes from first to third on a single) that could be pieced together into a whole picture of a player's skills.

From this era of skepticism about statistics, Americans were weaned of their trust in percentage points, and the intellectually lazy adopted the position that so long as something was stated as a statistic it was probably false and they were entitled to ignore it and believe whatever they wanted to. It is not this skepticism, or this ability of statistics to mislead us, to which I refer. It is rather that baseball statistics, acquiring as they do special powers, acquiring as they do connotative meanings unlike those of any other statistics, wrapping us as they do in a ceaselessly unfolding literature of strife and glory, acquire also a special ability to mislead us, and to draw us toward false conclusions.

On a personal level, no one has been more affected by this than Jose Cruz, the great outfielder of the Houston Astros. When I say that this man is a great hitter, I mean that he is a great hitter—as good as, maybe better than, hitters like George Brett, Dale Murphy, Jim Rice and Bill Madlock. We won't reprint all the numbers here, because that isn't what this book is about, but if you look at their stats in road games over the years 1981–84 (about 250–300 games per player), it is obvious that, as long as all players were in neutral parks, Cruz was the best hitter among that group; he outhit Rice, Murphy, and Brett during that period by more than thirty points (in road games) and also had a higher slugging percentage than any of them, including the man who won two MVP Awards during the four-year stretch.

But when the players went home, Dale Murphy went home to Atlanta, Jim Rice went home to Fenway Park, and George Brett went home to Royals Stadium—and all three of them magically became much better hitters. Jose Cruz went home to the Astrodome, the worst hitters' park in baseball, and magically lost thirty points off his batting average and 80 percent of his home run power.

And because that happened, the public at large never realized that Cruz was the great hitter that he was. Cruz' statistics have defrauded him. They have not told his story true and fair, but through an unfriendly interpreter known as the Dome. Cruz' stats, if interpreted by the network of standards which are used to transmogrify baseball statistics into language, and thus make them meaningful to the public, simply fail to reveal the true quality of the man's bat.

—Edited from the 1985 *Baseball Abstract*

On Wild Pitches and Passed Balls

The silliest distinction in the records is between a wild pitch and a passed ball. The official scorer should be assigned to make a factual record of what happens. He should not be assigned to record his opinions about why it happens or whose fault it is. In the case of the wild pitch and passed ball, what happens is precisely the same: A pitch gets away, and a runner advances. Absolutely the only thing that the official scorer has to do is decide who is at fault. It is an arbitrary distinction which creates the official fiction that Charlie Hough merely happens to be on the mound when the catchers develops fingers of stone, but Hough doesn't have anything to do with it. This is not a contribution to the record, but a distortion of it.

—1988

Section
V
RESEARCH

Summaries of Studies

One of the staple ingredients of the annual *Baseball Abstracts* was a series of scientific studies of baseball-related issues. This field of knowledge is called sabermetrics, and sabermetric articles were in a sense the guts of the book, the thing which most identified the book in the minds of the readers.

Science, even when one studies a game, is not a game itself; it involves unavoidable rigors. There are requirements of science which one is not free to dispense with merely because they create an ugly book. In reporting a scientific study, one must give details how the study was done sufficient to allow a reader to replicate the study if he chooses to do so. This requires the inclusion of technical material which cannot be written in such a way that it can easily be taken in by the average reader. In many cases it requires the inclusion of charts and data which is not an end product and thus is not interesting in and of itself. This is an awkward requirement for a popular book, but in my opinion it would have been dishonest not to have done it, and to have said simply that I did the study and you should trust me. Authority and science are an unholy combination; the scientist must never ask the public to accept his conclusions because of his own expertise.

However, after the studies have been published, it is acceptable to describe those studies in a more informal manner—understanding that this gives the reader the option of returning to the original source if he so chooses. That is the purpose of this section: to provide brief, informal summaries of the scientific investigations which appeared in the annual editions of the *Baseball Abstract*.

Most of the issues that I tried to investigate were so small that after a couple of years they retain little interest, and are really not worth recounting (such as a study of whether Reggie Jackson hits better in front of large crowds and a study of whether Rich Dauer had hit better when hitting second than when batting at the bottom of the order). There are other issues which I returned to over and over, and some methods which were used repeatedly, which will be explained here in a general way without specific references.

I also have edited since 1982 the *Baseball Analyst*, a small journal of sabermetric research. Some studies from the *Baseball Analyst*, by myself and others, will also be referenced here. There is no connection between this *Baseball Analyst* and the annual Elias publication of the same name.

I have tried to alphabetize these by subject . . . .

AGING PATTERNS, CHANGES IN
PERFORMANCE AS PLAYERS AGE

A long study of aging patterns was presented on pages 191–206 of the 1982 *Baseball Abstract*. The most essential conclusion of the study was that all groups of players (except knuckleball pitchers and those specifically selected because they had their best years at some other age) reach their peak value at the age of twenty-seven and decline thereafter. The peak period for ballplayers is not twenty-eight to thirty-two, as was once believed, but twenty-five to twenty-nine. Almost every accomplishment (twenty-win seasons, hundred-RBI seasons, winning a batting championship, winning a Gold Glove, etc.) is more common at age twenty-seven than any other age.

The study also reported:

1. That there is a clear relationship between the average age of a team's regulars and the probability that they will improve in the next season.

2. That all players as a group retain 77 percent of their peak value at the age of thirty, and barely over one-half of their peak value (53 percent) at the age of thirty-two.

3. That almost all groups of players (such as superstars, marginal players, pitchers, relief pitchers, etc.) follow essentially the same pattern as groups, although there are important differences because superstars reach the majors somewhat earlier and are able to stay in the major leagues much longer.

4. That contrary to popular belief, power pitchers age more slowly and last much longer than do "finesse" or "control" type pitchers.

Another article about aging patterns appeared in the August, 1982, edition of the *Baseball Analyst* (article by Dallas Adams). I also wrote about aging patterns in the December, 1985, edition of the same. Steven Roney in the August, 1987, edition of the *Baseball Analyst* reported on the percentage of home runs hit before and after age thirty.

THE AMATEUR DRAFT

The largest study that I have ever undertaken or published dealt with baseball's amateur draft; it was published as the first special edition of a newsletter that I ran for a couple of miserable years. The method used in this newsletter was to examine first the entire list of players drafted in spots one through fifty in the drafts of 1965–83, and to establish the value of each player taken in that draft. From the value of the players taken, I established the value of every draft pick, that value being the value of the average pick from a comparable position; in other words, the value of draft pick numbers forty through fifty was established by the number of good players who were taken with draft picks forty through fifty over a period of years. The value of the number one draft pick was obviously highest, and the value of each subsequent pick declined.

From there, categories of players were compared to the value of the draft picks which were invested in them—for example, all players drafted from the state of Florida were compared to the draft picks invested in them. A few of the questions examined by the study included:

1. *How many superstars are high draft picks?*

At the time of the study, virtually all of them. I made a list of Most Valuable Players from 1971 through 1983, and they were almost all first or second round draft picks. From 1984 through 1988, surprisingly, this has no longer been true; Dawson, Mattingly, George Bell, Willie McGee, and Jose Canseco are all low-round draft picks or undrafted. Many superstars still are among the first players drafted, like Roger Clemens, Kirby Puckett, Dwight Gooden, Darryl Strawberry and Kirk Gibson, but the pattern doesn't seem quite as clear now as it was five years ago.

2. *What is the chance that a number one draft pick will turn out to be a superstar?*

The draft usually produces one superstar somewhere among the top fifty picks. The chance of getting that player with a number one draft pick is about one in eighteen. The chance of getting a superstar with a number ten draft pick is about one in thirty. The chance of getting a superstar with a number fifty draft pick is about one in 130. The chance of getting a superstar with a number three hundred draft pick is probably about one in 2,500.

3. *What is the chance of getting a star player?*

With the first pick, about one in five. With the tenth pick, about one in nine. With the fiftieth pick, about one in sixty.

4. *What is the chance of getting at least a good ballplayer?*

With the first pick, a little better than 50 percent. With the tenth pick, about 1 in 3. With the fiftieth pick, about 7 percent.

5. *Is there a difference between players drafted out of high school and out of college?*

A tremendous difference. In the years 1965–83, draft picks invested in college players yielded a rate of return essentially twice that of draft picks invested in high school players. The difference is so great that it is apparent in almost every year's draft. In many of the early drafts, in the first fifty draft picks there would be forty players taken out of high school and ten out of college—and the ten college players taken would go on to do as much in the major leagues as the forty players taken out of high school. There was a night-and-day difference in the rates of return. Players drafted out of college were more likely to play in the major leagues, more likely to become major league regulars, more likely to become major league stars and more likely to become major league superstars.

Because of this, of course, teams stopped drafting players out of high school (with their top picks) and started drafting them out of college. Note what I am not saying: I am not saying that a young player should go to college, or that he will develop better if he does. It's the teams' drafting record that I was evaluating, not the players' options. It may well be that the reason for this difference was simply that the teams could scout and evaluate the college players more accurately than the high school players. But for whatever reason, the teams which drafted college players did very, very well in comparison with those who drafted high school kids. Players drafted out of college returned 160 percent of the value invested in their draft picks; players out of high school, only 87 percent.

6. *Was there a difference between pitchers and non-pitchers who were drafted high?*

Pitchers who were drafted *very* high (one through ten

spots) in the years 1965–83 proved on the whole to be terrible investments, returning only 56 percent of the value invested in their draft picks. After the number ten spot, however, there was no significant difference between pitchers and non-pitchers in this respect.

7. *What about players drafted from other positions? Any big splits?*

Nothing tremendous. Outfielders tended to pan out better than infielders, but the difference wasn't enormous.

8. *Were there any areas of the country which were over-scouted or under-scouted?*

I looked at this because I suspected that California players might be over-scouted and over-drafted. Scouts spend a lot of time in California because that's where they can always go to see a game, but that doesn't necessarily mean that that's where the best athletes are going to be.

This theory proved not to be true—California players have justified and indeed more than justified their investment, with a return rate of 116 percent—but I did find sharp regional patterns in the analysis. The South has been tremendously over-scouted and over-drafted, and almost every southern state has a poor rate of return. As a whole, players drafted from the south had yielded only 60 percent of the value of the draft picks invested in them. Florida, the state receiving the most attention in the draft other than California, had yielded a return rate of only 42 percent, meaning that a player drafted out of Florida had less than one half the chance of panning out of an average draft pick. On the other hand, players from the northern industrial states and the Great Lakes region had yielded out at a terrific rate, with players from Ohio, Michigan, Illinois, and Minnesota returning about 150 percent of the draft value invested in them.

In part, this may have been because the players drafted from the south tended to be drafted out of high school, while those from the Great Lakes region, like Dave Winfield, Bob Welch, and Paul Molitor, tended to be drafted out of college.

9. *When can a draft crop be evaluated?*

A group of players coming out of a draft will reach their peak value six to eight years later. The players drafted in 1989 will reach their peak value between 1995 and 1997.

I also examined the theory that the draft has created greater competitive balance in baseball. As George Steinbrenner has recently explained/complained about, baseball teams which finish well consistently don't get as many shots at the top prospects, and thus are dragged backward.

I found that the impact of the draft on baseball as a whole was, in fact, quite sufficient to create such an effect, and indeed sufficient to make it almost impossible for any team to become as dominant as the great teams of the past were. The amateur draft is, in all likelihood, in some measure responsible for the competitive balance of the 1980s.

ON ARTIFICIAL TURF SHORTENING CAREERS

A study on pages 179–81 of the 1986 *Baseball Abstract* examined the theory that artificial turf shortens players' careers. The method used was to go back to the 1973 season, and identify extremely similar players, one of whom played on artificial turf and one of whom did not. For example, Greg Luzinski of 1973 (twenty-two years old, .285 average with 29 home runs, 97 RBIs, very slow) was paired with Jeff Burroughs (also twenty-two years old, .279 average, 30 home runs, 85 RBI, also very slow). Luzinski played on artificial turf; Burroughs, on grass fields.

The study found no evidence that artificial turf was shortening players' careers. In fact, within the study (forty-eight matched sets), the players who played on artificial turf actually had substantially longer careers than the players who played on grass fields.

ARTIFICIAL TURF, TYPES OF TEAMS SUCCESSFUL ON

A number of studies in the *Baseball Abstract* first suggested and then demonstrated that the common idea of what type of team has an advantage on artificial turf (a fast team with high batting averages, a team with line-drive hitters who hit doubles and triples and play good defense) has no basis in fact. The first suggestion of this idea was on page 29 of the 1983 *Abstract*; it recurred on pages 40–41 of the 1984 *Abstract*. A study on page 257 of the 1985 *Baseball Abstract* looked at a group of ten very fast hitters to see whether they had hit better on artificial turf, and concluded that there was "no real reason to conclude that fast men do or do not hit better on artificial turf."

The first major study of the issue appeared on pages 195–98 of the 1986 *Baseball Abstract*. This study established a "statistical profile" of the type of team which is supposed to do well on artificial turf, and then compared every team of the years 1977 to 1985 to that profile, selecting the teams which were most similar and the teams which were least similar to the profile. The teams which fit the profile best were teams from the Royals and Cardinals, plus the 1983–84 Toronto Blue Jays and the 1979 Pittsburgh Pirates; all played on artificial turf in their home park. These teams, in fact, did *less well* on artificial turf than they could have been expected to do. They had small home-park advantages, and when on the road they performed better on grass fields than on artificial turf.

However, the study also identified teams which fit the profile of a turf team *least* well.The "poor turf-type" teams did, in fact, do very poorly on artificial turf.

In the February, 1987, edition of the *Baseball Analyst*, Sandy Sillman published a study which attempted to identify the real characteristics of teams which were successful on artificial turf. My study had started with the profile of teams which should have been successful and looked to their real records; Sillman's study started by identifying the teams which were in fact successful on artificial turf, and then tried to construct a profile of them. His study found that it was not possible to do this; the teams which were successful on artificial turf had essentially the same characteristics as other teams of the same overall ability. Sillman also looked at individual players to see what type of hitters hit well on artificial turf, and found that for hitters, the advantage lay not with speedsters but with power hitters. (Which makes a kind of sense when you think about it, because what artificial turf does is make the ball move faster. Who is going to be helped by that as a hitter—a slap hitter or a hitter who drives the ball? It would seem obvious that it would be a hitter who hits the ball hard—thus, a power hitter.)

Another related article by Robert Stewart Smith appears in the June, 1984 edition of the *Baseball Analyst*. An article by Craig Wright in the October, 1985, edition of the *Baseball Analyst* examines the effectiveness of ground-ball pitchers on artificial turf.

ASTROLOGICAL GROUPINGS IN TYPES
OF PLAYERS

An article by John Holway in *The National Pastime* suggested that there were astrological patterns in ballplayers—in other words, that certain types of players tended to be grouped under common birth signs. I did a study of this issue which was published in the April, 1988, *Baseball Analyst*. I studied the issue by identifying "most-similar" players for all major leaguers no longer active who played 1200 or more major league games. (For example, the most similar player to Willie Horton is George Foster. The most similar player to Nellie Fox is Red Schoendienst.) I found that there was no tendency of players with the same birth sign to show as most-similar, or as more similar than average. In short, there are no such patterns.

ATTENDANCE, PITCHER'S EFFECT ON

Many studies reported in the *Baseball Abstracts* of 1982–84 showed that only one pitcher during that time had an important impact on attendance at the games he pitched, that being Fernando Valenzuela. Outstanding pitchers did not, on the whole, draw more fans per start than poor pitchers, to any detectable extent.

BIORHYTHMS

An article on pages 258–59 of the 1984 *Baseball Abstract* examined the theory advanced in a 1977 book by Bernard Gittleson, a book entitled *Biorhythm Sports Forecasting*. That book claimed that the performance of athletes varied according to three cycles, a twenty-three-day physical cycle, a twenty-eight-day emotional cycle, and a thirty-three-day intellectual cycle.

The book argued that players would perform best when on a "triple high" and most poorly when on a "triple low." I charted the performance of eleven outstanding hitters over the course of the 1983 season. The players, as you might have expected, performed no better when theoretically on a triple high than when on a triple low. There were no observable variations in performance which would have been consistent with Gittleson's theory.

BIRTHDAYS

A study on pages 156–57 of the 1983 *Baseball Abstract* examined the performance of players on their birthdays, and reported that, in the 1980 and 1982 seasons, players having birthdays had hit an overall .290 (1980) and .337 (1982).

Subsequent studies of the 1983 and 1984 seasons did not show a similar effect. The 1983 study is reported on page 264 of the 1984 *Baseball Abstract*.

COLLEGE BACKGROUND, IMPACT ON DEVELOPMENT OF PLAYERS

On page 278 of the 1986 *Baseball Abstract*, I reported on a study which defined matched sets of players who did and did not have college backgrounds, and attempted to see whether there was a difference in their subsequent development. The study was based on the 1973 season; for illustration, George Hendrick was paired with Oscar Gamble. Each player was twenty-three years old, and their batting stats were very similar, Hendrick hitting .268 with 21 homers, while Gamble hit .267 with 20 homers. Hendrick had attended junior college for a year or two, while Gamble had not, so Hendrick represented the "college" group.

The indication of the study was not strong, but it suggested that players with a college background might have an advantage in future development. The players with college backgrounds played 12 percent more games after 1973 than those who had not attended college.

DH RULE, EFFECTS ON PITCHERS

A study on pages 105–06 of the 1983 *Baseball Abstract* examined the theory that the designated hitter rule was creating a strain on pitcher's arms which was causing pitchers to burn out early. The method used was to list all of the pitchers pitching two hundred innings in a season in each league, and then to ask how many of those pitchers were still doing the same one year later, two years later, three years later, etc.

The data resulting were consistent with the theory that there was a "DH burnout," which is to say that the percentages of repeating pitchers were distinctly higher in the National League than in the American.

ELEVATION, EFFECT OF ON HOME RUNS

A gentleman named Dick O'Brien has established (page 215, 1988 *Baseball Abstract*) to my satisfaction that the elevation at which a park lies has a major impact on how many home runs will be hit there—probably, in fact, a more major impact than the dimensions. The reason so many home runs are hit in Atlanta, despite normal dimensions, is simply the elevation of the park.

The first article by O'Brien about this appeared in the June, 1986, edition of the *Baseball Analyst*.

FARM SYSTEM, IMPORTANCE OF IN BUILDING A TEAM

A study on pages 141–43 of the 1984 *Baseball Abstract* examined the relationship between the amount of major league talent that had been produced by each major league farm system (how many stars, how many superstars, etc.), and the performance of that team over a period of years. That study concluded that there was a surprisingly weak relationship between the two, and therefore that the importance of a strong farm system to a strong team may have been overstated.

This conclusion was repudiated in a later *Abstract*, which studied the same issue in a different way and reached a more positive conclusion. In retrospect, I made one of the most basic mistakes in research: I concluded that because a relationship was not visible in the data that I assembled, no relationship existed. I should have realized that if you search every apartment in Manhattan for a Sasquatch and don't find one, that hardly proves that the Sasquatch does not exist; it may be simply that you have been looking in the wrong place. The correlation that I was looking for exists; I was merely looking in the wrong place.

Another article about farm systems appeared in the October, 1982, *Baseball Analyst*, an article by Craig Wright.

FREE AGENTS, IMPACT ON TEAM OF SIGNING

A study on pages 244–46 of the 1986 *Baseball Abstract* examined the impact of signing or losing a major free agent on the ball club's fortunes. After drawing up a list of the major free agent movements of the years 1974–84, I tracked what happened to four teams: the team which lost the player, the team which signed him, the team whose record over the previous two years was most similar to the team which lost him, and the team with the record most similar to the team which signed him.

The study showed that the teams signing free agents gained no advantage at all in the first year following, but gained a small advantage over a period of years—a matter of two or three games a year. The teams losing free agents were essentially unaffected by the loss *unless they sustained a series of free agent losses*, in which case they were usually devastated by the losses.

GOING FIRST TO THIRD ON A SINGLE

A study on pages 156–57 of the 1984 *Baseball Abstract* examined the ability of the members of the 1983 Texas Rangers to go from first to third on a single. The study found that there were distinct, even extreme, differences between individuals in this respect. While the team average was 30 percent (players on first base when a single was hit went to third base 30 percent of the time), individual figures for regulars and near-regulars ranged from 53 percent to 0 percent. I would like very much to see these records compiled and reported systematically, since I think the ability under scrutiny is relatively important and extremely easy to keep track of.

The study also found that Ranger players went first-to-third on a single to right 53 percent of the time, on a single to center 31 percent of the time, and on a single to left 18 percent of the time.

The 1986 *Abstract* passed along data from a similar study of the Seattle Mariners, a study done by Jeff Welch. That study found that the Mariners went from first to third on a single only 24 percent of the time, with individual figures ranging from 41 percent to 14 percent. The Mariners' figure was lower because, in addition to being a slow ball club, they play in a small ball park (meaning the outfielders don't have to play as deep) and were largely a right-handed hitting team (meaning that most of their singles went to left field). That study is on pages 97–99 of 1986 *Abstract*.

A related category which should also be recorded is baserunning errors—the number of times a player is put out on the basepaths when not forced out and not charged with a caught stealing. The two studies suggest that a team normally loses forty-five to fifty base runners in a season due to baserunning errors.

A somewhat related study by Dallas Adams was published in the March, 1987, edition of the *Baseball Analyst*.

ON HOT STREAKS

It is the suspicion of most sabermetricians and the conviction of some that hot streaks and slumps of players are primarily random fluctuations, and not in the usual case created by "momentum" or "seeing the ball well" or any other such factor. A study by Steven Copley (pages 230–31, 1986 *Baseball Abstract*) looked at the performance of members of the Houston Astros in the 1984–85 seasons to determine whether players hit better following a ten-game stretch in which they hit well, and found that there was no relationship; players as a whole hit no better when they had hit .350 in the previous ten games than when they had hit .150.

This may be obvious, but to be perfectly clear: It is the assumption of most baseball men and writers that when a player has been hitting well (when he is "hot") he will continue to hit well (at least for one more game, at least to some extent), and when he has been in a slump he is less likely to have a good day. Copley found that in fact a player who was perceived as being in a slump was neither more nor less likely to get a hit in any given game. If a player who has hit well in recent games continues to hit well, then it may be assumed that there is a "reason" or a "cause" for the hot streak. If, however, the hot streak evaporates at the moment of recognition, as Copley's study shows, then the hot streak is probably simply a random fluctuation, and its recognition has no real value.

A study of team momentum appeared on page 92 of the 1988 *Baseball Abstract*, and looked at the frequency with which teams followed a win with a win or a loss with a loss. The study found that in 1987 the average major league team followed a win with a win or a loss with a loss slightly less often than would be expected by random chance if there were no such thing as momentum, which is to say that they did so *much* less often than would be expected if there were such a thing as momentum. In simple English, teams developed winning streaks and losing streaks only to such an extent as luck should dictate, and not to the extent that one would expect if momentum or some other factor was creating fluctuations in their ability to win.

Another study of team momentum was published in the final edition of the *Bill James Baseball Abstract Newsletter*.

LATE INNINGS, RELATIVE IMPORTANCE OF

Many people believe that the difference between good teams and poor teams is in what they do in the late innings or at other crucial times. As one can easily see if one looks at the runs scored and allowed by innings, good teams in fact distinguish themselves from poor teams very early in the game. Good teams outscore poor teams or average teams in the first three innings and the middle three innings by just as much as in the late innings.

A study examining this issue was published on pages 75–77 of the 1983 *Baseball Abstract*. A related study was published by Scott Segrin in the June, 1985, edition of the *Baseball Analyst*.

LATE-SEASON SUCCESS, CARRYOVER VALUE OF

A study on pages 229–30 of the 1986 *Baseball Abstract* examined whether a team which finishes the season playing well tends to continue to play well in the following season. The study identified sets of teams with identical won-lost records for the season, but one of which finished the season playing well while the other finished the season playing poorly.

The study found that there was a significant carryover effect; the teams which finished the season playing well did, in fact, do substantially better in the following seasons.

THE LAW OF COMPETITIVE BALANCE

The Law of Competitive Balance states that all things in baseball are drawn powerfully toward the center. Teams which win a lot of games in one season show a powerful tendency to win fewer in the next year. Players who hit for a high batting average in any season have a powerful tendency to decline in batting average in the next season. These are among the many consequences of the Law of Competitive Balance, which is discussed at length in the 1983 *Baseball Abstract* (pages 220–22), an edited version of that article appears on pages 263–70.

LEADOFF MAN, IMPORTANCE OF GETTING ON BASE

A study by Chuck Waseleski of the Boston Red Sox' 1983 season revealed that the Red Sox scored 240 percent more runs (3.4 times as many runs per inning) in innings in which their leadoff man reached base as in innings in which the leadoff man did not reach. The study was reported on page 129 of the 1984 *Baseball Abstract*.

An article by Waseleski on a related subject also appears in the April, 1984, edition of the *Baseball Analyst*, with a response by Charles Hofacker in the edition of August, 1984, and an additional response by Dallas Adams in the edition of June, 1985.

LEFT-HANDED PITCHERS AND PENNANT RACES

A study in the 1983 *Baseball Abstract* (page 63) observed that, for no known reason, first-place teams tend to have more left-handed starting pitchers than do other teams; there is a surprisingly strong correlation between the number of left-handed pitchers (as measured by starts or innings pitched by left-handed pitchers) and the number of games won by the team. Over the period 1973–82, first-place teams had 44 percent more left-handed pitching than last-place teams, and, perhaps more strikingly, first-place teams had more than second-place teams, second-place teams more than third-place teams, third-place teams more than fourth-place teams, etc.

Although this tendency doesn't seem to make any sense, it has persisted and in fact grown stronger in the five years since the original study.

LEFT-HANDED PITCHERS, MATURATION OF

A study published on page 211 of the 1983 *Baseball Abstract* examined the theory that left-handed pitchers mature late. I have seen several people quoted as saying that left-handed pitchers don't mature until age twenty-six, and, however arbitrary the theory seems, I thought I should examine it.

The study found that there was no basis for the belief; left-handed pitchers mature gradually and in a normal progression, and nothing noteworthy happens to left-handed pitchers at the age of twenty-six.

LINEUP EFFECTS ON INDIVIDUAL BATTING PERFORMANCE

It is a popular theory among sportswriters that the hitter coming up behind a given hitter has an effect on the player's batting performance. I studied this issue on several occasions, and was never able to document such an effect; for example, although it was commonly reported that Dale Murphy hit much better when Bob Horner was in the lineup than when he was out of the lineup with an injury, in fact Murphy never had a season in which he hit dramatically better with Horner in the lineup, and over a period of years actually hit somewhat better with Horner out of the lineup than in the lineup. In 1987, when Bob Horner left the Braves, Dale Murphy had his best season. (Murphy's records with Horner in and out of the lineup for every year 1976–84 are given on page 258 of the 1985 *Abstract*. The data for 1985 are given on page 244 of the 1987 *Abstract*.)

It is my belief that the batting changes which are usually interpreted in this way, such as the increase in Tim Foli's batting average which occurred when he joined the Pirates in 1979, are in fact usually created by differences in ball parks, rather than by differences in the surrounding hitters.

MANAGERS, WHEN THEY ARE FIRED

A study in the 1986 *Baseball Abstract* (pages 86–88) attempted not very successfully to pinpoint the conditions under which managers get fired. The study found that when teams had poor seasons (finished six games worse than they could have been expected to finish in view of their record over the previous two years), they changed managers during or after the season 58 percent of the time. It also found, however, that when teams had highly successful seasons, they also changed managers during or after the season much more often than I would have expected (26 percent of the time).

MINOR LEAGUE BATTING STATISTICS

It is a common belief in baseball that minor league batting records are not a reliable indicator of a player's batting skill. It is my belief, originally proposed in a newsletter but explained and defended at more length on pages 5–15 of the 1985 *Baseball Abstract*, that minor league stats are exactly as reliable as a guide to future major league performance as are previous major league stats.

You have to remember that, even in the major leagues, batting statistics do not precisely represent batters' abilities; what a player hits in the Metrodome may be dramatically different from what the same player would hit in San Diego. In the minor leagues, the extremes of park effects can be much greater than they are in the major leagues, so that a player who hits .350 with 45 home runs at El Paso might hit .270 with 15 home runs at Syracuse. That creates powerful distortions in the records of minor league players, and that does make it difficult to perceive the player's ability accurately.

In addition, major league players actively spread the belief that minor league batting statistics are meaningless because this belief increases their job security. If executives realized that they could project what a player will hit in the major leagues based on his minor league performance, they would be much less reluctant to make changes which involve giving a major league job to a minor league player.

My article argues, and the study proves to my own satisfaction, that *if* you take the time and the trouble to adjust for the illusions of minor league parks, and if you adjust also for the better competition of the major leagues, then minor league batting statistics are a perfectly reliable indicator of a player's hitting ability. Another article relating to this issue appears on pages 160–64 of the 1985 *Baseball Abstract*. The March, 1987, edition of the *Baseball Analyst* published major league equivalencies for minor league players of 1986 who were candidates for regular season jobs—figures which have by and large proven to be extremely accurate projections of what those players would do in the major leagues.

In my opinion, this is the most important thing that I learned in my years of studying sabermetrics in terms of its potential ability to help a baseball team.

MVP VOTING, TEAMS WHICH
HAVE DONE WELL IN

A study on pages 33–34 of the 1983 *Baseball Abstract* compared the performance of teams in award voting to the performance of teams in the pennant race. The method developed was to award points to teams in one chart for winning the league championship, winning the division championship or finishing second in a pennant race, and to award points in another chart for winning MVP Awards, Cy Young Awards, the Rookie of the Year Awards. The key point is that since there were an equal number of points per league per season in each chart, over time there was a tendency of the two to balance out; most teams had won about as many points in one chart as in the other. For example, the Baltimore Orioles had 26.5 points in each chart, the Cincinnati Reds had 25 points in each chart and the Seattle Mariners had zero in each chart.

The goal of the study was to focus on those teams which had done better than expected or worse than expected in award voting. The two teams which had done the most poorly in award voting relative to the performance of the team were (at that time) the Pittsburgh Pirates and the Kansas City Royals, which between them had seven times as many "Performance" points as "Award" points. Since 1983 the Pirates have done nothing in either category, so would still be where they were. The Royals, however, have since then added a World's Championship, a division championship and two second-place finishes with only one individual award, so they would now stand out as the most "unlucky" or "victimized" team.

The most "over-awarded" team at that time was the Milwaukee Brewers, followed by the Twins and Red Sox. One of the surprises of the study was to find that the Yankees had won fewer awards than was justified by the performance of their team. Many people believe that the New York players have an edge in MVP/Cy Young voting, but on expanding this study so that it includes all New York teams and a longer period of time, it is evident that this is clearly untrue, and that in fact there may be "reverse discrimination" against New York players. New York teams since World War II have won markedly and consistently fewer awards than would be expected in view of the performance of their teams.

OFFENSIVE PLAYERS, TYPES OF

A study entitled "Pesky/Stuart," which appears on pages 5–10 of the 1982 *Baseball Abstract*, addressed the question of which is more valuable to a team: a high-average singles hitter (like Johnny Pesky) or a low-average power hitter (like Dick Stuart).

The study reported on a method (used in all subsequent editions of the book, with changes) which estimates the number of runs created by each individual player. The conclusion of the study is that the two types of players are essentially of equal value as types, the distinctions between them being those between individuals, and not anything as simple as one type being inherently superior.

An incidental conclusion of the study is that the most effective offensive player of all time was Babe Ruth (surprise, eh?), and that in his best season (1921) he created about 233 runs for his team.

OUTFIELD-TO-THIRD BASE CONVERSIONS, SUCCESS OF

In a couple of books I had commented that conversions of outfielders to third base almost never seemed to work. A reader (Steven Goldleaf) studied the issue and concluded that the outfield-to-third base conversion was successful about one-fourth of the time.

However, Steven was awfully generous in determining what was a successful conversion, and used a standard for inclusion in the study which automatically eliminated many of the most dramatic failures. It would seem to me that an estimate of 5 percent success would be as reasonable as 25 percent.

PARK EFFECTS

It is a general principle of annual *Baseball Abstracts* that the statistics of individual players, which many people regard as representing individual skills and accomplishments, are in fact to a tremendous extent derived from the context in which the statistics are compiled. For example, it is probably one hundred times easier for a player to lead the league in batting average while playing in Wrigley Field in Chicago than it would be to lead in batting average while playing in Shea Stadium or the Houston Astrodome. In the ten years 1976–85, the Chicago Cubs allowed fewer home runs in road games than any other team in their division; in their home park, they allowed more home runs than any other team. Over the same ten years, they also hit fewer home runs in road games than any other major league team; in their home games, they were second in the league in home runs. (Data given on page 187, 1986 *Baseball Abstract*; totals for all teams given throughout that book.) But park effects alter not only home run totals, which people are generally aware of although they underestimate the effect, but also every other statistic, including batting average, strikeouts and walks, doubles and triples, stolen bases and stolen base percentage, and in many cases to a huge extent.

A great deal of work on park effects has been done by Pete Palmer, author of *The Hidden Game of Baseball* and *The Hidden Game of Football*, who also compiled the home/road data for the Macmillan *Encyclopedia*. Articles about park effects also appeared in the June, 1982, edition of the *Baseball Analyst*, by Paul Schwarzenbart and Robert Kingsley, in the August, 1982, edition of the *Baseball Analyst*, by Craig Wright, by Jim Reuter in the February, 1983, *Baseball Analyst*, by Paul Schwarzenbart and Pete Palmer in the April, 1983, *Baseball Analyst*, and by Terry Bohn in June, 1984.

PLATOONING

A study on pages 9–15 of the 1988 *Baseball Abstract* asked a number of questions about the strategy of platooning. These included:

1. *How many players hit better the way they should?*

Over a period of three years, 87 percent of players studied hit better with than against the platoon advantage. However, it is clear in the data that the true percentage of players who hit better the way they should is even higher than 87 percent; over a period of enough time, in excess of 95 percent of players will hit better with than against the platoon advantage.

2. *How large are the differences?*

The normal platoon difference was 24 points in batting average, 53 points in slugging percentage and 34 points in on-base percentage.

The platoon advantage for left-handers was only very slightly larger than the platoon advantage for right-handers.

3. *Which players had the largest platoon differentials?*

The largest in the period 1984–86 were, in order, Rick Dempsey, Chet Lemon, Darryl Strawberry, Ray Knight, Von Hayes, Lou Whitaker, Jeff Leonard, Pete O'Brien, Mike Easler, and Tom Brookens. True platoon players (like Rance Mulliniks and Denny Walling) were excluded from the study because they didn't bat enough times against left- or right-handed pitching.

4. Do power hitters tend to have large platoon differentials?

No. The platoon advantage for power hitters is the same as the platoon advantage for singles hitters.

5. Do poor hitters tend to have larger platoon differentials than good hitters?

No. Surprisingly, the best hitters in baseball (George Brett, Don Mattingly, Wade Boggs, Tony Gwynn, Kirby Puckett, Dale Murphy, Andre Dawson, Pedro Guerrero, etc.) have platoon splits just as consistent and just as large as marginal hitters.

6. Do high-average hitters have smaller platoon advantages than low-average hitters?

No.

7. Do players who strike out a lot have large platoon differentials?

No. If anything, the platoon splits of players who strike out a lot are slightly smaller than the splits of those who rarely strike out.

8. Do players who walk a lot have large platoon splits?

The platoon differential for players who walk a lot does seem to be very slightly larger than for players who seldom walk.

9. Do young players have larger platoon advantages than older players?

No. If anything, the reverse is true; the platoon differentials of older players seem to be slightly larger than those of young players.

10. Are there any players who truly do not hit any better, over a period of years, when they have the platoon advantage?

There may be a couple—Robin Yount and Juan Samuel. That's about it. Virtually every hitter, over time, is better when he has the edge.

I know I'm repeating this, but the most important conclusion of the platoon study is that the platoon differential is not a "weakness" peculiar to some types of players, but is simply a condition of the game; almost every hitter and every type of hitter hits better over a period of time with than against the platoon advantage—good hitters, poor hitters, young and old, left and right, high-average hitters and power hitters. Although many people believe that we are "manufacturing" platoon players by not letting left-handers hit against left-handed pitchers, this clearly is not true, as is evident in the fact that the best hitters in the game, who have never been platooned, still universally hit better when facing a pitcher against whom they have an "advantage."

A brief note in the February, 1988, edition of the *Baseball Analyst* also deals with this issue, as do articles by Dick O'Brien and Tom Locker in the June, 1988, edition of the *Baseball Analyst*.

THE PLEXIGLAS PRINCIPLE

It is demonstrated in several editions of the *Baseball Abstract* that when a team improves in one season, they tend to decline in the next season; when they decline in one season, they tend to improve in the next season. In other words, resistance is a more powerful shaping force in baseball than is momentum, at least in this limited respect.

This also applies to individuals; a player who improves his batting average sharply in one season is extremely likely to decline in the next subsequent season. This is known as the Plexiglas principle, and is related to the Law of Competitive Balance. The most recent article about this appears on page 132 of the 1987 *Baseball Abstract*.

POWER PITCHERS AND EARLY-SEASON PERFORMANCE

In 1985 Joe Altobelli started Storm Davis on opening day, giving as his reason for so doing that hard throwers (like Davis) do better in cold weather than finesse pitchers, and therefore he wanted to get Davis more starts early in the season. In response to this, I did a "matched set" study which compared pitchers with identical won-lost records, one pitcher in each set being a hard thrower, and one pitcher being a finesse pitcher. For example, in 1963 Jim Maloney, a fire-balling youngster with 265 strikeouts, and the forty-two-year-old Warren Spahn each finished with a record of 23–7 on the season; they're one set. I identified thirty such matched sets.

The study found that the hard throwers had in fact performed dramatically worse in April than the finesse pitchers; worse in April but slightly better in May. From June through August the two groups were almost even, and in September the hard throwers had performed much better, leading to an overall won-lost record which was identical for the two groups.

The study was published on pages 134–36 of the 1986 *Baseball Abstract*.

POWER PITCHERS AND NIGHT GAMES

A study on pages 260–62 of the 1984 *Baseball Abstract* examined the performance of different types of pitchers in day and night baseball. I split all American League pitchers from 1983 into nine groups on a three by three pattern; high, medium, and low strikeouts, and high, medium, and low walks. The study found that, while all groups of pitchers were at least a tiny bit more effective at night than in day games, the difference was far greater for the power pitchers than for finesse pitchers. Pitchers who had high ratios of both strikeouts and walks per game posted ERAs almost a full run better at night than in day games; pitchers who had low ratios in both categories posted ERAs only .04 better at night.

Due to the increasing availability of the data, this advantage has become reasonably well known in the last five years. In particular, the comparative ineffectiveness of Dwight Gooden in day games has been widely noted.

THE PYTHAGOREAN THEORY

The Pythagorean theory of won/lost percentage states that the ratio between a team's wins and losses will be similar to the ratio of the square of their runs scored and the square of runs allowed. This fact is demonstrated in almost all of the annual *Baseball Abstracts*.

It can also be shown that teams which deviate from this relationship in a season tend to be drawn toward it in the next season; in other words, if a team wins ninety games with runs scored and runs allowed figures which should lead to only eighty wins, the odds are strong that that team will decline in the following season. This is known as the Johnson Effect. (See pages 106–07, 1983 *Baseball Abstract*.)

An article by Dallas Adams in the April, 1983, *Baseball Analyst* examines in more depth the relationships among runs, opposition runs, and wins. Other related articles are by Charles Hofacker in the December, 1983, *Baseball Analyst*, by David F. Hoppes in the June, 1986, edition of same, and by Dallas Adams in the edition of June, 1987. I wrote a comment in the February, 1988, edition of the *Baseball Analyst* which also relates somewhat to the issue.

ON THE QUALITY OF PITCHERS FACED BY A TEAM

In 1985 Garry Templeton observed that one of the reasons the Padres were having trouble following their championship season in 1984 was that the other teams were stacking their best pitchers against the Padres. I decided to study whether there was such an effect by sorting each pitching staff into "frontline pitchers" and "second-line pitchers," and then counting the number of frontline starters faced by each team.

I did these counts for both the 1984 and 1985 seasons to see whether the opposition had in fact increased the focus on the Padres in 1985. I found in this particular instance that the Padres had faced fewer frontline starters (and more second-line starters) than any other team in their division in both 1984 and 1985. The study is published on page 238 of the 1986 *Baseball Abstract*.

What was most surprising about the study was the discovery that the data in 1984 were distinctly imbalanced. While the 1984 Padres had faced only seventy-four frontline starters, the Cincinnati Reds had faced ninety-four, apparently not for any reason except the luck of the draw. This of course gave the Padres a significant advantage in their charge to the pennant.

I regret to say that I never repeated this study, and never extended it to any other division. I should have done so, because if differences in the number of quality pitchers faced by a team such as occurred in the NL West in 1984 are common, then it is something that we should be aware of, just because it helps us understand better what is happening and has happened. For example, in July of 1985 the Los Angeles Dodgers had a tremendous hot streak, which enabled them to take control of the division race. Many reasons were of course offered for this hot streak, but what I think no one realized at the time was that the Dodgers had just happened to get a run of luck in terms of facing quality pitchers; they faced only seven frontline starters all month. Unquestionably, that contributed to their success.

ROOKIES

The second-largest published study of my career dealt with rookies; it runs from page 33 to page 74 of the 1987 *Baseball Abstract*. Among the questions dealt with in that study are:

1. *How often does a Hall of Fame rookie appear?*

Almost every season produces at least one rookie who will eventually go into the Hall of Fame.

2. *Which season produced the most Hall of Fame rookies?*

The 1924 and 1925 seasons produced six each.

3. *What are the greatest one-team rookie crops of all time?*

Among the greatest are the 1909 Boston Red Sox, the 1924 New York Giants, the 1925 Philadelphia A's, the 1926 Pittsburgh Pirates, the 1942 St. Louis Cardinals, the 1948 Brooklyn Dodgers, and the 1958 San Francisco Giants.

4. *Which league produced the most rookie talent (in terms of what the players eventually did in the major leagues)?*

The National League in 1948.

5. *What was the worst rookie crop for a league?*

The American League in 1917.

6. *What was the greatest rookie crop of all time, counting both leagues and including quality players of less than Hall of Fame caliber?*

The 1913 season, and by a comfortable margin.

7. *How often does an outstanding rookie become an outstanding player?*

Discussing non-pitchers first, about one-third of players who win the Rookie of the Year Award will have brilliant careers and eventually go into the Hall of Fame. About one-third will be decent ballplayers or good ballplayers, but without developing substantially from the point at which they enter the league. About one-third will be distinct disappointments, fading out of the league after a few years.

To date, only six players have won the Rookie of the Year Award and moved on to the Hall of Fame; however, that figure will rise dramatically as players like Pete Rose, Rod Carew, Johnny Bench and Andre Dawson become eligible for the Hall of Fame.

For pitchers, there is very little relationship between success as a rookie and long-term greatness. Most of the great pitchers of the post-war era did nothing in particular as rookies, and most of the pitchers who did do well as rookies did not go on to great careers. Only four pitchers of the post-war era have had outstanding rookie seasons and gone on to Hall of Fame type careers.

8. Who was the weakest player to win the Rookie of the Year award?

Probably Chris Chambliss in 1971.

9. How many outstanding rookies are there in a normal season?

In a normal season there will be about three rookies who have seasons of the quality which normally can win a Rookie of the Year Award. In a normal year there are about eleven contributing rookies.

10. What factors help predict whether a rookie will or will not grow into an outstanding player?

By far the largest factor is age. If you compare a twenty-year-old rookie and a twenty-five-year-old rookie of exactly the same ability, the twenty-year-old rookie can be expected to play three times as many games and hit four times as many home runs in the major leagues as the twenty-five-year-old rookie. Even the difference between a twenty-one-year-old and a twenty-two-year-old rookie, for example, is extremely significant in predicting the future performance of the players.

In addition to this, players at some positions (catcher and second base in particular) show much less development as hitters than players at other positions such as center field. Rookies on good teams show slightly greater future growth than comparable players on bad teams. Players who have "young players' skills" (speed, hitting for average, etc.) tend to develop more in the future than players of equal value who have "old players' skills" (power, strike zone judgment, etc.).

Players with speed in general develop more and last longer than comparable hitters who lack speed.

Most surprisingly, the study found that when black rookies were compared to white rookies of precisely equal (or even somewhat better) ability, the black players as they aged showed dramatically better growth and durability. This did not result from superior speed, from the positions they played on the field, or from superiority as rookies in any other area of play.

An article by Dallas Adams about the effects of overwork on rookie pitchers appeared in the August, 1982, *Baseball Analyst*, with a response in the October, 1982, *Analyst* by Dick O'Brien.

RUNS SCORED AND RBI, IMPACT OF TEAM CONTEXT ON

A study on pages 175–77 of the 1985 *Baseball Abstract* examined the question of how much impact a player's team has on his individual runs scored and RBI counts. The study identified sets of players with extremely similar totals of at bats, hits, doubles, triples, homers, walks, strikeouts, and stolen bases, but who played for very different teams. In each "matched set" one player played for a very good-hitting team, and the other played for a very poor-hitting team.

The study found that it makes surprisingly little difference, the aggregate differences being 15 percent in runs scored and 13 percent in RBI. The reason the difference is so small is that the differences are largely offset by repositioning the player within the offense. A player who would hit seventh or eighth for a good team might be the leadoff man for a bad team, and thus might actually wind up scoring more runs with the bad team than with the good one; in fact, there were several occasions when this did happen, when the player with a poor team scored more runs than an almost identical hitter with a good team. A player who hits fifth or sixth with a good team might hit third or fourth with a bad team, and thus for the same reason might wind up with more RBIs.

In those relatively few cases where a player is so good or so bad he will hit in the same position no matter how good or bad the team, obviously the impact of the team can be larger than the 13–15 percent assessed in the study.

A related article by Dick O'Brien appears in the August, 1982, edition of the *Baseball Analyst*, with a follow-up by the same author in August, 1983.

ON RUSHING PLAYERS TO THE MAJOR LEAGUES

A study published on pages 111–13 of the 1987 *Baseball Abstract* attempted to examine the extent to which players of today are rushed to the major leagues in comparison with earlier generations. The study looked at all major league regulars of 1940, 1960, 1970, 1980, and 1986, and recorded two pieces of information about each: their age in their first season as major league regulars, and the number of minor league games that they had played before becoming major league regulars.

The study found that the average number of minor league games played by regular players was remarkably consistent over time; it was virtually the same in 1986 as in 1940, and at every point since 1940. The only change which had taken place over that time was a disappearance of the extremes. In earlier times there were more players who had spent many years in the minor leagues before getting a chance—but there were also more players who had come to the majors with no or virtually no minor league experience. Despite comments to the contrary, in fact there are fewer major league players now with very little minor league experience than there have ever been.

STOLEN BASES, IMPORTANCE OF IN AN OFFENSE

I tried many times and in many different ways to demonstrate the importance of stolen bases in an offense, and, after failing in every attempt, reached (and argued for) the conclusion that stolen base attempts in the ordinary case do almost nothing to increase or decrease the number of runs a team will score. Major studies relating to this issue appear in the following places:

1. Pages 96–97 of the 1983 *Baseball Abstract*; study shows

that teams which lead the league in stolen bases finish lower in the standings than teams which lead the league in any other significant offensive category (such as batting average, doubles, triples, home runs, walks, slugging percentage, or runs scored). Study also shows that teams which finish *last* in the league in stolen bases do *better* than teams which finish last in any other area of offensive performance.

2. Pages 114–15 of the 1986 *Baseball Abstract;* study by David Driscoll shows that Toronto hitters in the 1985 season hit, as a group, just .171 in plate appearances during which a stolen base occurred. Toronto opponents during such plate appearances hit only .134.

3. Pages 166–68 of the 1986 *Baseball Abstract.* This study attempted to evaluate how much of the St. Louis Cardinals' offensive success could be attributed to their base stealing. The method used was to identify a group of teams which were, as a group, virtually identical to the Cardinals in terms of batting average, doubles, triples, home runs, strikeouts, and walks, but which did *not* steal bases. The study estimated that the Cardinals in 1985 had scored twenty-five to forty runs more than they would have scored had they not been a base-stealing team.

4. An article in the September 6, 1982, edition of *Sports Illustrated* also deals with this subject, and is probably the best overall statement of my reservations about the stolen base.

Another comment about the issue appears on pages 162–63 of the 1983 *Abstract.* A study by Craig Wright of stolen bases in 1984 Ranger games was published in the April, 1985, edition of the *Baseball Analyst.* Another article by Wright, not related to this general point but making available a variety of extremely interesting information, appears in the February, 1986, *Baseball Analyst.* In studying 1984 scoresheets made available by Project Scoresheet, Wright learned, for example, that the only reason that base stealers have a higher percentage against left-handed than right-handed pitchers is that left-handers pick more runners off, resulting in "false caught stealing" (left-handed pitchers picked runners off first more than twice as often as right-handers).

STRIKEOUTS, EFFECT ON RUNS SCORED

Strikeouts have a negligible effect on runs scored; the belief that a strikeout is an especially negative out because it freezes base runners is essentially baseless insofar as it applies to major league baseball, though it might be true in, for example, high school ball. The reason for this is that while strikeouts don't advance runners, they also don't lead to double plays. When a ball is put in play but an out results, the negative side-effects (the runs lost because of double plays) balance the positive side-effects (that extra runs can result because of base runners' advancement).

This became apparent to me in the years 1976–82 when I was trying to perfect a formula to predict how many runs would result from any combination of singles, doubles, triples, home runs, walks, stolen bases, etc. I originally tried to make adjustments for strikeouts, just as I adjusted for every other recorded act. In time, it became apparent that the appropriate adjustment was so near .00 runs per strikeout—so near zero—that the impact of strikeouts was in essence negligible.

Later studies attempted to "improve the microscope" so that the impact of strikeouts, however small, would be visible. A study on pages 288–89 of the 1986 *Baseball Abstract* suggested that there was a loss of about one run for a team for each one hundred strikeouts (as contrasted to other outs). That means, as a frame of reference, that Dave Kingman probably cost his team in his career about eight runs by his strikeouts, if he is compared to a player of the same batting average and other batting statistics but who struck out only a normal amount. As I say, it's negligible.

STRIKEOUTS, IMPACT ON PLAYER GROWTH

On page 268 of the 1986 *Baseball Abstract*, I reported on a study which attempted to determine whether players who strike out a lot show less growth in their future careers than similar players who do not strike out as much. The study picked twenty-six "matched sets" of young players from the 1973 season, and then compared their future careers. The data were inconclusive, but suggested that there might be a small advantage in future production for the young players who struck out less.

A later study (pages 67–68, 1987 *Baseball Abstract*) examined the question of whether strikeout-to-walk ratio was an indicator of growth potential in a rookie, and concluded that it apparently was not.

SWITCH-HITTING, PLAYERS WHO ATTEMPT TO LEARN

It is my belief, based on the data but not on a systematic study of the data, that players who attempt to learn to switch hit after entering professional baseball often do their career far more harm than good. Most of these players are natural right-handed hitters who try to learn to hit left-handed "to take advantage of their speed." The problem is that many of these men (the group includes Kevin Bass, Julio Cruz, Mariano Duncan, Jerry Mumphrey, Gary Pettis, Tony Phillips, Johnny Ray, R. J. Reynolds, Alan Wiggins, and Mitch Webster, although not all of these are natural right-handed hitters) wind up with huge platoon differentials—that is, they hit far, far better one way than the other, usually hitting far better right-handed than left-handed. They wind up, in other words, with less production against right-handed pitchers than they would have if they just had a normal platoon disadvantage. Perhaps the worst examples are U. L. Washington, Tony Phillips, Mariano Duncan, and Julio Cruz, all of whom were terrific right-handed hitters, but screwed up their careers by trying to switch hit, and simply couldn't hit major league pitching left handed.

TALENT, DISTRIBUTION OF

Nothing in baseball fits the so-called "normal distribution curve," the bell-shaped curve which describes many different types of talent distributions. Major league baseball players represent the far right end of a bell-shaped curve, but are not themselves distributed in the same way. An article on pages 113–15 of the 1984 *Baseball Abstract* discusses the ramifications of this fact, and a response to that article by Charles Hofacker appears in the October, 1984, *Baseball Analyst*.

About the Author

From 1977 through 1988, BILL JAMES wrote, edited and compiled the *Baseball Abstract,* from which most of the articles in this book were selected. His work has also appeared in every major sports periodical that deals with baseball.

Mr. James lives in Winchester, Kansas with his wife, Susan Mc-Carthy, an artist; they have a baby and a yard young 'un, whose names are Isaac and Rachel. He is now at work on a different kind of book.

Mr. James wishes to deny the rumors that he has been signed to play centerfield for the Red Sox, and also claims not to have been involved in bank robbery or politics for more than a dozen years.